Ethics in Design and Communication

Ethics in Design and Communication

Critical Perspectives

Edited by
Laura Scherling and Andrew DeRosa

BLOOMSBURY VISUAL ARTS
LONDON • NEW YORK • OXFORD • NEW DELHI • SYDNEY

BLOOMSBURY VISUAL ARTS
Bloomsbury Publishing Plc
50 Bedford Square, London, WC1B 3DP, UK
1385 Broadway, New York, NY 10018, USA

BLOOMSBURY, BLOOMSBURY VISUAL ARTS and the Diana logo are trademarks of Bloomsbury Publishing Plc

First published in Great Britain 2020

© Introductions and editorial content, Laura Scherling and Andrew DeRosa, 2020

© Individual chapters, their authors, 2020

Laura Scherling and Andrew DeRosa have asserted their right under the Copyright, Designs and Patents Act, 1988, to be identified as Editors of this work.

For legal purposes the Acknowledgments on p. ix constitute an extension of this copyright page.

Cover design: Daniel Benneworth-Gray

A catalogue record for this book is available from the British Library.

A catalog record for this book is available from the Library of Congress.

ISBN: HB: 978-1-3500-7700-3
PB: 978-1-3500-7704-1
ePDF: 978-1-3500-7701-0
ePub: 978-1-3500-7703-4

Typeset by Deanta Global Publishing Services, Chennai
Printed and bound in India

To find out more about our authors and books visit www.bloomsbury.com and sign up for our newsletters.

CONTENTS

FIGURE CREDITS

PREFACE

The origins of this book can be traced to the conference panel, "Ethics in Design," which the editors co-chaired at the 2017 College Art Association (CAA) Annual Conference. The topic was due for a contemporary investigation, and we convened with colleagues from the City University of New York, Columbia University Teachers College, Politecnico di Milano, The Ohio State University, and the ArtCenter College of Design to discuss the multifaceted manifestations of ethics in the design field. The group shared much in common.

We had all witnessed and experienced the rapid digital transformation in design, the arts and humanities, and across scientific disciplines—from the emergence of immersive technologies, the Internet of Things, and machine learning, to the application of technology in all facets of life (reaching all the way into how we maintain friendships, and search for love). At the same time, we experienced changes with design's impact in society, in our communities, and globally. As the conference took place just months after the historic 2016 UK European Union membership referendum and the US presidential election, we questioned and rethought the role of design in the workplace, in education, in social media, big data, as well as in activist movements responding to these changes. What's more, competing for our attention was an array of challenges: the future of the Paris Agreement and the pressing need to combat climate change, police brutality against people of color, and the rise of neo-nationalism. These events further highlighted the potential impacts of design ethics.

We were brought together to consider a range of new ethical considerations and questions that might offer critical insights to designers, educators, and the next generation of young designers. This edited volume offers a twenty-first-century perspective on a conversation that has been happening for as long as designers have been creating. It collects twenty-four written works from twenty-eight authors, representing eleven countries, presenting a range of perspectives from new and established thinkers in the design community. The contributions address timely issues in design, communication, and technology.

Contemporary design work often involves collaboration between a variety of specialists from different disciplines. As technologies advance, the number of sub-specializations within the design field continues to increase. The boundaries in design *overlap*, *interweave* and *interrelate* in new ways that defy oversimplified "cookie-cutter" classifications. Accordingly, this book defines design ethics broadly and discusses a range of *designed* products, services, communications, and systems that affect us directly and indirectly at some point in our life journeys.

The contributors to this volume largely come from the design field. They include professionals, researchers, writers, and educators who engage with practical and theoretical ethical questions at work and in the classroom. Our aim is to provide readers with a compendium of research and provocations that touch on ethical questions in applied and theoretical settings and will reach readers both inside and outside of design. As we see clearly today, the choices that designers of products, services, systems, and communications make influence almost everyone. We all must grapple with the ethics of design.

ACKNOWLEDGMENTS

Numerous people have contributed to this volume. We would like to thank the Bloomsbury Academic team, Rebecca Barden and Claire Constable, and all the contributing authors for tirelessly working with us. The writers, who work as designers, educators, and researchers, bring invaluable insights on ethics in design from all over the world. We are grateful to be able to publish research coming from Argentina, Canada, Chile, Denmark, Germany, Iran, Italy, Portugal, Singapore, South Africa, South Korea, Spain, the United Kingdom, and the United States. We are also thankful for the support from Columbia University Teachers College and Queens College (the City University of New York). Laurence Wilse-Samson, George Njuguna, and Richard Jochum have provided tremendous feedback and insight. Our friends and family have been enormously patient throughout this process. We would also like to thank the contributing artists, illustrators, and photographers: Mona Chalabi, Ekene Ijeoma, Andrew Kuo, Gabriela Rendón, MICA's Center for Social Design, José Tomás Marchant, Belle Lee, Leonora Gonzaque, Cathy Laskiewicz, John W. Travis, the Center for Codesign Research (Copenhagen), Simeon Kondev, Charlotte Lucas, Claudia Corrales Garrido, and Thaddeus Miya. Finally, we acknowledge the ethicists, philosophers, designers, writers, and researchers who have inspired us to pursue this project.

INTRODUCTION TO THE SELECTION OF TEXTS

The chapters and provocations in this collection are organized into three sections and consider a range of ethical issues in design. Our motivation for each part of this book is to introduce, define, and interrelate critical, contemporary ethical dilemmas in design, embedded in social, theoretical, and organizational contexts. These essays and provocations, written by twenty-nine different authors, are divided into an "Introduction" to central themes; an exploration of "Design in Society," with a special focus on ethics in digital technology change and mass consumerism in design; "Theory and Communication," which probes ethical beliefs and systems, emphasizing activist theory, potentialities and notions of freedom; and finally, "Work and Pedagogy," which examines practical applications in work and educational settings.

"Ethics in Design" begins with an incisive note by Johanna Drucker, who challenges assumptions of agency in design, framing design in a Beckett-ian dilemma—"caught in the spaces between activist engagement and false consciousness"—where human complicity is often at odds with developing an equitable and sustainable world. Drawing on these insights, Laura Scherling examines the philosophical notions that ethics and ethics in design are drawn from, in order to give a prelude to the theoretical issues considered.

After the "Introduction," "Design in Society" explores macro-level concerns on design ethics for society-at-large. Jeffrey Chan questions whether ethics can be designed, scrutinizing the role of moral algorithms embedded in autonomous vehicles and the ethical questions raised by the design of dockless bikeshare systems. Chan's analysis also poses critical questions about emerging large-scale technological systems and the human moral agent operating them. In tandem with Chan's cautionary insights about design ethics and moral fallibility, Rachel Berger investigates the sanctity and reliability of information design by studying the 2016 US presidential election, analyzing a prominent election infographic: the *New York Times* needle. Berger challenges readers to think about what happens when complex data is reduced to a simplified infographic—especially at a time when data visualization has become increasingly ubiquitous—asking what the ethical implications of a "post-truth" world might be. Together with a post-truth world is a post-privacy world, explored by Michael Madiao and Sarah Edmands Martin. The authors envision the ethical design of civic machine-learning systems, arguing for greater citizen participation and digital literacy as a part of developing a sustainable framework.

Following these macro-level investigations in the first part of "Design in Society" comes a series of chapters that investigate the intimate relationships that people (or as users) have with personalized technology use, spanning digital, physical, and immersive interfaces and spaces. Considering technological intimacy and objectification in online dating apps, Martin (in her second essay) deconstructs the "Tinder Industrial Complex," stressing the importance of usability and ethical product design. Examining a more insidious level of user interaction,

Marc Miquel-Ribé reviews dark user experience, offering definitions, underscoring the absence of theoretical frameworks and empiricism to interpret "Dark UX" and "Dark Patterns," where individuals are intentionally manipulated and deceived by the digital products they engage with. Next, Michelle Cortese and Angela Zeller articulate the ambiguities of sexual consent in virtual reality (VR) meeting places and in VR design, arguing for body sovereignty as an essential VR design practice in which "all people should have complete ownership of their bodies and any interactions that should occur to them." "Design in Society" concludes with Heekyoung Jung's analysis of technology mediation in personal and professional healthcare applications, looking at the recent influx of apps for well-being that track some of the most intimate of one's personal information.

The second section, "Theory and Communication," seeks to make clearer the theoretical frameworks that motivate and drive ethical beliefs and systems in design. Peter Buwert unpacks the relationship between design and ethical crises, and design as an extension of potentiality, noting that "when design occurs, it brings ethical space into being." David Stairs, in his take on environmental and political crises, considers the role of design in sustainability, questioning whether design can be successfully used to mitigate "devastating" contemporary problems. Sara Velez Estêvão argues for the value of freedom in design and communication and points out instances where *freedom*, as a lesser recognized dimension of design, is impinged, and considers freedom broadly in terms of public use and public interaction.

The next three provocations in "Theory and Communication" examine different angles of design activism and activist theory. Maziar Rezai sketches an abbreviated chronology of design activism, analyzing the role of the activist designer in relation to Aristotelian philosophies. Tau Ulv Lenskjold and Sissel Olander weigh the complex relationships between design ethics, participatory design, and co-design, while also considering ethics in the context of a site-specific intervention in Copenhagen. Andréa Poshar assesses the symbolic nature of design and media activism by researching historical acts of resistance through a sample of designed campaigns.

In the section "Work and Pedagogy," authors share their insights into work- and education-related applications of design principles. Luke Jordan describes the deployment of *Grassroot*, a mobile app for community organizing in South Africa and the various design challenges with the deployment of an app suitable for a developing country's context. Iván Asin, in a provocation on sustainability in design practices, argues for circular design, highlighting the importance of environmentally conscious behaviors. Ciara Taylor and Samantha Dempsey assess awareness-raising tools and games for design ethics, for example by re-tailoring the "Modern Hippocratic Oath" for professional designers. Suna Jeong 정선아 analyzes the interpretation of cultural symbols in font development and considers the ethical challenges in the case of an East-Asian font library that strives to combine Chinese, Japanese, and Korean writing systems. At the end of the first half of *Work and Pedagogy*, Meredith James examines the complex ecosystem of digital media and describes several ethical dilemmas in user experience and information architecture, in addition to arguing for professional organizations in design to consider more stringent ethical codes.

The second half of "Work and Pedagogy," which focuses on ethics in design education, starts with Mariana Amatullo's work on social innovation pedagogy, reflecting on three case studies that include a pediatric burn rehabilitation center in Santiago, Chile, the development of new education spaces in Sunset Park, Brooklyn, and community-based approaches to reducing sexually transmitted diseases in Baltimore, Maryland. Kathryn Weinstein then assesses questionable practices in design internships, emphasizing the need for more diverse and inclusive hiring practices. Looking at components of diversity and inclusion in design education, Sabrina Hall and Anjali Menon outline how an AIGA/NY Mentoring Program workshop was used to foster dialogue on race and help to identify and confront racial and social injustice issues that students have encountered.

The concluding three chapters look at design ethics in curriculum design and development. In their provocation, David Gelb and Angela Norwood consider undergraduate students' engagement with research processes at a research university in Toronto, presenting several models to promote the use of value systems. Peter Claver Fine reflects on the design of a senior graphic design course to address the visibility of homelessness in Wyoming, demonstrating instances of "in-equality" by design. Finally, Paul J. Nini considers how design ethics can be embedded into design education programs, describing curricular "threads" where human-centric design research can be strategically integrated.

Each thematic area provides arguments for contemporary ethics in design discourse. We live in a complex time of both great digital technological change in how we absorb and communicate information, as well as of an existential threat from things such as climate change. This atmosphere provides an increased salience of the ethical questions designers face every day in their work. This collection provides no precise model, manifesto, or scripture to summarize and compartmentalize the inherent and complex nature of ethics in design. However, we hope to stimulate an understanding of the importance of ethical thinking about the design process for designers and all of us, as we are all consumers of design.

FOREWORD: ASSUMPTIONS OF ETHICS AND AGENCY IN DESIGN

Johanna Drucker

This timely collection brings together critical, analytic, historical, and practical studies to address what ethics means in the practice of design. The imperative toward ethical behaviors carries with it assumptions of agency. To call for intervention or activism is already to imagine that ethical values can be instrumentalized through the practice of design. Designers face the same challenges as all other human beings in the complex conditions of contemporary cultural life—choices about consumption, waste, exploitation, ecological damage, and political problems built into the supply chains and path dependencies on which the global systems of inequity currently balance precariously. But designers face the additional dilemma that their paid work is often complexly entangled with promoting the same systems such critical approaches seek to redress: how to reconcile this contradiction, among others, in seeking to chart an ethical course of action while still functioning effectively in the world.

The chapters in this book take up these questions across a wide spectrum of positions. In each case, the authors identify a way to produce resistance, critique, or some alternative discourse that poses itself in opposition to the dominant rhetoric of consumption. The positions are fraught with moral imperatives—the designer "should," "ought," "must," and "can" become an agent of transformation and social change. Who sets the agendas and evaluates the terms? How do we distinguish between the appearance of an ethical activity undertaken as salve to the conscience from work that makes structural change? Do digital environments and platforms require rethinking strategies that worked in print media and earlier communication systems?

In the late nineteenth and early twentieth centuries, design (in particular, graphic design, though industrial, applied, architectural, and other areas follow similar trajectories) emerged from a trade into a profession. Self-consciousness about the role of practitioners in the shaping of contemporary life and values emerged, and designers recognized that they were helping to change basic patterns of production and consumption at an unprecedented scale. The activist agendas of the early-twentieth-century avant-garde deliberately formulated connections between artistic engagements and social transformations. The utopian idealism that drove Russian designers as they became part of the Soviet experiment is one outstanding—but not unique—example of the belief that a new world required a new formal language, and that the relation between aesthetics and politics was vital. The design of workers' clubs and news kiosks, the creation of advertising campaigns for Soviet products like chewing gum and tobacco, and the design of posters in support of the Rural Electrification Program in the United States a decade later were the works of figures whose names have become canonical within the history of the field—Lazar El Lissitzky, Aleksandr Rodchenko, Lester Beall, and others. The works of activist designers in the 1960s through to the present in protests against the Vietnam War, the AIDS epidemic, Black Lives Matter, and the Occupy movement, to name only a handful of the most conspicuous, are also the direct result of ethical engagement in the service of social transformation, though the conceptual frameworks of social activism have shifted from invention to resistance. Without a doubt, such works have an impact. Moreover, like projects devoted to promoting information about health, water, safety, and justice in many parts of the globe and across many sectors of highly varied populations, they matter. The concept of "social design" pushed ambitious agendas around issues that could not always be solved within the terms imagined within the horizon of design practice.

Against such accomplishments and in relation to the recognition they deserve, several questions and caveats arise nonetheless. One is that such interventions make use of the same strategies that support corporate interests and campaigns, and even influence elections and policy with tactics able to be appropriated opportunistically across the political spectrum. Can exposing the workings of ideology change its overarching efficacy and control at a larger scale of cultural processes, or does the status quo remain? Another concern is the specter of self-congratulation for work done that salves the moral conscience without addressing the limits of efficacy or deeper issues of complicity, particularly among first-world practitioners. None of us stands outside of the systems we are trying to change, or is immune to the responsibility and accountability to our participation in and benefit from their operation. The remaking of the current world on ethical terms is a task not likely to be completed in our lifetimes—or perhaps ever—if the terms on which ethical values are negotiated are allowed to evolve. The scale of the transformation required for a fully ethical, holistic, social system that sustains equilibrium to emerge may always outstrip the capacity for intervention. The basic task of negotiating ethical values within a fully diverse society goes beyond the scope of design no matter how ambitious our aspirations are.

Finally, do we need to ask whether our concept of agency might delude us into imagining that these interventions are more effective than they actually are? What are the terms on which instrumental transformation can take place? Political action, if that is the goal of ethical design, has to result in a structural transformation of the systems of power by which decisions about the use and allocation of resources—human, natural, physical, and cultural—are carried out.

The chapters in this book offer starting points for considering these issues. What models of agency exist and whose values do they represent? Whose terms of responsibility are used to determine a just course of action? If we perform "ethical work" while continuing to practice and live within the very systems that perpetuate the abuse we protest, then how does this amount to an ethical agenda? A number of these chapters describe the modeling of ideas, concepts, and social beliefs. What is the role of design and the designer in understanding such issues as "freedom" and "information" or even "the social" as a domain? We know that design has played an enormous role in the fashioning of the very world that we are often attempting to correct. If such modeling is done deliberately, who determines, regulates, governs, and controls the agendas and issues to which this work is put? What are the unintended consequences of designing culture? Will the larger forces at work in global systems dwarf these actions? Are we delusional in thinking that a language of ethics can enact the necessary changes to go beyond mere trifles and small gestures and contribute to structural change, yet we can hardly shrug and walk away from challenges that feel central to human survival?

As the depth of commitment in these articles demonstrates, such questions are neither simply posed nor easily answered, but without this engagement, we are sentenced to business as usual and a sometimes troubling form of complicity. In the ongoing struggle toward an equitable and sustainable world, the talents of design and critical thought are required. So are realism and pragmatism about the limits of agency and the risks of imagining potency where there is none—or where it might unleash other ills. We are always in a Beckett-ian dilemma— caught in the spaces between activist engagement and false consciousness, unable to fully know how we are forming the basis of action or imagining our own efficacy, and yet, unable (for reasons of conscience, survival, ethical belief) to turn away from that engagement. The fact that such a wide array of practitioners, scholars, critics, and professionals are all committed to addressing these issues is already a positive sign. We simply must guard against confusing the coercive force of moral imperatives with the difficult process of ethical deliberation when conceiving a foundation for action.

Johanna Drucker

IN SEARCH OF A PHILOSOPHY
FOR DESIGN ETHICS

Laura Scherling

Recently, I dreamed about humanity's end. There was no fresh air, little food to eat, and radiation emitted by the sun had reached a toxic level. I hid in a makeshift shelter, crowded by blurry-faced avatars, clutching my iPhone. Along the perimeter of the shelter, I noticed a pool of pixelated lava surfacing and bubbling, much like out of a Nintendo game. Bewildered, I wondered if this was a simulated environment; perhaps I was trapped in a "hyperreality" where the borders between reality and its simulation were indistinct.[1] I then anxiously scrolled through my iPhone, in search of articles (and tweets) to help discern what was real and what was artificial. Eventually, I woke up and paddled my way back to the here. I found myself sleeping sideways, deliberating the possibility of a political, techno-social collapse.[2]

Looking back into much of the extant literature in philosophy, ethics, and moral psychology, many authors, philosophers, ethicists, and scholars have frequently used the concept of the end as a device to interpret and wrangle with contemplating, investigating, and negotiating fear of collapsing moral and social ecologies.[3] While this dystopian-dream-as-metaphor may seem too foreboding to begin a design ethics provocation with, it is used here to make a salient point regarding the contemporary, intersecting ecologies we are living within— where technological disruptions and a "wave of disillusionment" in a post-financial crisis reality has led to ethical crises which "hold social normalities hostage."[4] Ingrained in these confounding contemporary ecologies, there is just as much philosophical doubt, skepticism, and fiction as there is idealism and realism— which beckon us to make critical observations and challenge what is real, good, or just, as opposed to what is false, bad, or unjust. At times, it is hard to make these critical distinctions as we wade endlessly through "vaguely seductive, vaguely consensual" mediums and modalities.[5]

We perhaps may not deliberately philosophize as much as we should in the design disciplines. Designers, after all, are frequently entangled with materiality and design theory, and dueling with internal and external moral crises in regard to designing to market and advertising innovative products and services to consumers for use and misuse in our social, political, and economic lives. In design, we are frequently in search of an ethical philosophy or a guiding manifesto to ease the mental burden of engaging with conflicting sentiments. D. A. Drennan describes this conflict—a Cartesian doubt with social, political, and economic life—as the "insecurity of belief" in which we attempt to isolate what is true from what is false.[6] For many designers, creatives, and non-designers alike, this may instigate the pessimistic question: is a twenty-first-century collapse imminent? Will digital ecologies, physical (biological) ecologies, and political ecologies unravel in a dystopian fashion, where we systematically normalize commodification and inequality in global systems?[7] Can we find the pragmatic will to believe and human agency, and the necessary determination to see change for the better?[8] And perhaps a most urgent question persists: can designers interpret and fix these pressing societal, environmental, political, work, and education challenges?

This question begets more questions. Can designers "design" the much-needed solutions to make digital technology and artificial intelligence more equitable and resistant to "racial and gender biases" and catastrophic and "incidental harm"?[9] Can we design new models for design activism and designing activism? Is it possible to design interventions and social platforms to combat fake news and make information design accessible to "persons without the leisure to weigh evidence"?[10] Can we effectively design a more sustainable supply-chain to combat the rapid effects of climate change?[11]

These are substantial questions that draw on varied philosophical schools of thought. In this edited collection, these questions are approached through the lens of design and design ethics. The authors in this collection question the "appearance of ethical activity" in design and seek out new and innovative solutions in order to provide a rich dialogue on nurturing ethical frameworks in design.[12] It may become increasingly apparent as you read through the chapters that there may not be a singular model to solve these "wicked" design problems in society. It is therefore a combination of authors' models, frameworks, manifestos, and provocations on ethics in design that can inspire an open-minded approach to solving complex contemporary issues, aimed toward designing more livable, fair, and just systems.[13] By interrogating the nature of philosophical problems in design ethics, we hope to develop new critical perspectives that guide designers in addressing today's urgent ethical dilemmas.

Notes

1   See Umberto Eco, *Travels in Hyper-Reality Essays* (London: Pan Books, 1987); Jean Baudrillard, *Simulacra and Simulation*, trans. Sheila Faria Glaser (Ann Arbor: The University of Michigan Press, 1994).

2   Yuval Noah Harari, *21 Lessons for the 21st Century* (New York: Random House, 2018), 6.

3   See Stuart Sim, *Derrida and the End of History* (Duxford: Icon Books, 2000); D. A. Drennen, *Barron' Simplified Approach to the Methodical Philosophy of René Descartes* (Woodbury: Barron's Educational Series, 1969).

4   Harari, *21 Lessons for the 21st Century*, 5; Peter Buwert, "Design and Emergent Ethical Crises," in *Ethics in Design and Communication: New Critical Perspectives*, ed. Laura Scherling and Andrew DeRosa (London: Bloomsbury Academic, 2020).

5   Baudrillard, *Simulacra and Simulation*, 87; Michelle Cortese, "Designing Safe Spaces for Virtual Reality: Methods for Merging Body Sovereignty Theory into VR," in *Ethics in Design and Communication*, ed. Scherling and DeRosa.

6   Drennen, *Barron's Simplified Approach*.

7   Sarah Edmands Martin, "Swiping Left on Empathy: Gamification and Commodification of the (inter) face," in *Ethics in Design and Communication*; Jeffrey Chan, "Designing Ethics in Large-Scale Socio-Technical Systems," in *Ethics in Design and Communication*, ed. Scherling and DeRosa.

8   William James, *The Will to Believe, and Other Essays in Popular Philosophy* (New York: Longmans, Green, and Co, 1907); Johanna Drucker, "Assumption of Ethics and Agency in Design," in *Ethics in Design and Communication*, ed. Scherling and DeRosa.

9 Michael A. Madaio, "Who Owns the Smart City? Toward an Ethical Framework for Civic AI," in *Ethics in Design and Communication*, ed. Scherling and DeRosa; Luke Jordan, "Designing Tools for Low-Income Community Organizing," in *Ethics in Design and Communication*, ed. Scherling and DeRosa; bell hooks, *Teaching Community: A Pedagogy of Hope* (Hoboken: Taylor and Francis, 2013).

10 Rachel Berger, "All Models Are Wrong: Information Design in a Post-truth World," in *Ethics in Design and Communication*, ed. Scherling and DeRosa; William Edward Burghardt DuBois, "The Development of a People," *Ethics* 14, no. 3 (1904): 292.

11 David Stairs, "Design and Sustainable Development: Beyond Aesthetic and Functional Qualities," in *Ethics in Design and Communication*, ed. Scherling and DeRosa; Iván Asin, "All Models Are Wrong: Information Design in a Post-truth World," in *Ethics in Design and Communication*, ed. Scherling and DeRosa.

12 Drucker, "Assumption of Ethics and Agency in Design."

13 See Christopher J. Rowe and Sarah Broadie, eds, *Nicomachean Ethics* (London: Oxford University Press, 2002); Richard Buchanan, "Wicked Problems in Design Thinking," *Design Issues* 8, no. 2 (1992): 5; Nigel Cross, *Developments in Design Methodology* (Ann Arbor: John Wiley & Sons, 1984).

PART ONE

Design in Society

1

Designing Ethics in Large-scale Socio-technical Systems

Jeffrey Chan

Introduction: Designing Ethics?

In what ways are design and ethics connected? Philosopher Glenn Parsons outlines three major ways.[1] Firstly, ethics exists in the form of rules and norms to regulate conduct in design practices. Typically, ethics is framed in the form of normative theories.[2] For instance, utilitarianism or deontological ethics are applied to examine issues and dilemmas in design practices in order to evaluate their impacts and moral significance. This process produces ethical knowledge, which then guides responsible action. Secondly, ethics is also fundamentally concerned with what the designer creates. To rely on a drastic example here: should a designer elect to design a thermonuclear weapon—a weapon that exceeds all conceivable military purposes and armed only with the singular objective of annihilating large cities?[3] Perceived this way, this fundamental concern of ethics in design approximates what Horst Rittel described as the paramount question of "what to design and what not to design."[4] Finally, and in a reversal of directionality from design to ethics, the new possibilities engendered by design may transform existing ethical values. An instance of this is how technological design could normalize inequality, where a desirable advancement for a technologically privileged group is attained at the expense of an undesirable regression for other social groups that are either less technologically savvy or have little access to advanced technologies.[5] This reality has been routinely observed in how premium technologies (for example, fiber optic network cable)[6] that are embedded in new networks— which are also only connected to selected users and places while bypassing social groups and places that cannot afford them[7]—have hardened differences and intensified inequality in many smart cities.[8]

But is there also a fourth connection? Can ethics be designed? Or stated differently, how can ethics be changed or transformed by design? To visualize the possibilities implied by these questions, a threefold distinction is first necessary. Firstly, ethics often prompts design.[9] The discovery of a genuine ethical problem is often closely followed by figuring out what one ought to do—to devise a plan of action, which is to design. This is then Caroline Whitbeck's provocative analogy of "ethics as design."[10] The target of design here is likely a safer, or a more equitable, solution to an engineering problem. And as argued, this new design may also prompt changes in ethics. Even so, these changes, if any, are merely the unintended consequences— rather than the original and intended goals—of the design intervention. For example, Temple Grandin, professor of animal science, has spent many years designing slaughterhouses that are more "ethical" so that livestock could be less stressed before their final moments.[11] But her design has unintentionally raised an acute awareness on the rampant cruelty of the livestock industry that, in turn, has advanced food ethics.

Secondly, moral features could be built into the design, or what has been referred to as "designing in ethics."[12] As a recent development of institutional design,[13] "designing in ethics" argues that ethical relations are often mediated by institutions and technologies, and for this reason, their design can constrain possible and available ethical choices. In other words, it may be possible to design these institutions and technologies in ways that they are more likely to produce an ethical outcome. Here, consider the automated emergency hotline system: if the bot on the other end of the call has determined that the emergency at hand is not urgent by its triage logics, and furthermore could only offer preset options in response, then what ought the caller do? This caller, who is confounded by the many shades of any genuine real-life emergency, has little discretion either to persuade or to override the bot's automated judgment.[14] In this example, could the algorithm be redesigned to also include a moral "fail-safe," which will redirect the call to a human emergency responder among other comparable alternatives?

Thirdly, designing ethics is far more foundational; it aims to alter the moral ecology, which is an interdependent system comprising of reinforcing norms, values, and institutions. Here, the key variable for intervention is always humanity, and the outcome is inevitably a new human condition. Unlike "designing in ethics," which is designing the mediating institutions and technologies so that they are more likely to produce an ethical outcome, designing ethics is closer to the creation of a new set of moral codes—setting into place a new outlook for the human society that first jettisons existing moral codes and then fundamentally recalibrates what is good and bad, right and wrong. Throughout recorded history, entire moral ecologies have been periodically overhauled, for instance, during the Enlightenment, or more violently overturned, as witnessed in the Third Reich. While these examples are instructive evidence that moral ecologies exist, and moreover that sociopolitical turmoil tends to follow their destabilization, they neither offer any decisive insight on how new moral ecologies could be specifically designed with as little social destruction as possible, nor how to design them at scales far smaller than entire societies.

Research Questions, Methods, and Contributions

Admittedly, the primary question of "can ethics be designed?" and the conceptual terrain raised by this question has yet to be systematically broached in either design or ethics. On the one hand, design has been defined as the act of devising plans to change certain existing situations into preferred ones.[15] Conceivably, one could design an artifact, a process, a service, and even an organization.[16] However, what does the design of ethics entail substantively or procedurally? On the other hand, traditional ethics has frequently been concentrated on the problems of individual conduct, the moral qualities of human goals, obligations, and aspirations.[17] In this way, ethics calibrates the relational quality between persons as moral beings.[18] If so, then to what extent, and in what ways, is ethics even amenable to design? In nearly 3,000 years of Occidental ethics, perhaps the closest proxy has been the utopia—or what Karl Popper recasts in the language of design as "utopian engineering."[19] Instead of building a new society fit for people to live in, utopian engineering tries to mold people to conform to an ideal society, usually conceived by a single individual or a small group of visionaries.[20] Nevertheless, utopias—for example, the community of New Harmony as envisioned by Robert Owen (1771–1858)—tend to fail because, by necessity, they have to stabilize and control the dynamic processes that were once mobilized to build them.[21] And because the utopia is essentially an attempt to arrest change, which is unceasing for any complex system, the utopia tends to demand many improvisations in order to remain in an immutable state—improvisations that in turn lead to even more surprises that would ultimately derail its original ideal.[22] For these reasons, even if utopian engineering might suggest a concrete possibility for designing ethics, this form of large-scale social design is neither its most effective nor its most ethical benchmark.

Considering the untenable example of utopian engineering, this chapter instead broaches the idea of designing ethics by examining two contemporary design case studies of moral significance. They are, namely, dockless bikeshare programs and the controversy surrounding autonomous vehicles. These two cases appear to demonstrate the necessity for designing ethics—although in diametrically different ways. While the former case considers how ethics could be designed by modifying the artifact as well as the moral ecology of the dockless bike system, the latter case suggests the need to directly program autonomous vehicles (or self-driving cars), ex-ante, for moral reasoning. In sum, these two cases begin to demonstrate the relevance of designing ethics in large-scale socio-technical systems today.

The Dockless Bikeshare Program: Designing the Moral Ecology

The first bikeshare program (henceforth, BSP), Witte Fietsen (White Bikes), was launched in 1965 in Amsterdam. However, it is in recent years that BSP has experienced rapid growth and now finds adoption in cities around the world.[23] As a rough indication of the rapid growth of the BSP, thirteen cities operated a BSP in 2004 but by 2014, 855 cities had a BSP.[24] This number is surely set to grow even further based on the trend of new cities adopting the dockless BSP. The dockless system is the fourth generation of BSP, which is the most recent evolution of the bikeshare system after three successive generations of BSP: namely, the first-generation Witte Fietsen (White Bikes) BSP, the second-generation large-scale bikeshare launched in Copenhagen in 1995, and the third-generation BSP characterized by dedicated docking stations where one could retrieve and return the bicycles.[25] In the fourth-generation dockless BSP system, users first download a smartphone app, which subsequently unlocks the bicycle. And at the end of a user's journey, this user relies on the same app again to lock the bicycle. This technology allows the dockless bicycles to be parked anywhere, where they can also be left safely unattended.[26] Nonetheless, complaints and allegations of irresponsible parking and dumping of bicycles, vandalism, and theft pertaining to this fourth-generation dockless BSP have surfaced all around the world.[27]

Why have these widespread complaints and allegations surfaced across different cultures and cities? One possible explanation points to the intense competition between the providers of dockless bicycles for market share, which has often led providers to flood the city with too many bicycles amid regulatory gaps. And in a milieu desperate for alternative urban mobility that is not only environmentally friendly, flexible, and convenient, but can also be implemented at little or no cost to the city, cities today are enticed to first promote the dockless BSP and to deal with its many unintended and undesirable consequences later. Consider the example of Dallas, where as many as five startups armed with hundreds of millions of venture capital dollars have flooded the city with at least 18,000 bicycles.[28] In this deluge of bicycles and the myriad of users' behaviors that accompanies it, authorities are scrambling to write regulations[29]—a regulatory lag where the regulating institutions are still playing catch-up following the impacts created by the socio-technical innovation of the dockless BSP. In the meantime, in Dallas, Beijing, and Singapore among many other cities, bicycles continue to be irresponsibly parked—or more likely, dumped—in the most unlikely places, irking residents who have to maneuver around this mounting and unsightly nuisance in their everyday routines.

While these antisocial behaviors associated with the dockless BSP could be interpreted as the inevitable outcome of inadequate regulation, these behaviors can also be read as a deficit of responsible behavior associated with the usage of these dockless bicycles. Specifically, and to paraphrase Russell Hardin,[30] this is a moral problem where the good is being enjoyed at the cost of harm: where the freedom and the convenience of being able to leave or pick up the bicycles anywhere is enjoyed at the cost of inconveniencing and burdening many others in the form of irresponsible parking and dumping of bicycles. In other words, this also approximates the problem of moral hazard, when antisocial usage behaviors of the dockless BSP incur risk and costs that are instead borne by a third party. What then is the recourse?

There are at least two different approaches to address this moral problem. The first approach entails transforming the design architecture of the dockless BSP, which is a direct application of "designing in ethics." For example, many providers of dockless bicycles have sought for technological solutions to the problem of moral hazard. Locks, for instance, could be programmed not to work whenever a cyclist tries to park in an area predefined as an inappropriate parking spot. Another common design is to bar repeated offenders of antisocial behaviors from further participation in the dockless BSP.[31] In principle, these design interventions are structurally similar to Donella Meadows's example of designing a system for intrinsic responsibility; her hypothetical example required all towns or companies that emit wastewater into a stream to place their intake pipes downstream from their outflow pipe, which then effectively enforced responsible behavior.[32] This, then, is the approach of constraining behavior by changing the architecture.[33] Modifying the design of the architecture may decrease the likelihood of moral hazard; it may even deter antisocial behaviors. While these design countermeasures may be effective in discouraging antisocial behavior, they do little to cultivate the appropriate intentions and motivations behind responsible behaviors.

In contrast to the first approach of designing the architecture, the second approach views the dockless BSP as an apt opportunity for designing a moral ecology that can cultivate responsible behaviors. But what is a moral ecology? A moral ecology has been defined as the complex of interrelationships between moral norms, social institutions, and laws, which interact to produce beneficial social values.[34] Furthermore, it facilitates a dynamic exchange between people and their resource environment, balancing extractive tendencies with reinvestment obligations, thereby guaranteeing sustenance as well as the persistence of the overall system.[35] In neoliberal cities today, a moral ecology is also likely to be undergirded by a moral economy, which is an economy that embodies the norms and sentiments regarding the responsibilities and rights of individuals and institutions with respect to others in relation to the needs and ends of economic activity.[36] A moral economy recognizes the constitutive moral dimension in all economic relations—not only by the symmetrical goal of well-being that is shared by economics and ethics, but also that flourishing economic relations rely heavily on other agents behaving ethically.[37] In sum, through the galvanizing reinforcement of the moral economy, a moral ecology can build social capital, which in turn tends to reinforce trust and goodwill.[38]

Had the dockless BSP been conceived along the design of a moral ecology, users would not have been narrowly defined as the targets of anticipatory advertising, or for this new mobility to be suspected as a side effect of the providers' actual business model, which is monetizing the users' data.[39] Neither would the successful operation of the dockless bicycles been presumed on an economic model comprising of self-interested agents pursuing their own interests independent from other facilitating social relations, a model where nobody is required to know anyone else and where this anonymity and the lack of accountability are assumed to translate into the greatest possible freedom and flexibility for the dockless BSP. On the contrary, if enjoying the freedom and the convenience of parking and leaving the bicycles (nearly) anywhere is one of the primary design goals, then this goal would require the converse social relations of mutual respect, knowledge, and trust—all which are presumed by a community where users maintain relations with each other. To formulate this reality in the language of systemic design, the default ethics of the present dockless BSP conflicts with its intended goal.[40]

If so, can a new ethics be designed? Specifically, can a community bound together by a new moral code for the dockless BSP be designed? Perspectives on these questions are polarized. On the one hand, people today maintain (casual) relationships with a vast number of plural others in the city, where it has become impossible to agree on, and even much less to ground, the enforcement of any norms.[41] In this view, there is no sufficiently robust design that can effectively accommodate the plurality of norms. On the other hand, the enduring work of Elinor Ostrom makes a compelling case that moral ecologies in the form of common-pool resources do exist—for example, in the self-governance of common resources such as woodlands, pastures, and fisheries—and there are design principles that could be deduced from successful commons.[42] However, what Ostrom does not say is to what extent one could design a successful commons from the ground-up by relying on these principles, and how these design principles may apply in the urban environment of the city. If an enormous part of the debate about morality in the modern world today is about how individuals can be motivated to act morally,[43] then this discussion on the ethical design of the dockless BSP has just cast this perplexing debate into sharper relief.

The Controversy Surrounding the Autonomous Vehicles: Artifacts that can Engage in Moral Reasoning

In the near future, autonomous vehicles (or self-driving cars) will begin to replace the human driver—making many, if not all, of the ethical decisions involved in piloting the car amid unpredictable and often dangerous road conditions.[44] To operate responsibly in this complex environment, the autonomous vehicle (henceforth, AV) may need to maintain a sense of ethics similar to the human decision-maker.[45] In turn, this entails programming, ahead of time, decision rules about what to do in hypothetical situations characterized by unavoidable harm.[46] This means embedding moral principles in the operational algorithms of the AV.[47]

Even if such moral algorithms are feasible in the near future, what ought to be the moral principles that are embedded in these algorithms?[48] And to what extent are these moral principles acceptable in the larger system comprising of the regulators, the manufacturers of these AVs, the consumers, and other road users? As an intuition pump to draw out answers to these questions—and the many perplexities that they also connote—consider a sampling of the following four dilemmas that follow the structure of the famous Trolley Problem (see Figure 1.1):[49]

(Dilemma 1): In a situation of unavoidable harm, the AV has to decide between (A) killing five pedestrians or one passerby; (B) killing one pedestrian or its own passenger; (C) killing five pedestrians or its own passenger.[50]

(Dilemma 2): In a situation of unavoidable harm, the AV has to decide between (D) hitting a motorcycle and saving its own passenger, or swerving into a wall to avoid the motorcycle and risking its own passenger.[51]

(Dilemma 3): In a situation of unavoidable harm, the AV has to decide between (E) hitting an eight-year-old girl and hitting an eighty-year-old grandmother.[52]

(Dilemma 4): In a situation of unavoidable harm, the AV has to decide between (F) hitting a cyclist who is wearing a safety helmet, or one who is not wearing a safety helmet.[53]

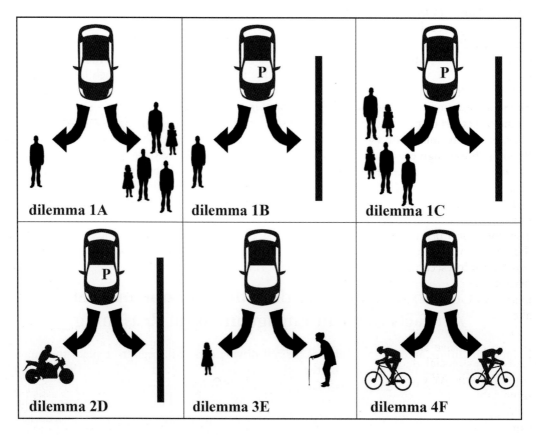

FIGURE 1.1 *An overview of the different moral dilemmas associated with the AV. Courtesy of Jeffrey Kok Hui Chan.*

To be sure, not only are dilemmas (1A) to (4F) reductively fixated on the moral complexities that could emerge from an individual AV interacting with some predefined and highly circumscribed road users, but they also do not consider the large system of other confounding variables present in any actual traffic situation today.[54] Furthermore, the Trolley Problem as an abstract thought experiment is structurally distinct from the complex realities of any actual accident, or traffic collision, situations.[55] Even so, these dilemmas remain useful as a starting point for revealing the different ethical challenges in the design of moral algorithms in AVs.

Specifically, what then are the ethical challenges invoked in these dilemmas? Dilemmas (1A) to (4F) could be read as dilemmas that presume some form of "crash-optimization" targeting technologies.[56] This implies that ex-ante, programmers will have to design algorithms that can assign and calculate the expected costs of various possible options, and further, to select the one with the lowest costs, which potentially determines who gets to live and who gets to die.[57] For example, consider dilemma (1A) and dilemma (4F). In dilemma (1A), if the AV has been programmed with the ethical principle of utilitarianism (that is, a principle that states that a greater number of lives saved is morally superior to fewer lives saved), then the AV has also been predetermined to target, and strike, that one passerby in order to preserve the lives of the five pedestrians. In contrast, in dilemma (4F), if the AV has been programmed with certain ethical principles of utilitarianism (for instance, more lives are expected to be saved over time if more cyclists comply to the rule of wearing a safety helmet when cycling on the road), then the AV is likely to target, and strike, the cyclist who is not wearing a helmet—ironically even when this action will likely result in a fatality relative to the cyclist who is better protected by wearing a safety helmet. In this way, the AV has no way but to follow an ethical rule to its repugnant conclusion.

If the above argument is sound, then the designer of the moral algorithm (assuming for a moment that this is possible using technology of the near future), no matter who (or what) he or she targets, is responsible for premeditated harm. The distribution of inevitable harm, prima facie, is neither immediately nor necessarily unethical; after all, to avoid the worst outcomes of flooding, flood engineers often have to make the hard choice—tantamount to a painful triage—on which communities to flood (and so to evacuate beforehand) and which communities to spare.[58] But premeditated harm in this case of the AV—especially without the consent of the victim if only because this specifically targeted victim can never be known ahead of time—is patently unethical. After all, risks become more acceptable to people if they give consent.[59] And even the moral principle of double effect, which can justify foreseeable but unintended evil in the pursuit of a good end,[60] is unable to justify this case of premeditated harm, where harm as evil is both foreseeable and intended. Because unlike the spontaneous reflexes of a human driver who strikes a single passerby while trying to avoid a crowd of pedestrians, the moral principles in any crash-optimization algorithm must be intentionally specified and then coded into the AV, ahead of time.

The moral complications of designing ethics are not merely internal to the designer and AV. An extensive study in this area suggests that the design of these moral algorithms can lead to new social dilemmas.[61] In this study, it was discovered that more surveyed subjects consent to the AV operating on the moral algorithm of utilitarianism, but paradoxically, these same subjects preferred the AV that could protect them at the expense of the pedestrians.[62] In other words, these subjects exhibit a moral inconsistency because while they prefer an AV that can save more lives by striking that single passerby down, they also prefer to save themselves, even if this means running over a greater number of pedestrians. The discovery of this moral inconsistency compounds the already complicated ethics of a moral reasoning AV.

Conclusion

In this chapter, the prospects of designing ethics were discussed through the case of the dockless bikeshare program, and the controversy around autonomous vehicles. Importantly, these two cases demonstrate that designing ethics could be broached through a contemporary account on the design of large-scale socio-technical systems. But just as importantly, these two cases are also distinct to the extent that while the dockless BSP suggests the immediate recourse of "designing in ethics" (changing architecture in order to change moral behavior), and an extended option of designing ethics by way of transforming the moral ecology associated with this sharing system, the AV entails the literal version of designing ethics by way of directly programming the moral algorithm into the machines. If the former case indicates that the human moral agent is still involved in designing ethics, then the latter case projects the possibility where the artificial moral agent (that is, the AV) may eventually have to play a larger role in designing ethics.

As both cases still involve some level of human involvement in designing ethics, they surface the ineluctable question of just how reliable it is even for responsible people, as morally inconsistent agents, to design ethics. Studies have demonstrated the moral fallibility of the human moral agent, whether as a rational individual or as a member of an irrational collective, who makes morally inconsistent and even morally dubious decisions.[63] What then can guarantee that the newly designed ethics is more robust than the ones that has just been displaced? Especially for the AV (or any other forms of moral artificial intelligence), the key question doesn't so much revolve around the technical challenges of representing ethics in algorithmic logic, but is instead centered on a deeper question of just how a morally imperfect human designer, relying on an essentially incomplete body of ethical knowledge at a certain point of the human civilization, can be expected to produce a morally superior artificial moral agent. While an artificial moral agent capable of functional morality may be able to follow an ethical rule more consistently than a human agent under duress,[64] contradicting conventional ethical rules to attain other moral goals in extreme situations—which justly could be perceived as a form of moral inconsistency— is however also evidence of genuine moral autonomy. The human moral agent's propensity for moral uncertainties and inconsistencies, may, after all, suggest not so much a genetic failing but instead, a genuine driver of moral progress.

Notes

1   Glenn Parsons, *The Philosophy of Design* (Malden: Polity Press, 2016).

2   Ben Sweeting, "Wicked Problems in Design and Ethics," in *Systemic Design: Theory, Methods, and Practice*, ed. Peter Jones and Kyoichi Kijima (Japan: Springer, 2018), 119–43.

3   Silvan S. Schweber, *In the Shadow of the Bomb: Oppenheimer, Bethe, and the Moral Responsibility of the Scientist* (Princeton: Princeton University Press, 2007).

4   Jean-Pierre Protzen and David J. Harris, *The Universe of Design: Horst Rittel's Theories of Design and Planning* (Hoboken: Taylor & Francis, 2010), 223.

5   Freeman Dyson, "Technology and Social Justice" (lecture, The Fourth Louis Nizer Lecture on Public Policy, Carnegie Council on Ethics and International Affairs, November 5, 1997).

6   Martin J. Murray, "Waterfall City (Johannesburg): Privatized Urbanism in Extremis," *Environment and Planning A* 47, no. 3 (2015): 503–20.

7 Stephen Graham and Simon Marvin, *Splintering Urbanism: Networked Infrastructures, Technological Mobilities and the Urban Condition* (London: Routledge, 2001).

8 Joshua J. Yates, "Saving the Soul of the Smart City," *The Hedgehog Review* 19, no. 2 (2017): 18–35.

9 Caroline Whitbeck, *Ethics in Engineering Practice and Research* (Cambridge: Cambridge University Press, 2011).

10 Ibid., 136.

11 Ryan Bell, "Temple Grandin, Killing Them Softly at Slaughterhouses for 30 Years," *National Geographic*, August 19, 2015, www.nationalgeographic.com/people-and-culture/food/the-plate/2015/08/19/temple-grandin-killing-them-softly-at-slaughterhouses-for-30-years

12 Jeroen Van den Hoven, "Introduction," in *Designing in Ethics*, ed. Jeroen Van den Hoven, Seumas Miller, and Thomas Pogge (Cambridge: Cambridge University Press, 2017), 1–10.

13 Russell Hardin, "Institutional Morality," in *The Theory of Institutional Design*, ed. Robert E. Goodin (Cambridge: University Press, 1996), 126–53.

14 Matthew Jewell, "Contesting the Decision: Living in (and Living With) the Smart City," *International Review of Law, Computers & Technology* 32, no. 2–3 (2018): 210–29.

15 Herbert Alexander Simon, *The Sciences of the Artificial* (Cambridge: MIT Press, 1996), 111.

16 Ibid.

17 Charles West Churchman, *Prediction and Optimal Decision: Philosophical Issues of a Science of Values* (Englewood Cliff: Prentice-Hall, Inc., 1961).

18 Roger Scruton, *On Human Nature* (Princeton: Princeton University Press, 2017).

19 Karl Popper, *The Poverty of Historicism* (London: Routledge, 2002), 61.

20 Ibid., 64.

21 David Harvey, *Spaces of Hope* (Berkeley: University of California Press, 2008), 173.

22 Popper, *The Poverty of Historicism*, 63.

23 Elliot Fishman, "Bikeshare: A Review of Recent Literature," *Transport Reviews* 36, no. 1 (2015): 92.

24 Ibid., 94.

25 Ibid.

26 Camila Domonoske, "Bike-share Firm Hits the Brakes in France after 'Mass Destruction' of Dockless Bikes," *National Public Radio*, February 26, 2018, www.npr.org/sections/thetwo-way/2018/02/26/588901870/bike-share-firm-hits-the-brakes-in-france-after-mass-destruction-of-dockless-bik

27 Dominic Rushe, "Why Can't We Have Nice Things: Dockless Bikes and the Tragedy of the Commons," *The Guardian*, November 5, 2017, www.theguardian.com/politics/2017/nov/05/why-we-cant-have-nice-things-dockless-bikes-and-the-tragedy-of-the-commons

28 Eliot Brown, "Dockless Bike Share Floods into U.S. Cities, with Rides and Clutter," *The Wall Street Journal*, March 26, 2018, www.wsj.com/articles/dockless-bike-share-floods-into-u-s-cities-with-rides-and-clutter-1522076401

29 Ibid.

30 Russell Hardin, *Indeterminacy and Society* (Princeton: Princeton University Press, 2013), 94.

31 Rushe, "Why Can't We Have Nice Things."

32 Diana Wright and Donella H. Meadows, *Thinking in Systems: A Primer* (Hoboken: Taylor and Francis, 2012).

33 Lawrence Lessig, *Code: Version 2.0* (New York: Basic Books, 2006), 126. See also, Richard H. Thaler, Cass R. Sunstein, and Sean Pratt, *Nudge: Improving Decisions about Health, Wealth, and Happiness* (New Haven: Yale University Press, 2008).

34 Peter L. Danner, "Affluence and the Moral Ecology," *Ethics* 81, no. 4 (1971): 287–302.

35 Michael Dove and Daniel Kammen, "The Epistemology of Sustainable Resource Use: Managing Forest Products, Swiddens, and High-Yielding Variety Crops," *Human Organization* 56, no. 1 (1997): 91–101.

36 Andrew Sayer, "Moral Economy and Political Economy," *Studies in Political Economy* 61, no. 1 (2000): 79–103.

37 Andrew Sayer, "Moral Economy as Critique," *New Political Economy* 12, no. 2 (2007): 261–70.

38 Robert D. Putnam, *Bowling Alone: The Collapse and Revival of American Community* (New York: Touchstone, 2001).

39 Rob Nikolewski, "How Can Dockless Bike and Scooter Companies Make Money?" *The San Diego Union-Tribune*, April 15, 2018, www.sandiegouniontribune.com/business/energy-green/sd-fi-dockless -profitable-20180415-story.html

40 Charles West Churchman, *The Systems Approach and Its Enemies* (New York: Basic Books, 1979).

41 Russell Hardin, *Trust* (Cambridge: Polity, 2008), 8.

42 Elinor Ostrom, *Governing the Commons: The Evolution of Institutions for Collective Action* (Cambridge: Cambridge University Press, 2008), 90.

43 Hardin, *Trust*, 7.

44 Jason Millar, "Ethics Settings for Autonomous Vehicles," in *Robot Ethics 2.0: From Autonomous Cars to Artificial Intelligence*, ed. Patrick Lin, Keith Abney, and Ryan Jenkins (New York: Oxford University Press, 2017), 20–34.

45 Patrick Lin, "Why Ethics Matters for Autonomous Cars," in *Autonomous Driving: Technical, Legal and Social Aspects*, Patrick Lin et al. (Berlin: Springer, 2015), 69–85.

46 Jean-Francois Bonnefon, Azim Shariff, and Iyad Rahwan, "The Social Dilemma of Autonomous Vehicles," *Science* 352, no. 6293 (2016): 1573–76.

47 Ibid.

48 Sven Nyholm and Jilles Smids, "The Ethics of Accident-Algorithms for Self-Driving Cars: An Applied Trolley Problem?" *Ethical Theory and Moral Practice* 19, no. 5 (2016): 1275–89.

49 See Eric Rakowski, "Introduction," in *The Trolley Problem Mysteries*, ed. Frances M. Kamm (New York: Oxford University Press, 2016), 1–7.

50 Bonnefon, Shariff, and Rahwan, "The Social Dilemma of Autonomous Vehicles," 1574.

51 Ibid., 1576.

52 Lin, "Why Ethics Matters for Autonomous Cars."

53 Ibid., 73.

54 Jason Borenstein, Joseph R. Herkert, and Keith W. Miller, "Self-Driving Cars and Engineering Ethics: The Need for a System Level Analysis," *Science and Engineering Ethics* 25, no. 2 (2017): 383–98.

55 Nyholm and Smids, "The Ethics of Accident-Algorithms for Self-Driving Cars."

56 Lin, "Why Ethics Matters for Autonomous Cars."

57 Ibid., 73.

58 Dik Roth and Jeroen Warner, "Rural Solutions for Threats to Urban Areas: The Contest over Calamity Polders," *Built Environment* 35, no. 4 (2009): 545–62.

59 Neelke Doorn, "The Blind Spot in Risk Ethics: Managing Natural Hazards," *Risk Analysis* 35, no. 3 (2014): 354–60.

60 Joseph M. Boyle, "Toward Understanding the Principle of Double Effect," in *The Doctrine of Double Effect: Philosophers Debate a Controversial Moral Principle*, ed. P. A Woodward (Notre Dame: University of Notre Dame Press, 2010), 7–20.

61 Bonnefon, Shariff and Rahwan, "The Social Dilemma of Autonomous Vehicles."

62 Ibid.

63 Ibid., 1575.

64 Wendell Wallach and Colin Allen, *Moral Machines: Teaching Robots Right from Wrong* (New York: Oxford University Press, 2010).

2

All Models are Wrong: Information Design in a Post-truth World

Rachel Berger

Introduction

Media coverage of the 2016 US presidential election produced a prodigious volume of information graphics, from months of dueling polls to CNN's "magic wall." Throughout the campaign, a new visual feature graced the homepage of the *New York Times*: an election forecaster in the form of a simple blue and red bar chart, blue for Democrat Hillary Clinton and red for Republican Donald Trump. From its debut through to Election Day on November 8, 2016, the bar resembled a matchstick (See Figure 2.1); mostly blue, with a narrow band of red. It communicated a clear message: "Hillary Clinton will win." On election night, as votes started coming in, the *Times* switched over to "the Needle," a meter with a jittery gauge displaying Clinton and Trump's chances of winning the presidency in real time (See Figure 2.2). By the end of the night, "the Needle" had flatlined in the red, and Donald J. Trump had won.

Information graphics are a ubiquitous and increasingly influential mode for communicating the news. The simplicity, visuality, and interactivity of data journalism can capture a distracted reader's attention and deliver a quick hit of information. Yet their easy appeal can also be problematic—an information graphic's visual form imbues it with a sense of accuracy regardless of the veracity of its content. What are the ethical implications of distilling complex news stories into simple graphics? How have modernist principles of "good design" lost legitimacy in a post-truth world? How are journalists, designers, and artists experimenting with the language of information design to rebuild trust?

This chapter is organized into three sections. The first explores the competing values of influential twentieth-century information designers Edward Tufte and Nigel Holmes, and how those ideologies perform in a contemporary context. The second section analyzes two examples of information design from the 2016 presidential election. The final section looks at three practitioners who are subverting contemporary norms of information design to offer new moral frameworks for the graphic visualization of data.

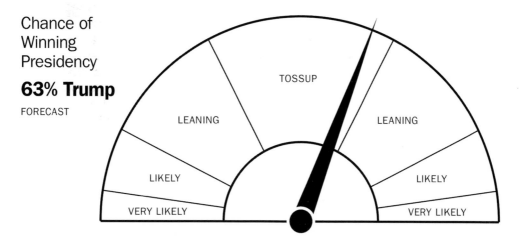

Election Forecast: **Hillary Clinton** has an **85% chance** of winning.

Clinton	Trump

FIGURE 2.1 *Election Forecast: Hillary Clinton has an 85 percent chance of winning, c. 2018. Courtesy of Rachel Berger.*

FIGURE 2.2 *Live Presidential Forecast: Chance of Winning Presidency, c. 2018. Courtesy of Rachel Berger.*

Defining Terms

This chapter explores the ethics of information design. Both "ethics" and "information design" are broad terms, so it is useful to define them. Various groupings of people—professional, religious, political, familial—define the moral principles that govern their behavior. There is no commonly accepted ethical framework for information designers, though there has been much commentary on the subject. Perhaps the most famous, popularized by Mark Twain, is "There are three kinds of lies: lies, damned lies, and statistics." Therefore, in this chapter, I look to journalism's ethical framework. The Society of Professional Journalists *Code of Ethics* is organized around four guiding principles: Seek Truth and Report It, Minimize Harm, Act Independently, and Be Accountable and Transparent.[1] Ethics are fundamental to journalism. Members of the public must be able to trust the integrity of their news sources. Otherwise, they will not have the information they need to be free, to make good decisions, and to make sense of the world. Journalism professors Cecilia Friend and Jane B. Singer argue that "the distinction between journalism and other forms of publication rests primarily on ethics."[2] This difference is increasingly important in the "open, participatory, and gloriously raucous online world."[3] It is also increasingly blurry, given the rise of fake news and the concurrent decrease in trust in the mainstream media. Moreover, it is evolving as new fields like data journalism become incorporated into journalism schools and the larger ethical framework of the profession.

There are many opinions on ways to categorize and define information design. For instance, in *Designing Data Visualizations*, Steele and Ilinsky recommend dividing information design into two categories: infographics and data visualization, based on the method of generation, the quantity of data, and the degree of aesthetic treatment.[4] Given the fluidity within these spectra, this chapter is not concerned with establishing a narrow definition of information design. Rather, it takes the broadest view, defining information design as "the visual display of quantitative information."[5]

Holmes vs. Tufte

In 1786, a young Scottish political economist named William Playfair published a book of charts entitled *The Commercial and Political Atlas*. It included the first known time-series graphs and bar charts. In representing data through graphics—rather than tables—Playfair aimed to make the information more memorable:

> A man who has carefully investigated a printed table, finds, when done, that he has only a very faint and partial idea of what he has read; and that like a figure imprinted on sand, is soon totally erased and defaced. . . . On inspecting any one of these Charts attentively, a sufficiently distinct impression will be made, to remain unimpaired for a considerable time.[6]

Playfair's work set the template for centuries of information design to follow (See Figure 2.3).

More than two hundred years after Playfair's seminal publication, leading information designers still credit his influence. Edward Tufte and Nigel Holmes, giants of late-twentieth-century design, both describe Playfair's achievement as "remarkable."[7] Tufte contends Playfair "developed or improved upon nearly all the fundamental graphical designs,"[8] and Holmes considered him the "forerunner of today's graphics journalist."[9]

Playfair's greatness is one of the few topics upon which Tufte and Holmes agree. In the 1980s, a feud erupted between the two men. Holmes is a humanist, interested in connecting with readers through an entertaining, illustrative style. He believes, "If I could get a reader to smile—a smile of recognition—then I was halfway to helping them understand the story."[10] Tufte is a strict modernist. He argues for the primacy of simplicity and clarity in information design. Both view themselves as Playfair's rightful heir, promoting the more memorable and appropriate visual solution, but they have fundamentally clashing views on the principles of good design. Moreover, their aesthetic priorities have assumed new connotations in recent years.

Nigel Holmes is a British-born graphic designer known for the charts he created for *TIME* magazine in the 1970s and 1980s. Holmes wanted to keep the magazine's readers engaged while ensuring they got the point of his graphics easily. He wraps quantitative information in a "visual vehicle" that would entice and entertain readers. Holmes believed that "to simply parade the numbers as a set of bars or a rising and falling line does only half the job. It gives no clue as to the subject being dealt with."[11] To visualize a story about fluctuating diamond prices, Holmes drew a bejeweled pinup girl whose fishnet stockings defined the grid and bent leg traced the plotted line. He graphed truck traffic on the side of a semi, government spending on the wing of an eagle, and congressional campaign expenditures in the mouth of a monster.

Readers responded to the accessibility, humor, and humanity of Holmes's style, but academics despised it. One of Holmes's critics was a Yale University professor named Edward Tufte. To date, Tufte disparages data presentation that has been corrupted by cosmetic decoration and distracting visual devices, calling it "chartjunk." In his books, he features Holmes's diamond price chart as a prime example of chartjunk, deriding it as "unsavory, chockablock with cliché

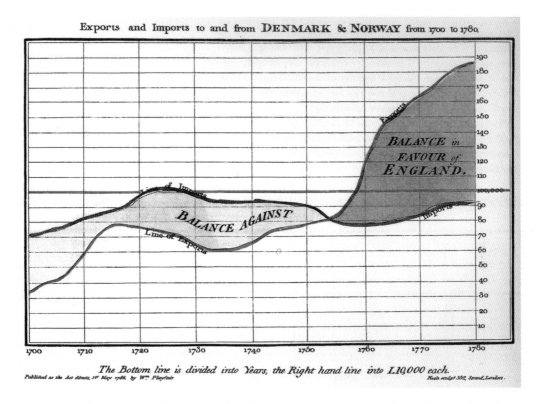

FIGURE 2.3 *The Commercial Political Atlas: Exports and Imports to and from Denmark & Norway from 1700 to 1780, c. 1786. Data visualization by William Playfair.*

and stereotype," and contemptuous of information and audience alike. Tufte believes chartjunk makes graphics less credible, asking, "Who would trust a chart that looks like a video game?"[12]

Tufte trained as a statistician and political scientist, not as a designer. His theory of data graphics originated in a series of seminars he and mathematician John Tukey taught at Princeton University in the 1970s. Tufte reified that theory in a trilogy of influential books: *The Visual Display of Quantitative Information* (1983, 2001), *Envisioning Information* (1990), and *Visual Explanations* (1997). In the books, Tufte offers principles for pursuing "graphical excellence" and thereby achieving timelessness, universality, and "graphical integrity."[13] According to Tufte, excellence largely comes down to eliminating chartjunk and maximizing "data ink,"[14] the proportion of a graphic's ink dedicated to non-erasable data information. Excellence means seeking the simplest, most efficient expression of a dataset.

Tufte's stance on graphical excellence aligns with the values of modernism. Great modernist designers like Dieter Rams, Paul Rand, Massimo Vignelli, and Ikko Tanaka championed similar principles to Tufte's. The last of Rams's famed ten principles for good design was "good design is as little design as possible."[15] Rand defined modernism as integrity, honesty, simplicity, clarity, and the absence of sentimentality and nostalgia.[16] Vignelli limited himself to a handful of typefaces and warned that the proliferation of digital typefaces "represents a new level of visual pollution threatening our culture."[17] Tanaka was the pioneering creative director for Muji, the Japanese "no-brand" brand known for rigorous simplicity and minimalism.

For the modernists, great design was not merely an aesthetic preference—it was a moral imperative. Rand truly believed that designers who abided by modernist precepts produced work that was more honest, clearheaded, and objective than those who did not. Like other modernists, Tufte tethers the moral to the formal. He provides plentiful art direction, like forbidding the use of illustration, and invokes ethical virtues to back it up. In making the case against chartjunk, Tufte calculates its "Lie Factor."[18] Elsewhere, he claims that the "operating *moral* premise of information design should be that our readers are alert and caring . . . not stupid."[19]

Despite his training in the social sciences, Tufte has yet to perform any empirical tests of his theory of data graphics. If he does, he might be disappointed. In a 2010 study of the effects of visual embellishment on comprehension and memorability of charts, "participants found the Holmes charts more attractive, most enjoyed them, and found that they were easiest and fastest to remember."[20] Holmes understands something that Tufte refuses to:

> I think [Tufte] missed the point of much that I was trying to do: TIME magazine charts were aimed at lay readers, not unintelligent ones, but busy ones. I knew they'd get the point quicker if they were somehow attracted to the graphic.[21]

His perspective manifests a simplicity Tufte could appreciate, but its consequentialism conflicts with Tuftean morality.

Holmes may have won readers, but Tufte won designers. His authoritative voice, compelling examples, and invocation of morality make a forceful case for minimalist, modernist information design. Tufte propagates a belief that removing embellishment and "non-data ink" makes a presentation more objective because the data "is allowed to speak for itself."[22] However, minimalism is no safeguard against bias. Designer and critic Michael Rock warns that images and charts "radiate a kind of false objectivity."[23] Innovation designer Ferdi van Heerden observes that designers inevitably "stamp a part of their personality" onto their work and have "an inherent cultural 'operating system' through which he or she turns meaning into expression."[24] When Tufte counsels his disciples that excellence "requires mastering the craft and spurning the ideology,"[25] he ignores their inevitable subjectivity.

Holmes and Tufte had opposing perspectives on the most appropriate way to present quantitative information, but they shared a belief that readers would trust that information. In the 1980s, when they came to prominence, neither could have anticipated the contemporary media landscape where data is available at an unprecedented level, images spread virally through social networks, fake news is proliferating, and trust in the government and mainstream media has been dangerously eroded.[26] In a post-truth world,[27] how can the ethical journalist seek truth and report it?

2016 US Election

The 2016 US presidential campaign and election were the subject of innumerable diagrams, charts, and maps. Throughout the campaign, mainstream data journalists sought to visualize the dynamic political landscape as simply, clearly, and accurately as possible. They followed the journalist's code of ethics, believing it would set their work apart from other forms of publication proliferating on the internet.

At the *New York Times*, the team producing a data-driven analysis of the campaign were good Tufteans. They created what I have come to refer to as "the Matchstick," a dynamic election forecast graphic for the paper's homepage that hewed closely to Tufte's principles of graphical excellence. The Matchstick was a simple bar chart with a blue section labeled Clinton and a red one labeled Trump. It was generated from a massive volume of polling data that had been combined and calibrated to balance the latest polls with polling trends from recent elections. It communicated complex ideas with clarity, precision, and efficiency. It was free of chartjunk and maximized data ink. Yet, it was a profoundly flawed piece of information design.

How can such a good chart be so bad? For three reasons: it relied on bad data, employed a bad format, and lived on a bad platform.

Bad Data: Inaccurate Polling

Polling data is notoriously inaccurate and getting worse.[28] Sixty-five years ago, journalist Darrell Huff wrote, "Polls, in general, are biased . . . toward the person with more money, more education, more information and alertness, better appearance, more conventional behavior, and more settled habits than the average of the population he is chosen to represent."[29] Today, the US population is much more diverse and response rates are much lower, making it virtually impossible to get a representative sample of the population. Even pollsters are sounding the alarm. David Moore, former managing editor for Gallup, worries that "media polls give us distorted readings of the electoral climate, manufacture a false public consensus on policy issues, and in the process undermine American democracy."[30]

Bundling many polls together and assuming that improves the credibility of the underlying dataset is like packaging subprime mortgages and reselling them with an investment grade rating. However, that is exactly what the *New York Times* and forecasting sites like FiveThirtyEight and PredictWise did when modeling the 2016 general election. Their models are based on combinations of polling data, and no amount of adjusting can turn bad data into good data.

Bad Format: Overstating Certainty

Despite their stylistic differences, Holmes and Tufte believe that the purpose of information design is to reveal the meaning buried inside a set of numbers.[31] They encourage designers to select formats that give their readers a clear, accurate understanding of data. The *New York Times* team that created the Matchstick believed that they chose a good format. They thought a quantitative forecast would help people gain perspective and avoid obsessing over the latest polls.[32] Instead, they created a false expectation in the minds of their readers.

On Election Day, November 8, 2016, the Matchstick was 85 percent blue, giving Clinton an 85 percent chance of winning. After the election, the team quickly realized the format they had chosen did not sufficiently convey the uncertainty inherent to forecasting models. Their readers are not good at interpreting a probability scale: they understand that a 50 percent chance is a toss-up, but they struggle to grasp the difference between a 75 percent and an 85 percent chance. In an election post-mortem column, editors Amanda Cox and Josh Katz admitted their mistake:

> We failed at explaining that an 85 percent chance is not a 100 percent chance. If we did it all again, we would probably emphasize uncertainty in a more visceral way, rather than using a simple statement of probability.[33]

Most of the *New York Times's* readers—and its Editorial Board—probably wanted to believe that Clinton's 85 percent chance *was* a 100 percent chance. In its endorsement of Clinton, the

Times called Trump "the worst nominee put forward by a major party in modern American history."[34] The *Times* also took the extraordinary additional step of publishing a second editorial, condemning Trump's candidacy.[35] The paper's leadership asserted an unusually partisan position on the election, which should have put the paper's data journalists on notice to present as nuanced a forecast as possible. Instead, their format suggested an unrealistic degree of certainty.

A bad format is exacerbated by many readers' faith in the relative objectivity of data graphics, especially those created in the Tuftean style. Creative director Leslie A. Segal writes of the implicit sincerity of charts and diagrams.[36] John Burn-Murdoch, a data journalist at *The Guardian*, reports that readers are much likelier to challenge data quoted in text than to question a graphic that uses the same data.[37] His colleague Mona Chalabi agrees, "A lot of data visualizations will overstate certainty, and it works. These charts can numb our brains to criticism."[38] A 2011 study found that viewers instinctively assume that maps that look good are more trustworthy.[39]

Bad Platform: Mobile Web

The 2016 election forecast chart lived on the *New York Times* homepage. Given the paper's reputation for excellence, its website should be a good platform for trustworthy data journalism. However, nytimes.com does not operate in isolation. It is part of the vast ecosystem of networked content that makes up the internet. Most Americans get at least some news through social media, most of it on mobile devices.[40] On these platforms, stories from the *New York Times* are difficult to differentiate from less reputable publications because their content is feed formatted by applications like Google AMP and Facebook Instant Articles. Journalist Kyle Chayka observes, "On a Facebook timeline or Google search feed, every story comes prepackaged in the same skin, whether it's a months-long investigation from *The Washington Post* or completely fabricated clickbait."[41]

Google's AMP (Accelerated Mobile Pages) project is an open-source library that allows people to create web pages that look good and load quickly on mobile devices. It launched in February 2016, and by October 2017, 4 billion AMP pages had been created.[42] AMP provides tools for building efficient, highly functional design. However, when all news is optimized to look the same, any of it could be fake. Days after the 2016 election, President Barack Obama held a news conference denouncing the spread of fake news. In it, he described misinformation that has been so well packaged it threatens our ability to discriminate between serious arguments and propaganda. He warned, "If everything seems to be the same and no distinctions are made, then we won't know what to protect."[43] As these platforms paper over the darkest corners of the internet with good design, they undermine the credibility of ethical journalism.

Good Format: The Needle

On election night, as returns started coming in, the *Times* debuted a new format: "the Needle," a meter with a jittery gauge displaying Clinton and Trump's chances of winning the presidency in real time. The Needle employed a distinctly different visual language from the forecast chart. It was illustrative and imprecise. It had a low data-ink ratio. It could have been a wireframe for a graphic that might appear in (gasp) a video game. The Needle was not quite chartjunk, but it was decidedly more Holmesian than the forecast chart. Moreover, it was not behaving according to plan.

Over the course of the night, as the Needle leaned further toward Trump, it twitched continuously, giving and taking a few electoral votes, a few percentage points. Clinton supporters following the *New York Times* election coverage despised the Needle. One Twitter user accused *The Times* of "peddling anxiety, not information."[44] Many were enraged when they realized that the jitter was hard-coded into the design and not precisely reflective of incoming data.[45] Jeremy Bowers, an editor at the *Times*, defended the Needle as a tool for "visualizing uncertainty," intended to provide a visceral understanding of the margin of error that is factored into electoral predictions.[46]

Despite its critics, the Needle is a good format. By wrapping data in a visual vehicle that gives people a true sense of the data—and the data's uncertainty—it achieves what the forecast chart could not. Of course, the Needle is still subject to the credibility challenges posed by the platform it lives on. On the mobile web, it is just one more viral infographic.

Three Practitioners

Two years on, the 2016 US presidential election remains mired in controversy. There are unanswered questions about Russian interference, Cambridge Analytica, and the role social media played in spreading fake news. Even before the election, leaders from both major parties suggested the process was rigged, and many Americans felt a generalized loss of trust in institutions. An October 2016 study found that 68 percent of Trump supporters distrust the economic data that is reported by the government.[47] Where statistics once provided a common ground, they have increasingly become a target for the populist right's critique of experts and elites.

Tufte and Holmes are still actively publishing and speaking on information design—Tufte's touring seminar on "Presenting Data and Information" sells thousands of tickets a year. Yet the world has changed dramatically since they were in their heyday. Holmes wonders,

Perhaps in today's political climate, the stuff I did in the late '70s and '80s might be more heavily criticized. If people today thought I was obscuring information, or trivializing it (as my critics did 35 years ago), might that add to a skepticism of the media?[48]

We live in a world that demands new approaches to information design.

This world needs data graphics that embrace Holmes's humanity without indulging in the clichés and imprecision that blunted his impact. It needs information design that lives up to Tufte's ideals while avoiding his false promise of objectivity. Mona Chalabi, Andrew Kuo, and Ekene Ijeoma are three contemporary practitioners who make work that subverts inherited notions of "good" information design. In radically different ways, their work offers alternatives to the data/format/platform trap that is compromising mainstream data journalism.

Mona Chalabi

Mona Chalabi is the data editor at *Guardian US*. She also writes and presents about data for television, radio, and film. In 2015, Chalabi started posting hand-drawn information graphics on Instagram, tagging them #datasketch. She views her data sketches as an extension of her work at *The Guardian*, with fewer constraints: "All of it is about informing as many people as possible, but particularly the groups who are affected by something."⁴⁹ Chalabi's Instagram audience is different from her *Guardian* audience. She published a recent data sketch about the side effects of hormonal contraception on Instagram in order to reach women who might be using that form of contraception. Her data is rigorously researched and cited, but her sketches are deliberately crude. In these sketches, Chalabi visualizes information using amateurish illustrations of simple shapes, body parts, and food, and she writes headlines in earnest cursive (See Figures 2.4 & 2.5).

Chalabi works in this style "so that people can see how imprecise the data is; so people can see that a human did this, a human found the data and visualized it."⁵⁰ Her shaky hand shows a vulnerability unimaginable to Tufte and Holmes. It invites readers to question the data, to check its accuracy for themselves, rather than trying to persuade them of its infallibility. Chalabi makes data sketches about whatever interests her: politics, race, orgasms, yoga. She is not charting her personal life; she is finding a way to make data feel more personal.

Chalabi's data sketches are "small data," a human-scale alternative to the unfathomable expanse of big data. Her philosophy of information design is illustrated by her data sketches and anchored by a framework she suggests readers use to evaluate data at any scale. She proposes three basic questions: Can I see uncertainty? Can I see myself in the data? How was the data collected?⁵¹ Chalabi offers these questions as a tool for readers, but they are equally relevant to designers and journalists. They suggest a new ethos of information design, one that prioritizes transparency, criticality, and humanity.

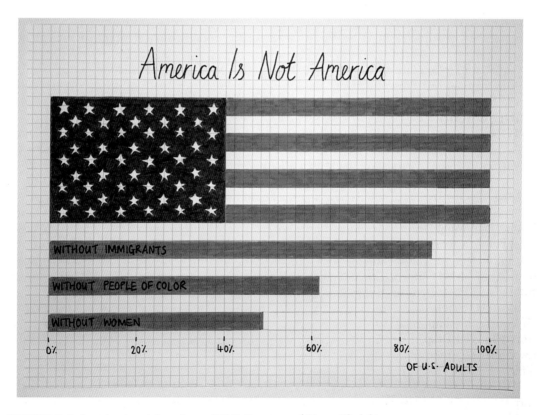

FIGURE 2.4 *America is not America, c. 2017. Courtesy of Mona Chalabi.*

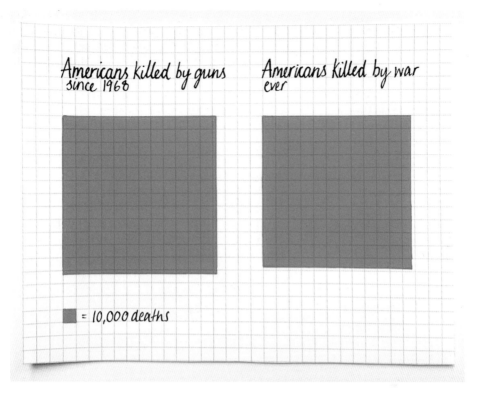

FIGURE 2.5 *Americans killed by guns, c. 2017. Courtesy of Mona Chalabi.*

Andrew Kuo

Andrew Kuo is an artist whose work attempts to express ephemeral emotions and experiences through meticulous charts and diagrams. From 2007 to 2015, he charted about pop music for the *New York Times* ArtsBeat blog. Kuo's charts are precise and seductive, with bold palettes and tight geometries. He borrows colors and compositions from modernist masters like Josef Albers, Barnett Newman, and Frank Stella, and overlays them with labels, axes, and arrows. Rather than using "real" data, Kuo charts his own idiosyncratic observations. A 2012 chart of Odd Future's song "Oldie" includes categories like "You can hide a forgettable song behind youthful energy once, but it's a lot harder to do it twice."[52] Kuo also uses titling to hint at the unorthodox nature of his data graphics, for example (See Figure 2.6): "The Walk Home After Being Racially Slurred/I'm Not Tall, Dark or Handsome, 2011."

In a perversion of Tufte's dogma, Kuo admits, "I'm not really concerned with accuracy. Of course, it's important to fall back on accurate data, but what interests me most is the storytelling."[53] Despite this seeming sacrilege, Kuo is no propagandist. He is concerned with *emotional* accuracy, conveying the truth about a subjective experience. He is engaged in the difficult work of quantifying things that cannot be compared to anything.[54]

Kuo is an artist, not a journalist or a designer. He favors the chart format because it is a way to talk about more than one thing at once, "literally plotting one idea against the other within the same eyeshot."[55] Charts and diagrams are good formats for Kuo's hip, semi-ironic

FIGURE 2.6 *The Walk Home After Being Racially Slurred/I'm Not Tall, Dark or Handsome, c. 2011.* Courtesy of Andrew Kuo.

testimonials. And Kuo's work, with its implied critique of the sanctity of modernist form, is good for information design.

Ekene Ijeoma

Ekene Ijeoma is an interdisciplinary artist and designer whose data-driven work raises awareness about social issues. In 2015, Ijeoma created "Wage Islands," an interactive installation that submerges a topographic map of New York City under water to show the parts of the city low-wage workers can afford to rent in (See Figure 2.7). Wage Islands has a sensuality that traditional information design lacks. Ijeoma believes that "data can be visceral and poetic, not just literal and pragmatic" and aims to make work that bridges feelings and facts.[56]

Despite his work in nontraditional media, Ijeoma has a more traditional perspective on information design than Chalabi or Kuo. He does not exhort people to question the data, nor does he commandeer conventional formats in service of personal expression. Ijeoma likes working with data precisely because of its objectivity. His interest is in finding formats that enable people to experience datasets emotionally, as well as intellectually. As he explains it, "A lot of the projects I did could have just been interactive maps, but I thought that they should have dedicated, committed mediums."[57] Ijeoma's epic, multisensory works elevate information design beyond the reach of undifferentiated feed formatting and platform optimization.

FIGURE 2.7 *Wage Islands, c. 2015. Courtesy of Ekene Ijeoma.*

Conclusion

The post-truth world is hard on ethical journalists and information designers. An increasing number of readers are less likely to trust news articles that reference quantitative data than those that stick to qualitative anecdotes.[58] Fake news spreads further, faster than real news.[59] Tufte's rules of graphical excellence have been co-opted by bad actors.

The 2016 US presidential election revealed the fragility of traditional information design in a contemporary context. The way forward requires that the authors of information design admit to the uncertainty in their data, pursue new formats and platforms for telling today's data stories, and let their humanity feature in their work, rather than ignoring or denying it.

Notes

1 "SPJ Code of Ethics," Society of Professional Journalists, September 6, 2014, www.spj.org/ethicscode.asp

2 Cecilia Friend and Jane B. Singer, *Online Journalism Ethics: Traditions and Transitions* (East Sussex: Routledge, 2015), xxiii.

3 Ibid., xvi.

4 Noah Iliinsky and Julie Steele, *Designing Data Visualizations: Representing Informational Relationships* (Sebastopol: O'Reilly Media, 2011), 4–7.

5 Edward Tufte, *The Visual Display of Quantitative Information* (Cheshire: Graphics Press, 2001).

6 William Playfair, *The Commercial and Political Atlas: Representing, by Means of Stained Copper-Plate Charts, the Exports, Imports, and General Trade of England, at a Single View* (London, 1786), 3–4.

7 Nigel Holmes, *Designer's Guide to Creating Charts & Diagrams* (New York: Watson-Guptill Publications, 1984), 18; Tufte, *The Visual Display of Quantitative Information*, 9.

8 Tufte, *The Visual Display of Quantitative Information*, 9.

9 Holmes, *Designer's Guide to Creating Charts & Diagrams*, 14.

10 Holmes, email message to author, September 10, 2018.

11 Ibid., 9.

12 Edward Rolf Tufte, *Envisioning Information* (Cheshire: Graphics Press, 1990), 34.

13 Tufte, *The Visual Display of Quantitative Information*, 13.

14 Ibid., 91–105.

15 Dieter Rams, "Ten Principles for Good Design," n.d., www.vitsoe.com/us/about/good-design

16 Paul Rand, *Paul Rand: A Designer's Words* (New York: School of Visual Arts, 1998), 7.

17 Massimo Vignelli, "Massimo Vignelli's A Few Basic Typefaces," Fonts In Use, last modified August 13, 2016, fontsinuse.com/uses/14164/massimo-vignelli-s-a-few-basic-typefaces

18 Tufte, *The Visual Display of Quantitative Information*, 57.

19 Tufte, *Envisioning Information*, 34.

20 Scott Bateman et al., "Useful Junk? The Effects of Visual Embellishment on Comprehension and Memorability of Charts," in *Proceedings of the 28th International Conference on Human Factors in Computing Systems*, ed. Elizabeth Mynatt (New York: ACM, 2010), 2573–82.

21 Nigel Holmes and Steven Heller, *Nigel Holmes: On Information Design* (New York: Jorge Pinto Books, 2006), 76.

22 Bateman et al., "Useful Junk?."

23 Michael Rock, "Since When Did USA Today Become the National Design Ideal?" *I.D. Magazine*, March/April 1992, 86.

24 Ferdi Van Heerden, "Foreword," in *Data Flow: Visualizing Information in Graphic Design*, ed. Robert Klanten et al. (Berlin: Gestalten, 2006), 8.

25 Tufte, *Envisioning Information*, 35.

26 William Davies, "How Statistics Lost their Power—and Why We Should Fear What Comes Next," *The Guardian*, January 19, 2017, www.theguardian.com/politics/2017/jan/19/crisis-of-statistics-big-data-democracy

27 Nick Enfield, "We're in a Post-truth World with Eroding Trust and Accountability: It Can't End Well," *The Guardian*, November 16, 2017, www.theguardian.com/commentisfree/2017/nov/17/were-in-a-post-truth-world-with-eroding-trust-and-accountability-it-cant-end-well

28 Jill Lepore, "Politics and the New Machine," *New Yorker*, November 16, 2015, www.newyorker.com/magazine/2015/11/16/politics-and-the-new-machine

29 Darrell Huff, *How to Lie with Statistics* (New York: W.W. Norton, 1954), 26.

30 Lepore, "Politics and the New Machine."

31 Holmes, *Designer's Guide to Creating Charts & Diagrams*, 9.

32 Amanda Cox and Josh Katz, "Presidential Forecast Post-Mortem," *The New York Times*, November 15, 2016, www.nytimes.com/2016/11/16/upshot/presidential-forecast-postmortem.html

33 Ibid.

34 The Editorial Board, "Hillary Clinton for President," *The New York Times*, September 24, 2016, www.nytimes.com/2016/09/25/opinion/sunday/hillary-clinton-for-president.html

35 The Editorial Board, "Why Donald Trump Should Not Be President," *The New York Times*, September 25, 2016, www.nytimes.com/2016/09/26/opinion/why-donald-trump-should-not-be-president.html

36 Leslie A. Segal, "Introduction," in *Graphic Diagrams: The Graphic Visualization of Abstract Data*, ed. Walter Herdeg (Zurich: Graphis Press Corp., 1983), 9.

37 John Burn-Murdoch, "Why You Should Never Trust a Data Visualization," *The Guardian*, July 24, 2013, www.theguardian.com/news/datablog/2013/jul/24/why-you-should-never-trust-a-data-visualisation

38 Mona Chalabi, "3 Ways to Spot a Bad Statistic," *TED: Ideas Worth Spreading*, February 2017, www.ted.com/talks/mona_chalabi_3_ways_to_spot_a_bad_statistic, 4:15.

39 Nurul Hawani Idris, Mike Jackson, and Robert J. Abrahart, "Map Mash-ups: What Looks Good Must be Good?" in *GISRUK Conference 2011* (Portsmouth: GISRUK, 2011), 1–8.

40 Elisa Shearer and Jeffrey Gottfried, "News Use Across Social Media Platforms 2017," *Pew Research Center's Journalism Project*, September 7, 2017, journalism.org/2017/09/07/news-use-across-social-media-platforms-2017

41 Kyle Chayka, "Facebook and Google Make Lies as Pretty as Truth," *The Verge*, December 6, 2016, www.theverge.com/2016/12/6/13850230/fake-news-sites-google-search-facebook-instant-articles

42 David Besbris, "AMP: Two Years of User-first Webpages," *AMP Project Blog*, October 19, 2017, www.ampproject.org/latest/blog/amp-two-years-of-user-first-webpages

43 Barack Obama, "Remarks by President Obama and Chancellor Merkel of Germany in a Joint Press Conference," Whitehouse.gov, https://obamawhitehouse.archives.gov/the-press-office/2016/11/17/remarks-president-obama-and-chancellor-merkel-germany-joint-press

44 Laureen Ancona, "Sorry, I Should be More Specific: This is Peddling Anxiety, not Information, and Disappointing to Say the Least," Twitter, (n.d.), https://twitter.com/laurenancona/status/796201871937511425

45 Alp Toker, "Looking for Trends in @nytimes's Presidential Forecast Needle? Don't Look Too Hard—the Bounce is Random Jitter from Your PC, not Live Data," Twitter, (n.d.), https://twitter.com/atoker/status/796176641600974851/photo/1

46 Nancy Wartik, "NYT Needle Returns to the Spotlight: The Internet Notices," *The New York Times*, December 14, 2017, www.nytimes.com/2017/12/14/reader-center/nyt-needle-election.html

47 Marketplace and Edison Research, "Economic Anxiety Index," https://cms.marketplace.org/sites/default/files/anxiety-index-data.pdf

48 Holmes, email.

49 Mona Chalabi, phone interview with author, September 7, 2018.

50 Chalabi, "3 Ways to Spot a Bad Statistic," 5:22.

51 Ibid.

52 Andrew Kuo, "Charting Odd Future," *ArtsBeat*, April 3, 2012, artsbeat.blogs.nytimes.com/2012/04/03/charting-odd-future

53 Andrew Kuo in Fresh *Dialogue Nine: New Voices in Graphic Design: In/Visible: Graphic Data Revealed—New Voices in Graphic Design*, ed. John Maeda (New York: Princeton Architectural Press, 2009), 5.

54 Andrew Kuo, "Charlie Rose Tomorrow—Andrew Kuo," interview by Charlie Rose, February 23, 2008, www.charlierose.com/view/interview/89567

55 Andrew Kuo, "Artist Talk: Andrew Kuo," interview by RxArt, November 8, 2011, rxart.net/blog/artist-talk-andrew-kuo

56 Ekene Ijeoma, "Ekene Ijeoma Combines Data and Design to Tackle Pressing Global Issues," *Design Indaba*, December 2017, www.designindaba.com/videos/conference-talks/ekene-ijeoma-combines-data-and-design-tackle-pressing-global-issues, 17:57.

57 Ibid.

58 Davies, "How Statistics Lost their Power."

59 Soroush Vosoughi, Deb Roy, and Sinan Aral, "The Spread of True and False News Online," *Science* 359, no. 6380 (2018): 1146–51.

3

Swiping Left on Empathy: Gamification and Commodification of the (Inter)face

Sarah Edmands Martin

The phrase "swipe left," now synonymous with universal rejection, is a colloquialism emblematic of the online dating gesture and its ubiquity.[1] Its prevalence is unsurprising when one considers how the dating app Tinder, to which the phrase is native, is globally renowned and available in over forty languages.[2] The swipe gesture designed into mobile dating interfaces, a left or right flick of the thumb, connotes instant approval or instant veto. It is a binary that, through its simplicity, also erases nuance. Moreover, when the same gesture is used to signify the desire to buy, as is the case on e-commerce apps like Stylect, Blynk, and Grabble, what are the ethical consequences of treating people like this season's pant trend? Is it ethical to commercialize and gamify the image of a person's face?[3] When the Tinder Industrial Complex (a term referencing the potentially nefarious and aggressive commercialization of mobile match-making by corporations) is more interested in commodifying the experience of dating—incentivizing users to browse, ad infinitum, a seemingly endless stack of romantic choices, or, offering pay-only options to filter by race—users encounter the ramifications and second-order effects of de*person*alizing the digital search for romance.

This chapter critiques the design decisions and methodology that leads to dating app interfaces dehumanizing their users, drawing upon scholarship from social theories and humanist design theory. This research also uses speculative design to visualize alternate, more ethical designs. These include prompts for users to be more empathetic that could arrest and clarify, for a moment at least, the blur of aestheticized gesture. Moreover, this chapter surveys contemporary artists and designers, such as Ben Becker, Elliot Glass,[4] Marcello Gómez Maureira, and Matei Szabo,[5] as well as projects like "Humanitarians of Tinder," by Cody Clarke,[6] and "Tinder Nightmares" by Elan Gale,[7] which disrupt, through their practice, the (digital) surface of modern romance.

Finally, this chapter asks the question: how does the objectifying swipe gesture (emblematic of other designed interactions) act as a transformational agent effecting human behavior that ultimately enacts an ideology through design?

Introduction

Simulating the referent of its brand name, the dating app Tinder has caught fire. According to the Apple Store, 20 billion matches have been made since the app's debut in 2012, while daily traffic on Tinder racks in around 26 million matches per day.[8] With its place in vernacular consciousness firmly entrenched, the app needs no grandiose introduction. Tinder's DNA is born of a powerfully simple functionality: the binary sorting of people. Assembling a profile on the app can be accomplished in under two minutes if a user already has a Facebook account (and most people do: Facebook has cited 2.23 billion users as of June 2018, which means 30 percent of the world's population is on Facebook).[9] Constructed from a few photos and a 500-character description, a user's profile can then begin location-based matching for potential romantic and/or sexual partners.

It is worth noting the etymology of the name, itself: of Old English origins, tinder derives from *tynder*, or a "dry, inflammable substance." The symbolism, of course, is that the titular app encourages sparks that inflame a passionate connection. Tracking that metaphor backward, however, suggests a disturbing narrative: the users are, themselves, the fuel. This chapter further argues that Tinder UX/UI users and their subjectivities become consumable commodities—the kindling, the *tynder*—burned to ash.

This chapter mainly focuses on Tinder, owned by umbrella company Match Group, Inc. Match owns several other dating applications (OkCupid, Match.com, and PlentyofFish) which provide a variety of tailored, shopping-for-a-mate experiences.[10] This research will briefly engage with Bumble and Grindr, but mostly scrutinize Tinder as its popularity has had the widest impression on so many users and society at large. Specifically, this chapter will examine the user experience (UX) and user interface (UI) through the lens of feminism as it defines theories of self and subjectivity. As the success of Tinder's UI continues to influence new app design (what one might call the Tinder Industrial Complex), more and more apps integrate, sometimes mindlessly, the swipe gesture for binary decision-making. That is, to say, one has to start somewhere and this chapter starts at the beginning, with Tinder.

Tinder was co-founded in 2012 by Sean Rad, Jonathan Badeen, Joe Munoz, Justin Mateen Dinesh Moorjani, and Whitney Wolfe and is a location-based method of romantic communication between two mutually interested users.[11] It has become synonymous with either finding a relationship or finding a "hookup," such that Urban Dictionary, the arbiter of online vernacular, defines "Tindering" as "Looking for a match (date)," followed by a paradigmatic sentence model: "'I was tindering during class because the lecture was boring.'"[12] Bumble is a similar app, founded in December of 2014 by Whitney Wolfe, also a co-founder of Tinder but who left after she filed a sexual harassment lawsuit.[13] Bumble is marketed as the "feminist" Tinder because, in heterosexual matches, only women may initiate conversation. It should be noted that "feminist" will remain in quotes until Bumble embraces the tenants of feminism. As bell hooks writes,

> The soul of feminist politics is the commitment to ending patriarchal domination of women and men, girls and boys. Love cannot exist in any relationship that is based on domination and coercion. Feminist thinking and practice . . . emphasizes the value of mutual growth and self-actualization in all relationships, their emotional well-being. . . .A genuine feminist politics always brings us from bondage to freedom, from lovelessness to loving.[14]

This chapter will show how empathetic design pulls from the tenants of feminism, and how without a responsible treatment of intersectional selves, the experience of a user can be lost to destructive modes of commercialization and commodification. To do so, this chapter will also define and unpack UX/UI principles that become important when discussing ethical, loving design.

Tinder's Interface

Tinder is an app that owes its success to reduction. At the core of its front-end interface exists one binary decision: left or right, yes or no. While other dating apps are packaged with extensive profiles, algorithmic pathways, questionnaires, pomp, and gimmicks, Tinder has but one interaction. The app presents the user with a virtual stack of faces on their mobile device—photographic representations of real people who geo-locate within a self-defined radius set by the searching user. An age range may also be set. Beyond these incidental filters, almost all of a smartphone's five-inch diagonal retina display is dedicated to the avatars of hopeful mates (almost 85 percent of the on-screen real estate, as of July 2017. See Figure 3.1).

75%

FIGURE 3.1 *Percentage of screen devoted to the face on Tinder's UI (as of Tinder's July 2017 redesign), c. 2017. Courtesy of Sarah Edmands Martin.*

That is a lot of face on the interface. Typically, this manifests as a tightly cropped composition focusing on the user's eyes, mouth, cheekbones, jaw, and hair (and sometimes bust and shoulders). This kind of composition does not accommodate detailed or nuanced descriptions of self. The face-centric interface offers no coherent biographical narrative. Instead, the featured photo asks users to base instinctive decision-making on the attractiveness of visage alone. Thus, the representation of a person on Tinder, their self-constructed composition of the face, is more akin to an avatar.

The term avatar is typically associated with illustrative or symbolic iconography attached to identities in the virtual world. Yet, the way Tinder profile pictures allow individuals to "express (or suppress) various physical and psychological traits" in such a reduced digital landscape aligns with the contextual definition of an avatar and the economized nature of personal information on Tinder.[15] The photographic Tinder avatar becomes encoded with binary decision-making power. As psychologist Dr. Liraz Margalit describes,

> Each image presented on Tinder also has a subtext. People use their photos to make identity claims—symbolic statements to convey how they would like to be seen . . . [like] behavioral residue . . . [which are] clues inadvertently included in the chosen photos. For example, smiling without a head tilt signals high self-esteem, selecting a close-up photo shows confidence and willingness to share minor flaws, and choosing a long-distance shot may indicate low self-esteem and a desire to hide flaws.[16]

Ironically, between one swipe and the next, the face of a potential match on Tinder does not actually get much face-time. A user's photo does not arrest the motion of a rapidly swiping thumb for long. The swiping user is urged onward by the next *carte de amour* peeking from below the current card, subtly pressuring a user to move on (see the next section for more on the metaphor of reality). An avatar on Tinder only has a few seconds to communicate its worth. It must rely on encoding (zero-degree-head-tilt-smile or close-up-confidence) that abstract the multitudinous real self into a compressed, symbolic image curated and designed to win the binary coin toss of Tinder's interface. It is almost entirely based on a gut reaction to the attractiveness of a face.

These portraits resemble hopeful tarot cards at the top of a deck, waiting to be read, accepted, and folded into someone's real life. According to one of the co-founders, the app's design embraces superficiality because life itself is superficial. "We built an experience that we wanted and a flow that emulates interactions in the real world," Tinder founder Sean Rad explains. "What we're striving to do with Tinder is understand what are the sort of social dynamics, physical dynamics, the flows of where you start with a request or desire to make a new relationship and how that progresses."[17] Trying to capture this natural flow, Tinder's front-end design relies exclusively on how people represent themselves in digital space. Rad argues realism from this digital displacement: "I just sort of am who I am and I walk in and I have relationships and discover about other people and share about myself as I progress."

That does not match (no pun intended) the metaphor created by the app. In real life, one does not have a near-limitless supply of disposable lovers readily available. There is a volumetric difference between reality and Rad's virtual reality. Yet, science has shown (the now-famous Milgram experiments on obedience to authority, for example) that falsely constructed realities can shape how a user perceives right and wrong, reality and consequences.[18] How a UX/UI designer constructs the metaphor of reality within an app can deeply shape the psychological experience of a user.

UI/UX: The Metaphor of Reality

When designing for virtual environments, UX/UI designers know that matching experience with expectation is incredibly important. To this end, the metaphor of materiality is a unifying theory of rationalized space and motion in UX/UI, as it grounds the experience in a tactile system everyone can understand. After these foundations are laid, a UX/UI designer can then play within that technological space in order to open a user up to imagination and magic.

The use of familiarly tactile attributes helps users to understand digital affordances quickly.[19] The flexibility of these virtual materials can then create new affordances that supersede those in the physical world, without breaking the rules of physics.[20] The fundamentals of light, surface, and movement are key to conveying how objects move, interact, and exist in space and in relation to each other. There is the gesture of your hand, as well as the responsive gesture of the animated, two-dimensional surface that follows. The semantic illusion of swiping an item out of the screen's frame is an example of skeuomorphism—a motion that mimics a functional action from the real, physical world.[21] An example is the design of a faux button that appears to depress beneath a finger tapping the glass of a screen. To achieve this effect, a designer will most likely code a shift in color between the pre-pushed button and the pushed button. In app design, skeuomorphism is an example of form-over-function, as the physics depicted within the digital metaphor is technically unnecessary within a virtual world. Proponents of skeuomorphic design argue that this helps novice users to navigate the gap between real-world interactions and virtual interactions.[22] The fact remains, however, that the careful design of digital gravity is but an allusion, a virtual artifact made to reference an embodied experience in the real world.

This synthetic motion reminds a user of motions from reality, such as grabbing products from a supermarket shelf or sweeping trash off a table and into the trashcan. For the swipe gesture almost all real-world connotations lie within the category of obtaining or rebuffing commodities. Yet, no one uses such a simplified gesture to dismiss others from their actual lives, to banish a face from one's presence.

The Swipe Gesture

Tinder's chant-like 2018 campaign slogan, "Swipe. Match. Chat," reads at a syncopated clip.[23] The cadence of this slogan in the mouth mirrors the rhythm of the app in the fingers: Swipe right. Swipe left. "Keep," or "throw." "Smash" or "pass." The swipe gesture lives at the heart of the brand's identity.

Although the physical gesture is slight, the implications are significant. To begin with, the swipe is not a straight, horizontal pan. Instead, the card moves across the screen on an arched trajectory, imitating the authentic path of a card operated on by gravity. The face is not a flat representation, a ghostly digital image, but has weight, following the illusion of physics. As described earlier in this chapter, the metaphor of reality is thus conflated—a virtual rejection becomes entangled with the disposal of an actual object. The faces of hopeful matches become objectified beyond the encapsulation of a photo as a user either collects them into their back pocket mobile repository or discards them into a cyber-dustbin.

The semiotic and ethical implications of the swipe gesture fundamentally debunk Rad's claim that the UX/UI reflects natural dating "flow." His argument specifically buckles under the sheer quantity and velocity with which one can view and dismiss other people. In many cases, the rapid cadence of the swipe can become addicting. In fact, there is a premium function that capitalizes on this gamification: "Rewind." When a user gets so caught up in the mindless swiping and accidentally rejects a photo of someone in whom they are interested in, Tinder Plus offers the "Rewind" function. With this function, a user may go back in time, rescinding their default declining judgment. That is, if a user forks over premium Tinder membership: $9.99 for users under thirty years old, $19.99 for over thirty-year-olds.[24] Thus, there is not only a monetary premium on youth built into the interface but also an association with the age of thirty having to pay more for greater access to love.

Indeed, the swipe gesture works well within commercial contexts. Shopping apps such as eBay, Amazon, Zappos, Poshmark, Nordstroms, and Asos all have the swipe gesture in their interfaces, helping navigate product purchasing. Gaming apps, too, like Broken Sword: Director's Cut, Temple Run, and New Star Soccer, all use the swipe gesture to reinforce addictive, entertaining functionality instead of intimately introducing one person to another.

When the practice of rapidly judging others' appearances unites with addicting, game-like interaction, a user may "feel like eating candy, a relatively harmless indulgence that starts to feel disgusting if you have trouble stopping."[25] When the human face becomes a commodity, depersonalized from the multiplicity and complexities that make each person unique, there is a loss of subjectivity and, ultimately, empathy in the design. The differences, the things that make a person unique and idiosyncratic, collapse under the endless blur toward a grayness of the same.[26] Tinder feeds itself, like a positive feedback loop: the spike of adrenaline jolts a user out of the mundane blur, ever seeking the next face in this spectral economy. Indeed, the app's photo-first profiles are designed to be swiped-through while a user stands in line at the grocery store: shopping while shopping.

Within the Tinder Industrial Complex, the same process by which the capitalist worker has been reduced to a commodity (namely, their labor), the individual has been reduced to the commodity of their attractiveness level—to the detriment of users on both sides of the interface. Other Tinder-like apps, such as Grindr, provide the option to filter by "tribes," or self-identified niche groups such as "daddy" or "twink," as well as by height, weight, body type, and ethnicity. The metaphor of the shopping cart returns. The danger in these "tribe" designations parallels the danger of Tinder's objectification—the symbolic system built into the interface sanitizes what does not fit designated categories, these surface levels of identification and relation.

In 2014, Sean Rad described how Tinder is "a casting session and you're in the director's chair," while speaking to the *Rolling Stone Magazine*. "At the end of the day," he says, "it's just one big party, and you're just sitting there saying, 'Yes, no, yes, no.'"[27]

Given the feminist and social revolutions of 2017 and 2018, including #MeToo movement and widespread sexual assault accusations, Rad's imagery here is particularly repulsive. The paradigm of the self that has gained ascendancy in the US popular culture and in Western philosophy (that Rad here posits as the "casting director" archetype) is derived from the experience of the predominantly white and heterosexual, mostly economically advantaged man who has wielded social, economic, and political power, dominating the arts, literature, media, and scholarship.

Feminist theory offers a path forward: intersectional and reconstructive approaches to self that are not from such a problematic perspective of privilege and commodification.

Affecting an Ideology

With the above arguments made, how does the swipe gesture act as a transformational agent—effecting human behavior, and ultimately, enacting an ideology through design?

Philosopher and theologian Emmanuel Lévinas describes the face-to-face encounter between two people as the foundation of all ethics. "The face resists possession, resists my powers," he says. "In its epiphany, in expression, the sensible, still graspable, turns into total resistance to the grasp . . . the face speaks to me and thereby invites me to a relation incommensurate with a power exercised."[28]

Tinder's UX/UI is so reliant on faces, yet does those very faces an incredible disservice. The homogenization enacted by commercial, spectral blurring also erodes that unique otherness that Lévinas finds "resistant to the grasp." Lévinas wrote extensively about finding an ethical path through life that contains encounters with The Other. To Lévinas, The Other is a *visage*: a living person beyond one's self that teaches a kind of perspective on life that adds to one's own. The design of an app that conditions people to treat the faces of Others like a stack of disposable objects needs reform.

The topics of "the self" and "the other" have long been central to feminist philosophy, as well, for "the self" is crucial to questions of personal identity, the body, sociality, and agency. According to early feminist philosopher Simone de Beauvoir, the Subject is diametrically opposed to the Other.[29] To be the Other is to be the non-subject, the non-person, the non-agent—in short, the mere body or a mere card, at the top of a deep stack. In feminist philosophy, if a person becomes objectified, they become severed from their subjectivity and agency.

A final note on material culture, by Albert Borgmann:

Just as the skill of reading animal tracks will not flourish in a metropolitan setting, so calls for the virtues of courage and care will remain inconsequential in a material culture designed to procure comfortable and individualist life. . . . Putting matters this way is to clarify also what is at the heart of real ethics. It is not finally the desire for greater scholarly circumspection or radicality, but rather the readiness to answer to the claim of eloquent things.[30]

Eloquent, ethical things are guided, too, by good design.

Discursive Interventions

Of course, not all users interact with a product in the way it is intended. Tinder has been publicly passed around at parties as a form of public entertainment or used as a simple means to kill time. It is not just these users that are subverting the scope of the app. Artists and designers have also taken a discursive approach to the digital landscape of Tinder's interface.

One notable intervention is by Dutch designer Marcello Gómez Maureira. Directly satirizing the commodification inherent to Tinder's binary swipe gesture, Maureira created *Tender—It's how people meat*, a robotic art installation that endlessly forced a raw steak to interact with Tinder's interface.[31] The tongue-like piece of meat is attached to a metal, rotating rod that swipes right on every available profile (See Figure 3.2). The proposed experience of mindless swiping through profile images reduces the user, on both sides of the app, to common, commodified flesh.

As the clockwork meat swipes on and on, skimming an infinite catalog, the faces detach from their individual subjectivities in what George Bataille describes as "one wave lost in a multitude of waves."[32]

Some designers have aped Tinder's entire interface in order to call attention to the absurdity of the binary premise. "Adoptly" was part of an "ongoing satirical art project" created in 2016

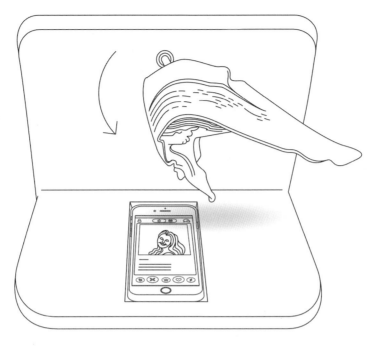

FIGURE 3.2 *A representation of the installation of Marcello Gómez Maureira's Tender—It's how people meat, c. 2015. Courtesy of Sarah Edmands Martin.*

by Ben Becker and Elliot Glass.[33] Designed to look exactly like an app in production (it went up on Kickstarter), the Tinder-like interface provided potential parents a platform to filter adoptable children by age, race, gender, and a few other characteristics. A user was presented with images of adoptable children and toddlers and could swipe either left or right to signify interest in bringing said infant into their family.

Beyond highlighting the shallow and tone-deaf stereotype of Silicon Valley investors and entrepreneurs, the app also drew attention to the original design's superficiality. That said, the Kickstarter campaign reached $4,000 of its $150,000 goal—which means a few people, at least, may have thought the app was a good idea.[34]

Another example of critique worth mentioning is the blog "Humanitarians of Tinder." The online archive, created by Cody Clarke, a New York filmmaker, documents examples of white, college-age Tinder profiles that feature themselves among people in presumably developing countries.[35] Typically, the construction of these featured photographs shows a white user staged next to, holding hands with, or embracing people (usually children) from a culture and country more disenfranchised than their own. The act of flaunting humanitarian efforts as dating props codifies itself in the repeated evidence of Clarke's screen grabs.[36] Although Clarke's blog does not offer written or immediate critique, it does starkly present the disturbing trope, evident after only a few minutes of scrolling through "Humanitarians of Tinder."

Finally, the intervention by the "Tinder Nightmares" Instagram account, created by Elan Gale, offers a discursive response to the Tinder Industrial Complex. "Tinder Nightmares" reveals some of the most hilarious, grotesque, and bizarre interactions on the app. Like "Humanitarians of Tinder," "Tinder Nightmares" documents interactions between real users. These conversations may begin, for example, with an innocuous "hello," yet quickly spiral into the discovery that the other person likes bathing in marinara sauce.[37] More disturbing interactions are brusque, rude, or abusive invitations for sex. Creator Elan Gale approaches the complex and sometimes-horrifying social interactions fostered by Tinder with absurdist humor: "The days of right answers are over. We live in an age of insanity and lies. And that's when you get upset, when you expect things to be clear and linear and make sense."[38] Gale's strategy seems to be to laugh or cringe his way through questionable mobile dating app design. At the very least, this creates a community of shared experiences in which everyone who has had their own Tinder nightmare may find solidarity.

Sincere Interventions

The agenda of this chapter is not to re-stigmatize the landscape of online dating. These criticisms are made in the service of creating healthy and safe online dating spaces. With millions of users, one might say that Tinder is ethically obligated to assess and reassess its responsibilities to users.

Thus, the following is a sincere proposal for intervention to the current UX/UI. A designer should understand the dominance of market forces, rooted in the Western culture of consumption, as well as how these can be shifted to prioritize empathy and connection. Can an ethical relationship to the Other on mobile dating apps be encouraged, or otherwise gamified?

What if the interface contained tiny breaks, moments of pause or reflection, designed into the interaction? Every ten swipes there is a prompt: "Go outside and list five things you hear," or "What are you grateful for today?" (See Figure 3.3). These prompts ask the user to check in with themselves on what they consider important in a relationship. Psychological relief prompts could also build compassion and empathy for the users on the other side of the interface, deepening the user's understanding of Self and Other. These relief quizzes could earn a user rewards like the "Rewind" function (instead of a flat fee), thus promoting self-reflection and emotional

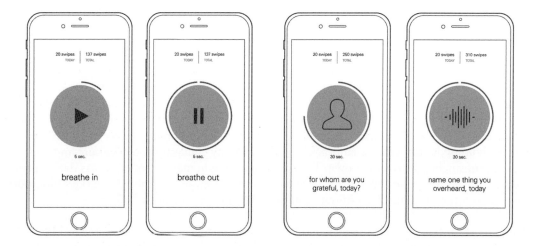

FIGURE 3.3 *Speculative designs for ways to encourage more empathy into Tinder's interface. Courtesy of Sarah Edmands Martin.*

health while still searching for love on a mobile app with a simple UX/UI. Alternatively, these recordings could be shared with potential matches, revealing the depth and nuanced reflection to each person's profile. This kind of content could expand, in a meaningful way, the data set of a user's information.

An additional opportunity to use the interface of Tinder in a less objectifying manner is exemplified by the 2017 philanthropic ad campaign by Ogilvy Africa to preserve the last male northern white rhino. The campaign embedded its content into the native experience of the dating app, creating a profile for the northern white rhino, Sudan, who is the last of his kind. Working in partnership with Ol Pejeta Conservancy, a nonprofit wildlife conservancy in Central Kenya, swiping right on Sudan raised money for an endangered species.[39] The money raised funds for research on artificial reproductive techniques, with which the rhino can find a mate and preserve the species. Here, the opportunity to donate to research breaks the endless blur of objectified faces, creating a delightful and empathetic experience in the service of altruism. This connects users, momentarily, to a compassionate deed very different from the judgmental one in which they have been here to fore participating. This is an example of the app being used or having space for opportunities to make a positive social change.

Design and Empathy: A Conclusion

If Tinder's UX/UI is based on reality, as co-founder Sean Rad urges, then that reality leaves much to be desired. As feminist theory asserts, we are daily intersections of idiosyncratic selves, deserving of much more than the homogenized flattening that occurs between swipes. To visualize a space for the intersectional self is to be an ethical dating app designer. Otherwise, as this chapter has sought to lay out, the experience of a user can be lost to destructive modes of commercialization and commodification. Tinder, for example, reduces the complexity of a person through the front-end interface. The binary built into the core of its user experience forces superficial judgment upon another person's face: swipe left or swipe right, yes or no. The swipe gesture, in particular, bases its semiotics on real-world connotations that almost always exist within the category of obtaining or rebuffing commodities. Linking that simplified gesture to repetitively dismissing real people from a user's life creates an ethical dilemma.

Dating apps should not forego authentic forms of connection, and by extension, the dignity of a fellow user. There is a real person beyond the face, beyond the avatar. Ethical design respects and embraces users with complex stories, fears, and fantasies. Just because an interaction is designed to exist on a mobile app does not justify the flattening of the intersectional self. Moreover, ethical design is not just for profit. Returning, once more to bell hooks and her assertion that "a genuine feminist politics always brings us from bondage to freedom, from lovelessness to loving,"[40] it follows that Tinder, an app invested in people and love, may need to take a closer look at the gestures it makes in the (digital) surface of modern romance.

Notes

1   Raju Mudhar, "Tinder's Swipe Interface Gets Swiped by Other Apps," *The Star*, August 6, 2014, www.thestar.com/life/technology/2014/08/06/tinders_swipe_interface_gets_swiped_by_other_apps.html

2   Tinder Inc., "Tinder on the App Store," App Store, August 3, 2012, https://itunes.apple.com/ke/app/tinder/id547702041?mt=8.

3   Yuyu Chen, "Swipe Right to Buy: E-commerce Apps Take Design Cues from Tinder," Digiday, March 15, 2016, https://digiday.com/marketing/swipe-right-buy-e-commerce-apps-take-design-cues-tinder

4   Jacob Kastrenakes, "Adoptly, the Tinder for Adoption, Was Actually an Art Project," *The Verge*, January 31, 2017, www.theverge.com/2017/1/31/14455622/adoptly-app-tinder-child-adoption-art-project-reveal

5   Marcello Gómez Maureira et al., "Tender—It's How People Meat," *Vimeo*, 2014, vimeo.com/111997940

6   Cody Clarke, "Humanitarians of Tinder," H of T, 2018, http://humanitariansoftinder.com/

7   Hannah Jane Parkinson, "Tinder Nightmares Founder: 'I Hate Dating So Much,'" *The Guardian*, December 7, 2015, www.theguardian.com/technology/2015/dec/07/elan-gale-tinder-nightmares-interview

8   ESilverStrike Consulting Inc., "Tinder Information, Statistics, Facts and History," Dating Sites Reviews, n.d., datingsitesreviews.com/staticpages/index.php?page=Tinder-Statistics-Facts-History#ref-ODS-Tinder-2015-18

9   Facebook, "Company Info," Facebook Newsroom, n.d., https://newsroom.fb.com/company-info

10 "MATCH GROUP, INC. (MTCH) IPO," NASDAQ.com, n.d., www.nasdaq.com/markets/ipos/company/match-group-inc-905768-79612

11 Felicia Williams, "Tinder Wins Best New Startup of 2013 | Crunchies Awards 2013," *TechCrunch*, February 11, 2014, https://techcrunch.com/video/tinder-wins-best-new-startup-of-2013-crunchies-awards-2013

12 "Urban Dictionary: Tindering," Urban Dictionary, n.d., www.urbandictionary.com/define.php?term=Tindering

13 Alyson Shontell, "Ousted Tinder Cofounder Sues For Sexual Harassment, And She's Using These Nasty Texts As Evidence," *Business Insider*, July 1, 2014, www.businessinsider.com/tinder-lawsuit-and-sexual-harassment-text-messages-2014-7?IR=T

14 bell hooks, *Feminism Is for Everybody: Passionate Politics* (New York: Routledge, 2015).

15 Katrina Fong and Raymond A. Mar, "What Does My Avatar Say About Me? Inferring Personality from Avatars," *Personality and Social Psychology Bulletin* 41, no. 2 (2015): 1.

16 Liraz Margalit, "Tinder and Evolutionary Psychology," *TechCrunch*, September 27, 2014, techcrunch.com/2014/09/27/tinder-and-evolutionary-psychology/

17 Carrie Yury, "Turning Desire into an App: 5 Questions for Sean Rad, CEO of Tinder," *Huffington Post*, June 7, 2014, www.huffingtonpost.com/carrie-yury/sean-rad-ceo-of-tinder-on_b_5087420.html

18 Stanley Milgram, "Behavioral Study of Obedience," *The Journal of Abnormal and Social Psychology* 67, no. 4 (1963): 371.

19 Victor Kaptelinin, "Affordances," in *Encyclopedia of Human Computer Interaction*, ed. Mads Soegaard and Rikke Friis Dam (Hershey: Idea Group Reference, 2013).

20 Sharon Correa and John Schlemmer, "Making Motion Meaningful," *Google Design*, September 23, 2016, https://design.google/library/making-motion-meaningful

21 Tom Page, "Skeuomorphism or Flat Design: Future Directions in Mobile Device User Interface (UI) Design Education," *International Journal of Mobile Learning and Organisation* 8, no. 2 (2014): 3–4.

22 David Pogue, "Apple's 5 Worst Attempts at Digital Realism," *Scientific American*, February 1, 2013, www.scientificamerican.com/article/pogue-apples-5-worst-attempts-at-digital-realism

23 "Tinder | Swipe. Match. Chat," *Tinder*, n.d., tinder.com/

24 Alison Griswold, "Are You 30? Tinder Has Officially Decided You're Old," *Slate Magazine*, March 2, 2015, https://slate.com/business/2015/03/tinder-plus-pay-for-passport-rewind-and-unlimited-right-swipes.html

25 Jonah Bromwich, "Finding Love, the Old, Shallow Way," *The New York Times*, October 25, 2013, nytimes.com/2013/10/27/nyregion/finding-love-the-old-shallow-way.html

26 Mark Featherstone, "The Eye of War: Images of Destruction in Virilio and Bataille," *Journal for Cultural Research* 7, no. 4 (2003): 441–43.

27 Vanessa Grigoriadis, "Inside Tinder's Hookup Factory," *Rolling Stone Magazine*, October 27, 2014, www.rollingstone.com/culture/culture-news/inside-tinders-hookup-factory-180635

28 Emmanuel Lévinas, *Totality and Infinity: An Essay on Exteriority* (Pittsburgh: Duquesne University Press, 1969).

29 Cynthia Willett, Ellie Anderson, and Diana Meyers, "Feminist Perspectives on the Self," in *Stanford Encyclopedia of Philosophy*, ed. Edward N. Zalta (Stanford: Stanford University, The Metaphysics Research Lab, 2016).

30 Albert Borgmann, "The Moral Significance of Material Culture," in *Technology and the Politics of Knowledge*, ed. Andrew Feenberg and Alastair Hannay (Bloomington: Indiana University Press, 1995), 92.

31 Maureira et al., "Tender—It's How People Meat."

32 Featherstone, "The Eye of War: Images of Destruction in Virilio and Bataille," 441–43.

33 Kastrenakes, "Adoptly, the Tinder for Adoption, Was Actually an Art Project."

34 Marie Claire, "Tinder: The Online Dating App Everyone's Talking About," *Marie Claire*, November 28, 2017, www.marieclaire.co.uk/life/sex-and-relationships/tinder-the-online-dating-app-that-everyone-s-talking-about-112522

35 Sydney Brownstone, "Meet the Super Sexy, Super Conscious Humanitarians of Tinder," *Fast Company*, February 25, 2014, www.fastcompany.com/3026878/meet-the-super-sexy-super-conscious-humanitarians-of-tinder

36 Clarke, "Humanitarians of Tinder."

37 Elan Gale, *Tinder Nightmares* (New York: Harry N. Abrams, 2015), 85.

38 Parkinson, "Tinder Nightmares Founder."

39 Angela Natividad, "The World's Most Eligible Bachelor on Tinder Is Literally the Last of His Kind," *Adweek*, May 25, 2017, adweek.com/creativity/the-worlds-most-eligible-bachelor-on-tinder-is-literally-the-last-of-his-kind/

40 hooks, *Feminism Is for Everybody*.

4

Dark User Experience: From Manipulation to Deception

Marc Miquel-Ribé

Introduction

Hassenzahl defines user experience (UX) as "the momentary feeling (good or bad) while interacting with a product or service."[1] While this definition—or any other UX definition—does not state that users' experiences should be positive, the importance of experiencing positive emotions while interacting with a device is accepted as a best business practice. The equation "better UX = more business"[2] is the motto that contributed to industries embracing this area of the design field, and at the same time, opened a path for UX to go outside of usability guidelines. It seems clear that by designing to the needs of users, users will be more satisfied, more engaged, and there should be positive outcomes for business.

Nevertheless, some companies are willing to reach their financial goals at any cost, regardless of whether their customers feel satisfied after getting what they need. These companies instead wonder: how can we design the user interface in order to increase the possibilities of reaching our objectives in a more effective way? Metrics related to purchase conversions as well as user retention and engagement become the focus of design, and any UX research conducted is aimed at understanding the users' needs or preferences for this purpose alone. In these cases, design is mainly aimed at increasing the company's revenue, and companies sometimes cross ethical lines. Such a phenomenon is called Dark UX.

Dark UX applies knowledge about users in order to design for the companies' benefit, even if that implies making users do actions they did not intend to do and would not have done in other circumstances. One of the most recognized Dark UX practices is called Dark Patterns (also known as interfaces designed to trick) and they are frequently encountered in many types of technology applications, from e-commerce websites to video games. Such interfaces are unethical because they facilitate negative consequences the user would have avoided had they been informed on the matter. This is precisely where the power lies. These interfaces are effective because the user is unaware of the goal, of the way they work, or of its existence altogether.

In this chapter, I identify Dark UX practices according to the way they *manipulate* and *deceive* users. The aim is to denounce some technology-derived ethical problems and help us find ways to deal with them, either helping users to develop dark design awareness or promoting the suitable changes in the current consumer rights legislation to prevent Dark UX practices ex-ante. The chapter represents a step toward a better understanding of Dark UX and a useful starting point for further discussion in the design community.

Dark User Experience: Design Not in the User's Benefit

What are Dark Patterns?

Dark Patterns are defined by the website darkpatterns.org as "tricks used in websites and apps that make you buy or sign up for things that you didn't mean to."[3] Harry Brignull coined the term in 2010 on the wake of interaction design patterns,[4] defined as "general repeatable solutions to commonly-occurring usability problems."[5] The difference is that Dark Patterns are not aimed at solving user problems, but at helping businesses to increase their income, often setting an almost adversarial relationship between the user and the business. In fact, Dark Patterns mean more than the adaptation of the mischievous door-to-door seller into the digital era; they come with objectives such as obtaining more subscriptions, helping a headline go viral, making the user disclose personal information and, obviously, increased income.

It may seem surprising that the term was proposed after more than a decade since the consolidation of the web. There were previous attempts to define ethics for persuasive technology[6] and discussions about the techniques that bad-intentioned interfaces employ.[7] Yet, the need for framing the problem wasn't entirely visible until the eruption of e-commerce websites. The web-based library darkpatterns.org, which classifies these patterns into several categories, has become popular on the internet and in the general media.[8] The objective of the website is to help users understand how Dark Patterns work and warn them about the dangers of becoming victims.[9] In some cases, publicly shaming the companies by exposing their Dark Patterns with some step-by-step screenshots has forced them to rectify or delete the dark pattern.

While most of the Dark Patterns are usually crafted deliberately during the interface design process, it is nonetheless possible that some of them are not purposely created to trick. Yet, when websites, apps, or any digital services are running, it is easy to realize their positive effects on the business. Consequently, they are not removed as they give positive results in A/B testing, that is, the statistical tests used to check which design gives a better performance in relation to one metric (for example, click-thru rates).[10]

Today, Dark Patterns are present in all sorts of environments. In video games, Zagal, Björk and Lewis have defined them as patterns "used intentionally by a game creator to cause a negative experience for players that are against their best interests and happen without their consent."[11] Although the definition does not mention that they are aimed at benefiting the game publisher, this is obviously the case: Dark Patterns not only push the player into spending more money but also trick them into spending more time and lower their social value by spamming their contact list, among other harms. In video games, Dark Patterns design is not only inscribed in the user interface but also on the rules, the mechanics, and the rest of the game elements. While these sorts of Dark Patterns are hard to distinguish, they also fall under our definition of Dark UX since the player eventually tends to regret some played sessions, terming them as, in the best-case scenario, a waste of time.

How Can We Spot a Dark UX?

Another reason why the term Dark Patterns became popular in mainstream media is its different clear labels to some particularly unethical technological experiences (such as "disguised ads" or "hidden costs"). Nonetheless, despite continuous e-mails with submissions made by internet users, the darkpatterns.org site has not increased its list from the initial ten to fifteen patterns. This is because, in some cases, the classification of one pattern into categories may not be straightforward or clear, since some tricks, due to their complexity, may fall at the same time into two or three categories, while in other cases, patterns sent by users are nothing but complaints of business deals or services rather than a thorough description of how the website worked.

As the scarce previous literature[12] suggests, classifying Dark UX into specific categories is challenging. Instead, I argue that the process of spotting Dark UX could be divided into two simple steps. First, ask how a particular dark pattern can be profitable for your company. Such profit can either be directly beneficial economically or can occur by means of other intangible benefits that eventually turn into profit. Second, in order to understand how Dark UX functions, I propose focusing on two communication concepts: *manipulation* and *deception*. I believe such concepts will help us understand how Dark UX operates and ultimately help us find strategies to counter them.

From Manipulation to Deception

How Do They Work?

Manipulation and deception are two classic concepts that have been long investigated in connection with persuasion studies in research fields such as Social Psychology and Communication. While in these fields, researchers focus on communication in its multi-modality—where verbal cues co-occur with gestural, facial, and prosodic cues. In digital applications such as websites, mobile apps, computer software, or video games, communication always takes place through user interfaces and in the interaction with their spaces and mechanisms. In fact, the use of multiple modalities such as the audiovisual is a key characteristic of technology along with persistence, anonymity, ubiquity, and personalization that endows it with a higher capacity for persuasion over human persuaders.[13]

In this sense, interaction designers pay attention to the use of typography, words, visual representation, and interface behavior in order to ease the users' tasks, and in some cases, influence them. This is what Anderson calls "seductive interaction design."[14] The mere fact that designers want to exert influence is not necessarily bad—such as easing the process of taking a necessary pill or of doing tedious work—as benevolent deception can sometimes be positive to the user experience.[15] However, in Dark UX, this influence comes in the form of manipulation and deception, and it is never aimed at the user's advantage.

Manipulation aims to change the behaviors or perceptions of others through abusive, deceptive, or underhanded tactics.[16] Although *deception* is sometimes included as part of the manipulation repertoire, it does not exploit the victim's vulnerabilities. Rather, it is limited to the inaccuracy of the information communicated. For this reason, I prefer discussing how each is applied to create Dark UX separately below.

Manipulation

In all cases, manipulation involves knowing the psychological vulnerabilities of the victim to determine which tactics are most effective.[17] Some of these tactics require tailoring the communication in order to drive the user motivation into the desired direction. In his book, *Evil by Design*, Nodder[18] uses the seven capital sins as metaphorical categories to explain how to communicate or interact with the customer in order to lead them to the desired actions.

One of the most manipulative internet tricks based on user's interest is called "clickbait."[19] It consists of using a short headline aimed at attracting the users' attention and obtaining their clicks—for example, sometimes using mysterious phrases like "and you will not believe what happened next." Beyond the headline hyperlink, there is often a piece of information not as valuable as to fulfill the previously set expectations, and users leave the site disappointed while having helped the website increase its number of page views. This is manipulative mainly because the same information could have been included in the initial headline, and the role of the page behind the hyperlink being that of expanding the headline with some additional information. However, in most cases, this descriptive headline would have been sufficient according to the user's interest in the topic. Other times, the information which follows the "clickbait" does not deliver the promised content at all, being a practice closer to deception.

Other manipulative tactics based on motivation try to tailor the context in which the user interacts, so it is harder for them to say no to a particular action at a given moment. For instance, in online multiplayer video games, "monetized rivalries" is a dark pattern that exploits player competitiveness.[20] In games that contain it, the player can initially enjoy the game even without spending any money until, at a given moment, the game mechanics drive to competitiveness between players that encourages them to buy some in-game options in order to achieve a status they would never reach otherwise. This is called "pay to win" or "pay to cheat" since players who use it do not rely on their skills to win. These Dark Patterns based on motivation are usually harder to identify since they are subtler. They smoothly create a situation in which players are faced with a choice they cannot refuse. "Privacy suckering"[21] is a similar dark pattern usually implemented in websites, which instead of asking for money, tricks users into sharing information about themselves (even information unrelated to the action they are doing or the product they are buying). Such a pattern is based on users' high interest in order to force them to disclose private data.

Some other manipulative tactics are based on people's lack of accurate visual perception. In fact, most of the usability principles were created in order to avoid mistakes due to these human factors. But once designers know how such principles work, they can deliberately turn them against the users' interests. For instance, knowing that people usually choose default options[22] may be used to make customers subscribe to predefined options and eventually pay more than they would if such an option had not been automatically selected. Likewise, there is a known usability fact which states that people do not read carefully but only scan documents,[23] and this is precisely at the base of the dark pattern "trick questions."[24] Users are asked to answer questions, which at a first glance seem to require a particular kind of answer, but upon reading more carefully, turn out to be totally different. In "tricky questions," several sentences are similarly or differently phrased in order to confuse the user into assuming the opposite (See Figure 4.1). Some advanced versions of this dark pattern combine tricky questions with relevant information hidden in long paragraphs instead of using a proper structure with headlines, subtitles, and visual hierarchies. Perception-based Dark Patterns are designed to play on users' vulnerabilities and exploit human cognition errors in a not-too-obvious way.

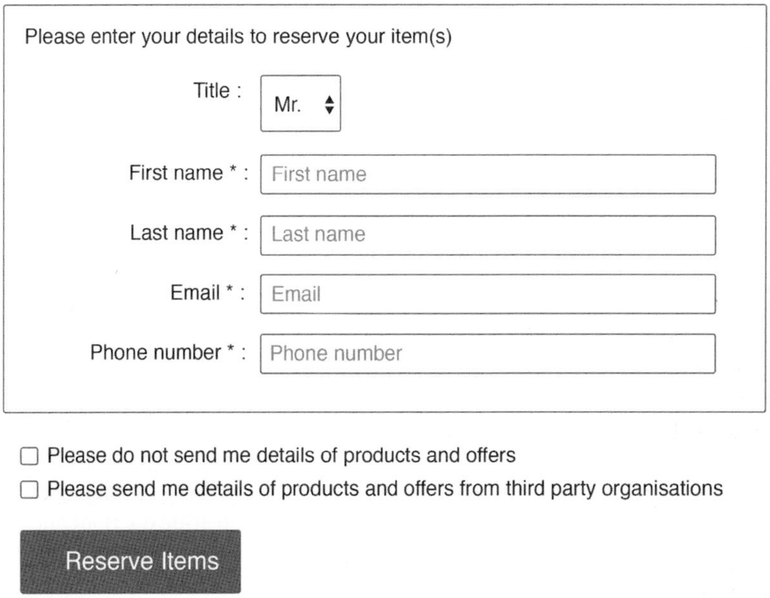

Please enter your details to reserve your item(s)

Title : [Mr. ⬍]

First name * : [First name]

Last name * : [Last name]

Email * : [Email]

Phone number * : [Phone number]

☐ Please do not send me details of products and offers
☐ Please send me details of products and offers from third party organisations

[Reserve Items]

FIGURE 4.1 *Trick question example, c. 2018. Courtesy of Marc Miquel-Ribé.*

Other tactics are "disguised ads,"[25] banners that are designed to appear exactly like the real information but which are actually paid ads; or "misdirection,"[26] which implies hiding relevant information or options by means of size and color while, making other options and information salient to distract users from the relevant ones. Unfortunately, the possibilities to create different variations of "misdirection" patterns are immense.[27]

One last type of manipulative tactic is based on creating frustration and disorientation so the user eventually gives up and tacitly accepts the current situation—whether it is paying a monthly fee or maintaining personal data on a server. This is a tactic commonly used in both online and offline processes of subscribing and unsubscribing. While in the latter case, customers are usually asked to call a number and provide detailed information in order to be able to unsubscribe, in the former case, the website's architecture and usability principles are designed to hinder navigation. The "roach motel"[28] dark pattern is aimed at making it difficult for users to reach what they are looking for. All the aspects that the information architecture field pays attention to, from menu to label clarity, can be perverted to create a great labyrinth where the exit that allows unsubscribing is always far. In fact, this dark pattern combines perfectly with the previously explained "misdirection," as they both take advantage of the user's lack of visual perception.

Deception

Contrary to manipulation, deception is intended to propagate information that is not true or to omit relevant information.[29] Thus, deception comes with different shades of grey depending on how clear or unclear communication is, and therefore, whether it allows the user to make decisions freely. For instance, "bait and switch"[30] consists of first showing how a part of the interface works, and later changing it without warning the user. The user is taught the meaning of a particular button, so when he sees others of the same color or shape, he is induced to infer that these new buttons will respond in a similar way to the previous one. However, such new buttons, which share the same appearance with the previous one, accomplish a different function. For example, in Figure 4.2, we can see a pop-up asking the user to update their operating system. In this case, and contrary to what all users learned from previous versions, clicking the close button activates the software upgrade instead of closing the pop-up. This is totally deceptive as there is no new information alerting of this behavior change.[31]

Other deceptive tactics are based on not explaining or disguising the real functioning of the service, so the user assumes it works in some controllable or expected way when in fact, it does not. These tactics have negative effects on game experiences. For instance, one such famous pattern is the "near-miss" in video gambling reel machines. In these games of chance, when the user draws three of the same items (e.g., cherries), the player wins a jackpot. When one of the three is different from the others, we say it is a near-miss. In terms of probabilities and rewards given to the player, the near-miss is nevertheless a non-win (like when all three drawings are different from one another), however, the effects of a near-miss on the player's behavior are powerful. Several studies[32] point out that near misses prolong the gambling. Hence, companies tend to display more near misses than there actually are in order to keep the player engaged and make him continue hoping and spending money. Such deceptive strategies that hide relevant information and let the users make incorrect inferences (i.e., that they are about to win) have been a controversial topic for decades.

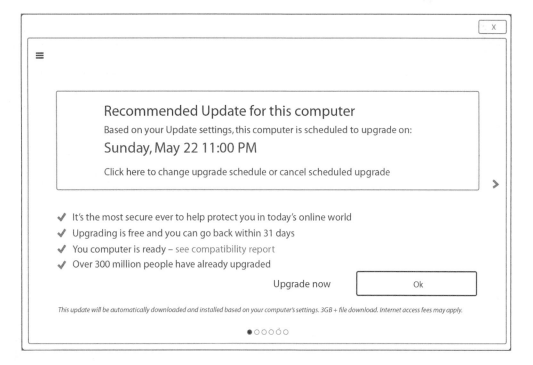

FIGURE 4.2 *Upgrade bait and switch detected, c. 2018. Courtesy of Marc Miquel-Ribé.*

Finally, one last type of deceptive tactics is based on hiding some relevant information at some key moments, such as, for instance, when decisions are being made. The Dark Patterns employing these tactics are usually directly related to spending money. For instance, the "hidden costs"[33] dark pattern appears in a multiple-step checkout process which shows an attractive initial price, but which changes completely at the last step due to extra charges (whether taxes, shipping costs or "handling fees"). By the time the user reaches this last step, he has already invested effort in filling in all the details, so he might be willing to accept paying an extra fee rather than starting over with some other online shop. If all the information were given in advance, the user could compare prices and make informed decisions.

Another tactic that implies hiding information during critical moments is based on encouraging users to use "credits" or tokens during the game instead of real money.[34] Such a strategy is common in games (both in mobiles and in video gambling machines). In this case, the only time when the user is fully aware of the quantity of money spent is at the beginning and at the end of the game or experience. At any other moments, since the real currency is masked by a fictitious currency, the values spent during the experience do not trigger the same alert messages at a conscious level, which would otherwise moderate the spending impulse. The value of the credit can be related to an in-game narrative, and the player, completely engaged in the game, can even lose the interest for the credits more easily than he would for real money. While many games promote in-game purchases, not all of them make visible (or easy to remember) the equivalence between credits and the real currency, hence being even more deceptive.

Conclusions

Dark UX applies knowledge about the user, typically for the company's benefit, even pushing the user to do actions that he or she might not have intended to do and would have certainly not done in other circumstances. It is called "dark" not only because it is unethical in its tactics and outcomes but also because the user is usually unaware while it is happening. The Dark Patterns are a popular way to identify and expose Dark UX, and there have been several attempts to classify them into particular categories.[35] Considering that this classification process may be unclear at times, I proposed distinguishing between the tactics based on manipulation and those based on deception as a useful way to reflect on how particular Dark Patterns operate.

Manipulation implies taking advantage of users' psychological weaknesses and it can relate to motivation and perception. Many Dark Patterns are based on usability facts and principles aimed at improving the user experience, and which are now applied in the exact opposite direction with respect to their initial objective.

On the other hand, deception works by clearly changing or hiding relevant information in order to alter the decision-making processes. Deception tactics are not as subtle as the manipulative ones, and they can be identified in a clearer way. Nonetheless, some sites are more original and include Dark Patterns that are a combination of the two. I argue that the benefit of the suggested distinction (manipulation and deception) is twofold. First, people may better understand how Dark Patterns operate and avoid being tricked by them. As I already mentioned elsewhere,[36] manipulation-based Dark Patterns can be countered with better education and increased design awareness. As far as deception-based Dark Patterns are concerned (like "near misses" or "hidden costs"), since they are easier to identify, they are likely easier to counter with legislation, and indeed, some have already been banned in the European Union.[37]

Second, the limited approaches to studying Dark UX often lack theory and empirical investigation. In order to classify Dark UX, it is important to really understand its nature, components, and how people process it. Hence, key concepts such as manipulation and deception can directly relate to psychological limitations and information qualities, which allow operationalization and measurement of the Dark UX practices elements. Empirical research based on these concepts might inform users, researchers, and legislators on which practices are more deceptive or manipulative, and at the same time, which eventually will provide a stronger knowledge base to demand technological applications free from them.

Notes

1 Marc Hassenzahl, "User Experience (UX): Towards an Experiential Perspective on Product Quality," in *Proceedings of the 20th International Conference of the Association Francophone D'Interaction Homme-Machine*, ed. Éric Brangier (New York: ACM, 2008), 2.

2 Goran Paunovic, "The Bottom Line: Why Good UX Design Means Better Business," *Forbes*, March 23, 2017, www.forbes.com/sites/forbesagencycouncil/2017/03/23/the-bottom-line-why-good-ux-desi gn-means-better-business/#943104f23960

3 "What are Dark Patterns?" Dark Patterns, n.d., https://darkpatterns.org

4 Jenifer Tidwell, *Designing Interfaces: Patterns for Effective Interaction Design* (Sebastopol: O'Reilly Media, 2005).

5 Eelke Folmer, *The Glossary of Human Computer Interaction*, Eva Hornecker et al., The Interaction Design Foundation, 2015, www.interaction-design.org/literature/book/the-glossary-of-human-compu ter-interaction/interaction-design-patterns

6 Daniel Berdichevsky and Erik Neuenschwander, "Toward an Ethics of Persuasive Technology," *Communications of the ACM* 42, no. 5 (1999): 51–58; B. J. Fogg, *Persuasive Technology: Using Computers to Change What We Think and Do* (San Francisco: Morgan Kaufmann Publishers, 2003).

7 Gregory J. Conti, "Evil Interfaces: Violating the User," *HOPE*, July 2008; Gregory J. Conti and Edward Sobiesk, "Malicious Interface Design: Exploiting the User," in *Proceedings of the 24th International Conference on World Wide Web* (New York: ACM Press, 2010).

8 Harry Brignull, "Dark Patterns: Inside the Interfaces Designed to Trick You," *The Verge*, August 29, 2013, www.theverge.com/2013/8/29/4640308/dark-patterns-inside-the-interfaces-designed-to-trick-y ou; Bruce Sterling, "Dark Patterns: User Interfaces Designed to Trick People," *WIRED*, February 10, 2014, wired.com/2014/02/dark-patterns-user-interfaces-designed-trick-people

9 Harry Brignull, "Dark Patterns: Deception vs. Honesty in UI Design," *A List Apart*, January 23, 2013, https://alistapart.com/article/dark-patterns-deception-vs.-honesty-in-ui-design

10 Jeff Sauro and James R. Lewis, *Quantifying the User Experience: Practical Statistics for User Research* (San Diego: Elsevier Science, 2016).

11 José Pablo Zagal, Staffan Björk, and Chris Lewis, "Dark Patterns in the Design of Games," in *Proceedings of the 8th Conference on Foundations of Digital Games 2013* (Gothenburg, Sweden: Department of Applied Information Technology, University of Gothenburg, 2013), 3.

12 Conti and Sobiesk, "Malicious Interface Design"; Zagal, Björk, and Lewis, "Dark Patterns in the Design of Games"; Sebastian Boring, Jo Vermeulen, and Jakub Dosta, "Dark Patterns in Proxemic Interactions—a Critical Perspective," in *Proceedings of the 12th ACM Conference on Designing Interactive Systems*, ed. Saul Greenberg (New York: ACM, 2014).

13 Fogg, *Persuasive Technology*.

14 Stephen P. Anderson, *Seductive Interaction Design: Creating Playful, Fun, and Effective User Experiences* (Berkeley: New Riders, 2011).

15 Eytan Adar, Desney S. Tan, and Jaime Teevan, "Benevolent Deception in Human Computer Interaction," in *Proceedings of the 2013 CHI Conference on Human Factors in Computing Systems*, Jaime Teevan et al. (Paris: ACM, 2013), 1863.

16 Harriet B. Braiker, *Who's Pulling Your Strings?: How to Break the Cycle of Manipulation and Regain Control of Your Life* (New York: McGraw-Hill, 2004).

17 George K. Simon, *In Sheep's Clothing Understanding and Dealing with Manipulative People* (Little Rock: A. J. Christopher, 1996).

18 Chris Nodder, *Evil by Design: Interaction Design to Lead Us into Temptation* (Indianapolis: Wiley, 2013).

19 Jonas N. Blom and Kenneth R. Hansen, "Click Bait: Forward-reference as Lure in Online News Headlines," *Journal of Pragmatics* 76 (2015): 87–100.

20 Zagal, Björk, and Lewis, "Dark Patterns in the Design of Games."

21 "Privacy Zuckering," Dark Patterns, n.d, https://darkpatterns.org/types-of-dark-pattern/privacy-zuckering

22 Jakob Nielsen, "The Power of Defaults," *Nielsen Norman Group*, September 26, 2005, nngroup.com/articles/the-power-of-defaults

23 Steve Krug, *Don't Make Me Think!: A Common Sense Approach to Web Usability* (Berkeley: New Riders, 2006); Susan Weinschenk, *100 Things Every Designer Needs to Know About People* (Berkeley: New Riders, 2011).

24 "Trick Questions," Dark Patterns, n.d., https://darkpatterns.org/types-of-dark-pattern/trick-questions

25 "Disguised Ads," Dark Patterns, n.d., https://darkpatterns.org/types-of-dark-pattern/disguised-ads

26 "Misdirection," Dark Patterns, n.d., https://darkpatterns.org/types-of-dark-pattern/misdirection

27 "Trick Questions," Dark Patterns, id.

28 "Roach Motel," Dark Patterns, n.d., https://darkpatterns.org/types-of-dark-pattern/roach-motel

29 Judee K. Burgoon and David B. Buller, "Interpersonal Deception Theory," *Communication Theory* 6, no. 3 (1996): 203–42.

30 "Bait and Switch," Dark Patterns, n.d., https://darkpatterns.org/types-of-dark-pattern/bait-and-switch

31 "Two Dots: Free Puzzle Game for IOS and Android," Dots, n.d., www.dots.co/twodots

32 Denis Côté et al., "Near Wins Prolong Gambling on a Video Lottery Terminal," *Journal of Gambling Studies* 19, no. 4 (November 2003): 433–38; Luke Clark et al., "Gambling Near-Misses Enhance Motivation to Gamble and Recruit Win-Related Brain Circuitry," *Neuron* 61, no. 3 (2009): 481–90.

33 "Hidden Costs," Dark Patterns, n.d., https://darkpatterns.org/types-of-dark-pattern/hidden-costs

34 Nodder, *Evil by Design.*

35 Zagal, Björk, and Lewis, "Dark Patterns in the Design of Games"; Conti and Sobiesk, "Malicious Interface Design."

36 Marc Miquel-Ribé, "Throwing Light on Dark UX with Design Awareness," *UX Magazine*, no. 1268, July 2014, https://uxmag.com/articles/throwing-light-on-dark-ux-with-design-awareness; Marc Miquel-Ribé, "Using Open Experience Design and Social Networking to Stamp Out Dark UX," *UX Magazine*, no. 1508, July 2015, https://uxmag.com/articles/using-open-experience-design-and-social-networking-to-stamp-out-dark-ux

37 Council of the European Union and European Parliament, *Directiva 2011/83/UE del Parlamento Europeo y del Consejo, de 25 de octubre de 2011 , sobre los derechos de los consumidores, por la que se modifican la Directiva 93/13/CEE del Consejo y la Directiva 1999/44/CE del Parlamento Europeo y del Consejo y se derogan la Directiva 85/577/CEE del Consejo y la Directiva 97/7/CE del Parlamento Europeo y del Consejo Texto pertinente a efectos del EEE* (The European Union, 2011).

5

Designing Safe Spaces for Virtual Reality: Methods for Merging Body Sovereignty Theory into VR Design Practice

Michelle Cortese and Andrea Zeller

Many Virtual Reality (VR) designers now accept the ethical responsibilities of removing a user's entire world and superseding it with a fabricated reality. These unique immersive design challenges are intensified when virtual experiences become public and socially driven. As female VR designers, we see an opportunity to fold the language of consent into the design practice of virtual reality—to design safe, accessible, virtual spaces.

New Worlds, Old Problems

Imagine it's your first time entering a social virtual reality (social VR) experience. You quickly set up an avatar, choosing feminine characteristics because you identify as female. You choose an outfit that seems appropriate, and when you're done, you spawn into a space. You have no idea where you are or who is around you. As you're getting your sea legs in this new environment, all the other avatars look at you and notice that you're different. Strange avatars quickly approach you, asking inappropriate questions about the way you look in real life, touching and kissing you without your consent. You try blocking them, but you don't know how. You remove your headset fearing that you don't belong in this community.

This narrative is based on multiple public accounts of avatar harassment in social VR applications, reported by women. In 2016, Taylor Lorenz, a staff tech writer at *The Atlantic*, shared her experience in a virtual reality room:

> Within two minutes of walking into the welcome room in . . . a leading social VR app, I was given my first unsolicited "virtual reality kiss." Shortly after, my skinny brown-haired avatar was swarmed by male users rubbing on me and asking if I was as skinny in real life or just

a fatty behind an avatar. I felt ripped from the virtual world and transported back to middle school.[1]

Less than two years later, popular VR platform *VRChat* publicly vowed to make safety a top priority after a female VR game designer shared a graphic recording of sexual harassment in a *VRChat* room.[2] While these cases are unique in the broader harassment landscape, they are a notable facet of an emerging market. In a 2018 study conducted by Jessica Outlaw for VR communication service, *Pluto*, nearly half of the female-identifying VR participants reported at least one instance of VR sexual harassment.[3]

Abuse and harassment due to anonymity on the internet have been well documented since the 1990s,[4] from trolling in chat rooms to cyberstalking and bullying on various social media platforms. Moreover, as our communication patterns evolve from text-based to immersive interactions, the perceptual physicality of VR gives harassers troubling new ways to attack. As female-identifying VR designers, we consider it our social responsibility to address abuse and harassment from an ethical design perspective and bring safety, consent, and body ownership to these foundational stages of VR.

Defining Social Interactions with Proxemics

When designing communication in virtual environments, we can look to factors that make up our real-world environment. Proxemics—a term coined by anthropologist Edward T. Hall—refers to the relationship between your identity, your surroundings, and the social norms of the community around you.[5] Proxemics can be categorized into four distinct zones: intimate, personal, social, and public.[6] The boundaries of these zones help us understand appropriacy at various distances[7] (see Figure 5.1).

For example, your bedroom is a space where intimate distance interactions can be expected, while a living room—shared with close family members—would encourage personal interactions. In contrast, a shared workspace is set up for social distance interactions. At a public space, like a park, you're able to keep a distance from other people. In locations that lack the necessary space to maintain social or public behaviors, people may introduce additive factors, like headphones or arm placements, to convey their need for a personal safety zone.

The act of demarcating and protecting embodied personal space is a requirement for mediating who is let into intimate and personal zones. While proxemics can be implied for a space, people need to feel in full control in any space and be able to decide what happens to their body. Hall demonstrates that regardless of the collective understanding of any given space, participants still have the adjacency to decide how they interact.[8] This control over our decisions is rooted in body sovereignty, the sentiment that all people should have complete ownership of their bodies and any interactions that should occur to them.[9]

Challenges arise when spaces overlap these boundaries, like public trains. Public environments with intimate vulnerabilities have clearly defined behavioral rules to protect against inappropriate behavior between participants.[10] These guidelines, often referred to as codes of conduct, offer explicit rules for what sorts of behavior are acceptable and unacceptable within a space. Conduct codes empower body sovereignty by defining appropriacy, highlighting universal safety, and enabling participants to report misbehavior. When a code of conduct is not reinforced, additional methods of intervention can take place, often causing exclusion to those who need protection most. One example of an exclusionary experience is a female-only train

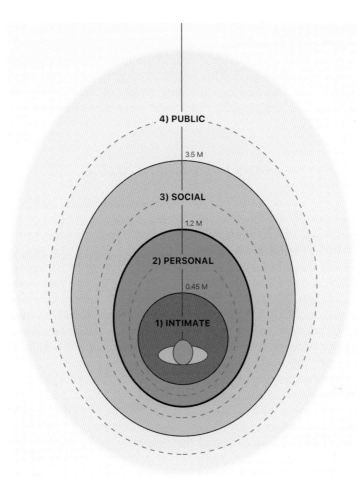

FIGURE 5.1 *Illustration of Edward T. Hall's Zones of Interpersonal Space, c. 2018. Courtesy of Michelle Cortese and Andrea Zeller.*

car, found in countries like Japan and Brazil. "Female-only carriages were first introduced in Japan in 2000, . . . as a way to stop sexual harassment."[11] When reporting options and justice procedures fail citizens, the systems are left to reactively redesign around threats, an ineffective way to build for inclusivity.

As social VR designers, we can aim to create implicitly and proactively safe social virtual communities. Using Hall's definitions of interpersonal space, we can define explicit structures for appropriate behavior and build natural boundaries in virtual social relationships.

Body Sovereignty as a VR Design Practice

In order to construct comprehensive safety features for social VR experiences, designers should understand the social and physical complexities of these experiences. Using Hall's "Zones of Interpersonal Space" as a spatial and emotional scale to analyze different aspects of spatial experiences with virtual bodies, we will develop a design language for safe, inclusive social VR. Starting from the inner circle of intimacy, we will break down characteristics at each stage of the interpersonal space spectrum and provide examples on how to bring body sovereignty theory into VR design practice, level-by-level. This results in suggestions for consent introspection at each level of the spectrum and develops building blocks of accountable social VR conduct codes. All offered solutions are considerations and recommendations, not requirements for implementation.

Zone 1: Intimate Space

Intimate distance is the closest zone to you and starts from 0–18 inches away (0–46 cm). Because of the proximity of the presence of another person, it may be overwhelming due to stepped-up sensory inputs like smell, touch, and sound. Physical contact or the possibility of physical contact is high. The challenge at this distance is to ensure that people who are within this close and intimate distance both want to be there and want to engage in activities at this proximity. Communication in real life at this distance is nuanced and complex, and virtual embodiment is no different. Therefore, we cannot assume that users electing to enter an intimate space together are automatically on the same page. Designers should set up proactive dialogs before the experience begins to ensure that all participants can curate their interactions to their own level of proxemic comfort. The closest, most intimate relations require the clearest, most explicit guidelines.

We can find inspiration for these proactive dialogs in the processes by which people in close relationships come to a mutual understanding of intimate experiences. We can look to paradigms for predetermining intimate agreements in various types of couplings, like "Yes, No, Maybe" charts and boundary setting tools for romantic relationships (see Figure 5.2). Couples use these tools to define the boundaries of their intimate experiences before they occur. As Rachel Kramer Bussel describes in her essay, "Beyond Yes or No: Consent as Sexual Process," it is beneficial for all participating members of an activity to have previously, and explicitly, stated their boundaries and desires; these are not contractual agreements binding participants to activities, but rather statements of previous interest or enjoyment.[12] Bussel instructs on the usage of "Yes, No, Maybe" charts, a procedure by which individuals in close relationships may list all intimate acts imaginable and then, "categorize them into things [they] enjoy/would like to do, things [they] don't ever want to do, and things [they are] not sure about or might try under certain circumstances."[13] This guideline allows participants to preemptively constrain all possible future experiences and limits interactions to those that are known to be comfortable for their own body or personal space.

Likewise, for individuals in polyamorous relationships—where truthful communication is required to define the experience for all parties involved—setting boundaries in advance is a critical component of healthy experiences.[14] Particularly, participants in nonmonogamous relationships "go through an explicit process of negotiation and boundary delineation, defining particular behaviors, emotions, and kinds of partners as either acceptable or off-limits."[15]

Furthermore, the process by which couples set comfort zones and outline emotional boundaries for their respective online social networking can be used as a parallel to how we may use proactive dialogs to build trust and satisfaction. The 2014 *Cyberpsychology* article, "Couple Boundaries for Social Networking in Middle Adulthood" posits that many married couples have preset boundaries for social networking and that these agreements are associated with

Yes, No, Maybe: Chart for Intimate Partners

Activity	Experience Yes/No	Willingness 0-5	Notes & Nuances
Biting	Y	3	Context-specific, ask about it
Body Paint	Y	4	
Corsets	N	0	Absolutely never, don't ask
Hugging	Y	5	Always fine
Intercourse	N	0	Possible but unlikely
Kissing	Y	4	
Rough Play	N	0	Absolutely never

FIGURE 5.2 *A hypothetical example of a "Yes, No, Maybe" chart. c. 2018. Courtesy of Michelle Cortese and Andrea Zeller.*

improved relational trust and satisfaction.[16] Opportunities for accidental breaches are limited when couples align on each other's intentions, this process also allows for greater freedom in the pursuit of common goals.[17]

Designing Safety for Intimate VR Spaces

In surveying predetermined, mutual understandings of complex and intimate experiences, we can extract several social VR design principles. We can empower users by allowing them to define their ideal experience up front to ensure that their experiences never violate their digital intimate space. One option is to supply granular controls and deploy opt-in setup dialogs *before* the user enters the social VR space. Everyone should feel that they have entered an intimate space with a clear understanding of what that relationship looks like—that they have delineated the bounds of all future interactions with ease and confidence.

Users should be prompted, through naturalized dialogs (in the software), to set their boundaries before any social interaction takes place. Experience curation should be part of initial setup, rather than reactively setting safety mechanisms following harassment or negative experience. We should provide users with sliding scales of safety precautions for personal customization: many users with experiential concerns do not want to participate in an overprotective or limiting experience. Allowing users to pick and choose safety options allows them to curate an ideal experience, providing them with a safe environment while still preserving the feeling of adventure. To facilitate the sliding scales of safety options, we must offer granular controls. There is a difference between a block and a mute, and there should be some natural negotiability between these states.

Zone 2: Personal Space

Personal distance starts at 18 inches (46 cm) and goes until about 4 feet (122 cm). It is the zone for people who are not in contact with each other. It can be thought of as a protective bubble that a person maintains between themselves and others but may allow people who they have an established relationship with (romantic, marriage, family, close friends) to be within this circle. The challenge for virtual environments at this distance is that people have different ways of communicating, and we need to provide equal tools to everyone to be able to feel comfortable interacting in this distance. At this personal level, users must have reactionary mechanisms for empowerment, understanding, and agency.

Designers can influence intuitive tools for safety and empowerment by looking at how clinical practices secure enthusiastic consent via nonverbal behaviors, subtleties, and other varying human communication capacities. The *Social Emotional Teaching Strategies* guidebook[18] unpacks various mechanisms for silently sensing the feelings of others, empowering children to identify and understand emotions via feeling faces, helping them understand and support the desires of others. Furthermore, the guidebook describes,

> One way to help children be more successful in developing friendship skills is to "teach" them to label, understand, express, and control emotions. . . . Children who don't learn to use emotional language have a hard time labeling and understanding their own feelings as well as accurately identifying how others feel.[19]

Conjointly, the United Kingdom's Mental Capacity Act was created to protect and empower adults who may lack the mental capacity to make their own treatment decisions. The Act describes variabilities in understanding and communication and advises on adapting consent dialogs to "A way that is appropriate to [the patient's] circumstances" and reinforcing this dialog by prompting the patient for ongoing feedback.[20] Similarly, the United States' National Institutes of Health has a set of rules for sensitively seeking consent from deaf and hard-of-hearing participants in clinical trials, asking that clinicians "develop informed consent materials that are responsive to the variations of language used by deaf and hard-of-hearing people [and] consider visual information such as symbols, pictures or diagrams on the consent form to enhance understanding."[21]

Designing Safety for Personal VR Space

These custom-tailored consent acquisition paradigms outline a framework for creating inclusive dialogs and reactionary tools that allow all users (regardless of their comfort levels, safety needs, or communication modes) the basic tenets of consent and experiential control. To manifest these sorts of clinical consent frameworks in social VR, designers can consider providing intuitive safety gestures to allow users to react to personal space violations quickly and fluidly. Employing gestures for this procedure feels intuitive, natural, and empowering: "We commonly think of gestures, actions, and expressions of people as being more or less characteristic of them, as embodying or revealing aspects that are more or less central to them."[22] Established, codified gestures are often used in personal interactions to communicate volumes without removing immersion.

Another consideration is to emotionally check in on our users and keep an eye out for users who may be having negative experiences. For example, if a user has become noncommunicative or attempts to report an incident and does not complete, it may be helpful to assist them. Just as we should check in during any consensual activity to make sure all parties are still participating with willful intent, we should keep track of our user's levels of active, affirmative interactions.

Additionally, we can aim to provide violation-reporting tools that do not punish users by degrading their experience. Ideally, these tools should not remove the user who accesses them from the experience or provide a lessened experience during or after blocking another user. Reporting should feel safe and integrated. These tools should be intuitive, easy to access, and provide immediate protection when deployed. Designing these tools may require consideration outside of the standard Flag, Block, and Leave actions depending on the unique dangers of the experience for which we are designing. Empowering people to report is core to ethical design. If people cannot report abuse, the community cannot build in protection.

Zone 3: Social Space

Social space is the zone for impersonal transactions, and we rely solely on what we can hear and see. Impersonal interactions and co-working tend to use this social distance. The challenge for social distance is that community behavior is guided by delicately maintained localized etiquette. In this niche of social environments, participants rely on soft, unspoken rule systems to determine and validate prospective behaviors.

We can learn how to instate protective, localized behavior rules by studying the places and circumstances which have unspoken, location-based conduct agreements to keep participants safe and reduce redundant consent discourse.

First, we can look to localized social conduct codes set by colleges to prevent on-campus sexual assault. In 2014, California Governor Jerry Brown signed a Senate Bill, informally known as the "Yes Means Yes" bill, into law, enacting "a definition of sexual consent known as 'affirmative consent' for all state-funded colleges in California." This bill establishes and instates a specialized, context-specific, soft rule set for all consent-adjacent interactions within California schools. Colleges and universities found that failure to enact said rules might lead to denial of their contracted state funding.[23] College campus social codes promoting affirmative consent first became a part of popular culture in the early 1990s when Antioch College adopted the "Sexual Offense Prevention Policy" (SOPP). SOPP provided "a definition of consent that requires an active, verbal offering of permission, as opposed to a lack of refusal, to a sexual encounter of any degree,"[24] to prevent sexual misconduct. At Antioch, opting into life on the premises served as a silent agreement to laws of SOPP.

As mentioned earlier, in specialized social spaces like community gyms and swimming pools, participants follow unspoken rules, routines, and rituals to respect the private space of the fellow patrons around them.[25] Susie Scott notes that participants perform as "disinterested strangers" and are surprisingly "orderly and civilized"[26] due to an unspoken agreement to respect other people's personal space and experiential intention. Individuals who opt to enter these sorts of specialized spaces silently consent to the soft, localized laws of the area and do so to maintain the experience of all participants.

Designing Safety for Social VR Space

Localized rules and behavioral agreements in niche social environments provide a framework for implementing soft laws into our social VR spaces. This is particularly important when our virtual worlds reference real-world locations. For example, popular social VR app, *Rec Room*, borrows the metaphor of a real-world space, without considering the real-world codes of conduct in that space. Katharine Schwab describes the *Rec Room* virtual space as resembling a recreational facility run by the *YMCA*, a charitable organization and wellness center "where participants can play games like dodgeball and paintball in a group. When first-time users enter the space, they begin in a locker room that everyone shares."[27] She goes on to describe her own experience entering the space and her previous frame of reference that a locker room may not be an inclusive environment and is "a space that's already fraught with misogyny for many women."[28]

To prevent the discomfort experienced by Schwab in *Rec Room*, one consideration is to exhibit specialized rule sets fit the unique social needs and challenges of a space's use case. Just as all specialized real-world spaces have unique and unspoken behavioral agreements, all specialized, mid-size virtual spaces require unique consideration for the prospective boundaries that should exist to maintain the intended experience of the space, for all users. "Different VR systems or types of [Virtual Embodiments] provide different frames for our encounter [and] if this applies to individual encounters and how we present ourselves to each other, it will also apply to larger groups."[29]

We can maximize user comfort by proactively understanding subtleties in interactions as an ongoing service to our users' emotional experience. Because VR can actuate a full gamut of emotions that can be internalized as real,[30] we should be on the lookout—via signals users provide us—for such trauma. It is our responsibility as designers to use this information in a positive, constructive, and accountable way, to better understand emotional distress in our users and dispatch helpful prompts in at-risk events.

Zone 4: Public Space

Public space describes the 12–20 foot (3–6 m) communication distance from which it is harder to read body language and tone. Comparative to shopping malls or public parks, public spaces are open to any and all people. We can prevent the design of lawless and dangerous worlds, both physical and virtual, by fostering spaces that provide capacity for communication and expression, the opportunity to exercise free will, and accountability for offensive actions. We should do so by building small sets of hard laws and respective consequences—based on legal definitions of safety and consent—for world-scale, public social VR experiences.

We can look to real-world law systems—their definitions of consent, evaluations of behavior violations, and the consequences that befall conduct criminals—to find inspiration in designing ethical social VR infrastructure and contributing to a universal VR behavioral code.

First, we could survey legal definitions of consent and the hardline laws that support them. In the United States, consent has no federally standardized legal definition. The State of California defines consent as "positive cooperation in act or attitude pursuant to the exercise of free will. The person must act freely and voluntarily and have knowledge of the nature of the act or transaction involved."[31] Despite varying legal definitions of consent, sexual acts are universally considered nonconsensual or criminal in various instances. Many of these universally criminal incidences exist when a participant is incapable of understanding their circumstances, whether due to intoxication, mental deficiency, or through being "under the age of legal consent, [or] of an age where sex is not lawful."[32]

Additionally, we can look to repercussions for nonconsensual behavior and their effect on the public collective consciousness: "The convictions and sentences of rape cases, especially in the age of new media, preach a moral lesson about who and what the U.S. legal system identifies as an actor in sexual assault."[33] In England's *R v Sussex Judges* case, Lord Hewitt argued, "Not only must Justice be done; it must also be seen to be done." High-profile, publicly documented consent violation trials help to "invigorate the movement for more comprehensive consent education"—public lessons gleaned from these cases have the opportunity to fuel conversation and "build momentum for greater awareness and attention to sexual assault and consent."[34]

Designing Safety for Public VR Space

The examples provided so far address how we publicly establish law, consequence, and behavioral expectation concerning consent and violations of consent in the real world. By studying these legal structures, we can derive key principles for designing universal ethical codes and behavioral expectations in public social VR experiences, and across the industry.

In order to design truly safe, public VR spaces, one approach is to establish a universal policy system to protect against unethical behavior and commonly offensive content. In the paper, "Real Virtuality: A Code of Ethical Conduct," Madary, Michael, and Thomas K. Metzinger stress that high-level ethical systems in VR help to reinforce user agency.[35] They go on to posit that certain types of VR content and experiences should be discouraged in various ways, "obvious candidates for such content would be sex (virtual pedophilia, virtual rape) and violence."[36]

We should also ask our users to consider the proxemic comfort zones of our real-world bodies and the bodies of those they interact with when participating in public social VR experiences. This reconsideration is not as far-fetched as it seems; contemporary developments in cognitive neuroscience and body ownership describe the "rubber hand illusion" in which a "visible rubber hand that is located in a plausible position in front of [a test subject] results in the illusion that the rubber hand is their hand."[37] In the same way, "Virtual reality can transform not only your sense of place, and of reality, but also the apparent properties of your own body."[38] We can utilize this embodiment to set conduct rules that mirror standards of the acceptable social experiences for our real-world bodies.

> A reasonable starting point on this issue would be to treat avatars in an analogous manner to personality rights relating to the publication of photos. . . . Just as many accept the right of an individual to control the commercial use of his or her name, image, likeness, one might, for example, interpret the "right to my own avatar" a property right as opposed to a personal right.[39]

This option is not always possible—particularly for commercial experiences—but helps foster user agency when available.

Lastly, we should establish universal conduct expectations by administering timely and appropriate consequences to violators. Public VR spaces should echo the public laws we live within every day, because, "virtual identification can cause real suffering, and real suffering is relevant for the law."[40] Moreover, virtual repercussions for behavior violations in virtual space could be good for our real-world lives, as it has been noted that "virtual reality experiences have lasting effects even after users have left a virtual environment."[41] What is good for the virtual world could be good for the physical world.

Beyond the Zones

As social VR designers, we hold the unique opportunity to create worlds unbound by reality's constraints. When approaching the responsibility of constructing new social environments—regardless of how surreal they may be—we should remind ourselves to treat virtual embodiment with the same respect given to physical bodies. It is our responsibility to design innately safe virtual spaces and interactions, laying the groundwork for a future of inclusive, secure and empowering VR communities.

Finally, when applying this methodology of virtual body sovereignty, remember that it is a singular framework and not an end-all solution. As social VR matures, more opportunities will arise to translate real-world ethics into virtual ethics. We should be actively and continuously looking to real-world interaction frameworks—like Hall's zones of interpersonal space—and appropriating relevant ethical structures into our VR creations.

A safe future is in our virtual hands.

Notes

1 Taylor Lorenz, "Here's What Happened When I Was Surrounded by Men in Virtual Reality," *Mic*, May 26, 2016, mic.com/articles/144470/sexual-harassment-in-virtual-reality#.zqMVIy4Hh

2 Jamie Feltham, "VRChat Dev Vows to Address 'Harmful' User Behavior in Open Letter," *UploadVR*, January 12, 2018, uploadvr.com/vrchat-dev-vows-address-harmful-users-open-letter/

3 Jessica Outlaw, "Virtual Harassment: The Social Experience of 600+ Regular Virtual Reality (VR) Users," *The Extended Mind*, April 4, 2018, https://extendedmind.io/blog/2018/4/4/virtual-harassment-the-social-experience-of-600-regular-virtual-reality-vrusers

4 Kaveri Subrahmanyam, David Smahel, and Patricia Greenfield, "Connecting Developmental Constructions to the Internet: Identity Presentation and Sexual Exploration in Online Teen Chat Rooms," *Developmental Psychology* 42, no. 3 (2006): 396–97.

5 Edward T. Hall, *The Hidden Dimension: An Anthropologist Examines Man's Use of Space in Public and Private* (New York: Anchor Books, 1982), 2.

6 Edward T. Hall, "A System for the Notation of Proxemic Behavior," *American Anthropologist* 65, no. 5 (1963): 1004.

7 Hall, *The Hidden Dimension*, 2.

8 Hall, "A System for the Notation of Proxemic Behavior," 1003.

9 Jaclyn Friedman and Jessica Valenti, *Yes Means Yes!: Visions of Female Sexual Power Et a World Without Rape* (Berkeley: Seal Press, 2008), 171.

10 Susie Scott, "Re-clothing the Emperor: The Swimming Pool as a Negotiated Order," *Symbolic Interaction* 32, no. 2 (2009): 123–45.

11 Radhika Sanghani, "These Countries Tried Women-Only Transport: Here's What Happened," *The Telegraph*, August 16, 2015, www.telegraph.co.uk/women/womens-life/11824962/Women-only-trains-and-transport-How-they-work-around-the-world.htm

12 Friedman and Valenti, *Yes Means Yes!*, 45.

13 Ibid.

14 Rhonda N. Balzarini et al., "Perceptions of Primary and Secondary Relationships in Polyamory," *PLOS ONE* 12, no. 5 (2017).

15 Meg Barker and Darren Langdridge, *Understanding Non-Monogamies* (New York: Routledge, 2012), 16.

16 Aaron M. Norton and Joyce Baptist, "Couple Boundaries for Social Networking in Middle Adulthood: Associations of Trust and Satisfaction," *Cyberpsychology: Journal of Psychosocial Research on Cyberspace* 8, no. 4 (2014).

17 Ibid.

18 Gail E. Joseph et al., *Social Emotional Teaching Strategies* (Nashville: Center on the Social and Emotional Foundations for Early Learning, 2012), http://csefel.vanderbilt.edu/modules/module2/script.pdf

19 Ibid., 26.

20 Carol Tullo, ed., *Mental Capacity Act* (London: The Stationery Office, 2005), 6.

21 National Institutes of Health and The National Institute on Deafness and Other Communication Disorders, "Guidelines on Communicating Informed Consent for Individuals Who Are Deaf or Hard-of-Hearing and Scientists," *National Institutes of Health (NIH)*, February 16, 2016, www.nih.gov/health-information/nih-clinical-research-trials-you/guidelines-communicating-informed-consent-individuals-who-are-deaf-or-hard-hearing-scientists

22 Meir Dan-Cohen, "Responsibility and the Boundaries of the Self," *Harvard Law Review* 105, no. 5 (1992): 966.

23 Julia Frances Morrison, "Pedagogies of Consent: What Consent Teaches us about Contemporary American Sexual Politics" (master's thesis, Wesleyan University, 2017), https://wesscholar.wesleyan.edu/etd_hon_theses/1736

24 Ibid.

25 Scott, "Re-clothing the Emperor."

26 Ibid., 126.

27 Katharine Schwab, "VR Has a Harassment Problem," Fast Company, n.d., www.fastcodesign.com/90166592/vr-has-a-harassment-problem

28 Ibid.

29 Ralph Schroeder, "Social Interaction in Virtual Environments: Key Issues, Common Themes, and a Framework for Research," *The Social Life of Avatars: Computer Supported Cooperative Work*, ed. Ralph Schroeder (London: Springer, 2002).

30 Thomas Metzinger, *Being No One: The Self-Model Theory of Subjectivity* (Cambridge: The MIT Press, 2006).

31 Morrison, "Pedagogies of Consent."

32 Heather Corinna, "Driver's Ed for the Sexual Superhighway: Navigating Consent," Scarleteen, November 11, 2010, www.scarleteen.com/article/abuse_assault/drivers_ed_for_the_sexual_superhighway_navigating_consent

33 Morrison, "Pedagogies of Consent."

34 Ibid.

35 Michael Madary and Thomas K. Metzinger, "Real Virtuality: A Code of Ethical Conduct: Recommendations for Good Scientific Practice and the Consumers of VR-Technology," *Frontiers in Robotics and AI* 3 (2016).

36 Ibid.

37 M. Slater, "Place Illusion and Plausibility Can Lead to Realistic Behaviour in Immersive Virtual Environments," *Philosophical Transactions of the Royal Society B: Biological Sciences* 364, no. 1535 (2009): 3549–57.

38 Ibid.

39 Madary and Metzinger, "Real Virtuality."

40 Ibid.

41 Daniel Oberhaus, "We're Already Violating Virtual Reality's First Code of Ethics," *Motherboard*, March 6, 2016, https://motherboard.vice.com/en_us/article/yp3va5/vr-code-of-ethics

6

Who Owns the Smart City? Toward an Ethical Framework for Civic AI

Michael A. Madaio and Sarah Edmands Martin

Introduction

In New York City, the bridges over the parkways to Jones Beach were too low. At 9 feet between the overpass and the road, automobiles could pass underneath, but public buses could not, limiting access to Jones Beach for lower-income residents without cars since their construction in 1929.[1] Urban planner Robert Moses' inequitable bridge designs have become a canonical example of how design instantiates ethics.[2] Now, as the physical infrastructure of everyday life in cities becomes increasingly interleaved with digital infrastructure, we must grapple with the ethics embedded in the design of socio-technical civic systems. Particularly as civic technologies increasingly rely on methods from artificial intelligence, the inner workings of these civic AI systems are often opaque[3] and may encode biases into their design.[4] For instance, many police jurisdictions have adopted an approach known as predictive policing, which uses crime incident data to predict the risk level of neighborhoods to inform police patrol deployment.[5] However, this veneer of algorithmic objectivity masks the entrenched historical biases present in the data used to train such models, perpetuating biases under the guise of neutrality.[6]

As cities increasingly adopt the rhetoric of the much-hyped "Smart City," deploying networks of sensors to collect data throughout urban life, concerned citizens and designers of civic AI systems alike are at a critical juncture to interrogate the ethics imbued into these technologies. In this chapter, we describe how democratic values of participation, inclusivity, and citizen engagement can be instantiated into the design of the algorithms that may soon govern civic life. While municipal and federal governments have long used digital tools, two recent developments may threaten the democratic participation of citizens in the machinery of civic governance. These are (1) the turn toward corporatization of civic technologies through so-called smart-city initiatives, and (2) the turn toward the use of AI methods such as machine learning to build predictive models using historical data to inform municipal decision-making. This use of complex machine-learning algorithms coupled with the often-proprietary nature of corporate systems used in public life suggests a need for both an ethical framework with which to analyze such technologies and a design process to engage in a more democratic, participatory design of civic technologies.

In this chapter, the authors draw on theories of civic participation to articulate an ethical framework for the design of civic machine-learning systems, reading several high-stakes examples of these systems through this lens, such as predictive algorithms for policing and social services. We then propose a more democratic design process for civic machine-learning systems, drawing on design methods such as participatory design and speculative design, and on recent machine-learning methods such as "human-in-the-loop" and user experience design (UX) for machine-learning.[7] As machine-learning algorithms are developed and deployed in ever more areas of civic life, from education, public safety, transportation, and yes, even for the predictive maintenance of Moses' bridges, it is critical that these systems are designed to instantiate democratic values.

What is a "Smart City"?

With over 400 mayors signed up for the 2018 Smarter Cities conference[8] and over $80 billion in investment in smart-city sensors and data systems predicted for 2018,[9] there is clearly a great deal of money and technology flowing into proprietary data collection and analysis technologies in urban centers around the world. The term itself is a powerful rhetorical strategy. Who would want to live in a dumb city? However, considering the seriousness with which municipal leaders are buying into the rhetoric of the "smart city," it is critical to ask what is meant, what visions and ethics of civic life are embedded in the rhetoric, and what role there might be for the citizen in such a city.

Much of this investment is tied to the increasingly ubiquitous sensors deployed throughout civic life and the vast quantities of data they generate at incredibly high velocities. These include sensors to measure everything from energy grid usage to public transit data to pothole repair data and more.[10] One view of the smart city, perhaps the most common, fetishizes the idea of a synoptic, all-seeing, control center where city officials, playing out their most SimCity-esque fantasies, have all the data from their city at their fingertips. An optimistic reading of the hyperbolic rhetoric of these initiatives is that the smart city is better positioned to provide services for its residents, be that for public safety, transportation or energy infrastructure, public health, or social services.

However, data alone does not make a smart city. These data are then fed into algorithms designed to optimize for a set of outcomes, such as a more efficient source of energy or transportation grid, faster detection of blighted properties, or more efficiently targeting welfare services at the citizens who may need them most.[11] In such a smart city, will the average citizen have input into the outcomes these systems are optimizing for—or will these be proprietary decisions made by private companies unaccountable to the public? Civic agencies' decisions are increasingly being augmented by (or in some cases offloaded to) machine intelligence in the form of predictive algorithms known as machine learning.[12] In these models, historical data are fed into algorithms, which are trained to detect certain outcomes of interest in those data based on features in the input data. As an example, risk assessment has historically been central in informing decision-making in many civic agencies, and machine-learning predictive risk algorithms have had some success in increasing the efficiency and effectiveness of existing procedures.[13]

One recently popular use case for predictive analytics is in predictive policing, or, using data from historical crime incidents to make statistical predictions about the locations most likely to have a crime incident in the future—often likened to the movie *Minority Report*.[14] Police departments in many states are using these predictive policing approaches, often contracted out to independent contractors.[15] However, if the input data used to "train," the model is biased due to historical patterns of systemic bias in policing predominantly black neighborhoods as is the case in many cities, then this model may lead to more policing of those same neighborhoods, compounding the inequity.[16] Often, cities will enter into contracts with third-party companies without subjecting them to periods of public review or commentary. In fact, when one such company, PredPol, was initially pitched to the city council of the city of Cocoa, Florida, information about the methods involved was explicitly "exempt from public inspection," citing Florida statutes regarding protection of police surveillance methods.[17] One particularly egregious example of this is in New Orleans, where Palantir Technologies had developed a method to identify citizens likely to be a member of a gang based on data about their criminal histories, ties to current gang members, and social media data.[18] However, the contract was so secretive that not only did many members of the NOLA city council not know about the algorithm, the people accused of membership in gangs did not either, and thus could not appeal the algorithmic determination made about them.[19]

This is indicative of the increasing corporatization of civic technologies in the so-called smart city. The prevailing paradigm of the smart city treats citizens as *consumers*, as *users* of city services, but crucially not as *co-contributors* to the design of civic AI systems, whether for social services, infrastructure, public safety, or more. Many city councils are turning to private corporations to offload the task of gathering and analyzing data to inform decision-making in matters that should be of public concern.[20] The privatization of these civic processes results in the exclusion of citizens from the decision-making process, and masks these civic systems from public review and scrutiny, as seen with Palantir, PredPol, and many others, making them difficult to critique or hold accountable.

As a result, citizens are transformed from active participants in the development of their city into passive recipients of data-driven services. In such a socio-technical milieu, what is the role of the citizen? If the city is smart, how smart must the citizen be in order to contribute to its development? These questions are often left unaddressed in the hyperbolic discourse of investment in smart cities technologies. The unquestioned technocratic ethos of these systems imagines the citizen as a recipient of the purported benefits of their systems (if they think of them at all). Yet, the relationship between the citizen and the state is a fundamental question at the heart of democratic civic life. Are citizens merely generators of data and passive beneficiaries of systems designed and developed by third-party corporations? Can there be a more democratic method for designing civic machine-learning systems for smart cities? In the next two sections, we will outline an ethical framework with which to understand the nature of citizen participation in the design of civic machine-learning systems and describe a design process that may help contribute to more participatory, democratic smart cities technologies.

Ethical Framework for Civic Machine-Learning Systems

While machine-learning (ML) researchers have only recently begun proposing ethical guidelines for designing machine-learning systems,[21] urban planning theorists have been debating the role of the citizen in civic life for decades. In the following sections, we discuss some ethical considerations relevant for ML (e.g., equity, transparency and accountability, privacy, and consent) and we discuss how those have unique implications when applied to *civic* machine learning specifically. To understand why this is the case, we draw on ideas of citizen participation from urban planning and urban theory. Foremost among these is the highly influential model of the "ladder" of citizen participation, first proposed by public policy scholar Sherry Arnstein.[22] She proposed a set of "rungs," including nonparticipation, tokenism, partnership, and control. In the nonparticipation model, citizens are either manipulated by a centralized government or are at best recipients of benefits from the government. Then, in a tokenist approach, citizens are merely informed of decisions. In a partnership model, citizens are equal partners in deliberative decision-making. Finally, at the highest "rung," citizens have control over the civic decision-making process.[23] We also draw on sociologist Henri LeFebvre's argument that citizens have a "right to the city," which, in his work, was a right to the physical spaces as well as the digital representations of the city.[24] If the citizen has a right to move freely about the city, then we must engage honestly in a debate about what rights citizens have to data privacy, to freedom from surveillance, and to freedom from the algorithmic control of one's behavior. With the increasing corporatization of the smart city, it is even more critical to understand the rights citizens have over the algorithmic decision-making at work in civic life, and how citizens can be more involved in the design of these civic AI systems.

Data-driven Biases in Machine Learning

Recent research has highlighted the ways in which machine-learning algorithms across domains may perpetuate existing racial and gender biases from biases in the data they use to "train" their models, compounding existing social inequities.[25] This data-driven discrimination has been demonstrated in advertising,[26] where Google searches for names more often associated with black males return ads suggesting the presence of an arrest record at greater rates, and in image labeling, where, for example, images of a person cooking are consistently labeled as a woman,[27] among many other examples.[28]

In civic machine-learning applications, the two most often-cited examples of social biases being perpetuated due to biases in the data are in the criminal justice domain—as in the predictive policing work discussed already, and in a recidivism risk prediction algorithm ("COMPAS") used in many states in the United States to help judges make decisions about parole sentencing. For both of these systems, the data used to train the models may already be ethically compromised due to decades of systemic bias in the criminal justice system in the United States.[29] With COMPAS, the recidivism prediction algorithm is trained on family criminal history and demographic data of individuals, data which may be subject to decades of wrongful arrests, and which led to nearly double the misclassification error for African American parolees, erroneously misclassified as high-risk.[30] Despite the designers of the COMPAS algorithm—and others—[31]arguing that their system was overall fairer than judges, it was distinctly biased against African Americans in ways that were not revealed without conducting an audit of the system's outcomes at racial subgroup levels.[32]

Transparency and Accountability in Civic Machine Learning

While it is critical that civic AI systems be *equitable* in their use of data and in the predictions they make about citizens, without sufficient *transparency*, regulatory agencies and citizen watchdog groups will be unable to assess the equity of these systems. Thus, transparency and accountability are essential ethical considerations for civic machine-learning systems. In May 2018, the European Union's "General Data Protection Regulation" (GDPR) took effect, enshrining a right to explanation for algorithmic decisions that significantly impact people's lives.[33] A debate has been raging within the ML community as to how exactly to implement its requirements. In part, there are questions about what qualifies as an explanation and how to elicit explanations from neural network machine-learning models that are often black boxes even to their designers.[34] In a hearing for NYC's City Council, Dr. Julia Stoyanovich argued that NYC's recently proposed algorithmic transparency bill, while necessary, is insufficient without transparency of the underlying data used to train that algorithm, and without sufficiently interpretable algorithmic results.[35]

As an example of the implications of algorithmic transparency for civic ML, we look at three case studies of predictive models used in child welfare services. One, from New York City's Administration of Children's Services (ACS), used to predict repeat abuse investigations,[36] another by Allegheny County PA's Department of Human Services (DHS) to estimate the likelihood of a child in their welfare system being removed from their home,[37] and another where Illinois' Department of Children and Family Services (DCFS) in Chicago estimates the likelihood of serious injury or death for children with abuse allegations.[38] In Chicago, the model was discontinued after a series of high-profile failures of the predictive model to accurately predict harm for children.[39] However, all predictive models have some error, as do human judgments, with some children being mistakenly labeled at-risk when they were not (i.e., false positives) and some cases mistakenly labeled low-risk when they are high (i.e., false negatives). Similarly, there may be consistent error profiles by race or socioeconomic status (SES), potentially leading to disparate impacts such as the facial recognition algorithms that were shown to be significantly less accurate when detecting the faces of women of color.[40]

Civic agencies should thus establish review boards—including community stakeholders—to conduct ethical reviews of algorithmic impact on departmental decision-making.[41] In Pennsylvania, Allegheny County's DHS commissioned an independent ethical impact audit of their predictive algorithm.[42] However, ethical audits need access to the algorithms and data used to train the models. In the case of Chicago's DCFS, a third-party contractor owned the model, and thus, even DCFS itself was unable to access the code or data to conduct an ethical audit.[43] This approach, when applied to city-scale decisions, has the potential to cause widespread harm without allowing the public to debate the technologies used to govern their lives. However, full transparency may not always be desirable, given the sensitive nature of civic data. As HCI researchers Mariam Asad et al. argue, transparency manifests differently across civic life—from the more innocuous data used for maintenance of public works to the more sensitive of, for instance, police incident data on domestic violence, which may cause immediate harm to citizens if made public without care taken for privacy and anonymity.[44]

Privacy and Meaningful Consent

With the increasing scope of data collected on citizens in "smart cities," painting ever-clearer pictures of our lives, there are thus serious risks to privacy and serious questions about whether and how people can provide meaningful consent to this data collection. These privacy risks might come about from civic data collected on citizens' identity, movement, transactions, and communications, among many other aspects.[45] The goal of transparency for civic ML described above would thus seem to be at odds with citizens' data privacy, as the same open data that would make it possible to hold algorithmic decision-makers accountable may also threaten citizens' privacy. To address this, some have proposed that cities nominate independent auditors who will be entrusted with access to the raw data to conduct an ethical audit. It is not clear, however, who will audit the auditors.[46]

More critically, it is not clear whether, or how, citizens can meaningfully provide or revoke consent to data collection by city-scale sensor grids, or consent to the data traces of daily civic life used to power ML systems that drive public policy decisions. In other large-scale socio-technical systems, as in Facebook or Google, users can opt out of the service—to deactivate one's Facebook account, as many did in the wake of the recent Cambridge Analytica data access revelations,[47] or to use Bing or another search engine. In many modern cities, however, there is no realistic option to forego consent to having one's data collected and used by the city.[48] Must one disconnect from the city's energy grid? Avoid public transit? Wear a mask in public to avoid facial recognition? Not participate in the fabric of public life: not voting, not calling emergency services or using public transportation? This does not seem like a realistic option. Furthermore, it's not clear how one could inform citizens of the potential downstream uses to which their data might be put.[49] Once collected, how will it be used? By whom? Will it be aggregated with other data? Can citizens rectify mistakes in the data? Revoke access to that data once collected? None of these has clear answers, and all have serious implications for citizens' privacy and control over their data in civic life. As some have argued, data privacy may need to be treated as a public good and regulated as such.[50] Recently, aggregated data from the fitness-tracking app Strava revealed classified CIA bases around the world. In this situation, one could argue that each consumer made a choice to allow Strava to collect their data for their own individual health benefits, but the users could not foresee the civic-scale consequences once that aggregated data was made public.[51]

Finally, even if citizens are aware of and provide consent for the data that is collected from them, they still may lack the data literacy skills necessary to understand the implications of that data collection. As Asad et al. argue, it is not enough to simply make smart-city processes transparent, they must also be "legible" to citizens.[52] Simply having city agencies release their data publicly (as done in many "open data initiatives") does not guarantee that citizens will be able to make sense of such data. In order to foster citizens' participation in the design and use of civic machine-learning systems, we must consider methods for the design of these systems that will mitigate the obstacles citizens may face to meaningful participation. Only then can they hold civic leaders accountable for implementing ethical civic AI systems that are equitable, transparent, and private.

Design Methods for Ethical Civic Machine Learning

The nature of democratic life implies multiple, contested goals, making it difficult for a designer of civic ML to identify the single desired future for their system. These decisions are too important to be left to a single technologist or relinquished to private, third-party vendors. Deliberating about these trade-offs in desired civic outcomes is at the heart of public discourse about the nature of civic life. We present here one step toward an ethical framework for the design of civic AI systems. Inspired by recent work in civic technology, we draw on the traditions of participatory and speculative design, and from recent work in machine learning, we draw on approaches for "human-in-the-loop" design of AI systems to understand how designers can use machine learning as a "design material." We propose initial steps toward a process that designers of civic machine-learning systems might use to design systems that are equitable, transparent, private, and above all, ethical.

Participatory and Speculative Design Methods

Inspired by Arnstein's ladder for citizen participation, we draw on Asad et al.'s work in designing a "socio-technical playbook" for cities. They recommend strategies for holding participatory design (PD) workshops with both community members and city agency representatives, and to allow the potential tension between those groups' goals to generatively drive discussion around the values in the proposed civic process, whether for public works, public safety, or other domains.[53] One such citizen-driven data collection initiative in Atlanta led to increased community activism around fair housing advocacy.[54] They complement these PD sessions with speculative design methods, to imagine new possibilities for civic futures, and to move beyond the corporate-inflected vision promulgated by smart cities rhetoric. The "Fictions of a Smart Atlanta" design anthology presents one vision of these imaginary cities, imagining a smart Atlanta that serves its citizens' interests, which may often be at odds with municipal or corporate interests.[55] Particularly notable is their story of the citizen who sold parking spots on a vacant lot during game days, and who used speculative design to envision sensors to detect when nearby lots were full.

However, while PD and speculative design are useful and effective methods for increasing participation in design, there remain meaningful obstacles to participation in PD workshops for civic machine learning, such as data literacy skills. Additionally, machine learning, even more so than other civic technologies, often has an aura of mystique that shrouds the systems, sometimes exacerbated by researchers' reliance on technical jargon. There is also the risk, as Arnstein cautioned, that citizen engagement could tend toward tokenism, as designers merely inform citizens of the outcomes rather than allowing citizens to truly be equal co-participants in the design process.

Machine-Learning as a Design Material

To avoid this tokenism, some user experience (UX) designers are attempting to make designing with machine learning (ML) more accessible to the nonexpert. In their survey of UX designers who work with ML, HCI researcher Graham Dove et al. found that many designers were only involved at the end of the design process after the meaningful decisions were already made and merely contributed to the aesthetic design, rather than contributing to the fundamental design process.[56] To address this, HCI researcher Qian Yang et al. describes how machine learning can be used as a "design material," to be used by UX designers throughout the ML process.[57] For Yang, the traditional framing of the UX designer's role as first "designing the right thing" and then "designing the thing *right*" becomes the challenge of defining how the ML model can "*learn* the right thing" and then how it can "learn [to predict] the thing right." In other words, what outcome is the ML model optimizing for? Moreover, in what way—or, with what data—does it learn it?

The challenge for designers of *civic* ML systems thus becomes how to engage citizens at higher rungs on Arnstein's ladder throughout the design process, ideally as co-designers in defining the goals and methods of the model—not simply relegated to being generators of the data or passive recipients of the final output. However, as Yang et al. point out, the often-unpredictable black box nature of machine learning is at odds with the traditional UX design process.[58] Traditional forms of prototyping user experiences, such as wireframes, storyboards, and other low-fidelity prototypes are not designed to deal with the ways in which ML systems might have drastically different predictions and error rates over time, as new data is incorporated. For citizens involved in co-designing civic machine-learning systems, one role might be in helping to define the objective of the ML system. For a predictive policing system, perhaps, members of a community advocacy group could advocate for the algorithm to predict wrongful arrests or police violence, instead of the typical predictive policing neighborhood crime risk model. Further, citizens could be involved in helping identify the sources of data used to inform the model and may even be vocal about data they feel is discriminatory or unfair to include, such as demographic data (or other highly correlated data with demographics) used in predictive policing.[59]

Society-in-the-loop Algorithms

One proposed method to resolve the contested values of citizen and municipal stakeholders in civic machine-learning systems is the so-called "society-in-the-loop" approach, coined by MIT Media Lab director Joi Ito and MIT Media Lab professor Iyad Rahwan.[60] This is modeled after a "human-in-the-loop" approach to AI systems where a human's input is provided somewhere within the AI's decision-making pipeline. As they argue, modern democratic societies are in some sense already a "society-in-the-loop" model writ large, where the desires and goals of individuals are aggregated and (ostensibly) incorporated into societal decision-making.[61] The challenge for civic machine learning, though, is how to quantify the ethical trade-offs made in machine learning modeling. Decisions about model accuracy and bias, transparency and privacy, and trade-offs between error ratios of "false positives" and "false negatives," are, for Ito and Rahwan, ripe for input from humans' qualitative value judgments made at scale. This approach is exemplified in their "Moral Machine" project from MIT, where individual users log on to make decisions about the ideal outcome of an autonomous vehicle accident, which are aggregated to "tune" a fictional autonomous vehicle's decisions.[62] However, as Ito and Rahwan readily acknowledge, it is difficult to establish clear and consistent guidelines for how to quantify qualitative ethical value judgments. This challenge is even more urgent for machine-learning systems woven into the fabric of civic decision-making.

Conclusion

The democratic public sphere is by its nature contested and fractious. The most urgent challenges faced by cities are wicked problems, with multiple stakeholders with conflicting interests. Civic anxieties and systemic inequities have been layered on top of one another.[63] And into this fray steps the slickly marketed solutions offered up by corporate smart cities initiatives, promising that these problems can be solved with more sensors and more data. However accurately these smart-city algorithms may perform, without an intentional approach to the ethical, democratic design of civic machine-learning systems, they might instead reify existing inequities and lead to significant consequences for civic life.

Here, we have proposed some initial steps toward an ethical design framework for civic ML systems. We draw on a model of civic participation that values citizens' active engagement in governance, instead of acting as passive recipients of government services. With more transparent data collection and machine-learning algorithms, citizens may be able to critique data-driven biases in such systems and hold civic decision-makers accountable for their impact. Thus, designers of ML systems deployed in civic life should consider the latent biases in the data they use to train their models, audit their models' performance to assess the possible disparate impact their model has on various populations, advocate for developing transparent, open-source models able to be audited by independent auditors, and most critically, involve citizens throughout the design of civic ML systems.

Yet, there remain challenges to such a vision. Citizens' participation in civic technology design requires a certain amount of digital and data literacy, not to mention the desire to participate in civic processes. Given this, it may be difficult to solicit or sustain citizen input, particularly for less high-profile, clearly-controversial initiatives than predictive policing. To that end, some cities have begun sponsoring data literacy education initiatives, such as Pittsburgh's Data 101, organized by the Carnegie Library and the Western Pennsylvania Regional Data Center[64]. In addition, the topics of "explainable AI," "fairness, accountability, and transparency" in machine learning, and UX design for ML are all active, developing research areas, and thus there may not be a toolkit for participatory design for ML ready to use quite yet.

The next incarnation of Robert Moses' bridge may not simply prevent you from driving to the beach. Instead, it may prevent you from being offered a job, a loan, or access to education or social services. Without appeal, without recourse, and without transparency, citizens are relegated to the role of consumers of services provided by corporate-led civic technologies. As the city becomes ever "smarter," it will become ever more critical to rethink the role of the citizen in such a city. What agency should citizens have over the design of the civic algorithms that will increasingly govern their lives? We intend this chapter to be the first steps toward an ethical framework for the democratic design of civic machine-learning systems.

Notes

1   Michael Adno, "Robert Moses's Jones Beach," *Curbed NY*, June 21, 2017, https://ny.curbed.com/201 7/6/21/15838436/robert-moses-jones-beach-history-new-york-city

2   Langdon Winner, "Do Artifacts Have Politics?" *Daedalus* 109, no. 1 (Winter 1980): 121–36.

3   Frank Pasquale, *Black Box Society: The Secret Algorithms That Control Money and Information* (Harvard: Harvard University Press, 2015).

4   Safiya Umoja Noble, *Algorithms of Oppression: How Search Engines Reinforce Racism* (New York: New York University Press, 2018).

5   Jessica Saunders, Priscillia Hunt, and John S. Hollywood, "Predictions Put into Practice: A Quasi-Experimental Evaluation of Chicago's Predictive Policing Pilot," *Journal of Experimental Criminology* 12, no. 3 (2016): 347–71.

6   Kristian Lum and William Isaac, "To Predict and Serve?" *Significance* 13, no. 5 (2016): 14–19.

7   Graham Dove et al., "UX Design Innovation: Challenges for Working with Machine Learning as a Design Material," in *Proceedings of the 2017 CHI Conference on Human Factors in Computing Systems*, ed. Gloria Mark (New York: ACM, 2017).

8   Smart Cities Connect Conference and Expo, Smart Cities Connect Conference and Expo, 2019, https://spring.smartcitiesconnect.org

9   International Data Corporation, "Worldwide Semiannual Smart Cities Spending Guide," IDC, 2019, www.idc.com/tracker/showproductinfo.jsp?prod_id=1843

10 Rob Kitchin, "The Ethics of Smart Cities and Urban Science," *Philosophical Transactions of the Royal Society* 374, no. 2083 (2016).

11 Ibid.

12 Virginia Eubanks and Teri Schnaubelt, *Automating Inequality How High-Tech Tools Profile, Police, and Punish the Poor* (Old Saybrook: Tantor Media, 2018).

13 Cary Coglianese and David Lehr, "Regulating by Robot: Administrative Decision Making in the Machine-Learning Era," *The Georgetown Law Journal* 105, no. 5 (2017): 1147.

14 Alisha Jarwala, "Minority Report: Why We Should Question Predictive Policing," *Harvard Civil Rights-Civil Liberties Law Review*, December 4, 2017, harvardcrcl.org/minority-report-why-we-should-question-predictive-policing

15 Robert Brauneis and Ellen P. Goodman, "Algorithmic Transparency for the Smart City," *Yale Journal of Law and Technology* 103, no. 20 (2017): 103–76.

16 Lum and Isaac, "To Predict and Serve?"

17 Brauneis and Goodman, "Algorithmic Transparency for the Smart City."

18 Ali Winston, "Palantir Has Secretly Been Using New Orleans to Test Its Predictive Policing Technology," *The Verge*, February 27, 2018, www.theverge.com/2018/2/27/17054740/palantir-predictive-policing-tool-new-orleans-nopd

19 Ibid.

20 Paolo Cardullo and Rob Kitchin, "Being a 'Citizen' in the Smart City: Up and Down the Scaffold of Smart Citizen Participation in Dublin, Ireland," *GeoJournal* (2018): 1–13.

21 Michael Veale, Max Van Kleek, and Reuben Binns, "Fairness and Accountability Design Needs for Algorithmic Support in High-Stakes Public Sector Decision-Making," in *CHI 2018 Proceedings of the 2018 CHI Conference on Human Factors in Computing Systems* (Montreal: ACM, 2018).

22 Sherry R. Arnstein, "A Ladder of Citizen Participation," *Journal of the American Institute of planners* 35, no. 4 (July 1969): 216–24.

23 Ibid.

24 Joe Shaw and Mark Graham, "An Informational Right to the City? Code, Content, Control, and the Urbanization of Information," *Antipode* 49, no. 4 (2017): 907–27.

25 Nathan Kallus and Angela Zhou, "Residual Unfairness in Fair Machine Learning from Prejudiced Data," in *Proceedings of the 35th International Conference on Machine Learning* (2018). PMLR 80: 2439–448.

26 Latanya Sweeney, "Discrimination in Online ad Delivery," *Communications of the ACM* 56, no. 5 (2013): 10.

27 Jieyu Zhao et al., "Men Also like Shopping: Reducing Gender Bias Amplification using Corpus-level Constraints," in *Proceedings of the 2017 Conference on Empirical Methods in Natural Language Processing* (2017). Association for Computational Linguistics 2979–989.

28 Solon Barocas and Andrew D. Selbst, "Big Data's Disparate Impact," *California Law Review* 104 (2016): 671; Safiya Umoja, *Algorithms of Oppression*.

29 Lum and Isaac, "To Predict and Serve?"

30 Julia Angwin et al., "Machine Bias? There's Software used Across the Country to Predict Future Criminals. And It's Biased Against Blacks," *ProPublica*, May 23, 2016, www.propublica.org/article/machine-bias-risk-assessments-in-criminal-sentencing

31 Alex P. Miller, "Want Less-Biased Decisions? Use Algorithms," *Harvard Business Review*, July 26, 2018, https://hbr.org/2018/07/want-less-biased-decisions-use-algoriths

32 Anthony W. Flores, Kristin Bechtel, and Christopher T. Lowenkamp, "False Positives, False Negatives, and False Analyses: A Rejoinder to 'Machine Bias: There's Software Used Across the Country to Predict Future Criminals. And It's Biased Against Blacks,'" *Federal Probation Journal* 80, no. 2 (September 2016): 38; Alexandra Chouldechova, "Fair Prediction with Disparate Impact: A Study of Bias in Recidivism Prediction Instruments," *Big Data* 5, no. 2 (2017).

33 Bryce W. Goodman, "A Step Towards Accountable Algorithms? Algorithmic Discrimination and the European Union General Data Protection," in *29th Conference on Neural Information Processing Systems (NIPS 2016)* (Barcelona: NIPS Foundation, 2016).

34 Ibid.

35 Julia Stoyanovich, *Testimony of Julia Stoyanovich before the New York City Council Committee on Technology regarding Automated Processing of Data (Int. 1696–2017)*, (2017), https://dataresponsi bly.github.io/documents/Stoyanovich_VaccaBill.pdf

36 Ravi Shroff, "Predictive Analytics for City Agencies: Lessons from Children's Services," *Big Data* 5, no. 3 (2017).

37 Rhema Vaithianathan et al., *Developing Predictive Models to Support Child Maltreatment Hotline Screening Decisions: Allegheny County Methodology and Implementation* (New Zealand: Centre for Social Data Analytics, 2017), www.alleghenycountyanalytics.us/wp-content/uploads/2017/04/Develo ping-Predictive-Risk-Models-package-with-cover-1-to-post-1.pdf

38 David Jackson and Gary Marx, "Data Mining Program Designed to Predict Child Abuse Proves Unreliable, DCFS Says," *Chicago Tribune*, December 6, 2017, www.chicagotribune.com/news/wa tchdog/ct-dcfs-eckerd-met-20171206-story.html

39 Ibid.

40 Joy Buolamwini and Timnit Gebru, "Gender Shades: Intersectional Accuracy Disparities in Commercial Gender Classification," *Proceedings of the 1st Conference on Fairness, Accountability and Transparency, PMLR* 81 (2018): 77–91.

41 Shroff, "Predictive Analytics for City Agencies."

42 Vaithianathan et al., *Developing Predictive Models to Support Child Maltreatment Hotline Screening Decisions*; Alexandra Chouldechova et al., "A Case Study of Algorithm-Assisted Decision Making in Child Maltreatment Hotline Screening Decisions," in *Conference on Fairness, Accountability and Transparency* (2018).

43 Jackson and Marx, "Data Mining Program Designed to Predict Child Abuse Proves Unreliable."

44 Mariam Asad et al., "Creating a Sociotechnical API: Designing City-Scale Community Engagement," in *Proceedings of the 2017 CHI Conference on Human Factors in Computing Systems*, ed. Gloria Mark (New York: ACM, 2017).

45 Kitchin, "The Ethics of Smart Cities."

46 Stoyanovich, *Testimony of Julia Stoyanovich.*

47 Julie Beck, "People are Changing the Way they Use Social Media," *The Atlantic*, June 7, 2018, theat lantic.com/technology/archive/2018/06/did-cambridge-analytica-actually-change-facebook-users-be havior/562154

48 Janet M. Fulton and Marjorie D. Kibby, "Millennials and the Normalization of Surveillance on Facebook," *Continuum* 31, no. 2 (2016): 189–99; Jathan Sadowski and Frank Pasquale, "The Spectrum of Control: A Social Theory of the Smart City," *First Monday* 20, no. 7 (2015).

49 Leonardo A. Martucci et al., "Privacy and Social Values in Smart Cities," in *Designing, Developing, and Facilitating Smart Cities: Urban Design to IoT Solutions*, Marina Jirotka et al. (Thousand Oaks: Springer, 2017).

50 Zeynep Tufekci, "The Latest Data Privacy Debacle," *The New York Times*, January 30, 2018, www.n ytimes.com/2018/01/30/opinion/strava-privacy.html

51 Ibid.

52 Asad et al., "Creating a Sociotechnical API."

53 Ibid.

54 Amanda Meng and Carl DiSalvo, "Grassroots Resource Mobilization through Counter-Data Action," *Big Data & Society* 5, no. 2 (2018).

55 Georgia Institute of Technology's Public Design Workshop and Center for Urban Innovation, *Fictions of a Smart Atlanta: An Anthology of Smart City Use Cases* (Atlanta: Georgia Institute of Technology, 2018), https://serve-learn-sustain.gatech.edu/sites/default/files/documents/Toolkit-Docs/fictions_of_a _smart_atl-compressed.pdf

56 Dove et al., "UX Design Innovation."

57 Qian Yang et al., "Investigating How Experienced UX Designers Effectively Work with Machine Learning," *Proceedings of the 2018 on Designing Interactive Systems Conference 2018—DIS '18* (2018).

58 Dove et al., "UX Design Innovation."

59 Veale, Van Kleek, and Binns, "Fairness and Accountability Design Needs," 440.

60 Iyad Rahwan, "Society-in-the-loop: Programming the Algorithmic Social Contract," *Ethics and Information Technology* 20, no. 1 (2017): 5–14.

61 Ibid; Coglianese and Lehr, "Regulating by Robot," 1147.

62 Ritesh Noothigattu et al., "A Voting-Based System for Ethical Decision Making," *arXiv preprint arXiv:1709.06692*, 2017.

63 Asad et al., "Creating a Sociotechnical API."

64 Data 101, "What is Data?," Carnegie Library of Pittsburgh, carnegielibrary.org/event/what-is-data-b eechview/

7

Design Possibilities and Responsibilities in Framing Well-being

Heekyoung Jung

With busier schedules, abundant information, and complex social interactions, stressors are increasing, and have a significant impact on personal well-being. At the same time, with a greater expectation for emphasis on the quality of life, public interest in well-being is growing. People are making an extra effort at taking care of their health, managing stress, and leveraging their capabilities. Many consumer products and services support tracking activities and biometric data to encourage change in behavior and the achievement of fitness, dietary, or meditation practice goals. Some products infer emotional conditions and levels of stress from physiologic and contextual data, prompting a break and mood boost. While they support the practice of well-being in simple steps of setting and tracking health-related goals, the paths to well-being have become primarily commoditized, establishing standard goals in changing one's health conditions and lifestyles. Moreover, such technology applications, ironically, become another source of stress and anxiety with their constant connectivity and reminders about health goals.[1] In this chapter, I reflect on the evolving notion of well-being as sociocultural movements, elaborate tensions around technology-mediated practices of self-care, and discuss ethical issues in framing the design for well-being.

Well-being and Wellness as a Public Healthcare Agenda

As per dictionary definitions, well-being is the state of being happy, prosperous, and healthy, encompassing the notion of wellness, which is exclusively about physical or mental health. Often used interchangeably, the concepts of well-being and wellness have been closely related to each other, mutually evolving as social, cultural, and technological movements for public healthcare. An early written record of wellness in Western culture was found in a personal prayer, as an antonym of illness and sickness that was the result of sin, "the sin of improper behavior on the part of the individual, whether it be nutritional sin or sin regarding some other sort of behavior."[2] With the advancement of scientific knowledge about the human body and medical practice in modern society, public education on hygiene, healthy eating, and self-care lifestyle have been actively promoted in relation to religious tradition and consumer culture.[3] In the twentieth century, with the demographic changes coming from increasing life expectancy and chronic and lifestyle diseases, the quality of life and status of happiness came into focus for public health beyond curing illness. In 1948, the World Health Organization redefined health as "a state of complete physical, mental, and social well-being and not merely the absence of disease or infirmity."[4] Taking upon into consideration this holistic measure of health, statistician Halbert Dunn, a vital statistician, proposed the concept of "High-Level Wellness" with four steps to its promotion: (1) quantify positive health by sampling and indexing demographic and environmental factors; (2) know thyself based on the quantified knowledge base; (3) leverage resources for community wisdom and maturity of the growing elderly population; and (4) support creative expression for adventuring into the unknown in search of universal truth.[5] In the past few decades, the first three visions have been actively investigated with medical and public health research agendas by applying information and communication technologies to develop a medical knowledge base with electronic health records, personal informatics systems, and online communities and support groups. However, the last vision has primarily remained in religious and spiritual practices due to its abstract goals and action plans.

Later in the twentieth century, the notion of High-Level Wellness was developed into a series of public health education models (See Figure 7.1)—including (1) the illness and wellness continuum (i.e., health and wellness can change on a measurable scale); (2) the iceberg model of wellness (i.e., health is the tip of iceberg built on lifestyle, mindset, and spiritual realm); and (3) the wellness energy system (i.e., a person is an energy transformer, processing illness or wellness from tangible and intangible inputs from the natural, social, and spiritual environments).[6]

These wellness models for public education have influenced healthcare culture and been applied to corporate wellness programs in the 1970s concerning risk management initiatives at workplaces and incorporating well-being at the societal and organizational levels.[7] The holistic perspectives of wellness and well-being movements have empowered individuals to actualize their capabilities and democratized healthcare by lowering the healthcare costs with preventive and experimental wellness regimes. However, such integrative approaches, sometimes stigmatized by their advocacy of alternative medicine and spiritual practice, have raised tensions with strictly evidence-based medical healthcare practices. Also, marketing strategies for nutrition and beauty products have often exploited the original intentions of wellness movements by stimulating human desire as well as guilt about not doing well enough in self-care.[8] The notion of well-being has set itself apart from wellness with increasing initiatives to measure "happiness" with systemic indexes, such as the Gallup Healthways Well-Being Index and the United Nations World Happiness Index.[9] Although intended to provide a comprehensive and comparable indicator, different index systems can bring about different happiness measures for the same country. This implies that while there are growing needs to quantify well-being for its education and promotion, there is also the need to consider particular sociocultural contexts to standardize and institutionalize the measure and practice of well-being. The concept of well-being reflects evolving aspirations and concerns in human life; it requires constant reflections regarding what constitutes it and how to support it instead of imposing universal goals and measuring criteria.

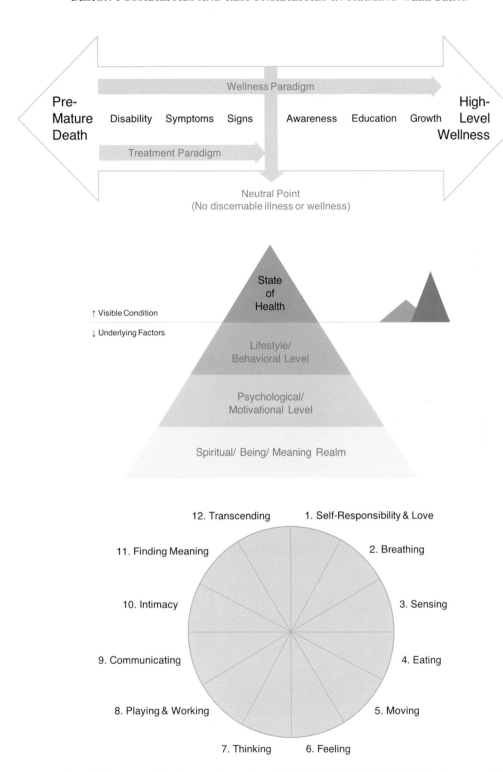

FIGURES 7.1 *Wellness models (top to bottom), c. 1972, 1978, 1988, 2002, 2004. Courtesy of John W. Travis.*

Technology-mediated Practice of Well-being

Recently, information and interaction technologies are blurring the boundaries between professional and personal health care. It has been a long-time vision of evidence-based medical practice to develop electronic health record systems that can provide more accurate and affordable health care services, with medical knowledge shared across hospitals and medical research institutes. Today, this agenda is further expanded to promote preventive and healthier lifestyles by synchronizing personal activity, biometric, and genetic data to medical research and service platforms and supporting personal reflections to encourage behavior change in daily contexts. Design practice presents more possibilities to intervene in self-care with various forms of consumer products, primarily mobile apps and wearable devices. Those products focus on different aspects of personal well-being, taking design approaches enabled by multiple properties of information and communication technologies:[10] (1) knowledge-based self-care through the access to medical databases and professional interventions (e.g., Ginger.io); (2) data-based self-reflection by self-reporting, automatic activity tracking, and data analytics (e.g., Fitbit, Pacifica, Moodnote); (3) community or professional support of therapeutic counseling in social media platforms (e.g., Koko, Talkspace, BetterHelp); (4) mindfulness and meditation guidance with

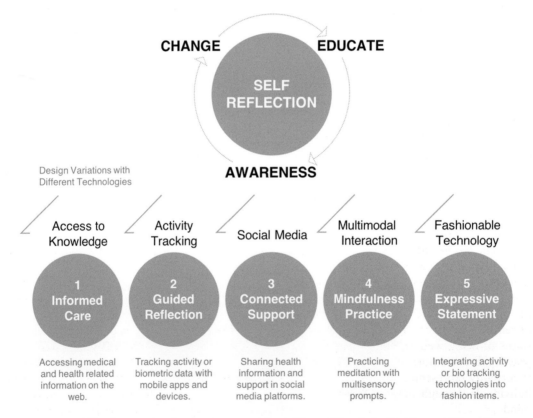

FIGURE 7.2 *Self-reflection. Heekyoung Jung and Jiani Zhou, "Trends in Mobile and Wearable Stress Care & Design Implications for a Culture of Wellness," in Proceedings of Academic Design Management Conference (ADMC) (Boston: Design Management Institute, 2016).*

audio, visual, and tactile stimuli (e.g., Pause, Doppel, Muse); and (5) fashionable technology accessories for tracking and inferring one's condition (e.g., MUJI to Sleep, Zensorium, Caden). These different approaches, not exclusive to each other, manifest how a general proposition of data-based reflective practice for behavior change—education, awareness, and growth for self-discipline[11]—take different product forms with digital technologies (see Figure 7.2).

In spite of the increasing number of personal tracking applications, questions have also arisen regarding their efficacy in healthy behavior changes[12] and side effects of constant connectivity and personal data sharing.[13] Most of their interactions are limited to passive tracking and visualization, easily ignorable and disconnected from the user's holistic experience. The status of well-being requires conscious awareness of one's condition through dedicated self-reflection and discipline, but such a process is often oversimplified in many commercial products, potentially deskilling the process of setting, measuring, and tracking goals. Simplicity and convenience tend to take over transparency and engagement in data collection and navigation. Design research, besides contributing to realizing technology-driven visions toward healthy behavior and lifestyle change, can play an instrumental role in addressing tensions around those visions and mediating them in promoting well-being.

Ethical Issues in Framing Design Approaches to Well-being

As creative approaches to personal healthcare are increasing from private sectors, including information technology, consumer product, and fashion industries, well-being and self-care practices are being promoted with various forms of consumer products. Still, their effects have not been clinically proven;[14] some products promise more than what is clinically or technologically proven. Moreover, due to convenient and intimate interactions, lightweight personal technology applications could be easily mystified as a replacement for expert knowledge or professional clinical treatment.[15] Experts have raised concerns that minor diagnostic errors could lead to severe health impacts and costs in the long term.[16] Sharing personal data for clinical knowledge base is well intended, but privacy is becoming a more pressing concern as workplaces and insurance companies attempt to access individual health and activity data for performance monitoring purposes. While personal healthcare applications make medical knowledge and interventions more accessible to the public, the quality, credibility, and limitation of such information need to be addressed transparently.

Design, by the nature of its practice, represents and aestheticizes desired values in the form of artifacts. However, aestheticization could misrepresent the ultimate design intentions, reinforcing stereotypical representations or instant gratifications about causal effects of human actions: "Design regularly encourages the creation of the mere impression, appearance and sensation of ethicality without engaging the presence of genuine ethical being."[17] That means, the design of self-care product could vicariously satisfy its users by making them experience the desired status of being well instead of actually acting on it with conscious self-disciplinary, reflective practice. Furthermore, it could limit other possible ways of achieving well-being, reifying how it is currently represented in marketed lifestyles. Earlier notions of well-being aimed to empower individuals through public education by emphasizing the wholeness of the human body and mind as well as spirituality. Today, with increasing design and technology interventions, the concept of well-being has been primarily reduced to data-based goal tracking or style-oriented product experiences. It is critical to simplify and aestheticize the steps of reporting and monitoring personal data to change behaviors and achieve goals. However, well-being is more than quantifiable and measurable goals, evolving in new social, cultural, and technological contexts. The focus of design for well-being needs to shift from *achieving* common goals to *navigating* personal goals and behavior strategies, acknowledging the time and effort for self-learning and disciplining before the result. Spiritual and creative practices also need to be more systematically integrated in personal practice of well-being, as Dunn envisioned with the concept of High-Level Wellness. Challenges remain regarding how to resolve tensions regarding about unscientific, alternative approaches with minimal marketing exploitations.

Today digital technology applications promote well-being but also often put it at potential risk with constant connectivity and data overload. The pervasiveness of digital technologies calls for different goals and strategies in self-care beyond imposing standard goals or rewarding instant gratifications through screen interactions. There are growing movements that advocate conscious disconnection from digital technologies and minimal screen interactions for human well-being, as seen in recent initiatives for "Time Well Spent"[18] and traditional community-based wellness retreats.[19] As briefly reviewed, well-being is a sociocultural construct; its practice and measure evolve according to emerging human aspirations and stressors. Design research and practice face more possibilities and responsibilities to address pressing human desires and concerns in framing and promoting well-being as a technology-mediated experience. Design can take a particular ethical stance regarding potentially conflicting values such as transparency versus simplicity of interactions with personal data, support for self-development versus market-driven consumerism, emphasis on self-disciplining process versus efficient goal achievement, and more. It is hard to separate one value from another, but ethical responsibilities of design lie in revealing those complex value systems and envisioning alternative ways of framing well-being instead of reskinning one given approach repeatedly. By describing in brief the context in which public healthcare agendas and recent design approaches for well-being have been shaped in modern Western society, I highlighted the possibilities and the responsibilities of design in framing and promoting it with emerging digital technologies beyond activity tracking for behavior change. To design for different cultural and technological contexts, further research about its meanings, concerns, and aspirations is consequently needed.

Notes

1 Kate Pickert, "The Mindful Revolution," *Time*, February 3, 2014, http://content.time.com/time/subscriber/article/0,33009,2163560,00.html; Tristan Harris, "What is Time Well Spent (Part 1): Design Distinction," *Tristan Harris*, September 30, 2015, www.tristanharris.com/tag/time-well-spent

2 James William Miller, "Wellness: The History and Development of a Concept," *Spektrum Freizei* 27, no. 1 (2005): 86.

3 Danya Glabau, "Fancy Feast: The Aspirational Fantasies in Photogenic Food," *Real Life*, September 21, 2017, http://reallifemag.com/fancy-feast/

4 James Strohecker, *A Brief History of Wellness* (HealthWorld Online, 2006), http://www.mywellnesstest.com/certResFile/BriefHistoryofWellness.pdf

5 Halbert L. Dunn, "High-Level Wellness for Man and Society," *American Journal of Public Health and the Nation's Health* 49, no. 6 (1959): 1.

6 John W. Travis and Regina Sara Ryan, *Wellness Workbook: How to Achieve Enduring Health and Vitality* (Berkeley: Celestial Arts, 2004).

7 Paul A. Schulte et al., "Considerations for Incorporating 'Well-Being' in Public Policy for Workers and Workplaces," *American Journal of Public Health* 105, no. 8 (2015): e31–e44.

8 Strohecker, *A Brief History of Wellness*; Glabau, "Fancy Feast."

9 Susie Ellis, "Wellness, Well-Being . . . And What About Spa?" *Huffington Post*, April 9, 2017, www.huffpost.com/entry/wellness-wellbeingand-wha_b_9641722

10 Heekyoung Jung and Jiani Zhou, "Trends in Mobile and Wearable Stress Care & Design Implications for a Culture of Wellness," in *Proceedings of Academic Design Management Conference (ADMC)* (Boston: Design Management Institute, 2016).

11 Richard O'Connor, *Undoing Perpetual Stress: The Missing Connection between Depression, Anxiety, and 21st Century Illness* (New York: Berkley Books, 2005).

12 Eric P. S. Baumer et al., "Reviewing Reflection: On the Use of Reflection in Interactive System Design," in *Proceedings of the 2014 Conference on Designing Interactive Systems* (New York: ACM, 2014); Petr Slovák, Christopher Frauenberger, and Geraldine Fitzpatrick, "Reflective Practicum: A Framework of Sensitizing Concepts to Design for Transformative Reflection," in *Proceedings of the 2017 CHI Conference on Human Factors in Computing Systems*, ed. Gloria Mark (New York: ACM, 2017).

13 Keith Hampton et al., *Psychological Stress and Social Media Use* (Pew Research Center, 2015), www.pewinternet.org/2015/01/15/psychological-stress-and-social-media-use-2/

14 Elizabeth Stinson, "Koko is a New Social Network Designed to Help You Deal with Stress," *WIRED*, December 16, 2015, www.wired.com/2015/12/a-new-social-media-network-to-help-you-deal-with-stress

15 Shaun Lawson et al., "Problematising Upstream Technology through Speculative Design: The Case of Quantified Cats and Dogs," in *Proceedings of Conference on Human Factors in Computing Systems (CHI)* (New York: ACM, 2015).

16 Christopher Labos, "There's an App for That Medical Issue. Should You Use It?" *Macleans*, April 11, 2016, www.macleans.ca/society/health/the-problem-with-wildly-inaccurate-health-apps

17 Peter M. Buwert, "An/Aesth/Ethics: The Ethical Potential of Design," *Artifact* 3, no. 3 (2015): 4.5.

18 Harris, "What is Time Well Spent?"

19 Mattie Kahn, "Jewish Rituals Are the Hot New Thing in Wellness," *BuzzFeed News*, December 18, 2017, www.buzzfeednews.com/article/mattiekahn/goop-shabbos

PART TWO

Theory and Communication

8

Design and Emergent Ethical Crises

Peter Buwert

How should we respond when technologies like the blockchain and social media threaten to dissolve the foundations of established centralized structures like banking, journalism, even government? How do our lives change when artificially intelligent machines can clean our houses, order and deliver our groceries, drive our cars, fight our wars, do our jobs, be our sexual partners, and keep us company and care for us in our old age? What does it mean to be human when we can edit our own genes, prolong our lives, and exist digitally beyond physical death? What does it mean to be a living thing when synthetic biology promises the creation of entirely new life forms at the same time as increasing numbers of existing species go extinct? As the global climate warms, the plastic-filled oceans rise, and we compete for finite resources in ever-smaller habitable territories, how do we attempt to continue existing in any form in a world we have made fundamentally inhospitable toward ourselves?

The Challenge and Opportunity of a Crisis

In everyday language, the word crisis is used to refer to any significantly unstable situation or event: financial, political, environmental, humanitarian, medical, marital, or personal. Crises can be characterized as "un-ness" events.[1] They are undesirable and unwanted. They typically catch us unaware and unready. They are unprecedented, unexpected, and therefore, often unimaginable and unforeseeable. The paradox of crisis management is that its core activities—prevention, preparation, mitigation, and recovery[2]—are almost ruled out from the start by the nature of the crisis itself.

At the heart of the crisis concept lie three core components of *threat, urgency,* and *uncertainty*.[3] While the specific threat of a crisis situation will typically be quite concrete, the general threat of a crisis is the perception of threat toward normality itself: the threat of an unpredictable process of the disruption and uprooting of established social structures and systems (whether that be at the scale of international relations, or family life).[4] The urgency of crises arises because of this threat posed to the larger social constructions from within which they emerge. Crises effectively hold social normalities hostage. If not dealt with, the prolonged impact of the disruption of the crisis moment threatens to bring down the whole structure. But more than anything, the experience of crisis is characterized by *uncertainty*. Full preparation for or prevention of crises is impossible. How can we prepare for or attempt to prevent phenomena, the parameters of which are characteristically uncertain, unknown, and unexpected?

For this reason, institutional crisis management processes and procedures are inadequate strategies for attempting to manage dynamic emergent crisis situations. There is no guarantee that anticipatory preparations based on lessons learned from past experiences will work today or tomorrow.[5] Crisis management strategies can nurture reactive resilience, encouraging and developing the dynamic flexibility to respond decisively to the unknown in the moment of uncertainty. However, acting decisively in the moment of uncertainty is the one thing that is hardest to do. The challenge of crisis mitigation is that crises emerge specifically as a result of our inability to make decisions as to how to mitigate within the context of a given situation.

In a crisis, we find ourselves at a crossroads with a number of paths available to us but are either unable to clearly determine which option is the optimal choice or are unable to take the actions necessary to set us on the path we would like to take. Crisis resolution requires the decisive, sifting,[6] judging action of choosing a path, and traveling down it to meet the unknown consequences that lie in wait. The paradox of crisis is that decisive action is required specifically in situations where we lack the critical knowledge to act confidently.

The uncertain fork in the road of crisis presents not only a threat but also an opportunity.[7] This is a moment in which the inadequacies of an existing complex system are brought to light, and a new resolution is urgently demanded. Thus, the goal of crisis resolution should not be to return to the status quo that gave rise to this crisis. To simply replace a system within which a crisis arose is to invite a repeat. The opportunity of a crisis is an opportunity to question and change these problematic underlying factors.

Therefore, the opportunity of a crisis would appear to be an opportunity for design. In our world, which certainly often feels like it is in a state of constant crisis, is design the tool, hero, or savior that we are looking for? This chapter explores some of the complexities and contradictions of the relationship between design and ethical crisis, considering that just as often as design turns up to save the day; it is caught red-handed at the scene of the crime. The implications of our understanding of the link between design and crisis are significant and far-reaching for how we think about the activity of design, its operations and its effects in and on the world.

Crisis and Artifice

Clive Dilnot argues that artifice (that which humans have made) finally eclipses nature and becomes the "horizon and medium of our existence"[8] precisely at the moment in which we come to realize both that we *can* (instantaneously through mutually assured nuclear destruction) and *are* (slowly but surely via Anthropocene-era global warming) designing our own collective extinction. At this global scale, we exist under constant threat of our own self-destruction. At the local scale, we find ourselves subject to an unrelenting stream of urgently demanding, threatening, uncertainty inducing designed interventions invading our personal realities.

How should we respond when technologies like the blockchain and social media threaten to dissolve the foundations of established centralized structures like banking, journalism, even government? How do our lives change when artificially intelligent machines can clean our houses, order and deliver our groceries, drive our cars, fight our wars, do our jobs, be our sexual partners, and keep us company and care for us in our old age? What does it mean to be human when we can edit our own genes, prolong our lives, and exist digitally beyond physical death? What does it mean to be a living thing when synthetic biology promises the creation of entirely new life forms at the same time as increasing numbers of existing species go extinct? As the global climate warms, the plastic-filled oceans rise, and we compete for finite resources in ever-smaller habitable territories, how do we attempt to continue existing in any form in a world we have made fundamentally inhospitable toward ourselves? The perpetual experience of crisis is the contemporary experience of living in our designed world.

We experience crisis and attempt to mitigate and recover, hoping to bring about new conditions of existence more stable and more amenable to us than those from which the previous crisis arose. We bring artifice into being to solve our problems, to ease our burdens, and to relieve our pain.[9] Yet all too often, our attempts to employ design to mitigate, resolve, and recover from crisis appear to bring new crises into being.

In nature, things simply are the way they are. Either the rain falls, or it doesn't. An acorn either grows into an oak tree or withers attempting to do so: it cannot grow into anything else. The nature of a rock is to remain a rock. Artifice, however, is a different story. Human-made things can always be different because their qualities can be changed in a multitude of ways. A rock is not simply a rock. It may be a tool or a weapon. Joined with other rocks, it could become a building. Cut and polished, it could become a symbol of an abstract concept like marriage. In artifice, reality can be transformed. It is by pulling on this thread that the full significance of the relationship between design and crisis begins to unravel.

All design involves transformation of one kind or another. Often, the outcome of a design process will involve physical change, some material presence, or impact in the world. However, such material transformation is only a secondary effect of the primary transformation of design, which is the transformation and expansion of potentiality.

Potentiality: To Be *and* Not to Be

The concept of potentiality is key to design.[10] Typically, potentiality is defined in opposition to actuality. In the simplest possible terms, actuality refers to things as they are. Actuality is what is. This is what is commonly perceived as "reality." Conversely, potentiality refers to the potential for things to be other than they are. Potentiality is what could be. It is the realm of possibility, capacity, imagination, and speculation. However, the relationship between potentiality and actuality is not as simple as it might first appear. For Aristotle, actuality is to potentiality as "that which is awake to that which is asleep; and that which is seeing to that which has the eyes shut, but has the power of sight; and that which is differentiated out of matter to the matter; and the finished article to the raw material."[11]

Aristotle's insight is that potentiality goes both ways. The potential-to-not-be (impotentiality) is just as significant as the potential-to-be (potentiality). The sighted person who closes their eyes chooses to not see while retaining their capability to see. The bricklayer on a coffee break is not currently building, but has not lost the capacity of bricklaying. The pianist is not always playing, but when sitting at the piano possesses both potentiality in the ability to choose to play, and impotentiality in the ability to choose not to play.

A lump of clay possesses actuality as what it is: it exists as a lump of clay. However, when considered by the designer, the clay may be perceived to possess potentiality to be given form as a cup, bowl, tile or any number of things. While the clay exists as clay, it also in the sense of impotentiality exists as *not-cup*, *not-bowl*, *not-tile*, and so on.

The act of designing is the act of bringing new possibilities into being by conceiving of novel configurations of existing elements within given contexts. In this sense, the fundamental act of design is the extension of potentiality. At the same time, design constantly involves the conscious act of choosing not to bring other potentialities into actuality. When the designer chooses not to bring a possibility into physical being, it does not cease to exist. The existence of the possibility persists as a potentiality within the designer's mind. The experience of designing is the experience of encountering the possibility of something both being and not being. When we design, we are constantly faced with choices to either attempt to bring this or that thing into being, or to suppress, inhibit, or deny its being.

Design's extension of potentiality is not limited to the activity of designing. Artifacts, the product of design, embody potentiality themselves. That which has been created possesses the implicit capability both to be and to not be. To encounter an artifact is to encounter something which is, but could not have been, and which both could have been and could yet be different. This encounter with potentiality has a profound impact on the individual encountering the design.

In 2013, Defence Distributed designed and published digital fabrication files online for the world's first functional 3-D printable gun, "the Liberator." Prior to this, I was aware that such an object was theoretically possible, but in terms of actualizable possibilities available to me, I was simply incapable of fabricating my own plastic firearm. Now, because I am aware of the existence of these files *and* I have the ability to access these files, *and* I have access to 3-D printing facilities, a change has been effected in me. I now possess the potential to print a gun. Before, even if I had wanted to, I would not have been able to print a gun. Now, even though I really do not want to, I must make the active choice to enact my impotentiality, my ability *not* to download those files from the dark corners of the web and attempt to print a gun.[12]

This experience of the encounter with potentiality—which is the fundamental experience of designing, whether it be brought about through the act of designing or through the encounter with designed artifice—is also the fundamental experience of the ethical.

Giorgio Agamben draws out the ethical implications of Aristotle's conception of impotentiality, writing that "the only ethical experience . . . is the experience of being (one's own) potentiality, of being (one's own) possibility—exposing, that is, in every form one's own amorphousness and in every act one's own inactuality."[13] To be capable of our own impotentiality, to embrace our human capability both to do and not to do, is to be ethical.[14] Conversely, Agamben maintains that the only true evil, that which negates and destroys the ethical, is the denial of our own impotentiality.[15] In the absence of the ability to choose to do or not do, we would be nothing more than automatons following predetermined programming. The ability to freely choose which of the multitude of potentialities available to us we do and do not enact is the ultimate root of our ability to extend potentiality by designing, and to recognize and be responsive to the potentialities presented to us by designed artifacts.

The Ethical

In everyday language, the words ethical and moral are effectively synonymous and interchangeable. Here, however, they are used to make a clear division between two quite distinct concepts.[16] The moral refers to the sphere of culturally embedded conceptions relating to the judgment of good and bad, right and wrong, and the core notion of "ought." Morality is primarily concerned with the judgment of what ought to be done. The ethical, on the other hand, is not concerned with judgment but rather with awareness and sensitivity to the possibilities available within a situation. The ethical precedes morality and is its necessary foundation. It is perhaps helpful to think of the ethical as the space within which the moral can take place. The activity of ethics is one of exploration and mapping: discovering how far the ethical space of a given situation extends, and becoming sensitive to the range of possibility available within this. To recognize the ethical dimension is to become aware that there is space in this situation in which things could have been, or could be, otherwise than they are. In other words, it is to become aware of potentiality. Wherever potentiality exists, the ethical exists.

Only when we are able to perceive a range of alternative possibilities for how things could be that it becomes possible to ask the moral question: how ought these things to be? Without the ethical, morality simply cannot take place. Using these words in the sense set out here, to say that something is unethical is not the same as to make the value judgment that this thing is morally bad. Rather, it is to say that there is no potentiality, no alternative possibility, here that could be judged morally better or worse. Something can be found to be unethical if it could not be otherwise than it is. In such a scenario, there is no room to criticize, judge, or imagine it being otherwise. In this sense, while nature may be unethical, artifice certainly is not.

When design brings artifice into being, it extends potentiality in multiple directions. This extension of potentiality simultaneously creates new ethical space—new possibilities to be explored and ultimately judged in the realm of morality. The problem is that as morality is culturally constructed based on collective prior experience, newly emergent potentialities always exceed the boundaries of established moral frameworks. Precisely, because they are new, we do not know where these possibilities might lead us. We find ourselves in uncharted territory.

To encounter the ethical in the absence of the safety net of morality is to find oneself exposed to the raw experience of sensitivity to a range of possible options, with no guiding principle to tell us what we ought to do. This experience of the moment in which morality fails us is the experience of ethical crisis.

Design and Ethical Crisis

What do we do when faced with the uncertainty, threat, and urgency of an emergent ethical crisis? We may attempt to turn to our established moral frameworks, rules, or codes to help us, but we will soon find that morality is almost completely unequipped to deal with ethical novelty. Philosopher John D. Caputo describes the situation using the metaphor of an accident:

> An accident is something that happens to us beyond our control and outside the horizon of foreseeability. Our theories and principles, whose whole aim and purpose is to prepare us for and foresee what is coming, we're still in bed at this early hour of the day. . . . As soon as something *new* or *different* happens ethical theory [morality] is struck dumb, the crowd gathers around the scene, and everyone starts buzzing, until finally it is agreed that we should all have seen this coming.[17]

The conditions of emergent ethical crisis are created every time design takes place and morality can only play catch-up.

More often than not, instances of design represent only incremental alterations of existing artifice;[18] minor extensions of potentiality, which can be assimilated into existing moral frameworks. Our attention is not always sensitively attuned toward noticing crises emerging through the extension of potentiality. Too often, we perceive the crisis only when it is too late after the "accident" (figurative or literal) has already occurred. One small step pushes us over the edge, exposing a complex mess of cumulative crisis. When substandard material specification allows a fire to spread quickly through an entire tower block, killing dozens of residents, systemic inequalities deeply designed into society are exposed. When a single poorly laid out ballot card causes voter error that swings an election, the flaws in democratic electoral systems are laid bare. When digital social networks ostensibly designed to bring us closer together so easily divide, polarize, manipulate, and exploit, our naïve assumptions about the stability and maturity of the societies we have constructed are brought into question. When an entire city runs out of water, we are faced with the reality that we cannot continue ignoring the effects of climate change and population growth and hoping that our lives will continue in the same way they always have. In such moments, the cumulative weight of all design's seemingly insignificant incremental extensions of potentiality reach critical mass and we find ourselves unavoidably faced with the threat, urgency, and uncertainty of designed crisis. From the smallest steps to these cumulative boil-over moments, design causes crisis wherever it goes whenever it extends potentiality.

Where does this leave us? How should we respond to the role of design in creating and sustaining the constant state of crisis of our artificial world? In conclusion here, I will discuss two possible approaches to the "management" of this worldwide design crisis. These are not mutually exclusive but are presented to illustrate some significant implications to be considered in the way we think about the relationship between design and crisis. The first approach is the attempt to regulate and control design through the application of moral frameworks. This moral approach foregrounds the question of what design *ought to do*. The second approach foregrounds the ethicality of design, asking first what design *can do* in light of the recognition that when design extends potentiality this opens up possibility and opportunity for both dark and light. Understanding design as fundamentally ethical in nature allows a shift in perspective. A crisis is not necessarily an undesirable side effect of design to be minimized or avoided. Understood in terms of encounter with potentiality, the ability of design to bring about emergent ethical crisis can be seen as a virtue to be carefully nurtured and embraced.

What Ought Design to Do?

The moralistic approach to the crisis of design privileges the question of what design ought to do. Society does need morality to function. It is a useful tool for understanding social conventions relating to what we collectively think the right thing to do might be. Moral regulation of design is well and good for what it is. Codes of conduct and professional certification schemes can serve certain practical purposes, but the limitations of the scope of such activities must be recognized. Collectively agreed upon moral frameworks can play aspirational, educational, and regulatory roles within a discipline. They play an important role in collective self-definition and retrospective judgment and criticism, but offer little help to the designer faced with the challenge of an emergent ethical crisis.[19]

The principles of moral frameworks are formed in response to experience and can only be applied to an emergent ethical crisis by way of analogy: "this new situation seems a bit like that old one; perhaps we should react in a similar way." Nevertheless, yesterday's answers do not always provide the solution to tomorrow's problems. Knowing where you have come from helps with understanding where you are, but it does not tell you where you are going.

Reacting to the inadequacies of principle-based approaches, particularist approaches to morality maintain that every situation is unique and must be dealt with not by following established conventions but also only according to the parameters of its own particular context. It would not be just to automatically incarcerate all drivers of cars involved in fatal road traffic accidents. It is important to establish the particulars of each case before apportioning blame and dispensing punishment. The difficulty with particularism is that without recourse to general guiding principles, we find it difficult to explain and justify our intuitive sense of what is right. Design is an activity that by its nature takes place in the territory of the new and unknown. Every act of design represents a fresh encounter with potentiality that must be confronted in all its particularity.

The challenge facing the designer in the act of designing is how to decide what ought to be done when faced with ethical novelty that does not conform to the pattern established by existing moral frameworks. To be able to adequately address the question of what design ought or ought not to do, the matter of what design *can* do (is capable of) in the context in question must first be addressed. This—which forms the foundation upon which a morality of design can be built—is the question of the ethicality of design.

What Can Design Do?

The act of design is the extension of potentiality. When design occurs, it brings ethical space into being. In this sense, design is by nature a fundamentally ethical activity. It cannot be separated from the ethical. It cannot exist without bringing the ethical into being.

Understanding the nature of potentiality is key to understanding the ethicality of design. Agamben draws a distinction out of Aristotle's thought on potentiality, distinguishing between two types: generic and existing. Generic potentiality is that which could in theory possibly come to be. In this generic sense, I have the potentiality to walk on the moon. However, it would be ridiculous for me to declare that at this current moment, I am simply choosing not to do so. Only when I have actually become an astronaut and am standing on the lunar surface in my space suit do I come to possess the *existing* potentiality to be able to choose whether to walk or not to walk.

The interaction with potentiality, which forms the basis of design's ethicality, comes in two forms. Design can *extend* potentiality by bringing generic potentiality into being, and design can *transform* generic potentialities into existing potentialities. The possibility of putting a human on the moon was imagined long before the necessary technologies had been developed. However, once this abstract generic potentiality was established as a desirable goal, the efforts of designers turned this theoretical possibility into a genuinely actualizable existing potentiality.

Generic potentiality presents us with the distant possibility of the threat and uncertainty of a crisis that may come to affect us at some point. The urgency of a crisis really arrives when a potentiality turns from generic to existing. The generic potentiality for self-driving cars has existed for a long time in the imaginative fantasies of science fiction. Now, advances in technology have rendered generic potentiality into existing, and we are urgently faced with deciding as to whether or not, and in what ways, we choose to use this capability. The uncertainty inherent in the potentiality for autonomous vehicles is that we have no precedent for integrating autonomous machines into our daily lives at scale: we simply do not know what this means.[20]

Our existing moral and legal frameworks are unprepared for and incompatible with the concept of mass-market artificially intelligent autonomous vehicles.

In transforming generic to existing potentiality, design has brought crisis upon us by bringing us face-to-face with various possibilities. At the utopian end of possibility, the self-driving car could mean the end of road traffic accidents. Yet, we perceive the real and undesirable threat that any sub-optimality in the system will inevitably lead to human deaths being actively caused by autonomous machines. The potential promise of massive increases in the efficiency of transportation both in terms of resource use and journey times is tempered by fears of the perpetuation of fundamentally environmentally and socially unsustainable modes of individual-oriented transportation based on a personal ownership model. Further down the tunnel of pessimism, there lie concerns about malfunction, hacking, and the robot revolution so regularly predicted in science fiction, but now a real possibility at very least in a generic sense.

The heart of the crisis of design is that we must be equally responsible for those potentialities which we choose to bring into existence, and for those possibilities that we choose not to bring into being. To comprehend design's potentiality fully is also to understand design's impotentiality: what it *can* choose *not* to do. Understanding this properly is a prerequisite to being able to begin thinking morally about what design ought to do.

The various activities of speculative and critical design (SCD) represent the attempt to approach design as an exercise in pure potentiality. SCD generally proceeds by asking, "do we or do we not want to bring this speculative potentiality into being?" The criticality of SCD tends to emphasize the *cannot* of impotentiality, presenting opportunities for what Cameron Tonkinwise (following Anne-Marie Willis and Tony Fry) calls prefigurative criticism:[21] the possibility to choose to design something out of existence before it comes to be in the first place.

The possibility of prefigurative criticism raises the question of whether it should not be the task of design to attempt to stop ethical crises from emerging in the first place. The truth is that we cannot know what we want to avoid until we encounter and experience these things. SCD can confront us with generic potentialities, offering us the chance to act to stop these theoretical possibilities from being developed into existing potentialities or actualities. This keeps the crisis at bay, under observation at a distance, but does not exorcize it entirely. There is no way to retroactively un-design a design: to stop it having been designed in the first place. Once design has brought potentiality into being, there is no way to prevent the crisis from occurring. Our only option is to choose how we respond to that which we have designed.

Design is radically disruptive in this sense. It destabilizes existing states of being, creating states of uncertainty. However, the crisis-inducing character of design is not something to be feared. I would argue that it should instead be cautiously embraced. Through creating these states of disorientating uncertainty, design offers us an opportunity and possibility itself. As Dilnot writes,

> design is the discovery of what the artificial can be for us. Since the artificial is also today the frame of our possibilities as human beings, to discover what the artificial can be for us is to discover what our possibility can be, and hence . . . it is also a discovery of what possibility can be.[22]

Cautiously Embracing Crisis

Instead of seeking to regulate design with normative moral frameworks, we should embrace design's nature as the producer of ethical crisis in our artificial world. When we extend potentiality, we can choose which potentialities to seek to bring into being, and which to work against (to quarantine as impotentiality). We can only intentionally do this if we are fully in control of and engaged with the design process. To fear design and to attempt to regulate and suppress its activity would be to disable our best conscious input into shaping this world for the better. Failure to recognize the ethicality of design suppresses our ability to recognize possibilities for both bad and good. It weakens design's ability to respond (to be both responsive and responsible in relation) to crises.

However, our embrace of crisis should be cautious. Techno-utopians place blind faith in artifice to improve our world.[23] This is unwise. We must be careful to proceed with the right attitude, an attitude of critical sensitivity to be able to recognize the shape of the new space of possibility created and what this means in context. Crisis offers opportunity and threat equally. It presents, as Agamben puts it, the potentiality for both darkness and light.[24] Embracing the ethicality of design exposes us more fully to the simultaneous possibilities for both good and bad. It is a risky strategy, and if we are to take it, we must prepare ourselves appropriately. The wise course of action is to invest in our knowledge and mastery of the design process in order to be able to more effectively control and manipulate the full spectrum of im/potentiality. Then, when we do inevitably encounter the undesirable, the bad, the evil, and the terrifying possibilities unlocked by our own explorations of potentiality, we will find ourselves better equipped and prepared to negotiate these crises.

Notes

1   Arjen Boin, "From Crisis to Disaster: Towards in Integrative Approach," in *What Is a Disaster?: New Answers to Old Questions*, ed. Ronald W. Perry and Enrico Louis Quarantelli (Philadelphia: Xlibris, 2005), 153–72.

    Kenneth Hewitt, ed., *Interpretations of Calamity from the Viewpoint of Human Ecology* (Boston: Allen & Unwin, 1983), 10.

2   Jonathan Bundy et al., "Crises and Crisis Management: Integration, Interpretation, and Research Development," *Journal of Management* 43, no. 6 (2016): 1661–92.

3   Arjen Boin and Paul 't Hart, "The Crisis Approach," in *Handbook of Disaster Research*, ed. Havidán Rodríguez, Enrico Louis Quarantelli, and Russell Rowe Dynes (New York: Springer, 2007), 43.

4   Boin, "From Crisis to Disaster," 161.

    Bundy et al., "Crises and Crisis Management," 1663.

    Matthew W. Seeger, Timothy L. Sellnow, and Robert R. Ulmer, "Communication, Organization, and Crisis," *Annals of the International Communication Association* 21, no. 1 (1998): 233.

5   Boin, "From Crisis to Disaster," 169.

6   The etymology of the word crisis itself can be traced to the Proto-Indo-European root *krei-. *krei- is the foundation for various words in ancient languages referring to sieves and sifting and leads on to the Greek *krinein* referring to the act of separating, distinguishing, judging.

7   Boin and 't Hart, "The Crisis Approach," 43.

8   This is a recurring theme in Dilnot's work. See for example:

    Clive Dilnot, "The Critical in Design (Part One)," *Journal of Writing in Creative Practice* 1, no. 2 (2008): 177–89.

    Clive Dilnot, "Some Futures for Design History?" *Journal of Design History* 22, no. 4 (2009): 377–94.

9   Elaine Scarry, *The Body in Pain: The Making and Unmaking of the World* (Oxford: Oxford University Press, 1985).

10 Clive Dilnot, *Ethics? Design?* (Chicago: Archeworks, 2005).

    Mark Jackson, "Ethics of Design," *Scope (Art & Design)* 4 (2009): 179–87.

11 Aristotle, *Metaphysics: Books VII-X, Zeta, Eta, Theta, Iota,* trans. Montgomery Furth (Indianapolis: Hackett, 1986), 9.1048b.

12 Peter Buwert, "Potentiality: The Ethical Foundation of Design," *The Design Journal* 20, no. sup1 (2017): S4459–67.

13 Giorgio Agamben, *The Coming Community,* trans. Michael Hardt (Minneapolis: University of Minnesota Press, 1993), 44.

14 Giorgio Agamben, *Potentialities: Collected Essays in Philosophy,* trans. Daniel Heller-Roazen (Stanford: Stanford University Press, 1999), 182.

15 Agamben, *The Coming Community,* 43.

16 Bernard Arthur Owen Williams, *Ethics and the Limits of Philosophy* (Abingdon: Routledge, 2006).

17 John D. Caputo, "The End of Ethics," in *The Blackwell Guide to Ethical Theory,* ed. Hugh LaFollette and Ingmar Persson (Malden: Blackwell Publishers, 2000), 111–28.

18 Buwert, "Potentiality."

19 P. Buwert, "Examining the Professional Codes of Design Organisations," in *Design Research Society International Conference 2018,* Erik Bohemia et al. (Limerick: Design Research Society, 2018), 172–86.

20 Despite the best efforts of science fiction's obsessive prophetic speculations on the implications of machine intelligence: from Samuel Butler's *Erewhon* (1872) to Isaac Asimov's *I Robot* (1950) to Clarke and Kubrick's *2001: A Space Odyssey* (1968) to the Wachowski's *The Matrix* (1999) and so on.

21 Susan Yelavich, Barbara Adams, and Cameron Tonkinwise, "Design Away," in *Design as Future-Making* (London: Bloomsbury Academic, 2014).

22 Clive Dilnot, "Ethics in Design: 10 Questions," in *Design Studies: A Reader,* ed. Hazel Clark and David Brody (Oxford: Bloomsbury, 2009), 184.

23 See for instance Invision's 2016 Design Disruptor's documentary: Invision, "Design Disruptors: The Future is Designed," *DESIGN DISRUPTORS,* July 7, 2016, www.designdisruptors.com

24 Agamben, *Potentialities,* 181.

9

Designing Ourselves to Death: The Politics of Progress Versus an Ethics of Survival in a Diminishing World

David Stairs

Some people may say that man's moral influence will suffice to rule them (machines) but I cannot think it will ever be safe to repose much trust in the moral sense of any machine.[1]

Cleverness

Many writers have joined Samuel Butler in reflecting upon humanity's infatuation with the risks of its own subtle inventions. In "Total Domination," part of her 1951 publication *The Origins of Totalitarianism*, Hannah Arendt wrote, "The ideological contempt for factuality still contained the proud assumption of human mastery over the world; it is, after all, contempt for reality which makes possible changing the world, the erection of human artifice."[2] She was referring to the rise of fascism, not design, but design played a significant role in the instrumentation of death devised by the Third Reich. It is now generally accepted that IBM Hollerith punch-card tabulators found at some of the death camps were crucial to the Final Solution,[3] while Wunderwaffe, "miracle weapons" like jet fighters and ballistic missiles, made it from the drafting table into the field. Albert Speer, Hitler's minister of armaments and war production, the man who kept the Third Reich war machine running between 1942 and 1945 in the face of inevitable defeat, was trained as an architect.[4]

American author, patent engineer, and singularity enthusiast Ray Kurzweil would likely take a different view of machines from Samuel Butler. He has gone so far as to argue that self-aware machines will supersede organic intelligence by the year 2040,[5] and IBM's Watson has already crushed the best human players at Jeopardy. This idea of humans made obsolete by sentient machines has had many evocations in literature and cinema, from some of its earliest appearances in Karel Capek's *R.U.R.* and Fritz Lang's *Metropolis* in the 1920s, to Charlie Brooker's television series *Black Mirror*. In such treatments, the outcome is usually similar to the dystopia ruled over by Skynet in the *Terminator* series, or the human incubators of the *Matrix*, suggesting that such reflections strike a chord of pessimism in many people.

The problem with Kurzweil's thinking is not that it proposes a narrative of future human enslavement as that it predicts the domination of all nature by an infinitely less resilient replacement since even machines designed by other powerful machines are still about four billion years behind natural selection.[6] Just as the physicists who have proposed that our universe is only one facet of a multiverse as a means of justifying their mathematical models of matter, energy, and time/space,[7] futurists looking ahead to a totally "planned" society like to refer to DNA as a "program," thereby framing their worldview of organic life in the terms most congenial to them, though not necessarily accurate or endearing to anyone else. As scientists did with DDT in the 1940s and 1950s, our obsession with ends often justifies an incautious application of means.

In his 2008 book, *Twilight of the Machines*, American anarcho-environmentalist John Zerzan traces human disassociation from its life-world to the ascension of so-called environmental mastery through agrarian domestication and the division, or specialization of labor in Neolithic times. He sees our current techno-capitalist society, so out of step with nature, as a "death-trip"—perverse, destructive, and anti-natural. According to him, it was the *gendered* division of labor that launched our patriarchal civilization. Zerzan equates the growth of technology with patriarchy. He observes, "Women experience the move from autonomy and relative equality in small, mobile anarchic groups to controlled status in large, complex governed settlements."[8] Unfortunately, the subjugation of women was only the first step on the road to social and environmental injustice.

Concurrent with the Neolithic origins of agrarian civilization, symbolism emerged in the form of art and writing. In a perfect storm of coincidence, what we have come to call "culture" arose with the development of various forms of symbolic notation, initially controlled by shamans and priests, and later dominated by patriarchal warrior emperors.[9] The problem with symbolic culture is its tendency to diminish the immediacy of human presence. Symbolism *re*-presents reality, thereby distancing people from nature and, by metaphoric *dis*-association, estranging them from one another. It is *dis*-embodying, precisely the effect of our current digital social media. According to Zerzan, "Symbolic means sidestep reality; they are part of what is going wrong."[10] This tendency toward abstraction, which affects our direct relationship with nature, is inherent in art, literature, music, and mathematics, and made the technological revolution possible. The symbolic linearization of writing led to technology's ultimate triumph over nature. In fact, technology has colonized the most powerful sense, sight itself, co-opting visual-symbolic representation and replacing both with machine language. Machine language is conscience-free. It is wonderful for rapid parsing and cross-platform communication, but a little myopic when it comes to determining the extent of human need, or the limits of the environment's carrying capacity.

> Design is essentially a middle-class profession that has delivered a comfortable life for middle-class people, while also indulging the wealthy. . . . The dark side of this success, however, is that it addresses the lives of a very small segment of the world's population and even within

that population it leaves out those with special needs such as the aged and the disabled. The majority of people in the world are not only without middle-class comfort, but many also lack the basic means of survival: adequate shelter, food, education, and health care.[11]

Loquaciousness

With increasing frequency, design ascribes much of human accomplishment to itself. Design world histories no longer begin with the Industrial Revolution, or even the Renaissance, but with the Neolithic advances in agriculture and metallurgy. In other words, design is part and parcel of the symbolic revolution. Since Nobel laureate Herbert Simon's 1969 *Sciences of the Artificial*, where he described design as the "core discipline for every liberally educated man,"[12] design's cultural footprint has expanded exponentially. This is due, in part, to the digital revolution of which Simon was an early proponent, but also to design's hunger for recognition and intellectual hegemony in spheres of human planning and making. In the last thirty years, design programs and publications have sprouted. Because design delivers recognizable results, and people like results, it has become a go-to discipline of integrative pragmatics. If one were accepting of society's status quo, which might include satisfaction with standard concepts of progress and growth, it would almost appear that the twenty-first century is poised to become the Century of Design.

Since art and design are two of the major disciplines implicated in any human obsession with symbolic manipulation (mathematics-based science, music, digital technology, and literature are among the others), design can also be indicted in the promotion of an unsustainable civilization, making all designers culpable, from Odysseus (the *Polymechanikos*) to contemporary practitioners. This is not the narrative propounded by the design profession, but historically the depth of design's collusion with "techno-capitalism," borne out by its traditional role as handmaid to commerce, does not leave wiggle room for its apologists. Recent efforts to change design's anti-natural image by incorporating sustainable solutions into design practice, like The Designers Accord Sustainability Toolbox, or some of IDEO's initiatives,[13] feel token when viewed through the lens of 400ppm of atmospheric CO_2.[14] Then there is the race to construct new buildings—so important to design competitions even though often at great cost to the environment—which seems criminal when cities like Detroit are being urged to tear down 40,000 structures.[15] This is not a problem isolated to just the American Midwestern post-industrial "Rust Belt," but is common in brownfields and redevelopment projects the world over. Yet economic development tends to turn a blind eye to environmental impact in the heat of momentary profit. In the face of a technical critical mass, one might ask: Does a design conscience regarding technological capitalism exist, or must design continue to serve progress so-called at any price?

One of the great roadblocks to sustainability is that ecological balance is truly difficult to achieve, and nearly impossible for an industrial economy. In Western Michigan, the Herman Miller Company has been striving for decades to reduce its environmental footprint. Having made a concerted effort to achieve 100 percent sustainability in everything from materials sourcing to power generation to greywater management, company representatives admit that it is difficult to move above 91 percent sustainable.[16] The problem begins with manufacturing and expands exponentially with the chain of supply. Herman Miller, like any large modern manufacturing enterprise, does business with several sub-contractors. It would take agreement with these entities that sustainability was in their best interest—a thing American society seems unable to do—to even begin to frame 100 percent sustainability as a realizable goal. Under the current free-enterprise capitalist model, this would be suicidal for smaller companies.

It is unfair to imply that design is wholly responsible for the difficulties we currently find ourselves in, but it is not inaccurate to state that, until very recently, designers did not consider themselves a factor in the need to reverse damaging trends.[17] Designers, focused on developing the skills to make things "look cool," are often more interested in conventional fashion than ethics, restraint, or sustainability. Even a famous worldwide practice like Frog, a firm that boasts "form follows emotion," is more market-driven and focused on solving the immediate and short-term business problematic than in protecting the homeostatic balance of our life-world. The questions might well be asked: If we can design whatever we want, why haven't we designed a world free from the devastating problems that arise in modern cities? If planning is design's core purpose, why has our foresight been so myopic? In effect, are designers speaking in tongues while trafficking in comforting clichés?

Wickedness

Then we roared along all night again and came to a much bigger town. There we stayed all day and all night; and right there I could compare my people's ways with the Wasichu ways, and this made me sadder than before. I wished and wished that I had not gone away from home.[18]

We know that cities concentrate commerce, wealth and, along the way, population with all its concomitant waste and pollution. Although social scientists are beginning to query the potential effects of climate change on human migration, urban planning, so crucial in super-concentrated environments, has not been terribly successful at anticipating human migratory patterns, let alone natural sustainability.[19] Perhaps the difficulty lies with the difference between shallow & fast versus deep & slow knowledge, a concept proposed by David Orr in *The Nature of Design*.[20] Even though design proceeds along an iterative trajectory, it develops at a faster pace than evolution—a fact that its advocates consider one of its strengths. However, the subtle genetic mutations and harsh empirical efficiencies imposed by nature on even its most successful species help to maintain a homeostatic and sustainable balance that no triple bottom line or six-sigma design program can hope to emulate.[21]

The suggestion of recent anthropological research that Paleolithic man was every bit the match for modern man in intelligence and resourcefulness, while living in a more egalitarian society that was respectful of women and the environment, gives the lie to patriarchic arguments about the superiority of Neolithic "advancements."[22] In fact, revisions in our understanding of the accomplishments and capabilities of "primitive" man have set this entire worldview on its head and continue to push back estimates of the first appearance of human tools. As Zerzan reminds us, "Ever-growing documentation of human prehistory as a very long period of largely non-alienated human life stands in stark contrast to the increasingly stark failures of untenable modernity."[23]

Proponents of civilization's "advances" will turn a mocking eye to the suggestion of even a partial return to simpler methods, the "primitivist" movement. The industrialized juggernaut that nearly destroyed Native American hunter/gatherer societies when it eliminated that people's food source by annihilating 75,000,000 free-ranging bison at the end of the nineteenth century has never been too terribly good at self-criticism. How often do we hear pronouncements about the successes of molecular biology or the medical miracle of increased human lifespan? Less frequently discussed are the trade-offs that have been made for such gains. Again, Zerzan says, "In language, number, art, and the rest, a substitution essence has been the symbol's bad bargain. This compensation fails to compensate for what is surrendered. Symbolic transactions deliver an arid, anti-spiritual dimension, emptier and colder with each re-enactment."[24]

American society's environmental movement did not even get underway until the second half of the twentieth century, with guidance from authors like Rachael Carson and Barry Commoner, and then it acted primarily as a bellwether. When deniers of environmental damage flocked to Washington in the wake of the 2016 election cycle, America faced the lowest November continental snowpack in recorded history, while wildfires ravaged the forests of the southeast. Yet many in the United States still seem to believe in the inevitability of continued economic and technological growth, as if they had no bearing on resource depletion or environmental imbalance, while recognition of the damage caused by tropical industrial deforestation seems to be viewed cynically by developing world governments desperate for foreign capital.

The conflict between design's acolytes and its critics is perhaps unresolvable. Capitalist systems reward initiative but ignore environmental piracy, concentration of wealth, and class stratification. Supporters of Kurzweil's theories, great believers in the establishment of human technological dominance over nature, would find little to celebrate in "equitable sufficiency," the argument Thomas Jefferson made for a pastoral society in Query XIX of *Notes on Virginia*.[25] Conversely, believers in the social and ecological "rightness" of homeostasis are convinced that the last 7,000 years have put us on the path to ecocide. Protests over the completion of the Keystone XL pipeline gained significant legal support because of the project's ill-conceived location on or adjacent to traditional First Nations reservation lands and water resources. Less prominent in the American press are stories about the devastation resulting from the mining of the Keystone oil from the Athabasca tar sands of Alberta, easily the dirtiest petroleum extraction process on earth.

For its own part in this seemingly impossible conflict, over the last thirty years, design has taken a series of these dichotomies, like development versus global warming, or urbanization versus population control, and defined them as "wicked problems."[26] Most designers understand that the definition of a problem is a certain first step toward rectifying it. Unfortunately, the problems confronting us have become so intractable that, to date, they have all but defied resolution by any means, let alone design intervention. How great the irony would be if design itself, and the human love of novelty resulting in the urge to constantly innovate, turned out to be the wickedest problem of all, the source and culmination of all wicked problems everywhere and always. Under those circumstances, one is tempted to ask: Would the world be a better place if design did not exist?

Freedom isn't an illusion; it's perfectly real in the context of sequential consciousness. Within the context of simultaneous consciousness, freedom is not meaningful, but neither is coercion; it's simply a different context, no more or less valid than the other. It's like that famous optical illusion, the drawing of either an elegant young woman, face turned away from the viewer, or a wart-nosed crone, chin tucked down on her chest. There's no "correct" interpretation; both are equally valid. But you can't see both at the same time.[27]

Conscientiousness

Paradigm shifts often happen subtly. Like the frog in a pot, the run-up to a tipping point can be masked by disagreement and contradiction, as has certainly been the case with global warming. But the alternative to our continuing denial of the current situation is the slow boil of climate change, driven by population growth, and resulting in environmental despoliation that also happens incrementally, until the wrath of nature or the reactions of culture lock in a death grip so cataclysmic it could result in the end of civilization as we know it. Apocalyptic cinema and literature, particularly of science fiction, have profited from this scenario many times over the last century. However, there is insufficient money to be made from this narrative of destruction either by entertainers or by those jokers who think they might eventually profit from the cleanup, to justify our continued evasions. How do we proceed in a world of shifting Gestalts?

Economist David Korten provided the basis for measured optimism with his 2006 book, *The Great Turning*.[28] According to Korten, a global social consciousness evolving away from control by governments and corporations of the north and toward the political, cultural, and economic re-enfranchisement of women, indigenous peoples, and civil society promises to overturn business as usual. "We facilitate the processes of awakening through our individual engagement and dialogue with others, creating cross-cultural experiences, encouraging deep reflection on meaning and values, exposing the contradictions of Empire, and spreading awareness of unrealized human possibilities."[29] This is more than pie-in-the-sky rhetoric, especially since the 2003 establishment of the high-level civil society activities of the United Nations Non-Governmental Liaison Service.[30]

In his 2015 book, *How to Thrive in the Next Economy*, author John Thackara addresses just this issue.[31] Utilizing dozens of case histories from both for- and nonprofit initiatives, Thackara analyzes the ways we maintain our life systems, like soil and water management, healthcare and transport design, proposing how we can do even better. In nearly every case, Thackara finds hope in the techniques of crowd-sourcing, commoning,[32] and what Ivan Illich termed *conviviality*. Thackara is not alone in this quest, by any means. In fact, a considerable number of people already practice "permaculture," responding to the environmental crisis in a variety of ways. It is significant that, while most design firms engage in some form of glossolalia toward the now mainstream concept of sustainability, Thackara believes it is not only attainable but is also optimistic about the possibilities for serious change, though not without admitting the need to overcome "feel good initiatives" and escape "the desert of the real" in the way we think about designing.[33]

John Zerzan is admittedly less sanguine than either Thackara or Korten. Many would take issue with his description of our society as "cynical," "dehumanized," and "bankrupt," or of techno-capitalism as a "malignancy." But it is sometimes hard to argue with Zerzan's reasoning: "Symbolic culture has atrophied our senses, repressed unmediated experience, and brought us, as Freud predicted, to a state of 'permanent internal unhappiness.'"[34] While educated and clever people obsess over the best ways to lure investment capital from the Shark Tank, our social and natural capital continues to erode. Levels of social alienation and disrespect for every form of life are at an all-time high. While Americans might here think of mass shootings, in capitals of the developing world the air quality is often so poor it can only serve as an indictment of progress.[35]

Where Zerzan criticizes technology's "hucksters" for enabling it to "continue to metastasize" while "impoverishing reality," Thackara calls for designers to be "transrational" and "interdependent" with earth's healthy systems, "assisting the one kind of growth that makes sense . . . the regeneration of life on earth."[36] In fairness to Zerzan, he and Thackara are criticizing the same political/economic system, one that combines capital and industry into an orgy of seemingly endless economic expansion. Unfortunately, resource competition has been at the root of human conflict since the dawn of time. Unless we voluntarily reduce our numbers or reign in our collective appetites, the future looms as a race to the bottom in an endgame of war for food, water, and energy. Then we are in the apocalyptic *Mad Max* world of George Miller's envisioning, where design exists to serve the few while everyone else subsists in chattel slavery.

One of Zerzan's most famous predecessors in the critique of techno-capitalism was Jacques Ellul who, from 1950 to 1990 published an increasingly pessimistic series of books about technological society. According to Ellul, technical systems are self-generating, but not self-reflective. In the *Technological Bluff*, he wrote, "Seeing the Hydra head of trickery and the Gorgon face of hi-tech, the only thing we can do is set them at a critical distance, for it is by being able to criticize that we show our freedom. This is the only freedom that we still have if we have at least the courage to grasp it."[37]

Over the quarter-century since Ellul penned this cautionary recommendation in his final book, it has become painfully obvious we will need more than courage to free ourselves from the delusions that enchain us. It will also take enlightenment on a scale that would exhaust an army of bodhisattvas. It will mean that designers, engineers, and visionaries of all sorts must relinquish rather than reinforce what Ellul called the "fascination" with technology, and we're nowhere near that point yet. It will take criticism surely, but also the willingness to accept that we not only don't have all the answers, but that some of the answers demand we abandon or at least redefine the idea of progress that has pervaded Western thinking since the Enlightenment.

Because techno-capitalism's illusion of possible universal affluence is so hypnotic, and design so persuasive, it will take a dramatic self-reckoning, especially an overcoming of our denial that the damage we have perpetrated has been created at the expense of the finite resources of our planet. We will need to finally admit the obvious role human agency has played in environmental destruction. It will require a willingness to put the world's long-term survival ahead of bottom lines and corporate balance sheets, quarterly returns, and personal investment portfolios. In fact, if design is to help make the world a better place rather than a worse one, it may even take the design profession's admission not only of its own past sins in the headlong pursuit of profits and professional growth, but an understanding of the limits, illusions, and real dangers of the visual-symbolic culture it so freely trades in. Designers, architects, and engineers can continue to plan prisons, design luxury cars, and conceive Super Bowl beer ads, or they could take a temporary leave of absence from these activities and design for the commonweal. As John Zerzan says, "We will all have to unlearn domestication."[38] In such a scenario, design could evolve to the heroic levels often ascribed to it, rather than being bogged down by so many of the trivial pursuits it has heretofore trafficked in.

All of this, and more, will be required for us to succeed as the caretaker species of our planet. It would be nice to think that designers could be an important part of the solution, but that is far from certain. Portentously, Zerzan says, "Commodification and aestheticization of the life-world proceed hand in hand. Consuming and ineffective, stylistic gestures prevail."[39] There are many well-meaning designers in the world, but whether a moiety will have the will to make the necessary sacrifices remains to be seen. We need to prove that capitalism has not made an oxymoron of design ethics, and that we can still see straight enough to know that the most compelling vision of the future is one where design functions not merely for profit, but for universal social and environmental health. Humanity has spent several millennia preparing for collective genocide. We would really be better off designing for life instead.

Notes

1   Samuel Butler, *Erewhon* (London: Trübner, 1872), 216.

2   Hannah Arendt and Peter R. Baehr, *The Portable Hannah Arendt* (New York: Penguin Books, 2003), 138.

3   Edwin Black, *IBM and the Holocaust* (New York: Crown, 2001).

4 Albert Speer, *Inside the Third Reich* (New York: Avon, 1971).

5 Ray Kurzweil and Alan Sklar, *The Age of Spiritual Machines: When Computers Exceed Human Intelligence* (New York: Penguin Audiobooks, 1999).

6 Juli Peretó, Jeffrey L. Bada, and Antonio Lazcano, "Charles Darwin and the Origin of Life," *Origins of Life and Evolution of the Biosphere* 39, no. 5 (October 2009): 395–406.

7 L. Mersini-Houghton and R. Holman, "'Tilting' the Universe with the Landscape Multiverse: The 'Dark' Flow," *Journal of Cosmology and Astroparticle Physics* 2009, no. 02 (2009): 6.

8 John Zerzan, *Twilight of the Machines* (Port Townsend: Perseus Book LLC, 2009), 16.

9 Ibid., 52.

10 Ibid., 7.

11 Victor Margolin et al., *Healing the World: A Challenge for Designers* (Chicago: Archeworks, 2004).

12 Herbert Alexander Simon, *The Sciences of the Artificial* (Cambridge: MIT Press, 1969), 83.

13 The design practice, IDEO, launched a nonprofit division, IDEO.org, in 2011.

14 In March 2015 global concentrations of atmospheric CO_2 surpassed 400ppm.

15 "Defining Blight in Detroit," *The New York Times*, May 27, 2014, www.nytimes.com/interactive/2014/05/27/us/Defining-Blight-in-Detroit.html

16 Staff conversation with the author at the Herman Miller, "Greenhouse," October 2012.

17 Also see Jessica Helfand and William Drenttel, "Ethics and Sustainability: Graphic Designers' Role" at the *Power of Design* conference (Vancouver, 2003) sixteen years after the Bruntland Report.

18 John Gneisenau Neihardt, Philip Joseph Deloria, and Raymond J. DeMallie, *Black Elk Speaks* (Albany: Excelsior, 2008), 173.

19 Richard Black et al., "The Effect of Environmental Change on Human Migration," *Global Environmental Change* 21, no. 1 (2011): S3–S11.

20 David W. Orr, *The Nature of Design: Ecology, Culture, and Human Intention* (Oxford: Oxford University Press, 2002), 35.

21 DFSS (Design for Six-Sigma) is a methodology that focuses development and production on process optimization.

22 Zerzan, *Twilight of the Machines*, 106.

23 Ibid., 108.

24 Ibid., 9.

25 Thomas Jefferson, *Notes on the State of Virginia* (Viginia: Prichard and Hall, 1781).

26 Horst W. J. Rittel and Melvin M. Webber, *Dilemmas in a General Theory of Planning* (Berkeley: University of Urban and Regional Development, 1973), 155–69.

27 Ted Chiang, *Stories of Your Life and Others* (London: Picador, 2015), 163.

28 David C. Korten, *The Great Turning: From Empire to Earth Community* (San Francisco: Berrett-Koehler, 2006).

29 Ibid., 316–23.

30 https://unngls.org/

31 John Thackara, *How to Thrive in the Next Economy: Designing Tomorrow's World Today* (London: Thames & Hudson, 2015).

32 Peter Linebaugh, *The Magna Carta Manifesto: Liberties and Commons for All* (Berkeley: University of California Press, 2009).

33 Thackara, *How to Thrive in the Next Economy*, 158–60.

34 Zerzan, *Twilight of the Machines*, 60.

35 On November 8, 2017, New Delhi's air quality index reached 999 ppm. The smog closed schools and caused traffic accidents. United Airlines canceled flights into Delhi.

36 Thackara, *How to Thrive in the Next Economy*, 169.

37 Jacques Ellul, *The Technological Bluff* (Grand Rapids: W. B. Eerdmans, 1990), 491.

38 Zerzan, *Twilight of the Machines*, 55.

39 Ibid., 72.

10

Freedom and Communication Design: An Ethical Approach

Sara Velez Estêvão

From all the ideals, freedom is the fairest. Synonym of dignity.
–VILÉM FLUSSER

Freedom is one of the highest values in democratic societies. One may ask if, and in what way, design should be concerned with freedom, particularly in a technologically complex world.

We rely on communication interfaces where technology plays a major role. In some cases, the information we access is selected based on algorithms. In other cases, it is chosen for efficacy. Recent political and media events have drawn attention to the proliferation of false news, issues regarding our data on social networks and websites, and our privacy. Design, specifically communication design, if considered as an intermediary that contributes to a public sphere, must also address these issues.

Communication design objects consist of signs and meanings that mediate perception. There are real effects on *actions* to be considered in the study of the role of design in the contemporary world. Be it in the form of agency, control, privacy, or lack of transparency among others, in all these events, communication design intervenes. The way these objects give form to that information influences the way we make decisions and take actions, thus shaping our worldview.

It is not difficult to evoke everyday, well-known examples, the literal and historical case of ideological, political, and scientific worldviews, which are the maps for creating models from which we orient ourselves. For instance, in traditional maps Africa appears smaller than it really is. In the year 2000, a badly designed voting ballot interfered in the results of the presidential elections and trust in the democratic process was shaken. With that, voters' freedom of choice and the interface design of voting machines may be called into question. While the value of information has overcome all other values, the everyday decisions we make and most of the actions we take have somehow mediated information as a basis that creates a limitation. This chapter argues for the concept of freedom as a dialogical response to the communication design object's dialectical dilemmas.

Placing Freedom in Ethical Thinking in Design

These concerns lead us to ethical questioning over the ways of designing and if freedom might constitute a reasonable ethical dimension. Albeit not new, ethical thinking on design has gained awareness in recent years. From a broad point of view, ethics arise in the theoretical discourse on the discipline as a result of its expansion. We may find the affirmation of this connection in authors such as Carl Mitcham, Bruno Latour, Victor Margolin, and Clive Dilnot.[1] Dilnot observes how the need to question the character of design relates to "our passage into a condition of being fundamentally defined by artifice,"[2] over which everyday design has a transformative capacity. "Ethics was not needed within design until quite recently because until quite recently, the activity known as designing did not play a prominent role in human affairs."[3]

The presence of design in human affairs leads us to concerns with the agency of design that have mainly addressed the ways in which this agency could be used to foster or nudge human behavior toward civic practices and imprinting a moral character in designing objects. To be able to influence human action and the way of life, the delegation of responsibility and morality fits in with the idea of the "consequentialist" ethics applied to design on which Carl Mitcham writes.[4] It is inherent in design as a practice that the intention in a project includes a pragmatic effect that will culminate in the activity. A study by researchers at the Cornell Food and Brand Lab[5] proposed a restaurant menu designed with certain typographic choices, visual composition techniques, and strong colors so that customers could prefer healthy eating while boosting the establishments' financial returns.

Attempts to incorporate moral values into design objects in order to moralize human actions first require a prior decision on this moral interference in the daily lives of potential recipients of design objects. Even if this moral interference is merely a nudge, it will only be so if this suggestion is stated. Otherwise, in this case, freedom of choice is compromised. This implies the acceptance that all the decisions made in the process of designing an object are moral decisions regardless of the goodness and good intentions of the morality inscribed in this design object. Ethics of consequentialism in design "would bring the moral character of action to the goodness or malice of its results."[6]

Victor Margolin also champions this humanist perspective as the moral code of design orientation in this age. Margolin considers that notwithstanding the values of the Enlightenment, the Universal Declaration of Human Rights (UDHR) must be maintained and reinforced as a reference for the reflection and practice of design in the information society.[7] Taking the UDHR as a reference to "moral authority,"[8] design would be integrated into the field of responsibility for all human activities. But this "moral authority" is jeopardized by the complexity of the contemporary production system that generates ambiguous situations. Design is inserted in this system in such an intricate way that the uncertainty is certain when finding the responsibility for an object's results. Let's take, for instance, a medical error in the diagnosis or treatment of a patient where a modern diagnostic device is used—one that computes a large and complex sum of the patient's data and crosses it with all possible diagnostics, which is operated by a doctor. Design intervenes not only on the device but also on the way this information is presented and how it is interacted with. How does one respond to the necessity of determining the responsibility of such an error? True to its dual art/technique characteristic, design conveys duplicity that also hampers its ethical evaluation. On the one hand, design objects are valued for their efficiency in accomplishing their goals; on the other hand, a depth of meaning in their form is sought.[9] Freedom in design fits into this ethical dimension as a fundamental human right upon which devices that partake in communication design can interfere.

Design and Freedom in the Public Sphere

The views for an ethics of design that do not separate our human existence from the artifices we create for ourselves, putting designed objects and communications as a part of our common existence, pose a political problem as design intervenes in the public sphere.

As communication design assumes a public role, one where it formats others' experiences with the intent of transmitting them, in the process of interpreting the phenomenon of communication, one cannot escape an interrogation about the truth of what is recorded and transmitted once subjected to the communication process. Hannah Arendt demonstrates this same concern in the chapter dedicated to the public sphere in her book *The Human Condition*, in which, when referring the term public, she writes, "For us the appearance—what is seen and heard by others and by ourselves—constitutes reality."[10] Design that is associated with the communication processes thus carries the characteristic of being a vehicle of communication, of dissemination, taken as reality.

One second meaning for the term public is the human-made world which we inhabit and where we, as humanity, relate to each other. It is our common sphere with a "world of things" that simultaneously connects us and separates us.[11] Just like design does and just as communication design does, it gives form and meaning to what we want to communicate, contributing to our dialogue and, at the same time, separating us by its impossibility in completely transmitting the experience. "The public sphere, as our common world, gathers us in the company of each other and, yet, avoids that we collide with each other" in the same way a table sits between people, guaranteeing a vehicle for them to relate while giving enough space and providing an obstacle so as not to feel the empty space.[12] Arendt tells us that for freedom to emerge, this public sphere must be guaranteed. Freedom, in this sense, coincides with politics,[13] so the Polis must be guaranteed.

The theme of freedom of human beings—or at least that of the pursuit of their liberation from what conditions them—serves as a motto for Arendt, as we can read on the first page of the prologue to *The Human Condition*.[14] The same is also a constant in Vilém Flusser's work. A thinker of Czech origin who lived most of his adult life in Brazil and later in France, he has dedicated himself to reflect on language, technology, communication, or design as processes of human construction of the world. A careful reading of his works will reveal freedom as a fundamental motivation in his thinking. The means for the transformation of the world in which, according to Flusser, one may include design, are then configured as means for this purpose. It is artifacts, results of artifice, of work, that "lend a certain permanence and durability to the futility of mortal life and to the ephemeral character of human time."[15] For Flusser, human artifice—in which the first artifacts, communication, and design are included in the same way— is constantly attempting to liberate humans from their natural condition.

So, in such an artificial society as ours, Flusser is concerned with yet another sort of conditioning—that of the apparatus in all its complexity. It would be through pure action (direct action between human beings without the intervention of matter), which for this author means freedom, that humanity can free itself from this other condition. "For now, this conquest of freedom must be fought, not so much against nature or against other men, but against the apparatus in its infra-human idiocy."[16] At the end of Arendt's work, there persists a professed expectation on the human capacity to act, and above all, in the activity of thinking as the pure activity that can supplant the rest in the human future.[17]

As Flusser argues, in such a time of abstract experience, it is up to designers to invent new forms where they will be playing with the apparatus instead of limiting themselves to a functional action. This game seems to correspond better to the political sense of Arendt's action, an approximation to the exercise of freedom. The contradiction seems to lie in the way design, being a discipline with purposes, intentions, techniques, and artifices, can contribute to a perspective that emphasizes pure action, politics. For Flusser, it is a question of ensuring that we are autonomous of the devices and that we cannot be independent of them; we must oppose our arbitrariness to the devices. Only in this way do we live in freedom.

The ability to project presupposes the ability to imagine the future, the capacity for hope. Choosing not to project, not to act, is, for Tomás Maldonado, a dangerous possibility. In a consumer society, despite its excess, choosing not to project under these conditions means rejecting hope and may seem more like an act of consent than of dissent.[18] That is, design that seeks to open a horizon of action that is articulated, coherent, and socially responsible for the human environment and its destiny.[19]

We may find a questioning akin to the above concerns in the writings of the German designer Otl Aicher, where he questions and places design on a political ground and its intricacy with the human way of existence. In fact, in design history, concepts of freedom appear embedded in the first modernist discourses and texts. Liberating the individual from unnecessary daily constraints would allow humanity to pursue their most noble aspirations. This assertion is, of course, linked to historical arguments for technological advancement that were picked by design discourse once design movements embraced mass production as a means for expanding well-designed objects that by being typified, would create harmony and equality. With this achievement, the collective society freed from day-to-day obligations due to new techniques and from the troubles of obtrusive objects could dedicate itself to act politically, to creating, and to thinking. These arguments are present in some of Deutscher Werkbund's members' discourses of their philosopher at hand, Georg Simmel's or Theo Van Doesburg's writings for *de Stijl*, or even in Walter Gropius's or Hannes Meyers's writings—a very different view from the one of postmodernism where this concept in relation to design shifts toward individual freedom, addressing specifically the designer's personal creative freedom. In more recent years, we find concerns about the value of freedom from speculative and critical design areas. Dunne and Raby's[20] position is akin to a vision of promoting concerns for freedom when designing. They defend clearly that although design may help shift behaviors, as in health and exercise, it should abstain from using its agency in a consequentialist manner and instead communicate the needs to change and always regard people as free agents. An exception is made in cases where people's behavior could harm others.[21]

However, it is Aicher who placed design as a political activity that, in this sense, should be concerned with the *freedom of others*, the *freedom in society* in general. Aicher's thinking on the role of design is linked to the time he founded the Ulm School (UFG) together with Max Bill and Inge Scholl, and the reflection process there originated. His reflections presented in *The World as Design*[22] see the world as the product of a civilization in which he recognizes the blurring of boundaries between nature and the artificial. He says, "Our world is no longer nature embedded in the cosmos. . . . We continue to philosophize about a world as 'being' and overlook the fact that it has become a design, a fabricated model that even includes nature."[23] He goes on: even the laws of nature "have left nature," becoming the basis of technology, being applied from machines and methods of production to the manufacture of products and the determination of their use and consumption.

Demonstrating affinities with the two previous authors (Arendt and Flusser), the author argues that design, as the possibility to project, emancipates us because it escapes the condition of determination of civilization. With its contribution, design leaves open the possibility of living in a pluralist and propositional culture that places the authority in the individual, providing a balance between the environment, the world, and us.[24]

Affirmed as the creation of realities, in this reflection, design is differentiated from science as a model and pronunciation of hypotheses. Under this model, design would open access to reality, to the world, because it is the responsibility of the discipline to pursue what has been done and what is possible and replace it with what should be, with the ideal. Replacing the existing with what should be is the idea also used by Flusser when referring to the human need to transform the world and human beings in what human beings should be. Design would thus represent an opening for a possible future world. To support this opening, Aicher relies on a certain dialectic that makes up design.

> Analytical and synthetic at the same time, specific and general, a concrete matter and one of principle. It keeps to the matter in hand and to demands, it goes back to facts and opens up new thinking spaces. It "counts the peas" and opens up perspectives. Calculates and opens up landscapes of possibility.[25]

The author's conviction also encompasses the possibility that by design, people may become themselves rather than remain as instruments. The question of freedom is equally important and serves as a corollary to Aicher. According to him, design should be concerned with freedom, a freedom that would occur precisely in this area of thinking that Arendt speaks of—that design occupies and connects to action. The human being "does not become free until he realizes freedom, manufactures it. In the freest societies, there can be slaves if people see freedom as a habitual behavior, not as concretization, development, design."[26] This is exactly how the American technology philosopher Carl Mitcham refers to design, "That intermediary between thought and action called design."[27] Aicher sees the role of design in this dialectic:

> Design is the creation of a world. It comes into being at the point at which theory and practice collide. But these do not cancel each other out. They both find ways of developing. . . . In design, man becomes what he is.[28]

Nevertheless, a world of apparatus is infinitely more complex. The unfolding of these conditions must be explored and questioned. Is design in fact the discipline that comes to challenge such conditions?

Distinct from visual thought seems to be the realization of an aesthetic experience that relates to the appearance of a free experience. "The realm of freedom is increasingly being reduced to the realm of aesthetics" because the aesthetic fact is taken as a fact,[29] hence his criticism of the world of communication design. The form that irremediably departs from the represented thing, breaking the analogy between the two, is a pure and aesthetic abstraction. The identity of a company is its example, most often as a surface design reflecting a surface world.[30] On the possibilities of digital means for design, John Thackara also touches on the issue of the freedom of decision-making by those made possible. While this new world of possibilities opened, the variety of the formal languages used was closing. The use of software, by definition, is limited because it does not allow designing features that do not already exist; the menu options are limited although the possible combinations are numerous.[31]

How the culture we produce programs and/or frees humans is a dilemma persistently present in Flusser's works. In the immaterial perspective configured in communication and in the information society we are addressing, the relevant element is always—as Flusser maintains—

the search for dialogue in view of the free existence of human beings. Particularly relevant are his arguments for the creation of dialogical objects capable of holding designers accountable, especially as regards to information technologies. We are all functionaries but for Flusser, the way to freedom is in a way the dialogical programming. Objects must promote dialogue.

Explorations in Dialogical Designing

For that to happen, it implies that the communication design in these devices is in accordance with this possibility of control and with the requirement of transparency for access to all the information. Under these conditions, it is important to examine the characteristics of design principles and their ability to respond to these dilemmas. Peter Hall, in "Bubbles, Lines and String: How Information Shapes Society,"[32] writes about the current enthusiasm for data and its visualization. Considering multiple decision-making in the process of visualizing information on what to omit and what information to prioritize, Hall comments on the contrast of this process with the authority, objectivity, and confidence that visualizations in general convey. However, usually, this is a neglected contrast in the discourse on the subject that ignores the theoretical problems that Johanna Drucker refers to in an excerpt also cited by Hall:[33]

> An empiricist assumption that what you see is what is there underpins their practice. The self-evident character of graphic entities—lines, marks, colors, shapes—is never itself brought into question, however much of the parameters on which they are generated or labeled might be criticized. That images themselves might be dialectical, produced as artifacts of exchange and emergence, is an idea foreign to the fields of engineering and information design.[34]

The richness and visual attraction that have, in a certain way, contributed to disseminating the notion that information is important and have made it an object of attraction are also reductive representations.[35] For Hall, these show a world without ambiguities as if "the disorganization of life had finally been conquered, organized and re-arranged as a refined form."[36]

The formal language of projects that begin by being experimental and critical is quickly adapted and replicated in commercial services to which the views attribute the sense of organization and refinement of life, losing the critical sense of the former. This is the case—referred to by Hall—of the visualization of the courses run in Manhattan, recorded by the Nike+ service on its website, and developed by Cooper Smith. This is an example of the trend that has taken place in order to collect exhaustively data from our entire lives. "Running is no longer just running, but measured, collated, and compared, tagged with personal targets and simulated rewards."[37] This view is inspired by Esther Polak's experimental project (2002), which equips sixty residents of Amsterdam with GPS locators, attempted to describe the city as lived by its inhabitants questioning the spatial difference of the city's experiences.[38] Information visualizations have also assumed the role of visually seductive objects as if this was an end in itself, promoting lifestyles and serving as a form of value attribution.

This value and "existential interest" assumed by the information, as well as the implications of the design objects that deal with it, motivate Drucker to argue for a humanistic, critical, and interpretive design. We recall Flusser's reflection on the interpretative characteristic of communication as opposed to explanatory when referring to the intrinsically human characteristic of communication.[39] Here is a long excerpt from Drucker's book, *Graphesis: Visual Forms of*

Knowledge Production,[40] which summarizes an argument and the ethical dimension of design in information technologies:

> When we finally have humanist computer languages, interpretative interfaces, and information systems that can tolerate inconsistency among types of knowledge representation, classification, fluid ontologies, and navigation, then the humanist dialogue with digital environments will have at the very least advanced beyond complete submission to the terms set by disciplines whose fundamental beliefs are anti-thetical to interpretation.
>
> The critical design of interpretative interface will push beyond the goals of "efficient" and "transparent" designs for the organization of behaviors and actions, and mobilize a critical network that exposes, calls to attention, it's made-ness—and by extension, the constructedness of knowledge, its interpretative dimensions. This will orchestrate, at least a bit, the shift from conceptions of interface as things and entities to that of an event-space of interpretative activity.[41]

In 2013, the Design Museum of London awarded the "design of the year" to the information portal for British citizens developed by the Digital Government Service. In addition to the surprise of a public office winning a design prize, the portal organizes the information in an almost typographic way, using hierarchy, trying to exploit a contextualized navigation and proclaiming the opening of information. The service that developed the portal includes a page where, reminiscent of the ten principles of Rams's good design, explains its ten design principles. However, these are procedural principles rather than indicative of the result. Thus, they seem to integrate some of the ethical perspectives referred to here. The list of principles includes a detailed explanation of each and its exemplification. They highlight the openness of information and the possibility of full access.

Even though it is a special design code, this set of principles shows signs of being integrated into a broader ethical perspective, which does not use the discourse of efficiency—which Drucker speaks of—and appears to be open to a critical position. Admittedly, this change in the UK government portal is probably related to the episodes of the selling of citizens' data to businesses in the United Kingdom, and, therefore, it is in part an attempt to gain the confidence of the citizens in the services of the state. This code and its explanation are representative of the notion that digital objects are the very reality in which we move.

Rarely is freedom placed as a dimension to be considered when designing, much less in communication design, although it makes sense that a fundamental human right is safeguarded. The discussion in this chapter intended, first, to bring this subject into conversation without pretending to be exhaustive and, second, to explore perspectives of designing that pay attention to freedom. Dialogical designing is inspired by Flusser's thoughts that in order to pursue freedom, communication objects must be open to dialogue. Nevertheless, questions remain about the real possibility of grasping the concept in practice, leaving room for further explorations on the matter. For now, a few ideas for designing with freedom in mind emerge from this work, such as declaring intentions, offering access to information, and creating room for interpretation and subjectivity.

Notes

1 Carl Mitcham, "Ethics into Design," in *Discovering Design Explorations in Design Studies*, ed. Richard V. Buchanan and Victor Margolin (Chicago: The University of Chicago Press, 1995); Clive Dilnot, "Ethics? Design?" in *The Archeworks Papers vol. 1*, ed. Stanley Tigerman (Chicago: Archeworks, 2005), 3; Bruno Latour, "A Cautious Prometheus? A Few Steps Toward a Philosophy of

Design (With Special Attention to Peter Sloterdijk)," in *Proceedings of the 2008 Annual International Conference of the Design History Society (UK) University College Falmouth, 3–6 September. HAL CCSD*, ed. Fiona Hackne, Jonathn Glynne, and Viv Minto (Falmouth: Universal Publishers, 2008); Victor Margolin, *Design e risco de mudança* (Vila do Conde: Verso da História, 2014).

2 Dilnot, "Ethics? Design?" 3.

3 Mitcham, "Ethics into Design," 174.

4 Ibid., 173–89.

5 Brian Wansink and Katie Love, "Slim by Design: Menu Strategies for Promoting High-margin, Healthy Foods," *International Journal of Hospitality Management* 42 (2014): 137–42.

6 Mitcham, "Ethics into Design," 180.

7 Margolin, *Design e risco de mudança*, 13–34.

8 Vilém Flusser, "The Ethics of Industrial Design?" in *The Shape of Things: A Philosophy of Design* (London: Reaktion Books, 1999), 67.

9 Mitcham, "Ethics into Design," 182.

10 Hannah Arendt, *A Condição Humana* (Lisboa: Relógio D'Água, 1958), 64.

11 Ibid., 67.

12 Ibid.

13 Ibid., 161.

14 Ibid., 11.

15 Arendt, *A Condição Humana*, 20.

16 Flusser, "The Ethics of Industrial Design?" 3.

17 Arendt, *A Condição Humana*, 395.

18 Tomás Maldonado, *Design, Nature, and Revolution: Toward a Critical Ecology* (New York: Harper & Row Publishers, 1972).

19 Ibid.

20 Anthony Dunne and Fiona Raby, *Speculative Everything: Design, Fiction, and Social Dreaming* (Cambridge: MIT Press, 2013).

21 Ibid., 160–61.

22 Otl Aicher, *The World As Design* (Berlin: Ernst, Wilhelm & Sohn, 1994), 179–89.

23 Ibid., 182.

24 Ibid., 185.

25 Ibid., 189.

26 Ibid.

27 Mitcham, "Ethics into Design," 173.

28 Aicher, *The World As Design*, 189.

29 Ibid., 36.

30 Ibid., 150–66.

31 John Thackara, *Design after Modernism: Beyond the Object* (New York: Thames and Hudson, 1988).

32 Peter Hall, "Bubbles, Lines, and String: How Information Visualization Shapes Society," in *Graphic Design: Now in Production*, ed. Andrew Blauvelt and Ellen Lupton (Minneapolis: Walker Art Center, 2012): 170–85.

33 Ibid., 171.

34 Johanna Drucker, *SpecLab: Digital Aesthetics and Projects in Speculative Computing* (Chicago: University of Chicago Press, 2009), 73.

35 Hall, "Bubbles, Lines, and String," 175.

36 Ibid.

37 Ibid.

38 Ibid.

39 Vilém Flusser, *Writings*, ed. Andreas Ströhl and Erik Eisel (Minneapolis: University of Minnesota Press, 2002), 3–20.

40 Johanna Drucker, *Graphesis: Visual Forms of Knowledge Production* (Cambridge: Harvard University Press, 2014).

41 Ibid., 178.

11

About the Ethics of Design Activism

Maziar Rezai

Thoughts about the impact of designers and their responsibilities in confronting societal ills have been changing as the role of design has expanded over time. Responsibility usually comes with many questions of ethics, including the obligations designers face with users of designed objects/services. These ethical matters take on another level when the designer becomes an activist.

Between the late 1960s and 1970s was a period of strong left-wing political activism in Europe, and the ethical underpinnings of capitalism were frequently questioned. Designers were inspired by critical writings such as *Silent Spring*,[1] an environmental science book that was published in 1962 by Rachel Carson. It documented the indiscriminate use of pesticides. Carson accused the chemical industry of spreading disinformation and public officials of accepting the industry's marketing claims unquestioningly.[2]

These years brought two significant concepts to design: one, that design is a social language and two, that design expresses lifestyle. At the International Council of the Society of Industrial Designers in London in 1969, the theme was "Design, Society and the Future," and designers aimed to contribute to a wider debate on the society they were helping to create.[3] At the same time, Herbert Alexander Simon stated that design is always about "courses of action aimed at changing existing situations into preferred ones."[4] Although devising courses of action is different from taking action, this proposition helped designers see the world as something that can be changed by their actions.

In 1971, Victor Papanek published *Design for the Real World*,[5] which quickly became a bible for the responsible design movement. Many designers now wanted to "save the world" through their actions and considered themselves responsible for the developments around them. Designers wanted to solve problems from abortion to the Vietnam War, and to abandon design for profit.[6] The old "form follows function" or "fitness for purpose" slogan was changed to "fitness for need" at the Design and Industries Association in 1975.[7] They also saw themselves opposing capitalist exploiters—a rather double-faced approach considering that the same companies simultaneously employed them.[8]

Years later, Nigel Whiteley, in *Design for Society*, pointed out that the conscious consumer of the 1990s expected a more ethical approach from companies, and many companies started considering ethical issues in their product development. Unlike in the 1970s, it was not only the designers who aimed toward a more ethical approach; the corporations were also inclined to produce new, morally conscious products.[9] Whiteley found a relation between the economic situation and the designer's willingness to consider moral issues.

Socially responsible design (represented by Papanek in the 1970s) resurfaced with a shift toward sustainable design. With his book *The Green Imperative*,[10] Papanek turned toward this approach. In 2005, John Thackara claimed that 80 percent of the environmental impact of the products, services, and infrastructures around us were determined in the design stage, and designers were urged to take moral responsibility more seriously.[11]

In 2003, historian John Heskett asked the question of whether designers are merely technocrats, devoting their skills to the highest commercial bidder without considerations of the ends they serve, or whether there is a dimension of social and environmental purpose requiring acknowledgment in their work.[12]

More recently, in 2017, Ezio Manzini and Victor Margolin, in an open letter to the design community, asked designers to respond to the crisis that democracy is undergoing.

> For many years, we lived in a world that, despite its problems, was nevertheless committed to principles of democracy in which human rights, fundamental freedoms, and opportunities for personal development, were increasing. Today, this picture has changed profoundly. There are attacks on democracy in several countries—including those where democracy had seemed to be unshakable.[13]

Manzini and Margolin asked the design community to take action. "Normal" ways of designing were not enough, and the role of designer in confronting the absence of democracy in the world needed to be changed.[14]

In 2008, Ann Thorpe had explored the activism phenomenon and its relation to design, stating that activism starts when groups within society call for change and society responds either by resisting or incorporating the values of activism. "I define activism as taking intentional action to instigate change on behalf of a neglected group."[15] Making a link between designers and activists, she continued, "Designers are working across a range of groups and issues, ranging from victims of war or disaster to minority groups."[16] Thorpe tells us that interest in public service design and design activism had been rising.[17]

Today, we can recognize what an activist designer can do in a society. Activist designers know their actions can change the social, cultural, and political situation. Moreover, they know their responsibilities, obligations and/or the ethics that drive them to do so, but how? In other words, how can ethics reinforce design activism?

Aristotle (384–322 BC), in *Posterior Analytics* and in *Nicomachean Ethics*, divided virtues into moral and intellectual.[18] He identified five intellectual virtues as the five ways in which the soul arrives at truth through affirmation or denial. These are then separated into the three classes (see Figure 11.1).

Aristotle claims that only the morally virtuous person will be able to be practically wise because only such a person will perceive what is and be motivated to carry out the appropriate actions. Because practical wisdom is in the service of action, and because human beings must choose some actions rather than others, they need to be able to deliberate well about what

Theoretical
Sophia(wisdom): rational intuition and scientific knowledge directed toward the highest and most valuable objects
Episteme: scientific knowledge of objects that are necessary and unchanging
Nous: rational intuition of first principles or self-evident truths
Practical
Phronesis: practical wisdom
Productive
Techne: craft knowledge, art

FIGURE 11.1 *Five intellectual virtues, c. 2018. Courtesy of Maziar Rezai.*

actions are needed. Someone who is both morally virtuous and has practical wisdom will perceive and deliberate well, and hence, choose well.[19]

Instead of using words of theoretical, practical, and productive virtues, we have changed these concepts to *science, technique, and art.* In science, cognition happens just in order to know. However, technique is not only for cognition, but also for *transformation.* Art is not a technique or a science. In art, cognition happens for transformation—transformation not for the sake of gain, but for the sake of beauty.

Ethics is also technique. In ethics, "I want to transform myself." In the other words, a designer or an activist designer, takes a "course of action aimed at changing existing situations into preferred ones." Therefore, ethics is a technique.

With Aristotle's definition, design activism is a moral phenomenon because its work is transformation, transforming products and systems to express a message or change a political, cultural, or social phenomenon. The big difference between design and design activism lies in responsibility. In design, the designer should design for users, based on their interests, culture, and physical and emotional needs. However, since the consumer is willing to pay for the product or service, designers align with markets, which sell consumers what they want even if it is harmful. This highlights a critical point for the designer: ethical responsibility. Ethical responsibility is the difference between being a designer and being an activist designer.

The key point here is what guided us as designers to produce a new concept and shape our role in society. For the activist designer, it is not only a desire to be an activist. Rather, it is a need and passion to be critical, more effective in tackling social problems, and to not being merely a "servant problem solver" or "service provider."[20] In my view, this need and passion in design that asks design to be something more is a kind of intellectualism.

Intellectualism, in modern use and not in mere philosophical meaning, refers to the responsibility of the communities' elite and reminds us of the Dreyfus affair and the reaction of Émile Zola and other French intellectuals in that historical case.[21].Furthermore, an intellectual's actions in society are based on responsibility and obligation and can be recognized as a moral phenomenon.[22] I believe that the designer's action within a design activism process is more than just being an activist. Rather, I believe it is creative enlightenment. Otherwise, how can we determine the border of the activist and the activist designer? Therefore it may be possible to divide the design activism area into two contexts—design by action and design intellectualism.

"Design by Action" is a term that comes from a phenomenon that had been analyzed before in design, called "Design by Use." In 2009, Uta Brandes explored this specific kind of design, in which people with no formal design training reappropriate and use things for different purposes than what they are designed for, thus converting them to new uses.[23] In short, they "misuse" them in the best sense of the word. Brandes and Michael Erlhoff describe this as non-intentional design (NID), a term meant to illustrate the everyday redesign of designed objects by users that do not create a new design, but through using an object, create something new or replace the old. This kind of redesign through reuse can make things multifunctional and cleverly combines them to generate new functions. It is often reversible, resource-friendly, improvisational, innovative, and economical.[24]

However, in Design by Action, there is no designer designing these creative actions. Design is made by people in an extraordinary situation, which naturally implies a perfect design thinking process every day and transforms every single element of the space into a meaningful tool based on their needs. Design by Action occurs quite often. Here, the creator is not a designer who is aware of his or her design action, but rather a non-designer. Design by Action can also be analyzed as an ethical phenomenon because although non-designers make it happen based on their needs, the people do this to save their lives and fill a necessary gap that occurs during tragedies. For them, Design by Action is an instrument for resisting.

The "design activism" phenomenon and the notion of the "Design by Use" shows that everyone can be a designer and is helping in democratizing design and providing a new understanding of it. However, considering the designer's absence is also a critical point as we review the concept of design activism.

We know that this absence could make a space for activists or non-designers to do what is necessary, but it also shows a challenge in the design activism discourse and raises the important issue: "What is the exact border between non-designers and activist designers?" I think there is a gap here that needs to be analyzed: How can we separate the results of non-designers who design by their ordinary actions and the designers who utilize their expertise?

Earlier, we analyzed these actions by people in the design activism area and we knew that they were not designers, activists, or activist designers. We need a new term to make the distinction. Therefore, I would like to call it "Design by Act." From my perspective, "Design by Act" is the exact term to express the situation of those people who design by their actions based on their social, political, or cultural needs.

In other words, the designer here is also the user; the people, who change their area, transform products, and design or redesign things for sending a message to other people, the government, or both. These messages are diverse and can be social, political, or cultural. By contrast, what an activist designer does is deliver this message through design, not merely through action. Design serves their actions in the purest way.

But who is an intellectual designer? In the design activism area, the intellectual designer is an activist designer who is first a thinker, who observes, discovers, analyzes and, with creative enlightenment, reacts by design. However, like an ordinary designer, his or her reaction can be a confrontation with society. This is the same perspective on design, which can help to reframe design as the result of an active and conscious thinking process that creates a strong social, political, and cultural message, action, intervention, or some other result that we may not be able to foresee.

In the design activism area, it is a necessity for the future of societies to aim at gaining a better understanding of how designers can effectively work and interact with social and political problems—problems that often need a kind of creative enlightenment for all parties involved in order to have a real and effective impact. Otherwise, the design work (the message) and the designer's role might disappear before reaching the audience.

Notes

1 Rachel Carson, *Silent Spring* (Mariner Books, Houghton Mifflin, 1962); Anna Valtonen, "Back and Forth with Ethics in Product Development: A History of Ethical Responsibility as a Design Driver," in *Opening the Black Box: Moral Foundation of Management Knowledge* (Paris: EIASM, 2006) 13–14.

2 Dorothy McLaughlin, "Special Reports—Silent Spring Revisited," *Public Broadcasting Service*, August 24, 2010, www.pbs.org/wgbh/pages/frontline/shows/nature/disrupt/sspring.html

3 Nigel Whiteley, *Design for Society* (London: Reaktion Books, 1993).

4 Herbert Alexander Simon, *The Sciences of the Artificial* (Cambridge: MIT Press, 1969).

5 Victor Papanek, *Design for the Real World: Human Ecology and Social Change* (Chicago: Academy Chicago Publishers, 1971). The book was first published in Swedish in 1970 as *Miljön och Miljonerna: design som tjänst eller förtjänst?* (Stockholm: Bonniers Boktryckeri) and then in German in 1972 as *Das Papanek-Konzept. Design für eine Umwelt des Überlebens* (München: Nymphenburger Verlagsbuchhandlung) before it was published in English in 1972.

6 Kathryn B. Hiesinger and George H. Marcus, *Landmarks of Twentieth Century Design: An Illustrated Handbook* (New York: Abbeville Press, 1993).

7 Ibid.

8 Valtonen Anna, "Back and Forth with Ethics in Product Development: A history of ethical responsibility as a design driver in Europe" 2006, www.academia.edu/972634/Back_and_Forth_with_Ethics_in_Product_Development.

9 Whiteley, *Design for Society*.

10 Victor J. Papanek, *The Green Imperative: Natural Design for the Real World* (New York: Thames and Hudson, 1995).

11 John Thackara, *In the Bubble: Designing in a Complex World* (Cambridge: MIT, 2005).

12 John Heskett, *Toothpicks and Logos: Design in Everyday Life* (Oxford: Oxford University Press, 2003).

13 Ezio Manzini and Victor Margolin, "Open Letter to the Design Community: Stand Up For Democracy," *Democracy and Design Platform*, March 5, 2017, democracy-design.org/open-letter-stand-up-democracy

14 Ibid.

15 Ann Thorpe, "Design as Activism: A Conceptual Tool," in *Changing the Change: Design, Visions, Proposals and Tools*, ed. Carla Cipolla and Pier Paolo Peruccio (Turin: Icsid, 2008).

16 Ibid.

17 Maziar Rezai and Mitra Khazaei, "The Challenge of being Activist-Designer: An Attempt to Understand the New Role of Designer in the Social Change Based on Current Experiences," *The Design Journal* 20, no. sup1 (2017): S3516–35.

18 Aristotle, *The Nicomachean Ethics of Aristotle*, ed. Hugh Tredennick, trans. J. A. K. Thomson (Lanham: Penguin Classics, 1976).

19 David Arnaud and Tim LeBon, "Key Concepts in Practical Philosophy: Practical and Theoretical Wisdom, And Moral Virtue, Practical Philosophy," *Practical Philosophy: Society for Philosophy in Practice* 3, no. 1 (March 2000).

20 Mahmoud Keshavarz, "Design-Politics Nexus: Material Articulations and Modes of Acting," 2015, https://pdfs.semanticscholar.org/6b0f/cd3b622eb41e15537f1b604881e5cb637097.pdf.

21 The Dreyfus Affair was a political scandal dividing the Third French Republic from 1894 until 1906.

22 With this definition, if an intellectual makes a mistake in its determinations and actions and breaks morality, intellectualism is still moral and that person's action should be examined from ethical aspects.

23 Miriam Wender, Uta Brandes, and Sonja Stich, *Design by Use: The Everyday Metamorphosis of Things* (Basel: De Gruyter, 2009).

24 Ibid.

12

Ethics in Contemporary Civic Engagements: Toward an Ethics of a Minor Design Activism

Tau Ulv Lenskjold and Sissel Olander

Over the past decade, the term design activism has gained increased attention in areas such as urban planning and architecture, product and interaction design, fashion and new media, social innovation, and social design.[1]Across this varied landscape, design activism is often rooted in, or shares an affinity with, social, cultural, or environmental issues engendered by the art and design avant-gardes of the 1960s and 1970s. The chief aim among these progressive and radical groups[2] was to challenge consumerism and devise strategies for reimagining design as a vehicle for bringing about societal change and creating more sustainable futures. In parallel, a somewhat different trajectory emerged in the 1970s and 1980s, namely the movement of participatory design.[3] Here, researchers and system developers introduced design methods to aid workers, and other groups, in their democratic struggle to counter the changes brought about by new technology.

The renewed interest in design activism today carries forth a political drive toward "relocating resources and . . . proposing non-mainstream models to create alternative constellations of people and artifacts and rearrange the channels between them."[4] While the provision of political agency to elicit societal change *in* and *through* design takes center stage in design activism, questions pertaining to ethics and values are often less explored.

Politics and ethics are complex concepts that intertwine in numerous ways. Even though the political drive is paramount to design activism, it "is often lost as it gets entangled in the pragmatic but necessary questions of its implementation."[5] Moreover, where the noise of getting things off the ground may hamper both considerations and expressions of explicit political aims, even less attention is directed to the contemplation of the inherent ethical stance of activist engagements. To unpack the ethics of design activism further, we begin from a provisional idea of how ethics and politics are both separated and entangled as particular modes of reasoning. In political philosophy, for example, a commonly held distinction sees ethics as *prescriptive* and politics as *descriptive*.[6] Ethics, then, is a series of prescriptions governing "our conduct regarding other persons and the world," while politics is a series of processes and "arrangements concerning the power to govern."[7] But in *the doing* of socially engaged design, with its multitude of different stakeholders and considerations, the practical discernment between prescriptive and descriptive actions is often imperceptible. If instead, we conceive of design activism as a politico-material practice with its own inherent values and norms, we may arrive at a more apt understanding of ethics—one that follows Hannah Arendt's suggestion of an ethics of plurality, that is, an ethics that is always intrinsic to action.[8] With this as our philosophical starting point, this chapter examines the implications of applying a pluralist and performative understanding of ethics to design activism. More specifically, we examine how this approach is related to what we have previously called *a minor design activism*.[9] The preposition "minor" denotes an approach to collaborative design research that foregrounds an inquiring attitude, always through the situated engagement, toward new possibilities of confronting dominant programs. The "minor"[10] is concerned with establishing a space of maneuverability for stakeholders. The purpose is to challenge stratification in organizations—for example, public institutions—in ways that enable a reconditioning of hegemonic (or major) discourses and objectives, and, specifically, for the discussion in this chapter, value systems.

Design Ethics and Ethics in Participatory Design

Taking stock of ethics in design and design research is a daunting task in every respect. It requires a cross-disciplinary perspective that considers the vast plurality of opinions and practices that unfold in constant operations of negotiation, alignment, and delegation of responsibility between designers, people, and materials. Moreover, a practice of ethics is shaped by overarching value imperatives, disciplinary traditions, and personally and socially constructed beliefs, as well as by the specific conditions, contexts, and arrangements that may promote or inhibit values in a design process. To engage such complexity from an analytical standpoint, we must begin from the assertion that ethics always gets articulated *in* and *through* practice. To accommodate a conception of ethics premised on practice, Stephen Loo[11] argues that "the shape of ethical considerations is intrinsic to the practices themselves," and further that "the form of ethics that arise out of these practices are specific—they make particular contributions to help human beings to find/make places in the chaos that is our world."[12] But to arrive at this position, Loo first makes another important incursion that we have yet to address. Design, like art, is different from epistemological practices, such as philosophy, law, or business: "Design becomes ethical because it performs a *distribution of the sensible*, supporting possibilities for life opened up in the space of indeterminacy."[13] French philosopher Jacques Rancière in his book *Dissensus: On Politics and Aesthetics*[14] writes about the distribution of the sensible. It is the way art distributes aesthetic values to cause disruptions, or dissensus, between reality and appearances. As argued by Loo[15] and Markussen,[16] this can be extended to design. The potent aesthetic value of art and design outputs (objects, activities, etc.) lies in their autonomy vis-à-vis expressive qualities charged with preestablished and identifiable values. Consequently, Loo tells us, design becomes ethical precisely because it is caught up in a constant oscillation between expression and autonomy; in other words, it is in *performing* the distribution of the sensible that design becomes ethical and capable of "supporting possibilities for life opened up in this space of indeterminacy."[17] It is precisely in this same indeterminate space, with all its inherent possibility for life, that we locate what we have called a minor activism.

However, before we take a deeper look at our proposal for an ethics that relates to design activism and to the minor, we need to briefly consider the way our design research practice and ethical make-up is shaped by our own rooting in the Scandinavian tradition of participatory design. In the *Routledge Handbook of Participatory Design*,[18] Robinson and Wagner define the ethical principles of the discipline. Here, we might add, though the authors themselves do not, that the ethical principles of any discipline are indebted to particular morals. This is because the latter denotes "the codified 'performance criteria' that should evidence the presence of [the former],"[19] which is what one would expect to find in a handbook. The core ethical principle of participatory design, according to Robinson and Wagner, is "that people have the basic right to make decisions about how they do their work and indeed any other activities where they might use technology."[20] Closely related to this principle are two others: (1) people who are involved in a particular activity are those who know it best, and (2) design tools and processes should enable stakeholders to learn from each other, which, as the authors point out, is based on the ethical stance that "different voices need to be heard, understood and heeded if a design process is genuinely participatory."[21] Underlining these principles of what "the good" entails as a premise for participatory design and research practices, then, is a clearly expressed political agenda in favor of human rights and civil society. Moreover, the historical roots of Scandinavian participatory design in the workplace movement of the 1970s carried with it a pronounced emancipatory agenda that links participatory design directly to the governing ethos of activism. What is of significance is that the examples from practice detailed in the case that follows resonate well with the authoritative ethical principles listed here.

Activist Design and a Minor Design Activism

Discussions of both design activism[22] and design ethics[23] point to Victor Papanek's book *Design for the Real World*[24] as an important historical point of ascent for contemporary considerations of both agendas. In the present, Papanek's criticism has been taken up under the relatively new notion of design activism across many different design disciplines and adjacent practices in architecture and art. In the design research literature, design activism has been defined as: the creation of counter-narratives to drive positive social change in design,[25] as a political design inquiry into the conditions of democracy,[26] and as the political potential of aesthetic disruptions by means of activist artifacts.[27] These definitions have different theoretical underpinnings in philosophical frameworks ranging from political to aesthetical philosophy. The latter stems from Rancière's notion of dissensus as a key to conceiving a performative ethics.[28] If we are to extract a common trait in design activism, pace Fuad-Luke, Markussen, and Disalvo with specific relevance for the ethical considerations of a participatory practice, it is that they all endeavor to promote the acts (variously termed: *disruption*, *contestation*, or *counter-narratives*) as a confrontation with hegemonic conditions.

This is also the case with the concept of a minor design activism. The *minor* moment must be understood as the realization of potentials that run counter to the prevailing order of things. But what distinguishes this kind of activism is that (1) It works from design experimentation embedded in everyday life situations and collaboration with the people who have their daily lives there. (2) It works from within public welfare institutions and their attendant hegemonic agendas. 3) The notion of becoming minor derives from the concept of *minoritarian* in the philosophy of Gilles Deleuze, Félix Guattari, and Marie Maclean.[29] It signifies a different kind of political action made possible by collective engagement and becoming. (4) It is associated with the making of an aesthetical entity—in the example discussed here, the making of cultural activities around a new library. (5) It is theorized as a tactical principle in co-design processes, characterized by bringing forward marginal or marginalized people and ascribing them new roles and agencies.

A Participatory Program for Research Engagements

One characteristic in research traditions of participatory design and co-design is the explicit commitment to societal change. On a practical and methodological level, this promise is usually articulated in a so-called design program.[30] The program functions as a kind of framing device to orient a line of inquiry, yet such programs for change through research may vary a great deal in both form and content depending on research environments and institutional traditions. These programs are also imbued with a mixed bag of prescriptive values, comprised of an uneasy fusion of research agendas and public or private managerial aims. In a Scandinavian context, at least, over the last twenty years, the university institution itself has transformed. In rather simplistic terms, we may talk about the university as a once distant and privileged space for analysis and reflection and, today, as a neoliberal organization measured on its ability to solve "here and now" societal problems. Design, through various versions of design thinking, user-centered design, and co-design, seems to embody the promise of creativity and innovation. As a result, new funding initiatives have emerged and participatory design researchers have been invited to work with design methodologies for inclusion and deliberation in different public-sector innovation programs often in complex project constellations with both public and private partners. Many of these projects require long-term engagements and are tied to large-scale plans around urban transformation with broad yet quite abstract ambitions to, for example, lift an entire neighborhood or overcome unemployment and social problems. This effectively means that many practice-based design researchers work from within quite explicit change programs formulated by government institutions. Design researchers work in complex project constellations with both public and private partners, who all have their different agendas. In constellations like these, a design researcher is often assigned a smaller task to support the larger project, and typically has little influence on the overall project frame or vision of the project or how results are evaluated. The challenge then, in terms of ethics, politics, and activism, is not only how to position oneself as a practice-based design researcher, but also how to pursue and perform ethics in particular contexts in collaboration with users and citizens, who are the actors the design researcher is assigned to involve and empower.

Civic Engagement Around a Future Liberty

To think through the challenges of both ethics and (minor) activism as performed and staged on the ground, in the following, we offer a small empirical example from a public-sector innovation program revolving around the design of a new library and cultural center in an international suburban neighborhood in Copenhagen. The two-year project was funded by the Cultural Counsel of Denmark. The aim of the project was to mobilize residents of the neighborhood in the design of their new and future high-profile library. The focus was not only on the design of the interior space of the building but also on promoting cultural and social activities to build a stronger and more resourceful community. The future library, as part of a bigger development plan for the area, was intended to lift the international neighborhood to a more promising future. The neighborhood figures with high unemployment rates and social problems in national statistics. The new building, already well underway as the two-year project began, was planned and designed by architects and decision makers following a previous ten-year process, which had also included various user involvement activities, for example, idea-generating workshops with residents. The final proposal was delivered by an architectural firm, with only small changes around the interior left open for negotiation. The two-year funding program harbored visions and ideas of the future of public libraries, and in accordance with these visions, the administration of Copenhagen libraries around the same time had issued a new strategy for their library services. This strategy promoted particular images of both library services and library users, with a focus on a digitalized future.

A digitalized future where users operate loan services online and without assistance from librarians while other citizens act as local entrepreneurs envisioning, arranging, and executing cultural events for the benefit of the entire community. Amid these future visions, architectural drawings, and some practical challenges on the construction site itself, the two-year project was intended to deliver a catalog of proposals to be implemented in the new building once it was ready to open for the public. However, no technique or co-design method can contain nor transgress the many different agendas and concerns held by residents as a response to the decisions made and visions articulated on their behalf. From a practice-based design research perspective, working with community building, and from a genuine ambition of distributing democratic deliberation, we can hardly rely on classical representational procedures to create new openings for an ethics of plurality. When co-designers are embedded in this kind of complexity and tight protocols of overall plans, there is a real risk that the plurality, for example, given form in the concrete material of a resident's idea-catalog is quickly translated to reinforce the very same images and visions that they were in fact intended to open.[31] At the same time, methodologies—the way the researchers approach the field to engage with complex issues—are critical in determining whether or not alternative futures can slowly be opened up. Elsewhere, we have argued that this constitutes the nexus of contemporary co-design[32] and that it evolves in a combination of synthesis by giving form to the concrete, for example at workshop events, and full-scale trying out of prototypical practices. In the case of the library research project, the concept of a future maker space in the library became the catalyst for rethinking and restaging what could be termed the plurality of the present.[33] To engage residents in a future of their own, the project had to redirect its focus to what was already taking place in the neighborhood. Instead of inviting residents to a series of workshop events in order to produce ideas, researchers began to prototype different maker activities with residents—activities that were already part of everyday cultural and social activities in the neighborhood. By hosting an open repair café and inviting for small events in the basement below the old and soon-to-be-closed library, slowly, a maker community started to build in parallel with the ongoing work at the construction site. Although such a move may seem in opposition to the dominant visions and ideas tied to the progress of the project, it may also be understood as an experimental upshot that actually feeds off prevailing images, as a kind of minor activist move, perhaps both parasitic and productive. This on-the-ground somewhat under-the-radar- and un-extraordinary day-to-day work is not really trying to overthrow the dominant vision, but rather, to stage and re-articulate what has perhaps been left out by architects and managers (see Figure 12.1).

Practically, this is done not only by performing an alternative maker community through a series of events and small projects, but also by documenting and accounting for what is going

FIGURE 12.1 *Left: Prototyping an alternative space for making in the library project. Right: Ad-hoc newspaper about maker activities for residents, librarians, and cultural workers. Courtesy of Center for Codesign Research, Sissel Olander.*

on in this community through small stories, images, and film. Dominant images of citizens and libraries became reference points for developing alternative visions for how citizens could step forward as makers. During the two-year engagement, this work included not only creating a platform for citizens, library staff, and researchers to collaborate around maker activities, but also accounting for this work in ways that could be carried on to management and architects while still enabling residents to recognize themselves in the material. This requires an ongoing production of different communication materials like quickly edited videos, photos, small leaflets, and invitations on social media as well as consistency in everyday engagement with residents in the neighborhood.

Toward an Ethics of a Minor Activism

The way of working and positioning oneself as a researcher *and* an activist doesn't come without its challenges. From a performative ethical stance, the attentiveness toward the socio-material potentials of designing—in this case for increased civic engagement—may run counter to the researcher's disciplinary ethos that different voices need to be heard and understood. On the other hand, the experimental attitude governing a minor activist approach could be successful in reconditioning relations between people in the neighborhood and thus unleash new desires on the type and quality of cultural events the library should facilitate.

In this respect, a performative ethics in design "that defies immediate codification"[34] is mirroring the ethical ambitions of a minor activism, or put differently: under the specific conditions outlined as a prerequisite for a minor activism, a tactical principle in co-designing (everyday life, public institutions etc.), ethics *is* understood as design that inquires and challenges prefigured moral conventions.

It is, however, with a note of warning that we will end this discussion. The practical conditions on the ground when doing civic design engagements can seldom—if ever—be purely described and understood as a performative ethics. The reality of the ethical pluralism encountered in design(ing) is—for the most part—a complex and uneasy negotiation between a transformative ethics and moral and professional codes. If ethics, at its core, is about responsibility, design is, first, a precarious balancing act and labor of accommodating different ethical conditions and aims. And for that, there is no fail-proof formula.

Notes

1 Thomas Markussen, "The Disruptive Aesthetics of Design Activism: Enacting Design Between Art and Politics," *Design Issues* 29, no. 1 (2013): 38–50.

2 Peter Lang and William Menking, *Superstudio: Life Without Objects* (Milano: Skira, 2003).

3 Pelle Ehn, *Work-Oriented Design of Computer Artifacts* (Stockholm: Arbetslivcentrum, 1989).

4 Guy Julier, "From Design Culture to Design Activism," *Design and Culture* 5, no. 2 (2013): 215–36.

5 Ibid.

6 Elizabeth Frazer, "Max Weber on Ethics and Politics," *Politics and Ethics Review* 2, no. 1 (2006): 19–37.

7 Ibid.

8 Alice MacLachlan, "An Ethic of Plurality: Reconciling Politics and Morality in Hannah Arendt," in *In History and Judgement: IWM Junior Visiting Fellows' Conferences, Vol. 21*, ed. Vienna A. MacLachlan and I. Torsen (Vienna: Institut für die Wissenschaften vom Menschen, 2006), Available online: https://www.iwm.at/publications/5-junior-visiting-fellows-conferences/vol-xxi/alice-maclachlan/ (accessed July 29, 2019); Frazer, "Max Weber on Ethics and Politics."

9 Tau U. Lenskjold, Sissel Olander, and Joachim Halse, "Minor Design Activism: Prompting Change from Within," *Design Issues* 31, no. 4 (2015): 67–78.

10 Gilles Deleuze, Félix Guattari, and Marie Maclean, *Kafka: Toward a Minor Literature: The Components of Expression* (Baltimore: Johns Hopkins University, 1985).

11 Stephen Loo, "Design-Ing Ethics: The Good, the Bad and the Performative," in *Design and Ethics: Reflections on Practice*, ed. Emma Felton, Oksana Zelenko, and Suzi Vaughan (London: Routledge, 2012): 10–20.

12 Ibid., 16.

13 Ibid., 14.

14 Jacques Rancière and Steve Corcoran, *Dissensus: On politics and Aesthetics* (London: Continuum, 2010).

15 Loo, "Design-Ing Ethics."

16 Markussen, "The Disruptive Aesthetics of Design Activism."

17 Loo, "Design-Ing Ethics," 15.

18 Toni Robertson and Ina Wagner, "Ethics: Engagement, Representation and Politics-In-Action," in *Routledge International Handbook of Participatory Design*, ed. Jesper Simonsen and Toni Robertson (New York: Routledge, 2013), 64–85.

19 Cameron Tonkinwise, "Ethics by Design, or the Ethos of Things," *Design Philosophy Papers* 2, no. 2 (2004): 129–44.

20 Robertson and Wagner, "Ethics," 65.

21 Ibid.

22 Julier, "From Design Culture to Design Activism"; Alison J. Clarke, "Actions Speak Louder," *Design and Culture* 5, no. 2 (2013): 151–68.

23 Clive Dilnot, "Ethics in Design: 10 Questions," in *Design Studies: A Reader*, ed. Hazel Clark and David Eric Brody (Oxford: Berg, 2009): 180–91.

24 Victor Papanek, *Design for the Real World: Human Ecology and Social Change* (Chicago: Academy Chicago Publishers, 1971).

25 Alastair Fuad-Luke, *Design Activism: Beautiful Strangeness for a Sustainable World* (Sterling: Earthscan, 2009).

26 Carl DiSalvo, "Design, Democracy and Agonistic Pluralism," in *Proceedings of the Design Research Society Conference* (Montreal: Design Research Society, 2010) Available online: http://www.drs2 010.umontreal.ca/proceedings.php (accessed July 29, 2019); Carl DiSalvo, *Adversarial Design* (Cambridge: MIT Press, 2012).

27 Markussen, "The Disruptive Aesthetics of Design Activism."

28 Loo, "Design-Ing Ethics."

29 Deleuze, Guattari, and Maclean, *Kafka*.

30 Thomas Binder and Johan Redeström, "Programs, Experiments and Exemplary Design Research," in *Proceedings of Design Research Society Wonderground International Conference*, ed. K. Friedman, T. Love, and E. Corte-Real (Lisbon: Design Research Society, 2006).

31 For a detailed account of the translation of design proposals in co-design, see Jens Pedersen, "War and Peace in Codesign," *CoDesign* 12, no. 3 (2015): 171–84.

32 Lenskjold, Olander, and Halse, "Minor Design Activism."

33 Alex Wilkie, Martin Savransky, and Marsha Rosengarten, "The Lure of Possible Futures: On Speculative Research," in *Speculative Research: The Lure of Possible Futures* (London: Routledge, Taylor & Francis, 2017): 1–17.

34 Loo, "Design-Ing Ethics," 18.

13

Graphic Design and Activism: Reflecting on Interactions

Andréa Poshar

Activism is a relatively new term. It was introduced in the mid-1970s to refer to the ability to act and produce changes within society. From this perspective, one can say that activism represents a struggle that can be fueled by reactionary tendencies and aims.[1] Manifested by violent or nonviolent acts, these reactionary tendencies can be taken as expressions at the core of all processes of social changes. Here, we relate these expressions with visual graphic demonstrations such as billboards, fanzines, journals, and pamphlets. In line with this, Umberto Eco[2] once affirmed that in the past, if one wanted to be politically empowered, it was necessary to be part of the army or take part in policymaking. Nowadays it is necessary to be involved with the media—in other words, one must take part in the creation of alternative means of communication or "mass dissent" media, which are equally powerful and effective as mass media.[3]

Thus, like in a remediation process,[4] it is by retaking and repurposing the use of media devices that activists communicate their main ideas. Thus, we must consider an act of resistance as, according to Henry Giroux and Brad Evans,[5] "a creative act that leads to the creation of new forms of thinking and alternative ways of living," which can be taken as a creative act of media activism itself.

Within this context, Cammaerts and Carpenter[6] affirm that media should be understood not only as a medium to communicate, propagate, and interact, but also as a "symbolic arena" where the struggle for social change is expressed and where meanings of the world and ideas of what citizenship entails compete. This is in essence what Eco once defended as "semiotic guerrilla warfare"[7]: the act where complementary systems of communication should be considered and developed against its own system, that is, dominant culture.

Eco defended the argument that it is not by taking TV studios that the production of massive ruling images is going to stop. This "can be frightening and can also seem utopian."[8] Instead of taking the control, media activism—considered a broad category of activism—repurposes mass media to use it as a basis for the development of a "new" and cheaper means of communication through which the minority can visually express their social and political issues. Hence, to exercise "semiotic guerrilla warfare" or media activism is to use "forces of expression" with little and alternative mediums where dominant culture has no power or control.

In line with this context, the role of the designer is important. Tracing them from this perspective is to wonder about his/her engagement within social movements and to also start seeing him/her as an activist. For Tim Jordan and Gül Çağalı Güven,[9] for instance, being an activist does not only mean being someone who chains himself or herself to bulldozers, hacks websites, or attends endless meetings. It also means to achieve the point that social solidarities and sustaining campaigns against exploitations become central to the building of a new and better society.

Anyone nowadays can find himself or herself beginning to recognize his or her potential for creating new social forms. "Small actions are just as central to activism as larger ones."[10]

With the help of designers, particular activist movement's visuals were constructed, marking an era and the history of the movement to which designers engaged.

Let's take the Russian graphic designer and artist Aleksander Rodchenko as an example. Heavily influenced by the upheaval within the Russian revolution of 1917, Rodchenko was one of the main versatile artists to emerge during the revolution. During his life, his works were always socially engaged and innovative.

To bring Rodchenko's example is to illustrate how designers have for a long period of time engaged with social movements and activist causes which, according to Julier,[11] has to do with the fact that many creative makers are no longer willing to lend their "ethical surplus" to the hegemonic culture:

> Beyond a realization of the straightforward exploitation of their own "ethical surplus," designers share a broader set of tumultuous political and economic circumstances in the West that may bring about politicization and a search for alternative models of everyday practice.[12]

Just like the term "activism," these alternative ways of everyday design practices may be also traced back to the mid-1970s, leading to the period of radical thinking in the field. This includes new ways of working, which coincide with geopolitical, economic, and environmental crises.[13]

In line with that, Markussen argued that "design is not a boycott, strike, protest, demonstrations, or some other political act, but lends its power of resistance from being precisely a designerly way of intervening into people's lives."[14]

For Scalin,[15] to work with design and activism is "about using the incredible power of visual communication as a tool for making a positive transformation in our world—specifically by raising the voices of individuals & groups that would be normally overlooked in our current communications" dynamics.[16]

Within the tools of the dominant culture, Scalin can create an alternative channel of communication and share his knowledge within society, that is, to break the limits of our own "bubble." As mentioned previously, to be an activist is not just to participate in violent or nonviolent protests. In fact, it is to be the agent responsible for the creation of alternative ways of producing, disseminating, and structuring society's culture.

When designers intentionally use design to talk about an activist argument or cause, whether they are working by themselves or with a nonprofit design agency explicitly built with altruistic objectives, it can be considered as "design-led activism."

> There are many actors, agents and stakeholders within activist scenery that intentionally or unintentionally use . . . design processes to deliver their activism. Intentional use of design

may involve the commissioning of professional designers by organizations or individuals with an activism orientation.[17]

It is important to stress this distinction between intentional and/or unintentional use of design processes since the topic here relies on the distinction between intention and skill. Not all participants from an activist movement have the knowledge that a visual communication designer has, although their intention is the same, that is, to catalyze social and cultural change.

For that reason, design has long been associated with social and political discourse and propaganda. The voice of designers generally becomes more obvious during times of social and political change, either in the service of clients' needs or with concerns raised by the designers themselves. The latter is a good example of design-led activism.

If we take the poster as one of the many visual historical references, we might see that the visual production of a non-designer might be somehow effective, but it will not have the kind of details related to certain trained skills that only designers have. This is a demonstration that design has a central role to play in activism's wider purpose.

What we want to reflect here is that within activist movements, designers are active agents with a cultural capital that is capable of reproducing, rebuilding, and reshaping a culture by improving its methods, practices, and tools of communication. Through design's ability to interact among those fields, designers are considered a determining factor in the production, organization, sharing, and diffusion of culture and knowledge. They operate in an area in which any other professional does not speak on behalf of ordinary people, who are actively struggling against dominant culture—which makes us think of design's ethical involvement with the movement and with society.

Key skills in the design process, says Macdonald,[18] include being able to conceptualize and weigh-up a multidimensional problem, consider scenarios of use, think laterally and creatively, evaluate ideas, and communicate effectively. Hence, to use these skills in favor of activists and social movements is, according to Glasser et al.,[19] at its best an action fueled by empathy where the idea is always to keep in mind that other people matter. In this sense, to "designerly dissent" is to break established patterns of design—be it as a study, be it as a practice—and to engage with a social cause/issue:

> Throughout history, in a constant struggle to create a better and more just world, people have raised their voices in protest against corruption, wrongdoing, and the exploitation of power. The most effective designers have used their skills, and the means at their disposal, to create graphic responses that educate and spread these messages of defiance.[20]

Through knowing how to capture and disseminate events as they happen, creating particular social and political messages, designers can immediately respond to current issues and social events. That is the challenge of the current situation of a designer as a professional and as an individual: to bring about social changes in the most effective and ethical way possible.

Notes

1   Bart Cammaerts and Nico Carpenter, *Reclaiming the Media: Communication Rights and Democratic Media Roles* (Bristol: Intellect, 2007).

2   Umberto Eco, *Towards a Semiolical Guerrilla Warfare* (1976), www.kareneliot.de/downloads/Um bertoEco_Towards%20a%20Semiological%20Guerrilla%20Warfare.pdf

3 Ibid.

4 Jay David Bolter and Richard Grusin, *Remediation: Understanding New Media* (Cambridge: MIT Press, 2000).

5 Henry Giroux and Brad Evans, "Disposable Futures," *Truthout*, June 1, 2014, truthout.org/articles/disposable-futures/

6 Cammaerts and Carpenter, *Reclaiming the Media*.

7 Eco, *Towards a Semiolical Guerrilla Warfare*.

8 Ibid., 13.

9 Tim Jordan and Gül Çağalı Güven, *Activism!: Direct Action, Hacktivism and the Future of Society* (İstanbul: Kitap, 2002).

10 Ibid., 154.

11 Guy Julier, "From Design Culture to Design Activism," *Design and Culture* 5, no. 2 (2013): 225.

12 Ibid.

13 Ibid.

14 Thomas Markussen, "The Disruptive Aesthetics of Design Activism: Enacting Design Between Art and Politics," *Design Issues* 29, no. 1 (2013): 38.

15 Noah Scalin and Michelle Taute, *The Design Activist's Handbook: How to Change the World (or at Least a Part of It) with Socially Conscious Design* (Cincinnati: How Books, 2012).

16 Erin Mays, "Design Activism," *Print Magazine*, January 3, 2014, www.printmag.com/featured/design-activism

17 Alastair Fuad-Luke, *Design Activism* (London: Earthscan, 2009), 24.

18 Nico Macdonald, "Can Designers Save the World? (And Should They Try?)," in *New Design*, September/October 2001, https://www.lucs.lu.se/wp-content/uploads/2017/01/kkeg17_littsem-1_can-designers-save-the-world.pdf

19 Milton Glaser et al., *The Design of Dissent: Socially and Politically Driven Graphics* (Beverly: Rockport Publishers, 2017).

20 Ibid.

PART THREE

Work and Pedagogy: *Work*

14

Designing Tools for Low-income Community Organizing

Luke Jordan

Grassroot is a nonprofit technology start-up in South Africa. It creates and deploys simple, purpose-built tools for activists and movement builders in low-technology, marginalized communities. As of writing, those tools have reached over 150,000 people and helped call over 20,000 meetings, votes, and actions. The tools have a "net promoter score" (a measure of how likely users are to recommend a product to others) only slightly below that of Netflix, Amazon, and Apple. Within the first two years of adoption, two-thirds of communities reported a significant improvement in the quality of life through more cohesive and effective community action.[1]

Grassroot's home is South Africa. The country has a history of community organizing and activism. In the Apartheid years, such organizing was conducted by the United Democratic Front (UDF), a major anti-apartheid coordinating body in the 1980s. The organizing coordinated by the UDF was vital to the "rolling mass action" that helped bring the Apartheid government to negotiations and gave the African National Congress the credible threat it needed in those talks.[2] In the early years of South Africa's democracy, there were plans to use the organizing infrastructure as the basis of participative budgeting, but this was discarded when the new government turned sharply toward neoliberal and managerial policies.[3] Formal organizing atrophied in the years after the mid-1990s. In the same period, the new democratic government made real gains in service provision, and the economy grew. However, youth unemployment grew rapidly, alongside violence and crime. In communities, collective action became entwined with patronage-based and factionalized politics. Then, from the late 2000s, organizing underwent a resurgence, now based on much more informal modes of action, focused on obtaining a response from an opaque local state, sometimes through the destruction of public property—an action characterized by the phrase, "the smoke that calls."[4]

This complex history is of extreme importance in how Grassroot approached the ethics of design in building its tools. A naïve but relatively harmless ethical lapse would have been to design and build in ignorance of user needs. In what is known as "civic technology," user-centric design is unfortunately rare.[5] But this would have been relatively harmless because the most likely outcome in our context would have been the absence of adoption, rather than positive harm. A set of tools that no one uses is a waste of resources, but not actively dangerous.[6]

If that were the only ethical risk, it would perhaps be worth treating more fully. But three others were more serious as they contained the possibility of actual harm. Those risks can be classified as follows: first, the tools would expose users to danger from outside; second, the tools would create unintended, perverse, or harmful effects within the groups using them; and, third, they would enable purely violent or criminal activity.[7]

The risk of harm from outside stemmed most obviously from surveillance risks. South Africa is a constitutional democracy with a strong and respected judiciary and active civil society. Nonetheless, the state security apparatus is known to monitor communications even when it should not, hoping this activity remains undiscovered.[8] In the rough politics of some provinces, assassinations of leaders of rival factions or social movements are not unknown. One of the largest social movements in the country, called Abahlali baseMjondolo and numbering fifty thousand "shack dwellers," has lost at least two branch leaders to killings. One (Thuli Ndlovu) was shot at home by hitmen hired by a local ward councilor, with all three later convicted and sentenced to jail; the other (S'fiso Ngcobo) was shot by a group of unknown men in May 2018.[9]

The tools in their most basic form relied on a mobile network protocol called unstructured supplementary service data (USSD). That protocol allows users with feature phones, or smartphones but no data, to use a flow of menus to control the application. It is core to the user value of the tools, but it does not allow for encryption—both the menus and the users' responses are carried as plain text over the mobile networks. For the outbound messages delivered to users, short message service (SMS) texts can technically be encrypted, but at an extremely high price in user experience (high enough that even Signal abandoned encrypted SMS).[10]

This dilemma had no easy answer. We could encrypt at so large a sacrifice in user experience that the platform's original purpose, bringing advanced capabilities across the digital divide, would be nullified, or we could naively accept the possibility of aiding surveillance. Ultimately, we found what we considered a "least bad" trade-off, by explicitly not requiring any information to be "real." The platform allows users to enter any name they like; to enter a location by any descriptor they like; to set aliases for specific groups; and to determine if their group even appears on public profile lists, with all defaults set to private. In training and awareness raising, Grassroot emphasizes these features to community groups and has made explicit to them that for highly sensitive, small-group communications they should not use the platform.

The second risk was subtler and more significant than the first. Surveillance and censorship tend to gather most of the attention in discussions of developing world technology-based activism, but entrenched interests have shown that they fear technology for its coordination capabilities much more than its broadcast ones. For example, the Chinese government censors attempts at coordination at a vastly greater frequency and intensity than it censors individual complaints or other individual speech acts. Modern autocrats spend much more resources sowing division among their opponents than they do silencing them.[11] In South Africa, the absence of accountability traces back not to an absence of reporting or speech, but to an absence of effective collective action to create power backing that speech, so undermining that power could be especially damaging.

The specific ways the platform might damage instead of improve group cohesion are multiple, arise again with every new feature, and are never fully solved. For example, who within the group could call meetings? Who could add members or remove them? We invested in a technically complex solution to enable groups to decide these questions individually, but then had to set defaults, and thereafter, to decide and adjust the defaults. At a more general level, we had to consider how differences in the friction of user experiences could bias group activity in unintended ways. For example, if it were too easy to call a vote, would groups start to avoid deliberation for the quicker but often more divisive process of a majoritarian vote?

As Grassroot, we would not pretend to have solved these problems. What we have done is attempted to iterate our way to a set of less bad trade-offs, doing so with our users rather than for them. As an example, following the advice of users, we invested considerable time (for a small development team) in building a highly flexible role-permission structure for groups so that our users could themselves choose what kind of members could perform which action (see Figure 14.1). However, we could not design a USSD flow that could accommodate so detailed a task as setting and adjusting these permissions. USSD only allows presenting the user with one menu or free text input at time, so setting and adjusting permissions through it would require the user to sequentially respond to a dozen or more menus. Our approach was to set a default that we called "open"—only organizers could manage the membership list, that is, add and remove members, but any member could initiate a meeting, vote or action item. In time, we found that this was inappropriate for large groups, so we created multiple permission templates and let users pick "closed" or "open" during group creation.

On the broader issue of biasing group action, we have not tried to pretend that we can avoid any effect. We have accepted the responsibility of having explicit beliefs about group

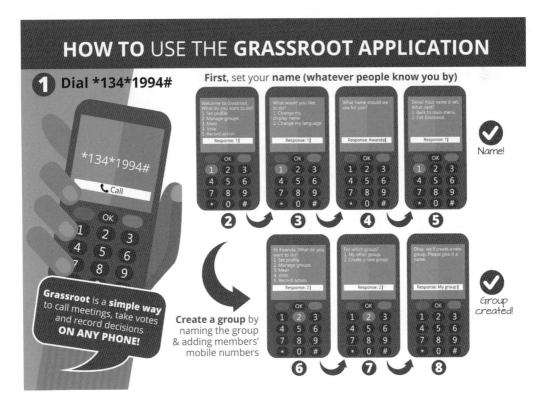

FIGURE 14.1 *Guide to setting up groups, c. 2017. Courtesy of Grassroot.*

effectiveness. We believe that rich, face-to-face and offline deliberation, of the kind in public community meetings, is central to group effectiveness, followed closely by public and accountable calls to offline action. Online decision-making and record keeping are useful and important, but ultimately as supports of the former.[12] We have consequently made an explicit prioritization of the meeting-related functions and they account for the dominant share of platform use. Between August 2015 and August 2018, over twenty thousand tasks were called through Grassroot, with meetings accounting for just over 60 percent, versus 20 percent each for votes and action items.

We have of course made mistakes. The most serious resulted from an over-eager response to user requests for a feature. Soon after we launched the early version of our Android app, several users in awareness workshops would ask us to add a group chat function. Rationally, we knew this would be a bad idea because we would in effect be cloning WhatsApp group chat, with fewer features. But some in our development team were eager to build it, and we kept getting these requests. We failed to interrogate the context—users' first introduction to the app, when in the mental frame to look for features similar to those they knew—or to think about competing priorities properly. We ended up building the feature at a significant cost in developer time. Worse, we confused some users, who expected the group chat messages to be distributed by SMS and were confused and unhappy when it did not. In all, we had low uptake and caused confusion, a worst possible outcome. We took the decision to remove group chat from the app six months after launching it. We did not abandon or turn back on co-creation as a result. We have attempted to get better at interrogating the context of feedback, guarding against our own impulses, and, for major feature builds, reserving the right to exercise judgment counter to user input. This is a balance that we believe we are becoming less bad at striking, rather than a problem we think we have solved.

Finally, there is the risk of the platform being used with the explicit intent to do harm. That is a risk that has gathered much attention of late in public as it pertains to enormous scale information platforms like Facebook and Twitter. We have had in our terms of use from the start that we will remove from Grassroot any group that is formed for criminal activity or with violence as its primary end. We have not built means to detect such activity. That is not from neglect, but rather a conscious decision taken and periodically revisited. We believe that the tools do not provide a material advantage to criminal groups, who are liable to buy smartphones or data and who already have means to gather, call meetings, make decisions, and so forth, and to do so with greater protection from detection than our tools allow. While Grassroot's tools do not require users to post a public record, they are fundamentally oriented toward public action. Our tools similarly provide few-to-no affordances for the spreading of disinformation, except as would happen in offline deliberations with or without us. We may be wrong on either of these fronts, and at the first evidence that we are mistaken, we will invest in both improved reporting and proactive detection. Until then, we will continue to keep such risks foremost in mind, while balancing among them and investable resources and our users' privacy.

Some of these decisions will alter in our next set of tools. Most significantly, we are developing a service to integrate with WhatsApp that will use machine learning to enable community leaders to find each other across disconnected social graphs. Given the dominance of WhatsApp among our user base, and the value of finding others undergoing similar struggles and ideas and knowledge with them, we believe such a service could be transformative. However, it raises a host of risks, among others, bad actors mimicking activists to be connected to them, draw out information, or plant misinformation. To mitigate them as much as we can, we are working through design issues related to intermediation, ladders of engagement and trust, and tiers of reputation. We will deploy the service only once we have some confidence that such risks have been mitigated enough that the risk of catastrophic harm has been removed, and the risks of incidental harm have been contained sufficiently that the benefits of the service are at least an order of magnitude greater than them.

Notes

1 Data taken from Grassroot system directly through real-time reporting, at April 24, 2018. Net promoter score and reported community improvement from a user-survey conducted in March-April 2018 (N= 200).

2 Mark Swilling, *The United Democratic Front and Township Revolt in South Africa* (Johannesburg: Association for Sociology in Southern Africa, 1987); Ineke Van Kessel, *Beyond Our Wildest Dreams: The United Democratic Front and the Transformation of South Africa* (Charlottesville: University Press of Virginia, 2000).

3 Gianpaolo Baiocchi, Patrick Heller, and Marcelo Kunrath Silva, *Bootstrapping Democracy: Transforming Local Governance and Civil Society in Brazil* (Stanford: Stanford University Press, 2011).

4 K. Von Holdt and Adèle Kirsten, *The Smoke That Calls: Insurgent Citizenship, Collective Violence and the Struggle for a Place in the New South Africa: Eight Case Studies of Community Protest and Xenophobic Violence* (Johannesburg: Centre for the Study of Violence and Reconciliation, 2011).

5 Heike Baumüller, "The Little We Know: An Exploratory Literature Review on the Utility of Mobile Phone-Enabled Services for Smallholder Farmers," *Journal of International Development* 30, no. 1 (2017): 134–54; Tiago Peixoto and Jonathan Fox, "When Does ICT-Enabled Citizen Voice Lead to Government Responsiveness?" *IDS Bulletin* 41, no. 1 (2016): 23–39.

6 In this regard, we have differed from Paul Nini, "In Search of Ethics in Graphic Design," *AIGA*, August 16, 2004, www.aiga.org/in-search-of-ethics-in-graphic-design

7 Focusing on these risks is a slightly different approach taken in Ibid by expanding the third point of responsibility. We believe the risk of harm is a dominant concern and hence, have focused on it more than other responsibilities in this case. Similarly, we foreground the risk of unintended "dark patterns," using Marc Miquel's terminology, "Throwing Light on Dark UX with Design Awareness," *UX Magazine*, July 7, 2014, https://uxmag.com/articles/throwing-light-on-dark-ux-with-design-awareness

8 As reported, for example, in Dean Workman, "R2K: South African Govt Is Spying on Mobile Users," *IT News Africa*, August 24, 2017, www.itnewsafrica.com/2017/08/r2k-south-african-govt-is-spying-on-mobile-users

9 On size, see Dennis Webster, "Unfreedom Day Rally: Freedom a Figment of Elite Imagination, Say 50,000 Shack Dwellers," *Daily Maverick*, April 24, 2018, dailymaverick.co.za/article/2018-04-24-freedom-a-figment-of-elite-imagination-say-50000-shack-dwellers/#.Wup8QJdrw2w. On assassination, see GroundUp, "GroundUp: Another Abahlali baseMjondolo Member Assassinated," *Daily Maverick*, October 2, 2014, dailymaverick.co.za/article/2014-10-02-groundup-another-abahlali-basemjondolo-member-assassinated/#.Wup8Ipdrw2w

10 For USSD explanation, see Michel Hanouch, "What is USSD & Why Does It Matter for Mobile Financial Services?" *CGAP*, March 8, 2017, www.cgap.org/blog/what-ussd-why-does-it-matter-mobile-financial-services. On encrypted SMSs, see: Moxie0, "Saying Goodbye to Encrypted SMS/MMS," *Signal Messenger*, March 6, 2015, signal.org/blog/goodbye-encrypted-sms. Signal is an encrypted messaging and communications tool.

11 Zeynep Tufekci, *Twitter and Tear Gas: The Power and Fragility of Networked Protest* (New Haven: Yale University Press, 2017); Gary King, Jennifer Pan, and Margaret E. Roberts, "How Censorship in China Allows Government Criticism but Silences Collective Expression," *American Political Science Review* 107, no. 02 (2013): 326–43.

12 Tufekci, *Twitter and Tear Gas*; Hahrie Han, *How Organizations Develop Activists: Civic Associations and Leadership in the 21st Century* (Oxford: Oxford University Press, 2014); personal observation in the field.

15

Design and Sustainable Development: Beyond Aesthetic and Functional Qualities

Iván Asin

We live in a time of great concern over human activities and how these activities affect the systems that provide our most basic needs. Indeed, these systems of survival are in danger of collapsing, and in some cases, beyond a point of possible retrieval.[1] Given the undisputable reality of our global environmental crisis—which has been accelerated by our imprudent use of natural resources—we ought to think more seriously about the road-maps that might be necessary to guide designers to participate in the development of products more sustainably.[2] This chapter aims to incite designers to think about the issue of sustainability and the practices that might allow them to be agents of change from within the industries in which they operate.

In recent decades, there has been an increasing effort in the field of design to articulate what sustainability means. Designers are now thinking about their work in broader terms than the traditional notion of design as a mere contributor to production strategies and economic growth. It has been evident that in recent times designers have shown concern for understanding the implications of the materials they use and the environmental consequences of their practice.[3] We are now moving away from thinking that sustainability is only of concern to the industry and consumers, and that designers are somehow outside of responsibility for creating sustainable systems in their professional practices. These practices have received more attention thanks to the increased exposure that industrial design, architecture, fashion design, and graphic design—among many other areas—have enjoyed in recent decades.

In 1992, the *Hannover Principles* paved the way for how designers may think about sustainable practices.[4] These principles articulated a need for

- coexistence between nature and humanity;
- interdependence between design and the natural world;
- connecting material and spiritual consciousness;
- accepting the responsibility for the consequences of design;

- understanding the issue of longevity in the products we design;
- minimizing waste;
- using natural energy;
- understanding the limitations of design; and
- ongoing improvement of design practices through knowledge sharing.

Sustainable Development as a Design Concept

The main goal of sustainable design is to develop systems and practices that guarantee the well-being and balance of the main three elements of sustainable development: economic, social, and environmental.[5] In the 1990s, the *Ecodesign*—an exclusively environmental movement—began to gain traction, and, later, Design for Sustainability (D4S) expanded on the concept, by integrating economic and social considerations.[6] As a freestanding concept, sustainability is a paradigm for thinking about a future in which environmental, economic, and social considerations are balanced,[7] and where we can meet the needs of the present without affecting future generations' ability to meet their own needs.[8] Within that concept of sustainability, designers contribute to our society and human relationships through their unique role as generators of visual meaning and forms. This contribution carries a social and ethical responsibility, as the work of designers in many ways holds a mirror up to society. Naturally, this element has been somewhat controversial as designers are able to make environmental claims or make companies look more sustainable as a mere marketing tool. Widely known are cases of companies labeling products as "natural" or "green" without any proof to back such a claim. In an effort to avoid false or misleading claims—also known as *greenwashing*—the Danish Consumer Ombudsman (DCO) issued guidelines for green marketing in 2011.[9] However, the issue of accountability continues to be a burning issue among corporate responsibility leaders.

Designers play a critical role in the development of products, manufactured objects, and visual culture.[10] They also play an important role in minimizing the environmental footprint during the manufacturing of products and establishing sustainable practices within the industrial world. Indeed, they make important decisions about the materials that are to be used and direct the processes that need to be followed in order to manufacture the products they design.

Sustainable development is fundamentally about materials.[11] Therefore, it is critical that designers think beyond the aesthetic and functional qualities of the designs they produce and take into consideration that designing, producing, using, and disposing of a product requires thinking about materials and their entire lifecycle. We must be conscious that the manufacturing process that transforms these materials into things will generate waste, which will be inevitably released into the environment, atmosphere, water, and soil. For example, the buildings we design are in most cases built with concrete. Given that concrete is the most widely used building material, its production has a significant environmental impact. Indeed, about 7 percent of the carbon dioxide—a greenhouse gas contributing to global warming—released into the atmosphere comes from the production of cement.[12] Therefore, we need to think about materials as a basic ingredient for creating a sustainable context and as a platform for designing sustainably.

As key players in the development of products, designers need to work on the basis that a product is only sustainable if it is conceived within a sustainable context. Such a context exists when we achieve a balance between economic, social, and environmental stability. It is also crucial that we have a serious plan for what the product or service's lifecycle looks like. In this sense, we must honestly assess all aspects of what goes into producing, using, and disposing of the products we design. What are the resources needed to develop prototypes? What are the resources needed to produce? What kind of packaging will be necessary to transport these products to their destination? What will be the ecological footprint of the use of these products? What will be the plan for disposing the product when it is no longer usable? Can this product be recycled? If so, is the product designed in ways that it can be easily disassembled? To answer these questions and to understand the relationship between the products we design and their users, the concept of *circular design*—which works on the basis of circular economy systems—has emerged as a way of assessing the lifetime of a product and its ability to be successful at the economic and environmental level.[13]

Design for Economic Sustainability

Economic stability is an essential element of sustainable development and a central objective of sustainable systems.[14] Design contributes to a dynamic economy through innovation and creativity, which is used as part of strategies to boost the competitiveness of enterprises.[15] Traditional economic thought suggests that we should aim to develop products efficiently and in ways such that the cost of production can be minimized. However, economic prosperity—at least in capitalistic societies—is also associated with increased consumption. This is problematic for designers interested in sustainable practices, given that the capitalist-oriented markets in which they usually thrive, are in the business of convincing people to consume.[16] Sustainable development, on the other hand, urges people to consider precisely the opposite. Therefore, sustainable practices in design need to be conscious of social, economic, and environmental issues.[17]

Currently, designers work within values that are typically in line with marketing strategies carried out within a worldview in which prosperity is measured in complete disregard for long-term societal well-being.[18] This economic thought, which sees consumption as a virtue, is one that can be particularly challenging for those designers interested in developing sustainable practices, for they play a critical role in the development of products, manufactured objects, and visual culture.[19]

Design for Social Sustainability

Globalization has not only transformed the way industries conduct business, but also presented the world of design with a variety of new social issues that call for innovation. The benefit that people in our society obtain through the products we design is known as social sustainability. At the most basic level, design is a field that contributes to sustainability through creations that promote social inclusion, interaction with users, generating job opportunities, and creating innovative channels of citizen participation within social systems.[20] In this sense, designers are beginning to explore new media and ways of visual communication that are more attuned to real human needs, and they are moving away from merely pleasing people's aesthetic sensitivities and wants.

In relation to social impact, design can be a powerful tool to promote environmentally conscious patterns of behavior. By thinking about design in these terms, we contribute to the inclusion of the creative fields in the larger debate on sustainable development and we create conditions for developing a design culture in which the consumer benefits are as regarded as the economic gains.

In terms of social ramifications of design, we must also think about the opportunities and responsibilities that exist in our relationship with the internet and platforms of mass-participation. Our designs are now reaching unprecedented numbers of individuals, who in turn benefit from this visual dialogue and take these aesthetic ideas in other directions. In a sense, we can say that we are living in times of a great deal of co-creation and in which people are influencing others also in unprecedented ways.

Research in design has also benefited from globalization and social media. Designers are now able to understand more effectively the needs of users of the products they design. Through multiple channels, users are now able to participate in the design process. This is essential for sustainability, for these new opportunities allow the markets to better tend the needs of people through design.

Design for Environmental Sustainability

During their lifecycle, our designs make demands on nature. An ecological footprint is something that we must think about seriously. Design for environmental sustainability is concerned with minimizing the damage to the natural environment, the use of natural resources and with the creation of products that will have a low or no ecological impact. In this sense, "*decoupling*" is a concept that attempts to break the correlation between economic growth and environmental degradation.[21]

The field of design has been historically influenced by trends, therefore, it is critical for any initiative that promotes sustainable practices not to be understood as a transitory concept or merely a slogan. This isn't about what is fashionable; this is about the future of this planet. In that sense, it is important not to treat sustainability as a trend. Design exists within a larger system; therefore, initiatives toward sustainability need to penetrate all levels of production and ultimately the culture. This requires a vision and leadership in order to engage everyone involved in the process.[22]

We cannot afford to continue thinking about design as an element in a linear infrastructure of producing and selling. Design happens in an interconnected world in which natural, economic, and social systems coexist.[23] Unfortunately, the industries we work for have ignored this reality and it's up to designers to bridge the language barrier that exists between the goals of an industrial world and a sustainable world. Taking this on requires a broad *rethinking* of how we think and make things. We have to be able to debate visual contexts and our responsibility in the supply chain. We must be able to think about the lifecycle of the products we design, making sure that what we make will not negatively affect future generations. Ultimately, we want to develop and share design strategies that will help us contribute to society and will broaden the way we think.

Notes

1 Iván Asin, "The Sustainable Art Studio: Finding the Voice of Art in Education for Sustainable Development," *Green Teacher* 116 (Summer 2018); Nicholas Bayard, "Valuing Nature in Environmental Education," *Green Teacher*, no. 79 (Summer 2006): 27.

2 S. A. Waage, "Re-considering Product Design: A Practical 'Road-Map' for Integration of Sustainability Issues," *Journal of Cleaner production* 15, no. 7 (2007): 638–49.

3 Universidad de Palermo, *Introducción a la investigación: Diseño gráfico sustentable* (Buenos Aires: 2015).

4 William McDonough and Michael Braungart, *The Hannover Principles: Design for Sustainability* (New York: W. McDonough Architects, 1992).

5 Jong-Jin Kim and Brenda Rigdon, *Sustainable Architecture Module: Introduction to Sustainable Design* (Ann Arbor: National Pollution Prevention Center for Higher Education, 1998).

6 Garrette Clark et al., "Design for Sustainability: Current Trends in Sustainable Product Design and Development," *Sustainability* 1, no. 3 (2009); Tania H. Smith, "Sustainable Design and the Design Curriculum," *Journal of Design Research* 7, no. 3 (2008): 259.

7 UNESCO, *Education for Sustainable Development: Sourcebook* (Paris: UNESCO, 2012).

8 United Nations General Assembly, ed., *Report of the World Commission on Environment and Development: Our Common Future* (Oslo: United Nations General Assembly, 1987).

9 Susie Stærk Ekstrand and Kristine Lilholt Nilsson, "Greenwashing?" *European Food and Feed Law Review* 6, no. 3 (2011): 167–73.

10 Richard Firth, Einar Stoltenberg, and Trent Jennings, "Using an Outdoor Learning Space to Teach Sustainability and Material Processes in HE Product Design," *International Journal of Art & Design Education* 35, no. 3 (2016): 327–36.

11 Michael F. Ashby, Jordi Segalas Coral, and Didac Ferrer Balas, *Materials and Sustainable Development* (Amsterdam: Elsevier, Butterworth-Heinemann, 2016); Michael S. Hopkins, "How Sustainability Fuels Design Innovation," *MIT Sloan Management Review* 52, no. 1 (Fall 2010).

12 Christian Meyer, "Concrete Materials and Sustainable Development in the USA," *Structural Engineering International* 14, no. 3 (2004): 75–81.

13 Marcel Den Hollander, "Design for Managing Obsolescence: A Design Methodology for Preserving Product Integrity in a Circular Economy" (doctoral thesis, Delft University of Technology, 2018); Marc Hassenzahl, "The Thing and I: Understanding the Relationship between User and Product," in *Funology 2: From Usability to Enjoyment*, ed. Mark A. Blythe and Andrew Monk (Springer 2018); P. Lacy et al., *Circular Advantage: Innovative Business Models and Technologies to Create Value in a World without Limits to Growth* (Chicago: Accenture, 2014); Ruth Mugge, "Product Design and Consumer Behaviour in a Circular Economy," *Sustainability* 10, no. 10 (2018): 3704.

14 J. J. Schul, "Sostenibilidad en el diseño y ejecución de proyectos: Implicaciones prácticas," *Información Comercial Española*, 2002. Office for ECOSOC Support and Coordination United Nations (2008). *Achieving Sustainable Development and Promoting Development Cooperation: Dialogues at the Economic and Social Council*. UN.

15 M. V. Navarro and J. R. Martínez, "Diseño sostenible: herramienta estratégica de innovación," *Revista legislativa de estudios sociales y de opinión pública* 4, no. 8 (2011): 47–88.

16 Angharad Thomas, "Design and Sustainable Development What Is the Contribution That Design Can Make? A Case Study of the Welsh Woollen Industry," in *Design Research Society Conference, 16-19 July 2008* (Sheffield: The University of Salford, 2008).

17 Marc A. Rosen and Hossam A. Kishawy, "Sustainable Manufacturing and Design: Concepts, Practices and Needs," *Sustainability* 4, no. 2 (2012): 154–74.

18 Kim and Rigdon, *Sustainable Architecture Module*.

19 Firth, Stoltenberg, and Jennings, "Using an Outdoor Learning Space to Teach."

20 Navarro and Martínez, "Diseño sostenible."

21 Clark et al., "Design for Sustainability."

22 James W. Marcum, "Design for Sustainability," *The Bottom Line* 22, no. 1 (2009): 9–12.

23 William McDonough and Michael Braungart, *Cradle to Cradle: Remaking the Way We Make Things* (London: Vintage, 2009); Madeleine Sclater, "Sustainability and Learning: Aesthetic and Creative Responses in a Digital Culture," *Research in Comparative and International Education* 13, no. 1 (2018): 135–51.

16

Designing Ethics Tools for Self-reflection, Collaboration, and Facilitation

Ciara Taylor and Samantha Dempsey

Introduction

Who are we, as designers, and who do we want to be? We first began to consider this question in 2015 at an Interaction Design Association (IxDA) meeting in Boston, Massachussetts, where we explored the ethics of gamification.[1] After exploring actual and imagined scenarios where gamification encouraged behavior that was against a person's best interests, small groups of participants were assigned different pieces of the Modern Hippocratic Oath and collectively altered them to be relevant to design. The Modern Hippocratic Oath is a document outlining the ethics of medical practice. Traditionally, all medical doctors swore to uphold the Hippocratic Oath, which bound them to a common set of ethics relevant to their practice. Participants were able to draw inspiration from the structure of the Modern Hippocratic Oath while altering the specifics to be relevant to design practice. We put their pieces back together to create one oath and all signed it, swearing to uphold our ethical duty as Boston interaction designers.

This was the first of several ethics tools we created. This case study traces the evolution of tools that we designed to prompt discourse about ethics among designers and explores how ethics tools are being used for self-reflection, collaboration, and facilitation in the design profession and education system today. In this work, an "ethics tool" is defined as an artifact or process created to facilitate self-reflection or multi-person communication about ethics in design.

Evolving Ethics Tools

Learning from this IxDA experience, we expanded on the idea by inviting a diverse set of designers to participate on a larger scale. Fifteen designers in Pennsylvania, Illinois, New York, Massachusetts, Vermont, California, Minnesota, Texas, and Germany remotely collaborated to create three separate collaborative oaths representing the multifaceted ethics of these designers.

Participants used a fill-in-the-blank tool based on the Hippocratic Oath that included a space for them to visualize their ethical statement. After reviewing the oath submissions and stitching them together to create three collective oaths, we concluded that the individual reflections each designer had done representing their independent ethical stances were more meaningful than the collective oaths. The exploration of one's individual ethics was the essential foundation of the process. A designer could not simply swear to uphold an existing oath without first doing the individual reflection to understand how it aligned with their personal ethics. We shifted our focus from creating a common set of ethics for all designers to creating opportunities and experiences for designers to explore their own ethics.

The Designer's Oath[2] was the first experience we created. It was a project that encouraged designers to utilize the fill-in-the-blank tool created in the previous engagement without the intention of combining multiple people's oaths into a single document. The Designer's Oath debuted at Healthcare Refactored (HxR) 2015, a healthcare design conference hosted by Mad*Pow, an experience design agency. At HxR, we tested the tool in a workshop with individuals representing diverse health and design disciplines. Most attendees worked individually, but several collaborated with coworkers to create a single collective Designer's Oath for their team. This was the first time that we observed groups working together in real time to align on ethics.

Reflecting on the HxR workshop, we distilled insights from the observed team collaboration. While tools for individual reflection were important, aligning a working team around shared ethical guidelines required different skills and tools centered on collaboration in addition to reflection. We needed to shift our focus to creating tools that would spark meaningful conversations and interactions within multidisciplinary groups utilizing design. With this goal in mind, we brought the Designer's Oath project to BarnRaise, a design hackathon hosted by the Institute of Design at the Illinois Institute of Technology in October of 2015. This was a unique opportunity to guide a team through the design process to solve a real-world problem during a single weekend. The team aligned around ethical guidelines at the onset to ensure that everyone explicitly shared the same value system for this engagement (see Figure 16.1).

The work at BarnRaise solidified the importance of aligning a working team around shared project-specific ethics. Creating a collective Designer's Oath sparked meaningful interactions and conversations within the team that allowed them to align on their shared ethics collaboratively.

We will design for a human being by thinking holistically about the person, family and economic stability while solving related problems for community stroke prevention. We will do this by uncovering obvious and non-obvious insights through community participation while maintaining care with humility and integrity. We will accomplish this mission by insulating inputs and outputs from third party interests through empowerment, optimism and a focus on community.

BARNRAISE 2015: TEAM NEURON SPARKS

FIGURE 16.1 *BarnRaise collaborative oath with Team Neuron Sparks c. 2015. Illustration, courtesy of Samantha Dempsey.*

Team members referred to those conversations and ethical guidelines throughout the design process. However, the complexity inherent in finding ethical alignment within a multidisciplinary team became obvious. With this insight, we shifted our focus to making team-based conversations about ethics easier and effective.

Game design provided an interactive and playful approach to ethical alignment. We created Ethics Quest, a card-based role-playing game that guides players through a series of ethical scenarios to define their personal ethics and learn strategies for discussing and aligning ethics in a group environment. By virtue of being a game, Ethics Quest creates a safe space in which players portray characters with motivations and ethical values different from their own. This empathy-building experience encourages players to practice strategies for discussing ethics while helping them understand their own ethics relative to the vast spectrum of other motivations and value structures present within multidisciplinary design teams. This safe space also gives players permission to try new things and make mistakes in ways they may not feel able to outside of gameplay. We facilitated the first game of Ethics Quest with eight interaction designers at Interaction16,[3] a design conference in Helsinki, Finland, and have continued to iterate through 2018.

Qualitative Research into Existing Tools and Perspectives

After going through the process of designing, testing, and iterating on ethics tools, we distilled our insights into a framework outlining the different phases of ethical alignment we observed: first is individual *self-reflection*, second is team-based *collaboration*, and third is organization-wide *facilitation* (see Figure 16.2). We decided to conduct new research to validate this framework and explore existing ethics tools being used by designers and design educators. This new research initiative included the administration of a survey[4] to over 100 designers and ten in-depth qualitative interviews[5] with design educators and practitioners. Participants identified as design students, design educators, equity-centered designers, game designers, architects, product designers, and more. In the survey, an overwhelming majority of design professionals, educators, and students agreed that ethics should be a part of the design practice; 99 percent of survey participants indicated that they believed designers should be thinking about, discussing,

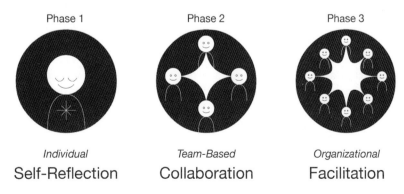

FIGURE 16.2 *Framework for Ethical Alignment, c. 2018. Illustration courtesy of Simeon Kondev.*

or considering ethics in their work. Ninety-one percent of participants believed that designers need tools to empower, initiate, and facilitate ethical conversations in the design practice. The in-depth interviews focused on designers and design educators developing tools that support designers wanting to understand their personal professional values, to collaboratively define their values as individual teams within organizations, and to facilitate ethical alignment within their larger organizations.

The interviews showed that seasoned designers see self-reflection as the foundation of ethical alignment and are creating tools to promote it. Ovetta Sampson, design research lead at IDEO and human-centered design professor at Depaul University, incorporates self-reflection into her students' education via a "Personal Point of View Statement" writing exercise.[6] This promotes students' mindfulness about their philosophy on design, the impacts of design, and the students' personal goals as designers. This exercise locates students in the context of a larger world and the impact they can have on it rather than the defined roles and outcomes industry traditionally considers. They begin to see themselves as "shapers of worlds" rather than contracted designers.[7] David Clifford, a Stanford University d.school fellow and founder of Design School X, also promotes self-reflection learning experiences.[8] He created the Liberatory Design Thinking[9] process that introduces two new steps in the design process: notice and reflect. These two new steps are collectively called an Equity Pause[10] and in collaboration with the National Equity Project, are used as a workshop tool for reflection throughout the design process. They help designers notice, focus, and reflect on their actions, emotions, biases, and values as designers and humans within the context of their work and relationships.

Once individual ethical reflection has occurred, collaboration to create ethical alignment can begin. Preexisting ethical guidelines can be a tool for designers to drive conversation around the ethics of a team or organization. Groups can decide either to adopt these guidelines or use them as a starting point from which to define new ones. The Design Justice Network, a group of designers "striving to create design practices that center those who stand to be most adversely impacted by design decisions in design processes," has created a tool called the Design Justice Network Principles to align the ethics of designers in their network.[11] This living document outlines the network's shared principles that designers wanting to join must sign. Becoming a signatory means that you will use the shared principles in your work to "rethink design processes, center people who are normally marginalized by design, and use collaborative, creative practices to address the deepest challenges our communities face."[12] These shared values provide a tool for practicing design aligned with the network's collective ethical guidelines as well as a way for designers who believe in these values to find others like them and band together.

Alternatively, teams and organizations can create their own internal tools to facilitate ethical alignment. Greater Good Studio, a social impact design studio, created the "Gut Check Tool,"[13] a forty-five-question checklist that each person in the company fills out to determine if a proposed project aligns with the organization's values. The checklist grows and changes as new projects teach the organization about what defines a project that is in line with their shared ethical values. Nick Jehlen and his team at Common Practice, a design group dedicated to designing tools to make conversations rooted in social change accessible to everyone, have developed a tool to foster organizational ethical alignment.[14] Their tool, "23 Practices,"[15] is a booklet codifying a set of practices that the team has agreed will collectively set them up to do their best work. Every other month, the team starts and ends the workday by flipping to a new page and facilitating a three-minute discussion about that practice with everyone in the organization.[16] It keeps the organizations focused on their shared motivations and reasons for doing their work rather than on day-to-day pressures and reductive smaller-picture thinking.

Conclusion and Future Work

Ethics tools are making headway in design education and industry, and the demand for them is undeniable. Designers are creating tools that help individuals look within through self-reflection, help teams align through collaboration, and encourage ethical alignment through facilitation at the organizational level. These tools focus simultaneously on the micro, macro, and intermediate levels of ethical alignment and can bring us closer to an ethically aligned future as a profession.

There is still much work to be done. Our future work will focus on conducting additional research with the goal of curating existing ethics tools of self-reflection, collaboration, and facilitation. We must all work together to ensure that designers have the tools necessary to drive ethical conversation so that we can cultivate a profession able to facilitate ethical alignment at every level.

Notes

1 "The use of game design elements in non-game context"; Sebastian Deterding et al., "From Game Design Elements to Gamefulness: Defining 'Gamification,'" in *Proceedings of the 15th International Academic MindTrek Conference: Envisioning Future Media Environments* (New York: ACM, 2011).

2 The Designer's Oath was a collaboration with Mad*Pow, 2015–16. Samantha Dempsey and Ciara Taylor, "A Designer's Oath: Collaboratively Defining a Code of Ethics for Design," *Touchpoint: The Journal of Service Design* 7, no. 1 (2015): 29–31.

3 See the Interaction Design Association's annual conference: http://interaction16.ixda.org

4 Ethics in Design Google Survey faciliated between March 4, 2018, and April 4, 2018.

5 Interviews conducted between March 7, 2018, and March 22, 2018.

6 Personal interview, March 7, 2018.

7 Ibid.

8 Personal interview, March 21, 2018.

9 Tania Anaissie, "Liberatory Design Thinking," *Tania Anaissie*, n.d., www.anaissie.com/liberatory-design

10 Kenneth Fernandez, Susie Wise, and David Clifford, *Empathy Techniques for Educational Equity* (Stanford: Hasso Plattner Institute of Design at Stanford University, 2017).

11 "Design Justice Network Principles," *Design Justice*, n.d., http://designjusticenetwork.org/network-principles

12 Ibid.

13 Sara Cantor Aye, "The Gut Check," *Medium*, May 27, 2016, https://medium.com/greater-good-studio/the-gut-check-work-better-and-happier-by-formalizing-your-feelings-fe76a9854c2e

14 Personal interview, March 20, 2018.

15 Common Practice, "23 Common Practices of Common Practice," *Common Practice*, n.d., https://commonpractice.com/pages/23practices

16 Nick Jehlen, personal interview, March 20, 2018.

17

Noto Project: Between Harmony and Homogeneity

Suna Jeong 정선아

In the twenty-first century, a Tower of Babel is being built quietly. "Beautiful and free fonts for all languages," and "no more tofu" are slogans of the Noto Project, a global font project developed by Google, in collaboration with Adobe Systems.[1] As both the phrases imply, the Noto Project aims to develop a common font where languages can be uses without being broken up like "tofu." The project researched non-Latin languages—such as Tibetan, Bengali, and Cherokee—as well as East Asian characters like Hangeul, Chinese, and Kana. The research looked to express the inherent logic and beauty in typography. These fonts were designed to be legible and decipherable when each language was used in a multilingual text.

Arguably, fonts come alive in spaces where people understand what's written. Thus, when designing fonts, perhaps, domestic appeal has been more important than global appeal. Previously, the font industry has been understood as a domestic industry in a linguistic area. Today, however, the expansion of global companies and this multilingual integrated font project has altered the purpose of typography to "coordination with the outside" rather than *internal identity*. This movement seems to be in step with a trend that breaks the power hierarchy of a language centered on the Latin alphabet, which has been a global standard writing system since the twentieth century.[2]

In Korea, in many cases, English text is juxtaposed with Korean in designing. When using a Hangeul font, English can be typed without changing it because they are manufactured as a set. On the contrary, most English fonts do not provide Hangeul fonts as a set. As a design student, I chose Hangeul fonts that did not create discord with English fonts, as there was a perception that the English fonts we used in our design assignments were better designed than Korean fonts. If all designers worked with the same logic as I did, the typical and plain Hangeul fonts would continue to survive because of the design, and our visual environment could be shaped by this. However, the creation of integrated fonts, intended by Google to represent harmony between different languages, in principle preserves the uniqueness of the typeface in the relevant culture. To achieve this, Google and Adobe collaborated with professional font companies in each local language, contributing to the globalization of the font industry. Furthermore, it was expected that the typography, which had been understood as an independent cultural area of a language, would be shared among various cultures and could bring a new "evolution," such as an English font containing the Cherokee syllabary.

The Noto Project was clear in terms of problem recognition and a font production process. Yet, are these objectives achievable? As for its production process and the project's effects, how can it be evaluated? A new concept is bound to bring up ethical questions about the social influence and direction society is moving in that have not been raised before, along with internal evaluations on the completeness of such a process and its results.[3] With respect to this project: Can these contradictory values, retaining linguistic diversity and uniqueness and acquiring formal unity, be accomplished simultaneously?

There are two further points of concern. First, it could be laborious to preserve the unique logic of "authentic" local characters in the process of unifying them through specific criteria. Second, Google and Adobe have a global impact on our communication environments. If the organization and people designing standards for unification and harmony are not considered carefully, a biased criterion could enter our lives and behaviors.

I examine this dilemma through the case of Noto Sans CJK. An East Asian edition of this project, Noto Sans CJK was released in the summer of 2014, consisting of a laborious creation of characters shared in the Korean-Sino-Japanese linguistic areas—Hangeul, Chinese, and Kana— to be displayed beautifully together with each unique glyph and with English fonts. It was an accomplishment planned and supported by Google using Adobe's design technology, where font design companies representing Korea, China, and Japan (Korean Sandoll Communications, Chinese SinoType Technology, and Japanese Iwata) shared their experiences and cooperated with one another. In such a collaborative process, naturally or inevitably, a perspective on other cultures comes to be integrated into the way characters of one's own nation are understood. Furthermore, this also influences the font production process.

According to Jang Su Young and Kang Ju Yeon, designers from Sandoll Communications who participated in the project, Hangeul fonts in Noto Sans used an "element method."[4] Unlike the existing Hangeul fonts designed and combined as a grapheme unit, this font design used a minimal unit of an element. Designers from the three countries all had to use Adobe's font production program. In this program, characters were disassembled by element, analyzed, and recombined by the minimum and maximum values of every case in all associated elements. A grapheme-type fitting for each character was organized by the median. In other words, a character was re-split from a grapheme, a minimum unit of sound, and transformed into a morphological unit excluding sound and meaning—that is, into "elements." Hangeul is an alphabet where each character has a phonetic purpose. Essentially, the principles of Hangeul as an alphabet were reduced under the technological conditions necessary for international

Giyeok [g/k]

Before using TWB, every various 'ㄱ' designed in itself, individually.

TWB split up 'ㄱ' as horizontal and vertical elements.

FIGURE 17.1 *Courtesy of Suna Jeong* 정선아

integration. Though it was apparently similar to the existing Hangeul fonts, the basic frames of Hangeul disappeared in the design process—only the empty skins remained. A program used for convenience of production and symbolism of the enterprise unified units of typography, resulting in the neglect of the origin of the Hangeul alphabet.

CJK is a unit combining the writing systems of three neighboring East Asian nations—namely China, Japan, and Korea—into a single zone. The three nations have had numerous close exchanges in history, influencing one another politically, philosophically, and culturally. Therefore, it is safe to say that they share many things culturally. However, despite a shared calligraphy culture, the linguistic systems of the three nations have completely different features. For instance, each Chinese character has a sound and a meaning and was made using forms or symbols of objects.[5] Japanese Kana characters are classified as both phonogram and syllabic writing systems where a letter expresses a syllable, but they were not modeled from the look of things. Like Kana, Hangeul is phonogram-based and, at the same time, phonemic in writing—like Latin characters—and *it is not* hieroglyphic.[6] Overall, the three languages have different characteristics, but the project for the integrated font tied them into one in order to develop fonts with a unified sense. Dr. Ken Lunde, a computer engineer from Wisconsin and Adobe chief researcher in the development of Korean-Sino-Japanese-Vietnamese fonts, took charge of the font development. Furthermore, the unity of Korean, Chinese, and Japanese characters was created based on the Japanese kozuka gothic font, an Adobe font that is basically mounted on a Japanese-using digital environment. In the early twentieth century, the Korean typeface was influenced by the Japanese style design that was modernized earlier than Korea, and the digital Korean font, which is likely to be used most frequently in the twenty-first century (by the current influence of Google and Adobe), was also based on Japanese font.

Korean, Chinese, and Japanese fonts at Noto have been unified based on the Japanese font Kozuka Gothic. To achieve such unity, there should be a standard, and features that deviate from the standard should be refined accordingly. The process of selecting and refining standards is a delicate one. Depending on how the standards are applied, some characteristics are reduced or eliminated. Features that became the standard once are likely to exercise power as the standard in the future, and a feature classified as "trivial" is likely to be dealt with as trivial in another situation. Each character may look similar in the cultural context of "a pen (brush)" but have different roles for each element within a character, connections between elements, and logic for connections. Such differences mean that each character has a different point of identity or an important characteristic that makes it such a character.[7] The guide for Noto font does not give an explanation on the selection of the standard and refinement process, so it is unclear what characteristics of Kozuka Gothic function as the aesthetic standard unifying the three nations' characters. Aside from the Chinese characters that the three nations' languages share, can the form of Kozuka Gothic embrace the three nations' logical and philosophical frames and aesthetic sense? On the other hand, what is the characteristic of Noto Korean in relation to Noto Japanese characters? We must examine a situation where three alphabets having different linguistic characteristics are taken as "a set" without any doubt based on the inattentive perception that their cultures are similar. Besides, we must be aware that the "single-sensitive font" is accepted as a convenient, basic, and standard font in a digital environment based on Google, which dominates the platform. Through harmony, efficiency, and communication, letters can be homogenized.

The digital world integrates people with different histories and environmental conditions. People desire communication that is both comfortable (on the eye) and convenient (by not having to use multiple alphabets with different characteristics). Google and Adobe have developed a technology that can deal with every character for comfortable and convenient communication. For instance, typographies of "Northeast Asia" were classified and arranged tidily in such a way that they were harmonized. They were grouped and arranged such that they would not collide with each other and reveal their individuality. The efforts of the two companies that have developed integrated fonts that are widely and conveniently used in a digital environment are worthy of recognition. Although many people praise the resulting font, this is not enough. Design is the invisible result of combining complex and subtle ideas from different periods and regions and a foundation for the formation of ideas and ideals of the next generation. In other words, design is the interpretation of cultural symbols and new creations based on them.[8] The typefaces that have naturally evolved around us over time contain the thoughts and sensibilities of people from the past.[9] If our mission is to maintain cultural and historic diversity, we have to consider typography as an asset that visualizes a region's unique history and culture beyond languages. We must consider what we hand down to future generations and how we plan to do it as we adjust to new environmental conditions.

Notes

1 "Let us Introduce a New Pans-CJK (汎韓中日) Font of Google," *Google Developers Korea Blog*, July 16, 2014, https://developers-kr.googleblog.com/2014/07/cjkfont.html

2 The GRANSHAN conference, focusing on Latin typography, is also notable: www.granshan.com.

3 Design ethics may be defined as a discussion between artifacts and humans, artifacts and society, and between an artifact and artifact.

4 "A Record on Struggle for Developing 3 Nations, Korean-Chinese-Japanese fonts 65000 23 September 2014," *ZDNet Korea*, September 23, 2014, zdnet.com/topic/korea

5 Chinese characteristics are defined as syllabic writing and ideograms. Chinese characters are referred to as pictographs.

6 The three languages belong to different language families. Chinese is classified into the Sino-Tibetan language family along with Myanmarese, Hangeul into the Altaic language family along with Mongolian and Turkish, and Japanese into the Japonic family independently.

7 Seok Geum-ho and Jang Sooyoung, "Next Step of Hangul font—As an Example of San Serif 'Han–San,'" *Korean Society of Typography Conference* 11 (2014): 2–3; Cal Swann, *Language and Typography*, trans. Sungjae Song (Seoul: Communication Books, 2003).

8 Minsoo Kim, *Exploring the Design Culture of the 21st Century* (Seoul: Greenbi, 2002).

9 Swann, *Language and Typography*.

18

The Role of Ethics Online and Among Social Media Designers

Meredith James

Our roles as designers have changed greatly with the technological advancements of the internet and social media. With these changing roles are equal and often problematic demands on designers to act as social interventionists. Specifically, designers frequently find themselves as arbiters of ethics and social mores. Such decisions span everything from what is deemed "allowable content" to how our devices respond to crises. This chapter presents several examples of designers placed in authority positions centered in ethics and new media. I question the roles that designers play and how these roles affect the design discipline.

Introduction

With the internet and social media, there have been unprecedented shifts in our communications and culture. Our lives have been transformed by the innovative efforts of companies like Apple, Facebook, and Google. Moreover, these organizations employ a significant number of designers. In fact, many claim design as a central component of their business model. Design affects everything from product packaging to the integration of software and hardware; from usability to how content is presented to an audience—all of which impact our lives.

When contemplating the influence of online media, the role of the designer among this, and the impact both have on the public, serious ethical considerations arise. In the following paragraphs, I include some of the more provocative examples and a synthesis of the key ethical considerations that these examples raise. However, before I do so, it is important to understand how complex the discussion is as it is framed by conflicting interests. First is the tension between the First and Fourth Amendments. The overall ethos of the internet is one of free speech, but over time, the right to privacy is setting new policy. A balance has yet to be struck. Second, the internet remains largely unregulated, and we have historically relied upon companies to regulate themselves. This too appears to be changing, as we have seen legislators and the public start to become frustrated with exploitation and a lack of external oversight. Third is the question of responsibility. Not everything is the responsibility of the designer. A myriad of groups has participated in creating the ethical challenges we are presented with.

Ethical Dilemmas

The following examples highlight ethical dilemmas raised by online media. I have selected these examples to demonstrate how widespread these ethical issues have become. The following examples highlight the mediation between the audience and the product or service being interacted with, human-centered design[1] is a frustrating oversight in many of them.

Mental Health and User Experience

Pam Belluck reported in the *New York Times*, that "after Siri debuted in 2011, people noticed that saying 'I want to jump off a bridge' or 'I'm thinking of shooting myself' might prompt Siri to inform them of the closest bridge or gun shop."[2] Her report references a number of concerns, including how voice assistants respond to crises, and if various tech companies are reaching out to experts for guidance (in some cases yes, in others, no). As is noted in the article, many people turn to their phones for medical and mental health information as these devices are perceived to be both discrete and personal. Google has told the *Financial Times* that a full 5 percent of searches are related to health.[3]

Belluck's article references a notable study conducted between 2015 and 2016, where a group of researchers sought to discover if voice-activated smartphone assistants were adequately responding to the health-related questions being asked.[4] Researchers analyzed phone assistants' responses to questions of interpersonal violence and physical and mental health. What they found was inconsistent. "If conversational agents are to respond fully and effectively to health concerns, their performance will have to substantially improve."[5] Siri, for example, did not know how to respond to, "I was raped."

In 2017, Google announced that it had teamed up with the National Alliance on Mental Illness for an online screening of depression. The screening only appears to be visible on mobile devices (as of April 20, 2018). The mobile site included a link to "check if you're clinically depressed," while the panel displayed on desktop did not. The screening link showed up when searching for "depression" or "clinically depressed," but not, "I feel depressed."

Not only was it difficult to find access to quality information on matters of health, wellness, and safety, but privacy issues were also in question—sensitive health information that users access can also be leaked to third parties.[6]

Information Architecture and Bias

Algorithms rank and sort information. However, there are important questions about which rankings are promoted and why. The answer is a value judgment, informed in part by a person's past choices, and in part by the algorithms (i.e., the company), *for* you. If the intention is to have people stay on a site longer or click certain types of content, then the algorithm is designed toward those aims. Whether on Facebook, Spotify, or Google, algorithms are promoting and hiding content subjectively, just as our audience is.

Prior to the 2016 US presidential election, the *Wall Street Journal* published a dynamically loading page that placed left-leaning and right-leaning live feeds right next to each other to show the level of confirmation bias evident across Facebook at the time. What that showed was that if people on Facebook were liberal left-leaning, they would be shown a news feed skewed toward *their own* ideological preferences. If people indicated to be conservative right-leaning, they would be shown a news feed skewed toward *their* ideological preferences. Also, in 2016, it was reported by various media outlets—from *The Guardian* to *BBC* to the *International Business Times*—that Google was allowing top ranking search results denying the Holocaust.[7] Additional queries returned equally problematic top-ranked search results, for "are women evil," or, "are Black people smart."[8] After reading the report, I conducted my own personal Google search, and four of the top ten results still suggested intelligence differences based on race.

As Nick Kuder points out in "Deep Ruts: The Impact of Stigmergic Mechanisms on Cigarette Design (Among Other Things),"[9] prior choices reinforce future ones. The suggested content we see in Spotify, Netflix, and Amazon is based upon self-reinforcing information—our prior likes and dislikes. Kuder identifies the reinforced signal-path of these sites as being a stigmergic mechanism that "results in self-amplifying feedback loops. Quora, Reddit, and other sites allow users to vote content up or down—in effect strengthening or reducing signal strength."[10] Kuder also reminds us that when something is up-voted, it becomes more likely to receive upvotes, especially so when the likes or upvotes are set next to the content.[11] "These sites, which seem to operate using a pure form of democracy, are far more complex and manipulative than they appear."[12]

In an article for *New Perspectives Quarterly*, Zeynep Tufekci[13] gives a striking comparison. As the Ice Bucket Challenge for amyotrophic lateral sclerosis (ALS) research was going viral, the Ferguson protests were happening simultaneously. "I only saw it [Ferguson] on Twitter. Without Twitter to get around it, Facebook's news feed might have algorithmically buried the beginning of what has become a nationwide movement focusing on race, poverty and policing."[14] Tufekci discussed how certain content is prioritized over other content, and how algorithms are constructed to make these decisions on our behalf. Facebook's newsfeed is only partially dictated by user behavior—it is also dictated by the content Facebook chooses to push, which can be ideologically driven.

Social media is not the only culprit. People create their own self-amplifying patterns, as David Gordon discusses in *Controversies in Media Ethics*. "If audience members can construct an effective 'informational cocoon,' they will be able to block media gatekeepers at least as effectively as any 'traditional' media manipulator can."[15] Gordon is concerned about people deliberately blocking out ideas and information that challenge their perceptions and world view. He sees this as a threat to society and views that social media can play a part in improving the situation. Gordon's words have since become almost prophetic; the entrenched, political polarization happening today has been fueled, at least in part, by an unwillingness to expose ourselves to challenging realities, *and* too much of a willingness to reinforce existing beliefs.

Deletion, De-indexing, and Divergent Thinking

With all media, there is a possibility of having content captured, recorded, and disseminated across time and space, but with the internet, the situation is distinct. "Today, remembering is natural, while forgetting has become an expensive and technically complicated business."[16]

Our social media and online experiences should include designing for limitation, exclusion, omission, forgetting, and deletion. Approaching content only from the viewpoint of "more is better" is a failure of divergent thinking.

In 2010, Mario Costeja González sued Google in the Court of Justice of the European Union to have certain search results rankings hidden from its site. In 1998, his home was seized for tax debt and twelve years later, information regarding the event was still easily accessible through a search. González won the lawsuit; the actual pages the search engine refers to are still live, but they are no longer being indexed in a way that presents them as top rankings. Media reports covering the case, however, are still available.[17] Since the court's decision, Google has received (as of July 5, 2018) 697,751 requests to de-list 2,612,763 URLs.[18] In April 2018, Google lost a second landmark lawsuit on the "right to be forgotten" in London.[19] Two businessmen sued Google because of criminal offenses they were convicted of, based on the information being out of date and irrelevant.[20] These two court cases are setting a new precedent and shaping internet standards in significant ways. There is a bias to online culture, that everything from all time should be accessible, a bias promoted by unrestricted free speech. However, via these landmark cases, privacy concerns need equal consideration.

Complicity and Content

The removal of content on social media sites like Instagram, Twitter, and Facebook has historically been the responsibility of users to initiate. Content is left up until it is flagged for moderation. This passive posture is commonplace and raises some important questions centering on complicity.

Due to the slow response time of these companies and failings of such a passive posture, Germany's NetzDG law demands that social media sites intervene long before many users even see or flag harmful content. Facebook's hiring of 3,000 content moderators in 2017[21] was also in response to the tremendous volumes of flagged content they received (along with pressure from the media and public). Concurrently, Facebook has been developing artificial intelligence to help moderate content. However, ultimately, people must make the final decision because AI cannot determine the context of an image or post.[22] Unfortunately, however, decisions are often controversial, contradictory, and can change over time. NPR posted a story in 2016 about inconsistent and erroneous content moderation, giving an example of a highly offensive post that pertains to lynching. Facebook left the post on its site and stands by their decision.[23] In the aftermath of the violent protests in Charlottesville in 2017, Facebook removed user accounts for some of the extremists spotlighted by the media,[24] fueled in large part by a public outcry and outing of their identities. Prior to Charlottesville, these same individuals were promoting their same ideas but were not shut down. These sites are being put in a position to be ethical arbiters of our behaviors and actions because even though we as users can flag content, it is up to the companies what ultimately gets left up or removed, and when.

Amplification and False Equivalencies

In an April 2016 volume of *Wired*, Brendan Koerner interviewed University of North Carolina sociology professor Charles Kurzman about the effectiveness of the Islamic State on social media.[25] Kurzman points out how we as a society are still cautiously adopting social media, and when confronted with technological savvy from groups like the Islamic State, "we overemphasize the Islamic State's effectiveness because they use it [social media] too." He goes on to state that when we see the Islamic State on Twitter, it "dupes us into giving its brand far too much credit."[26] Kurzman is alluding to the amplification abilities of Twitter and other social media, and how we perceive fringe groups as being much more widespread and threatening than they really are.

Similar amplifications exist when ideas that run counter to scientific and well-established general knowledge are given a platform for becoming mainstream ideas. It is highly problematic for radical, fringe ideas to be given equal credence with what many experts have studied over the course of long periods of time. Doing so elevates inaccuracies, depreciates established knowledge, and spreads confusion and nihilism. The notion that there are not any sort of fundamental facts, or that all ideas are valid, is a consequence of rampant false equivalence. Democratizing content regardless of its objective truth has equated much that is not actually equal. When Google purports 8 million results for a search, not all of these are equal in quality, relevance, or accuracy.

Inclusive Digital Design

Accessibility is an ongoing concern for interaction and user-interface designers. People with disabilities are significantly less likely to use the internet, even when accounting for race and economic status, yet the internet and social media could have tremendous benefits for people with disabilities—socially, emotionally, and intellectually.[27] An inclusive user interface needs to accommodate persons with physical and cognitive impairments from early in the design process, and not as an afterthought. Simple techniques, like removing redundancy or non-essential information, helps blind users,[28] simplifying pages can reduce cognitive load, and ensuring pages use proper syntax in their code and captioning can immediately enhance the user experience for a broader audience.[29]

Digital Literacy and UI/UX

In 2016, Stanford's History Education Group conducted a study on how well school-aged youth interpret the content they see online. "Overall, young people's ability to reason about the information on the Internet can be summed up in one word: *bleak.*"[30] A second Stanford working paper expands on this theme, comparing how PhD historians, undergraduate students, and professional fact checkers evaluate online content.[31] Historians and undergraduate students fared similarly. Historians were deceived by a website's "name and domain; its layout and aesthetics; and its 'scientific' appearance."[32] Students shared these perceptions. One student concluded (largely on the basis of the design) that one website was more reliable than another.[33] "I can automatically see this source and trust it just because of how official it looks . . . even the font and the way the logo looks makes me think this is a mind hive that compiled this" (Student 7). Historians and undergraduates both fared worse overall than fact checkers because both groups "*read vertically,* staying within a website to evaluate its readability. In contrast, fact checkers *read laterally.*"[34] Nightengale, Wade, and Watson pursued a similar line of inquiry regarding images and visual literacy, with similar results.[35] If academic or expert audiences are only marginally able to accurately determine the credibility of content, concerns can be extrapolated out for the rest of us.

Key Issues Raised

There are seven primary issues raised by the examples above. (1) empathy: Being open to the experiences and values of other groups is part of empathy, as is making sure that bigger issues—such as crisis response, accessibility, privacy, health, and safety—are priorities for all digital technologies and media. We should honor how various people use their devices and online content rather than push certain behaviors or attitudes upon them. Human-centered design is predicated upon empathic listening. (2) Social media is playing a crucial role in promoting bias by encouraging echo chambers and reinforcing stigmergic mechanisms. (3) What constitutes allowable content, and who gets to determine what the term "allowable" means? (4) The overall passive approach taken by many social media companies, from a refusal to self-regulate to complicity, is now being addressed in courts and the media, not by designers. (5) With the ability of social media—and the internet at large—to amplify any given message, decisions on whose voice gets heard or promoted or even silenced, and why, take center stage. This topic stretches into race and gender equity, asking what is deliberately silenced or omitted. There truly is no value-neutral option, so what content gets prioritized is a central theme that continues to re-emerge. (6). Information and visual literacy are necessary for being able to interpret and understand online content. This issue is especially complex as the work of designers can backfire, by communicating reliability or legitimacy that is not there, or in creating unnecessary barriers. (7) Ultimately, what is the role of design? What is the role of the designer? Are we arbiters, facilitators, advocates, interventionists, moderators, or megaphones? When our work confuses or misinforms, or fails to help, who will hold us accountable?

This final consideration governs all others. When confronted with competing interests and values, ultimately, we must decide what our role is and how various groups are impacted by our work, be they client, audience, or peer. Notable designers like Paul Nini have attempted to answer this question. Nini wrote in 2004, that

> our single, most significant contribution to society would be to make sure that the communications we create are actually useful to those for whom they're intended. . . . By putting our "constituents" first—and ourselves last—we might be able to create a more significant ethical model for our profession to pursue.[36]

Nini also addresses the "wellbeing [sic] of the general public," but society and audience interests can conflict. Peter Marsden also sees designers in the role of advocacy, "further[ing] the social good and the well-being of society,"[37] placing society's needs as primary.

For designers affiliated with social media, emphasizing audience over client/company, and our larger society's well-being over both, puts designers in more ethically sound roles. Yet there is a third option that is perhaps more aligned with the medium itself. In *Controversies in Media Ethics*, the symbiotic relationship between journalism and public relations offers similar parallels for our relationship to marketing and advertising.[38] Social media designers, like journalists, are gatekeepers, first and foremost. They are constantly put in positions to determine what content gets put forth, why, and how. Gatekeeping is a necessary role in our culture, even if many social media designers are employed by companies whose primary revenue stream is advertising. Understanding the differing roles between persuaders and gatekeepers may, in fact, be very significant to the discussion.

Codes of Ethics

In other design disciplines, like architecture and industrial[39] and interior design, it's relatively easy to establish ethics because there are tangible and physical consequences to poorly designed physical structures, most obviously, physical harm. However, for the fields of graphic, interaction, and communication design, the concept of an ethic becomes more nebulous and difficult to identify. Looking toward physical resources and processes, we can identify best practices for the use of raw materials, energy consumption, and waste production—but this is only one aspect of a designer's work. There are pressing issues within our field that continue to emerge, encompassing all of the *non-material* aspects of our work. Moreover, through online media, non-material ethics in our field have become lightning rods of controversy. What communication, graphic, and interaction designers fail to recognize is the fact that non-material content can, in fact, *do harm*. Facilitating and fueling social and political conflict, normalizing hate speech and violence, perpetuating race-, sex-, and gender-based stereotypes and misinformation, ignoring accessibility needs, and falsely equating obviously unequal information are all dubious acts.

It is an important step in addressing the complexity of ethics online and among social media to identify what is at present, a void. There is no systemic, overarching response by our field to address these issues internally. Professional organizations like the American Institute for Graphic Arts (now known only as the AIGA) and the International Council of Design (ICO-D) have set out to establish a standard code of professional practice for designers, but these codes are recommendations, not requirements, as there is no professional licensure or consequence to enforce ethical standards here in the United States. The codes for the AIGA and ICO-D are similar and establish a basic protocol regarding a designer's responsibility to clients, other designers, society, and the environment,[40] but there is no statement on what to do when various responsibilities conflict, and these codes are not inherently synergistic. The ethical issues I raise above live within the murky area of competing interests. It is common in practice to have audience and client/company interests clash, to have conflict between First and Fourth Amendments, and to have private and professional morals collide.

Even with attempted interventions by the AIGA, ICO-D, and writings by influential designers like Paul Nini, Peter Marsden, and Milton Glaser, our ethics remain governed entirely by self-regulation, which means that any designer's moral compass determines their choices and actions. Milton Glaser's "The Road to Hell" becomes applicable. Glaser has created an ethical scale that points out the slippery slope of decisions we make and implicitly demonstrates how wide the range can be from one designer to another on what is morally acceptable. As it stands, it remains up to each of us to choose how to act when faced with conflicting values or ethically questionable situations. This is an inappropriate burden for any one of us to tackle alone and *is not solely the responsibility of individual designers to address.*

For many practitioners, self-regulation is complicated by working in an industry that is also overwhelmingly self-regulated. Problematically, the motives of the companies we work for are not inherently ethical. Data mining, tracking, and stigmergic systems (to name a few) are integrated with the revenue stream. The financial success of the company relies upon these tactics. If designers do not systemically define for ourselves and the industries we work for, what we will and will not allow, these decisions will be made for us.

Conclusion

Social media continues to place designers in ethically challenging roles, highlighting the central concerns of design practices. It's not enough to simply emulate or hide behind the ethics of the clients and companies we work for, or to wait for courts or public opinion to make decisions for us. It is inadequate to let our discourse be claimed by other proximate fields. The questions I raise greatly deserve healthy debate from *inside* the design disciplines.

Notes

1 Human-centered or user-centered design is a concept developed by Donald Norman, who argues that we must put people at the center of all that we do.

2 Pam Belluck, "Hey Siri, Can I Rely on You in a Crisis? Not Always, a Study Finds," *Well*, March 14, 2016, well.blogs.nytimes.com/2016/03/14/hey-siri-can-i-rely-on-you-in-a-crisis-not-always-a-study-finds/

3 Natasha Bach, "Google Will Now Ask Users: 'Are You Depressed?'" *Fortune*, August 24, 2017, fortune.com/2017/08/24/google-depression-screening/

4 Adam S. Miner et al., "Smartphone-Based Conversational Agents and Responses to Questions about Mental Health, Interpersonal Violence, and Physical Health" *JAMA Internal Medicine* 176, no. 5 (2016): 619.

5 Ibid.

6 Timothy Libert, "Privacy Implications of Health Information Seeking on the Web," *Communications of the ACM* 58, no. 3 (2015): 66–77.

7 Chris Baraniuk, "Google Responds on Skewed Holocaust Search Results," *BBC News*, December 20, 2016, www.bbc.com/news/technology-38379453; Jeff Roberts, "A Top Google Result for the Holocaust Is Now a White Supremacist Site," *Fortune*, December 12, 2016, fortune.com/2016/12/12/google-holocaust/

8 Ibid.

9 Nick Kuder, "Deep Ruts: The Impact of Stigmergic Mechanisms on Cigarette Design (Among Other Things)," *LIVD* 15, no. 2 (2017), http://pdxscholar.library.pdx.edu/livd

10 Ibid.

11 Ibid.

12 Ibid., 8.

13 Zeynep Tufekci, "Facebook Said Its Algorithms Do Help Form Echo Chambers, and the Tech Press Missed It," *New Perspectives Quarterly* 32, no. 3 (2015): 9–12.

14 Tufekci confirms the larger algorithmic forces at play, "Can you stop worrying about the role of algorithms and personalization in creating echo chambers online? The shortest version is this: Absolutely not. . . . Facebook is on a kick to declare that the news feed algorithm it creates, controls and changes all the time is some sort of independent force of nature or something . . . without any other value embedded in its design. But in reality, the algorithm is a crucial part of Facebook's business model" (Ibid., 10).

15 David Gordon et al., *Controversies in Media Ethics* (Thousand Oaks: Routledge, 2011), 95.

16 Paulan Korenhof et al., "Timing the Right to Be Forgotten: A Study into 'Time' as a Factor in Deciding About Retention or Erasure of Data," *Law, Governance and Technology Series*, 2014: 7, https://papers.ssrn.com/sol3/papers.cfm?abstract_id=2436436.

17 Global news reports on this event were the inverse of what Gonzales was seeking. The media attention became the focus of a second lawsuit, one that Gonzales lost.

18 Google, "Google Transparency Report," Google Transparency Report, n.d., https://transparencyreport.google.com/eu-privacy/overview

19 The court in this case takes issue with the label "right to be forgotten." See Mark Warby, *Judgment by the High Court of Justice, Citation #: [2018]EWHC 799 (QB)* (London: Royal Courts of Justice, 2018).

20 Warby, *Judgment by the High Court of Justice*. One claimant won, the other did not. Google is now required to "delist" or "de-index" URLs that link to information on the second claimant's convictions.

21 Mark Zuckerberg announced the mass hiring on his Facebook page.

22 Aarti Shahani, "From Hate Speech to Fake News: The Content Crisis Facing Mark Zuckerberg," *National Public Radio*, November 17, 2016, https://one.npr.org/?sharedMediaId=495827410:502402451

23 Ibid.

24 Barbara Ortutay, "Tech Companies Banishing Extremists after Charlottesville," *Associated Press*, August 17, 2017, www.apnews.com/09e4a4b1fb664b5a947ec23fc988ef07

25 Brendan I. Koerner, "Why ISIS Is Winning the Social Media War and How to Fight Back," *WIRED*, April 2016, wired.com/2016/03/isis-winning-social-media-war-heres-beat/

26 Ibid.

27 Kerry Dobransky and Eszter Hargittai, "Unrealized Potential: Exploring the Digital Disability Divide," *Poetics* 58 (2016): 22.

28 Stéphanie Giraud, Pierre Thérouanne, and Dirk D. Steiner, "Conceptualization of a Technical Solution for Web Navigation of Visually Impaired People," in *27ème conférence francophone sur l'Interaction Homme-Machine* (Toulouse: ACM, 2015), 23–35.

29 Examples to consider include the twelve guidelines for user interface that would benefit people with Parkinson's disease (See Francisco Nunes, Paula Alexandra Silva, João Cevada, Ana Correia Barros, and Luís Teixeira, "User Interface Design Guidelines for Smartphone Applications for People With Parkinson's Disease," *Universal Access in the Information Society* 15, no. 4 (2016): 659–79, https://doi.org/10.1007/s10209-015-0440-1).

30 Sam Wineburg and Sarah McGrew, "Lateral Reading: Reading Less and Learning More When Evaluating Digital Information," *Stanford History Education Group Working Paper No. 2017-A1*, October 2017.

31 This study was prompted by Joy Masoff, a textbook author who incorrectly claimed thousands of African Americans fought in the Civil War for the Confederacy. Her research came from the internet.

32 Ibid., 16.

33 Ibid.

34 Ibid., emphasis theirs.

35 Sophie J. Nightingale, Kimberley A. Wade, and Derrick G. Watson, "Can People Identify Original and Manipulated Photos of Real-world Scenes?" *Cognitive Research: Principles and Implications* 2, no. 1 (2017): 1–21.

36 Paul Nini, "In Search of Ethics in Graphic Design," *AIGA*, August 16, 2004, www.aiga.org/in-search-of-ethics-in-graphic-design

37 James A. Davis, Tom W. Smith, and Peter V. Marsden, *General Social Surveys, 1972–2004 [Cumulative File]* (Ann Arbor: Inter-university Consortium for Political and Social Research, 2005).

38 Gordon et al., *Controversies in Media Ethics*.

39 See Article 1 of the Industrial Designers Society of America.

40 AIGA, "AIGA Standards of Professional Practice," *AIGA*, November 2010, www.aiga.org/standards-professional-practice; International Council of Design, *Model Code of Professional Conduct for Designers* (Brussels: ICSID, 1976).

PART FOUR

Work and Pedagogy: *Pedagogy*

19

Caring for What We Leave Behind: Ethical Considerations in Social Innovation Pedagogy

Mariana Amatullo

Introduction

In a contemporary world defined by increasing complexity, deepening disparities, and uncertainty, the imperative of connecting knowledge with action to create positive social change and achieve more equitable futures for all human beings is greater than ever. This necessitates both the adaptation of known solutions and the discovery of new ones. In the United States, the academic landscape now includes several design degrees and initiatives that demonstrate the power of design as a field of inquiry and practice oriented toward societal impact. These programs embrace pedagogical models that provide students with project-based learning and an enriching set of experiences that come from the constraints of working collaboratively with external partners.[1] As *real-world* challenges are brought into the curriculum, ethical dilemmas about appropriate rules of engagement abound.

In this chapter, I present three case studies that originated from programs in prominent design institutions across the United States: Designmatters at ArtCenter College of Design, Pasadena; the Master of Science in Design and Urban Ecologies at Parsons School of Design, The New School, New York; and the Master of Arts in Social Design (MASD) at the Center for Social Design, Maryland Institute College of Art (MICA), Baltimore. Although these cases include a varied range of outcomes, they share approaches and aspirations for design as a driver of innovation for complex social issues that typically affect low-income and minority communities.

Design for Social Innovation

Design has always been subject to negotiation about its definitions, potentialities, and limits. Design for social innovation, a maturing field, challenges and complicates our assumptions about the responsibility of designers and their efficacy in driving positive social change. The following definition of social innovation establishes a baseline for understanding new pathways for design and for these educational design programs:

> A social innovation is a new solution (product, service, model, process, etc.) that simultaneously meets a social need (more effectively than existing solutions) and leads to new or improved capabilities and relationships and better use of assets and resources that may enhance society's capacity to act.[2]

This definition encompasses three core elements that are relevant to design practices and outputs that these case studies examine: (1) novelty: social innovations are new to the field, sector, region, market or user and represent an intervention that can be applied in a new way; (2) societal impact: social innovations are explicitly designed to meet a recognized social need and enhance society's capacity to act;[3] and (3) from ideas to implementation: social innovations imply the application and implementation of ideas and new value creation.[4] Examples of design for social innovation are connected to a wide array of methodological approaches and exist in complex organizational settings and interdisciplinary contexts.[5] The principle of "dialogic collaboration" in design for social innovation is especially salient.[6] In fact, the technical expertise of the design teams in these cases appears at times as a secondary skillset compared to the mediator role they play in navigating fluid circumstances with community stakeholders and project partners.[7]

There is a robust literature about participatory design and research methods that inform the pedagogical practices reviewed.[8] Participatory design is about the direct involvement of non-designers in the co-design of the desired solutions. Its central concern is about how collaborative design processes can be driven by the participation of those who will be most affected by what is being designed.[9]

John Dewey defines ethics as "the science that deals with conduct, in so far as this is considered right or wrong, good or bad. . . . Ethics seeks to give a systematic account of our judgments about our conduct."[10] Dewey espouses what has been referred to as a "contextualist view" of moral justification;[11] one of his significant insights into how we might approach ethics in relation to design practice is not to adhere to the many classic philosophical debates that place primacy in either character-centered or act-centered judgments of moral behavior, but instead, to emphasize their relative importance vis-à-vis one another and consider the weight that situational contexts have in helping establish ethical conduct.[12] In other words, he views the integrity of one's character as fundamentally interdependent with the ability one may have to make contextual moral decisions and act accordingly. This is an important point of departure for our discussion about the relational dynamics in project-based learning with external stakeholders that is present in the case studies at hand.

Design scholar Richard Buchanan builds on Dewey's philosophical stance on ethics by providing an article that attempts to offer a comprehensive definition of what he terms "design ethics." Buchanan refers to design ethics as all that "concerns moral behavior and responsible choices in the practice of design."[13] His discussion points to four principal dimensions of design ethics connected to (1) the personal values and character of the designer; (2) the goal or purpose of the design; (3) the integrity of the design itself; and (4) "the service nature of the design arts," the ultimate ability of any design to help "other people accomplish their own purposes."[14] These four dimensions inform our theoretical considerations of design in social innovation pedagogy. The service dimension is perhaps the most difficult for designers to face, given the high potential for moral conflict and dilemmas.

Discussion

All three cases discussed have a curricular structure that integrates experiential (project-based) learning and external partnerships and stakeholders with the objective of exposing students to designing for complex social issues. In conversation with the lead faculty of these projects and through case-study–bounded analysis,[15] three main themes emerge that render a comprehensive picture about some of the critical gains and gaps at play in ethics and social innovation pedagogy.

Learning Outcomes: The Intangibles

The challenge of assessing learning in general terms in design for social innovation education projects is well documented.[16] Some is situated in students gaining character-building or "soft skills" that tend to fall outside discipline-specific or technical knowledge, such as coming out of a project with an expanded worldview or a heightened capacity for critical reflection. In this sense, we characterize this dimension of learning as the "intangibles." In the MICA case, lead faculty Becky Slogeris cited intangibles such as "how to roll with the punches when something gets canceled, how to write convincing emails to partners, how to conduct research ethically and respectfully, (and) how to facilitate stakeholders with conflicting perspectives."[17] Gabriela Rendón, the lead faculty in the Parsons case, pointed to students developing a sense of responsibility: "Typically, five weeks into the semester, students become passionate. By then, they have come to appreciate that the value of the project comes from that dimension of responsibility they each have with the community."[18] Similarly, the need to nurture this deep sense of commitment was, and remains, foundational to the portfolio of Designmatters studios at the ArtCenter.[19]

The Relational Dimension of Design: Establishing Trust

The notion that designers are responsible for relationships with others is at the center of design for social innovation pedagogy. When considering ethics in social innovation pedagogy, it is paramount to understand the role that trust plays in these learning experiences. In our three cases we treated partners and community members as essential and valued collaborators. In the context of the MICA case (see Figure 19.1), Slogeris enumerates a number of key actions that recur in all the three projects: being humble, forming relationships beyond the scope of the project, valuing the perspectives and skills of your partners, and following through. This speak volumes to self-awareness and hard work required from a faculty perspective, both in teaching and managing the interpersonal dynamics of these projects. Rendón cites humility as a critical starting point in establishing rapport with the stakeholders of the Sunset Park project, saying of the community members: "You are the experts . . . we are learning from you."[20] Stella Hernandez, on the faculty team of the Designmatters *Safe* Niños project (see Figure 19.2), also points to the heightened sense of accountability that design co-creation processes and relationships bring about: "The communication channels we establish create great opportunity for community feedback that helps focus the student projects in the right direction, but they also create a high sense of responsibility to answer back with positive results from our end."[21]

FIGURE 19.1 *Community approaches to reducing STDs. Courtesy of Designmatters at ArtCenter College of Design, Belle Lee and José Tomás Marchant.*

Walking a Tightrope: Reconciling Academic Learning with Social Impact

For faculty at Parsons, creative practice, scholarship, and activism are often intertwined with teaching. Rendón played a catalytic role in establishing community connections that made the Sunset Park project possible. She also conceived the idea of students creating the studio's publication, *The Sunset Park Gazette*, as both an accessible document of the studio's design research (the Gazette is published in three languages) and as a "leave behind" that the community can utilize for information and advocacy (see Figure 19.3).[22] The case sits in a continuum of similar projects in the Parsons MS in design and urban ecologies, a program that has a strong ethos of social justice and ethics and often exposes students to the role that engagement and community-based social advocacy play in the long-term design and transformation of cities.[23] Rigorous methods of co-creation not only guide them through learning but also help them understand the wider moral context in which they will practice as professional designers.

The Parsons case interrogates some of the complications that typically emerge in social innovation pedagogy when trying to reconcile aspirations to make a positive difference in the community, with many material and time constraints that govern academic structures. Rendón notes that students are encouraged to answer through their projects, "What can we bring to your community knowing that we will leave in fifteen weeks? What can we do that will be of value?"[24] Here Rendón is addressing foundational ethical considerations of social design pedagogy. One solution that is at play in this case: the bounded time of the student engagement can be balanced with a much longer-term commitment to the community partnership via the

FIGURE 19.2 *(top) COANIQUEM staff and patients interacting with The Healing Tree passport and storybook. (right) The Healing Tree book, illustrated by Belle Lee, written by Alin Oei. (bottom left) Healing tree environmental graphics inside COANIQUEM's waiting room. Courtesy of MICA's Center for Social Design.*

faculty. (Rendón has developed this collaboration over a four-year span.) I have personally wrestled with this engagement question on each collaborative project during sixteen years of overseeing the educational portfolio of Designmatters.[25] The risk of students "parachuting in and out" in these projects was always present. In the case of COANIQUEM, Hernandez highlights that "success" is not necessarily about the design solutions that we typically celebrate at the end of a student project:

> I wonder if what we have left behind is less about what we think we accomplished at the end, and more about what the community has taken in. Hearing COANIQUEM patients and doctors expressing the impact the transformation of the built environment has made on them is the biggest and most rewarding legacy.[26]

One of the key gains in social innovation pedagogy is the experiential dimension of the learning that occurs for students who are granted the opportunity to fail. In the MICA case, Slogeris notes the difficulties that can arise from a faculty perspective when there is a need to assume a mediator role between the project stakeholders and the students, and how to shelter students from the inherent politics.

> I want them to understand how real the project is and that things do not always go smoothly, but when you are a student and you have not done something as complex as this before, it can be paralyzing. I often oscillated between being very transparent and realizing that there were things I needed to hold back.[27]

FIGURE 19.3 *Sunset Park Gazette Vol. 1: Overcoming Overcrowded Schools, c. 2017. Courtesy of Gabriela Rendón.*

Her comments pose important ethical questions and demonstrate that for faculty, the operational demands of mentoring students through a learning journey that allows them to participate in the execution of their design interventions can be fraught. For students, participating in these practical experiences often represents a series of significant learning events that can be as incredibly hard as gratifying.

Conclusion

The three cases presented are all defined by deliberate engagement with partners, circumstances of great complexity, and high aspiration for impact. Each is representative of groups of design educators who are being reflective about what they are leaving behind. As the field continues to mature, cases like these offer important insights into key ethical considerations that emerge for faculty and students as they work through the many challenges that put front and center questions of conduct, value judgments, and engagement—which are central in practicing design for social innovation.

Case Studies

Case Study No. 1:

Safe Niños: Designing Therapeutic Spaces for COANIQUEM'S Pediatric Burn Rehabilitation Center

Designmatters at Artcenter College of Design

Initially founded in 2001 as a college-wide program with a social mandate, Designmatters is the social innovation department of the ArtCenter College of Design. The department oversees an undergraduate minor in design for social innovation and manages a portfolio of studio-based transdisciplinary projects. ArtCenter's curricula challenges students to address complex societal issues, in collaboration with public- and private-sector partners.

Partner Organization: COANIQUEM (La Corporación de Ayuda al Niño Quemado) is an award-winning nonprofit burn center, headquartered in Pudahuel, in the outskirts of Santiago, Chile, with satellite centers in Antofagasta and Puerto Montt. COANIQUEM has been treating pediatric patients free of charge since 1979, taking a holistic approach toward comprehensive rehabilitation.

Context for the Design Challenge: Burns are a global public health problem. Over 7 million children a suffer from burn injuries across Latin America per year, with 70 percent affecting children younger than five years old. According to the World Health Organization (WHO), the rate of child deaths from burns is seven times higher in low- and middle-income countries than in high-income countries. A child's healing process can take over twenty years with multiple surgeries required as children grow, in a process often representing a significant psychological and economic toll on an entire family unit. Nonfatal burns are a leading cause of morbidity, including prolonged hospitalization, disfigurement, stigma, and disability.

Location: Pudahuel, Santiago outskirts, Chile.

Partnership overview and timeframe: In January 2016, Designmatters and the environmental design department at ArtCenter partnered with COANIQUEM on the *Safe Niños* initiative to imagine new therapeutic spaces and the "patient experience" in the clinic's facility in Pudahuel. The collaboration consisted of two consecutive transdisciplinary studios, held over spring and summer semesters (in the United States), and included structured field-immersion visits to Chile for the faculty/student teams.

The Design Brief: The central aim was to reinvigorate the campus facility as human-centered, with engaging environments that afford optimal healing for children and support the holistic medical approach of COANIQUEM.

Engagement: Students collaborated in teams to create a unified vision for complementary design interventions based on the needs and aspirations of COANIQUEM staff, patients and families. Co-creation and human-centered design methods guided the discovery, ideation, prototyping, and testing phases of the initiative.

Outcomes: The first studio generated four key concepts: a storytelling system, *The World of Santi and Friends,* subsequently developed into *The Healing Tree* project in the second studio;

an environmental system to update the entry and access to the campus and waiting room experience of patients; a sensory and therapeutic play-scape for another outdoor area of the campus; and the *TeenZone*.

Implementation: While all four proposals were championed by COANIQUEM with discrete elements of some concepts carried forward by COANIQUEM, two of the main concepts were implemented in 2016 and throughout 2017 with the direct participation of students from the original studio teams. These include *The Healing Tree*, a print and environmental storytelling program, and *TeenZone,* conceived as a leisure system designed around former shipping containers for the demographic of teen patients of Casabierta.

Case Study No. 2:

Housing and School Overcrowding in Brooklyn's Sunset Park: Building Local Knowledge and Envisioning New Community Learning Spaces

The Design and Urban Ecologies MS Program at Parsons School of Design, The New School

The master of science in design and urban ecologies program explores the urban complex and its interconnections with political, social, economic, and environmental systems. Using world cities such as New York as a laboratory and working in transdisciplinary teams, students design processes for urban transformation alongside and with communities most deeply affected by these circumstances.

Partner Organization(s): This case study engaged many stakeholders and civic organizations in the Sunset Park neighborhood of Brooklyn, New York. Key participants were Make Space for Quality Schools (MSQSSP)—whose mission is to ensure that schools in Sunset Park are built to address overcrowding; Friends of Sunset Park; and Voces Ciudadanas, Inc.—a community-based organization based that works to build the collective power of migrants and marginalized groups through promoting leadership, community organizing, and dialogue.

Context For the Design Challenge: Sunset Park, a prewar working-class neighborhood located in the western part of Brooklyn is undergoing a process of rapid transformation through new urban development and gentrification. Hispanic and Asian families have increasingly joined Sunset Park's original population, mostly of European descent. The lack of affordable housing opportunities in New York City and limited affordable housing developments has pushed many low-income, immigrant households to live in precarious quarters and sometimes in substandard conditions. Eight out of ten elementary schools in Sunset Park are overcrowded, and on average, overcrowded schools reach 143 percent of their capacity. Lack of affordable housing and school overcrowding represent pressing issues that have grown hand-in-hand and affect the immigrant community of Sunset Park most severely. School overcrowding has well-documented negative effects on academic achievement, a teacher's ability to perform, and overall school environment.

Location: Sunset Park (Community District 07), Brooklyn, New York.

Partnership Overview and Time Frame: The studio took place in the fall 2016 semester with production and dissemination of the studio's publication, *The Sunset Park Gazette,* in spring 2017.

The Design Brief: In close coordination with local organizations and stakeholders in the community, the main aim of this project-based studio was to co-produce useful knowledge of the housing and school overcrowding crisis in Sunset Park in order to create new advocacy tools and strategic proposals to address the crisis by identifying new spaces for public schools and community learning places, as well as helping disseminate participatory-based solutions to prevent school crowding in the future.

Engagement: By considering public plans, urban development trends, and housing market changes and by conducting fieldwork, participatory research, and policy analysis, students gained a broad understanding of the complex forces that influence urban growth and development in Sunset Park.

Outcomes: The students produced *The Sunset Park Gazette Vol. 1: Overcoming Overcrowded Schools*, a free publication in an accessible format that synthesizes the research and design-based concepts from their learning in the studio and has as its main audience the community of the Sunset Park neighborhood. The research was translated into Spanish and Chinese and included information about the history of Sunset Park, demographic and economic changes, local education and jobs, housing conditions and new development trends, the current transformation of the waterfront, public plans, and zoning, and how all these aspects have affected public schools in Sunset Park. The research also focused on concrete proposals to address school overcrowding with schemes designed that considered immediate, short-, medium- and long-term design solutions and policy proposals (refer to the Gazette for detailed proposals).

Implementation: *The Sunset Park Gazette Vol. 1: Overcoming Overcrowded Schools* was widely disseminated in Sunset Park in spring 2017. The research and proposals generated by the students have informed many aspects of community planning underway. Because of the work and leadership of Make Space for Quality Schools in Sunset Park and the contribution of this studio to their efforts, by spring 2017, the School Construction Authority and the Department of Education committed to the construction of four new schools in the neighborhood, a pledge that represented a significant accomplishment for the studio and community members.

Case Study No. 3:

Community Approaches to Reducing STDs (CARS) Among Youth and the "Stay Sexy, Stay Healthy, Get Checked" Campaign

The Maryland Institute College of Art (MICA) Center for Social Design

The Center for Social Design at MICA utilizes a human-centered and collaborative process to understand and define social problems, identify opportunities, generate ideas, and make tools that support positive change. The Center (originally launched as the Center for Design Practice in 2007) coordinates practice-based studios and a one-year MA in Social Design (known as MASD), and a post-graduate fellowship program funded by the Robert W. Deutsch Foundation. Practice-based studios bring students from a variety of disciplines together with outside partners from government, nonprofit, and business sectors over a sixteen-week course to address a key issue.

Partner Organization(s): This case study engaged two main organizational partners: The Center for Child and Community Health Research (CCHR) at John Hopkins Bayview Medical Center, which is dedicated to improving the lives and the communities of disadvantaged children and youth by engaging in innovative, translational public health research according to the highest scientific and ethical standards; and The Baltimore City Health Department. As the oldest continuously operating health department in the United States (formed in 1793), the department collaborates with other city agencies, health care providers, community organizations, and funders to empower all Baltimoreans with the knowledge, access, and environment to enable healthy living. It has a range of responsibility, including acute communicable diseases, animal control, chronic disease prevention, emergency preparedness, HIV/STD, maternal-child health, restaurant inspections, school health, senior services, and youth violence issues.

The MICA students also benefited from the direct engagement with a Youth Advisory Council (composed of a group of young people from areas in Baltimore most impacted by STDs) identified by project partners who brought key lived experiences to the project.

Context for the Design Challenge: Baltimore has a long history of epidemic rates of sexually transmitted diseases (STDs) and is a city with racial and ethnic disparities in STDs that are two to four times the national average. In 2012, young people represented 70 percent of new STD infections reported to the Baltimore City Health Department (BCHD), including 60 percent for gonorrhea and 70 percent for chlamydia.[28] Youth between the ages of 15–24 make up one-third of the patients visiting BCHD clinics. Although many low-cost and no-cost options for testing are available locally, the city continues to experience high rates of STDs among young people, particularly among African American youth.

Location: Baltimore, Maryland.

Partnership Overview and Time Frame: The research was conducted in a practice-based studio through the 2016–17 academic year with key components of the "Stay Sexy, Stay Healthy" campaign and environmental design interventions implemented in summer and fall 2017. The campaign was part of the MICA Center for Social Design's "Impact Initiatives," which are long-term, multi-year funded research projects.

The Design Brief: In partnership with CCHR, The Baltimore City Health Department, and Baltimore youth directly affected by the challenge, students explored how to address the high incidence of STDs among youth in Baltimore by developing design interventions striving to increase access to STD testing among young people aged 15–24 in Baltimore.

Engagement: Following a human-centered, immersive, and co-design approach with studio partners and youth stakeholders, students researched attitudes about STD testing among Baltimore youth, identified opportunities for intervention, and created youth-centered messaging and design interventions to improve the testing experience and uptake of testing among this youth demographic.

Outcomes: The fall 2016 semester of the studio generated a rich set of insights as a result of a collaborative and iterative design research process with project stakeholders. The spring 2017 semester built on these insights and initial conceptual directions to develop two design interventions. These were: (1) effective sexual health messaging in a targeted campaign for youth, the "Stay Sexy, Stay Healthy" campaign, and (2) a physical redesign and patient service design that both reimagined the physical environment of a pilot clinic site (the Eastern Clinic) with environmental graphics and welcoming spaces intended to create a positive testing experience for youth.

Implementation: All components proposed for the "Stay Sexy, Stay Healthy" campaign were fully designed during the spring 2017 studio. The campaign includes print components (postcards, posters, and stickers) and online messaging for social media. Students proposed an initial pilot rollout and trial evaluation period of the campaign to be carried out under the Baltimore City Health Department UChoose program, which was selected because it has the audience and website platform to scale the campaign. However, the implementation of the campaign's print components was pending funding allocations. As of summer 2017, the patient journey experience and physical interventions proposed by the studio had been fully implemented at the Eastern Clinic site.

Notes

1 Academic programs with a social innovation orientation include the transdisciplinary design MFA (Parsons), the MFA in social design (School of Visual Arts), masters and PhD-level programs (Design School, Carnegie Mellon), and the MDes in design for social impact (University of the Arts)—to name a few.

2 Julia Culier-Grice et al., *The Theoretical, Empirical and Policy Foundations for Building Social Innovation in Europe* (Brussels: European Commission, DG Research, 2012); Frank Moulaert et al., "Towards Alternative Model(s) of Local Innovation," *Urban Studies* 42, no. 11 (2005): 1969–90.

3 Robin Murray, Julie Caulier-Grice, and Geoff Mulgan, *The Open Book of Social Innovation* (London: National Endowment for Science, Technology and the Art, 2010).

4 Culier-Grice, *The Theoretical, Empirical and Policy Foundations.*

5 Thomas Binder et al., *Design Things* (Cambridge: The MIT Press, 2011); François Jégou and Ezio Manzini, *Collaborative Services: Social Innovation and Design for Sustainability* (Milano: Edizioni Polidesign, 2008); Ezio Manzini and Eduardo Staszowski, eds., *Public and Collaborative: Exploring the Intersection of Design, Social Innovation and Public Policy* (DESIS Network, 2013).

6 Arturo Escobar, *Designs for the Pluriverse: Radical Interdependence, Autonomy and the Making of Worlds* (Durham: Duke University Press, 2018).

7 Ibid.; Ezio Manzini, *Design: When Everybody Designs. An Introduction to Design for Social Innovation*, trans. Rachel Coad (Cambridge: MIT Press, 2015).

8 Ezio Manzini and Francesca Rizzo, "Small Projects/large Changes: Participatory Design as an Open Participated Process," *CoDesign* 7, no. 3–4 (2011): 199–215; Toni Robertson and Jesper Simonsen, "Participatory Design: An Introduction," in *Routledge International Handbook of Participatory Design*, ed. Jesper Simonsen and Toni Robertson (Thousand Oaks: Routledge, 2012); Elizabeth Sanders and Pieter Jan Stappers, *Convivial Toolbox: Generative Research for the Front End of Design* (Amsterdam: BIS, 2013); Elizabeth B. Sanders and Pieter J. Stappers, "Probes, Toolkits and Prototypes: Three Approaches to Making in Codesigning," *CoDesign* 10, no. 1 (2014): 5–14; Jesper Simonsen and Toni Robertson, eds., *Routledge International Handbook of Participatory Design* (Thousand Oaks: Routledge, 2012).

9 Simonsen and Robertson, *Routledge International Handbook of Participatory Design.* See pages 1 through 17.

10 John Dewey, *Ethics* (Read Books Limited, 2016).

11 Gregory Fernando Pappas, "To Be or to Do: John Dewey and the Great Divide in Ethics," *History of Philosophy Quarterly* 14, no. 4 (1997): 447–72.

12 Ibid.

13 Richard Buchanan, "Design Ethics," in *Encyclopedia of Technology, Science and Ethics*, ed. Carl Mitcham (New York: Macmillan Reference, 2005).

14 Ibid.

15 Case study methodology and sampling allowed us to compare insights and extend theory. See Kathleen M. Eisenhardt and Melissa E. Graebner, "Theory Building from Cases: Opportunities and Challenges," *Academy of Management Journal* 50, no. 1 (2007): 25–32; Robert K. Yin, *Case Study Research: Design and Methods* (Thousand Oaks: Sage Publications, 2014).

16 Mariana Amatullo et al., "Educating the Next Generation of Social Innovators: Designmatters at ArtCenter," in *Public Interest Design Guidebook: Curricula, Strategies and SEED Academic Case Studies*, ed. Lisa M. Abendroth and Bryan Bell (New York and London: Routledge, 2018); Mariana Amatullo et al., *LEAP Dialogues: Career Pathways in Design for Social Innovation* (Pasadena: Designmatters at ArtCenter College of Design, 2016).

17 Becky Slogeris, in interview with the author, March 2018. See also Suzanne M. Grieb et al., "Identifying Solutions to Improve the Sexually Transmitted Infections Testing Experience for Youth through Participatory Ideation," *AIDS Patient Care and STDs* 32, no. 8 (2018): 330–35.

18 Gabriela Rendón, interview with the author, March 2018.

19 The scope of the Safe Niños project benefited from a team-approach to teaching and project management, supported by the Designmatters staff: Penny Herscovitch, Daniel Gottlieb and Stella Hernandez. See also https://4eyos01khlgv2ccw28adjy2x-wpengine.netdna-ssl.com/wp-content/up loads/2016/11/SafeNinos_Complete_Web.pdf

20 Gabriela Rendón, interview with the author, March 2018.

21 Stella Hernandez, interview with the author, March 2018.

22 The Sunset Park Gazette available at sds.parsons.edu/urban/portfolio/sunset-park-gazette/

23 For a comprehensive overview of the MS in Design and Urban Ecologies at Parsons refer to www.n ewschool.edu/parsons/ms-design-urban-ecology.

24 Gabriela Rendón, interview with author, March 2018.

25 During my tenure at Designmatters, our "real-world" studios were often co-created with partners; design briefs aspired to deliver feasible and viable design proposals, with a high rate of implementation, while keeping student authorship intact.

26 Stella Hernandez, interview with the author, March 2018.

27 Becky Slogeris, in interview with the author, March 2018.

28 Grieb, "Identifying Solutions to Improve the Sexually Transmitted Infections Testing Experience for Youth."

20

Perpetuating Class Divide: The Reality of Graphic Design Internships

Kathryn Weinstein

This chapter traces the economic and political forces that shape the internship economy in graphic design, the role of industry and colleges in the perpetuation of the system, and the resulting transformation of points of entry to the profession. It concludes with three examples that foster broader participation and pathways to the profession for students who have been historically marginalized from the field.

Introduction

At art schools everywhere, design programs emerged from their dusty crawl spaces, becoming proud engines of growth for colleges and gleaming beacons of opportunity for young artists who were drawn to digital tools and were unashamed to openly consort with commerce.[1]

In the last twenty years, graphic design has evolved from a narrow, specialized profession to an expansive field encompassing a wide-ranging set of skills, activities, and tools. As curators Lupton and Blauvelt note in the exhibition catalog of *Graphic Design: Now in Production*, the transformation of the field created opportunities for colleges and universities to attract students eager to embark upon lucrative, creative careers.[2] During a period of steady decline of enrollments in the United States from 20.6 million to 19 million in 2016,[3] colleges were expanding their programs in graphic design. Between 2006 and 2016, the number of new degrees and certificates nearly doubled, with current estimates of 2,500 college programs currently offering some type of instruction in the field.[4]

Other countries show similar patterns of growth of undergraduate design programs resulting in increased numbers of degree-bearing design graduates entering the workforce. From one stand-alone design school and a handful of programs in government technical institutes in 2004, India currently has over seventy institutions teaching design at various levels. With an estimated

FIGURE 20.1 *Photo collage by Lance Goddard, sophomore at Queens College, CUNY. When asked to submit an artist statement, Lance wrote, "This image was inspired and created by my desire to make a lot of money from a graphic design career choice that I am very passionate about. The image is a representation of my future goal to become very wealthy and successful businessman out of diving into the field of the highly profitable field of graphic design." The author found it of note that a black student used an image of a white man to represent the "plunge" into the professional field of graphic design, Lance Goddard was paid for the use of his poster in this chapter. c. 2017. Courtesy of Lance Goddard.*

7,000 qualified designers working in India and approximately 5,000 students currently pursuing design degrees, the popularity of the design degree in India shows no signs of waning. The National Institute of Design reports yearly increases in entrance exam applications, reporting 10,451 applicants in 2016 for 100 available seats for incoming students.[5] Within the past decade, enrollments in design studies have increased by 10.4 percent in the United Kingdom,[6] and China, with 1,951 higher-education institutions currently offering design majors, is building on average one university per week in a concentrated effort to develop a creative economy.[7] The growth of design programs in higher education is fueled by government and student desire for financial security of graduates to meet challenges of fluctuating economies.

The growing demand that college degrees demonstrate a positive effect on social and economic mobility, as measured by career outcomes for the individual as well as for demographic groups, is shaping priorities and curricula in higher education in the United

States and beyond.[8] A 2014 New America survey finds seven out of ten students list improved employment opportunities and higher income as top reasons to attend college.[9] Rising joblessness among new university graduates in both China and India[10] led to educational reforms in higher education aimed at skilling a labor force for a growing economy and increasing the employability of graduates.[11]

Although there may be an array of factors influencing student pursuit of a graphic design degree, the decision is often inextricably linked to the conviction that the degree leads to careers in the field. Speaking from experience, design educator Juliette Cezzar[12] notes, "Maybe one out of a hundred students would even attempt to question career being the ultimate end goal of college. 'Career' is very present even in discussing individual projects and classes." Increasingly, higher-education marketers are promoting their programs as bridges to careers using the promise of college internships as a persuasive recruitment tool to prospective students as the gateway to full-time employment.[13]

Despite the US Department of Labor's 2016–26 projections of sluggish growth in graphic design employment—4 percent compared to 7 percent projected growth for all occupations[14]—students remain optimistic (or oblivious) about future career pathways in the field. Student reporter Nishan Kafle writes that the scope of graphic design is boundless as students within the major are "flooded with internship and job opportunities,"[15] reiterating what seems to be a global trend of internships as an integral stepping stone to professional practice.

Who Designs?

Students keen to enter the profession may be ill-equipped, or ignorant, of the biases based on race, ethnicity, gender, or social class to be encountered in their endeavors to embark upon careers. "Where is Our Diversity" cites the institutionalized exclusion and underachievement that circumscribe the design careers of women and minorities in Australia,[16] a description that resonates within the US graphic design profession. Cheryl D. Miller notes a range of obstacles to black designers ranging from "family hostility to their career choice, to limited financial resources for acquiring an adequate education, to the dearth of mentors able to provide guidance and employment opportunities once the education has been acquired, and to ever-present prejudice."[17] Over a quarter of a century after Miller's article and with acknowledgment of major advances in the field, Antoinette Carroll writes about the lack of demographic diversity and notes that the absence of a culture of inclusion continues to characterize the field, estimating that 86 percent of professional graphic designers in the United States are Caucasian.[18] The lack of diversity within the field is troubling, both for the impact on individuals and the field. Carroll writes persuasively, "Interconnectedness in all its forms, including technology, multiculturalism, and globalism, make diversity and inclusion more relevant than ever in design. . . . (We) must openly embrace more diverse practitioners and retain them through inclusion."[19] The Design Council echoes the sentiment, identifying increasing the diversity of the UK's design workforce, currently characterized as young and male-dominated, as a priority to maintain the vitality of the field.[20] Lack of information on the demographics of professional designers in China or India prevents the identification of a culture of inclusion or exclusion within the design workforces of these countries. However, designer and writer Aboli Joshi[21] observes that the relative newness of design careers in India coupled with the steep tuition costs of design programs yields a workforce comprised primarily of individuals from privileged backgrounds.

Internships: Launchpad or Roadblock?

In a perfect world, all students would have access to entry-level, paid jobs that don't require prior experience, and their employers would have an incentive to invest time and money in training them so that they could meet mid-level and then, high-level expectations. A good first step, though, would be for all internships to be paid.[22]

Representing a bridge between academic studies and careers, the perceived value of a college internship has shifted from an additional benefit experienced by a few to a requirement of entry-level employment as employers increasingly prioritize relevant work experience over factors such as major or grade point average.[23] Today, prospective students are encouraged to evaluate an institution's ability to provide internship opportunities with the same importance as an institution's choice of majors, cost of tuition, and availability of financial aid.[24]

By 2014, nearly two-thirds of US students surveyed participated in an internship while attending a four-year college, and 46.5 percent were unpaid positions.[25] Recent graduates quickly discover that the lack of an internship within college will likely result in the need to participate in an internship after graduation before obtaining entry-level employment. It is currently estimated that 70,000 internships are offered annually in the United Kingdom, with 40 percent of survey respondents reporting participation in an unpaid internship, and over 10,000 graduates engaged in an internship role six months after graduation.[26] The Institute for Public Policy Research analysis of internship postings found twice as many internships than advertised job vacancies within the "creative industries" sector,[27] and these internship positions often require advanced skillsets of applicants and completion of degrees. The study strongly suggests that employers are using interns in place of employees as an ongoing source of labor.

Internships are a mandated requirement of degree completion for the majority of China's undergraduate programs[28] and a common requirement of undergraduate design programs in India. Both countries typically require two internships, a summer internship, and a thesis internship within a company, and the responsibility to find an internship often falls upon the student. Both Joshi[29] and Shi[30] state that design internships (in India and China respectively) typically come with some type of financial compensation—frequently, a token amount to cover lunch and transportation costs and rarely providing a living wage. Both noted that the amount of stipend was based on the prestige and type of institution, the more prestigious the brand of the institution the greater the amount of financial compensation tied to the internship.

The Rise of Unpaid Internships

During the recession of 2008, the numbers of unpaid internships in the United States began outpacing paid internships, created by an environment where companies could find competent student and recent graduates willing and able to accept unpaid internships in the hopes of launching careers.[31] This period marked a surge in growth in college graphic design programs and graphic design graduates, creating a saturated labor pool and greater competition for fewer opportunities. Design educator Maribeth Kradel-Weitzel wrote in 2011 of the obstacles created for those who do not have the luxury of working without pay and eliminating "potential opportunities for those already at a disadvantage and exclude many important voices representing all aspects of society."[32] Despite economic recovery, highly publicized lawsuits, and increased scrutiny questioning the exploitative nature of unpaid internships, the practice continues to flourish in undergraduate programs in the United States supported by the effective lobbying efforts of colleges and six major higher-education groups.[33]

In 2011, two former interns at Fox Searchlight Pictures filed a lawsuit alleging their employer violated the Fair Labor Standards Act (FLSA) by not paying them for work they did on the movie *Black Swan*. In 2013, a court ruled in favor of the interns, finding that their roles fell short of the 2010 Department of Labor's (DOL) Rule for unpaid internships that required for-profit employers[34] not to derive "immediate advantage from the activities of the intern."[35] The court ruling raised great concern within the creative industries, resulting in some companies' decision to retroactively pay their former interns and re-examine their internship policies. As a result of a class-action lawsuit, Condé Nast agreed to pay $5.8 million in the settlement to former interns[36] and simultaneously suspend their internship program. The 2013 court decision was reversed in 2015. The court held that a "primary beneficiary" test should be used to distinguish employees from interns, requiring courts to assess whether the benefit was primarily an economic benefit to the employer or an educational benefit to the intern.[37] On January 5, 2018, the DOL issued a seven-factor "primary beneficiary" test to distinguish interns from employees, but unlike the 2010 DOL's Rule, an unpaid internship need not meet any prescribed threshold related to the list—creating a less regulated environment for unpaid internships.[38]

Under UK employment legislation, anyone who is acting as a "worker," an official employment classification, must be paid. An intern with a promise of a future contract is considered a classified "worker" but internships tied to coursework or academic degrees, within charity/voluntary organizations, or deemed as work shadowing, are excluded from "worker" classification. Despite a recent initiative of the UK government to crack down on unpaid internships, action to date of the writing of this chapter has been limited to warning letters.[39] Exacerbating the problem of regulation is the tradition of circulating high-profile internship opportunities through private networks and personal connections, hindering public scrutiny of hiring practices and creating an unfair advantage to those students with social and financial capital.

There are no laws regulating interns in India[40] and China's regulation varies by province.[41] A study of a summer internship course in Hong Kong found that over half of respondents described their summer internship working experiences as exploitative,[42] an unsettling finding and in accordance with intern claims of exploitation in other countries.

Perpetuating a Class Divide

Critics of the internship economy charge that the system perpetuates class divisions between those who can afford to work for no wage and those who cannot, and poses roadblocks to groups who are historically disadvantaged in the labor force.[43] The Strategic National Arts Alumni Project (SNAAP) survey of recent arts graduates in the United States finds that paid internships function as an important pathway to degree-related employment; former interns find employment at a faster and higher rate than students who had not participated in an internship. The SNAAP analysis found unpaid internships to be negligible on career benefits as former interns find employment at the same rate as students who did not participate in any internship, the unpaid internship experience providing little or no connection to professional networks or pathways to entry-level employment. Additionally, the study finds women, black, Hispanic/Latino, and first-generation college students disproportionately participating in unpaid internships.[44]

The imbalance between paid and unpaid internships in graphic design raises concerns about producing a class divide of the profession. Design educator Aggie Toppins describes unpaid internships as a "form of systematic exploitation. It's dangerous to both design and designers" and urges access to resources like affordable education and paid employment as points of entry for those historically marginalized from the field.[45] One study that tracked career outcomes from one graduating class of graphic design majors found a college design internship the only statistically significant factor in relation to employment levels after graduation. Students without an ongoing financial support system were the first to exit the field, suggesting a key barrier to careers in the field was a lack of financial resources that enabled individuals to pursue low or unpaid roles to gain work experience after graduation. The same study found part-time employment (or under-employment) in graphic design was more likely to be reported by graduates characterized as female, Hispanic, or immigrant.[46]

Divides within Higher Education

Students attending prestigious colleges gain the advantage of access to an established network of professional connections, often maintained and fostered by college career development resource centers. Potential employers trust the schools' ability to prepare students for the workforce, based not only on the reputation of the school, but often from a personal relationship as an alumnus. Recently developed graphic design programs lack an established professional network created by alumni, and those in public colleges lack the resources to invest in the same activities provided to students of private colleges.[47] A study of five New York City graphic design programs[48] (two public, two private not-for-profit, and one private for-profit) notes public institutions rely heavily on faculty to forge connections with industry, whereas private institutions possess greater resources to create and sustain industry relationships through an array of activities provided by career centers.[49] Of the five colleges surveyed, only the public ones required internships (and neither requires internships to be paid) within the curriculum. The private colleges encourage but do not require internships,[50] which creates a perplexing conundrum—those students who potentially have the least ability to participate in an internship while attending college *and* the least access to internship opportunities are required to participate in an internship to complete the requirements of the degree. Moreover, if the student is a woman, black, Hispanic/Latino, and/or first-generation college student, there is a greater chance that the internship is unpaid and less likely to initiate a network of professional connections or lead to entry-level employment.

Equitable Pathways

It is predicted that automation of routine tasks will collapse low-skilled jobs in graphic design, just as the personal computer eliminated paste-up artists and typesetters. The workforce will still need highly skilled designers, but the acquisition and scaffolding of skills that were once assumed to begin in college and expand as a professional may prove to be an obsolete model for tomorrow's designer. To meet the needs of a future labor force, *The Chronicle of Higher Education* proposes an expanded role for employers, collaborating with higher-education institutions to help train students for employment before graduation, noting the inherent opportunity in such partnerships for employers to identify and hire the highest performing students.[51]

In addition to keeping the curriculum current and competitive, the responsibility to create equitable access to employment may ultimately fall upon design programs, and their ability to succeed will be dependent on the institution's ability and willingness to support such programming. Three examples are presented as models that foster broader participation and pathways to the profession for students who have been historically marginalized from the field of graphic design.

Leveling the Playing Field

Although highly contested, the reserving of 52.6 percent[52] within all higher-education institutions in India for students who are socially and educationally underprivileged or belong to marginalized caste/tribes attempt to level the playing field on the first day of college. From Joshi's experience as an alumna from the renowned National Institute of Design, reservation stops mattering the moment a student steps into a classroom and she believes the policy provides an equitable pathway for design students who demonstrate talent. To ensure student success, Joshi[53] argues for greater financial aid to economically disadvantaged students throughout their studies, but she states that for those students who complete their degrees, the booming demand for designers in India creates an opportunity for new designers, regardless of background, to secure entry-level employment.

Guided Experiential Learning (GEL)

Professors Yeh and Shin have spearheaded a new initiative through the Creative Technology & Design (CT&D) program at Fashion Institute of Technology (FIT), SUNY, that fosters collaboration between the school, students, and industry. The initiative creates a design studio within the school inviting projects from high-profile industry partners. Students are selected through a rigorous portfolio review and the number of participants (ranging from four to twenty-five) is dependent on the scope of the project. Each project has its own unique framework, which is designed to maximize students' learning and, at the same time, ensure that industry partners receive innovative design solutions at the end of the project. GEL projects are co-curricular, so students do not receive grades or credits; however, they do receive a stipend from the industry partner based on the duration of the project, which may range from two weeks to one year.

Professor Yeh does not consider GEL as a replacement for the traditional internship, but rather a missing link between theoretical academic studies and the often, unforgiving professional work environments. Yeh observes:

> Some of these things just can't be taught, you have to experience it, and the GEL project framework provides a "safe space" for that. . . . An important element that separates GEL from the traditional internship is the effectiveness of teaching and learning. Some of the industry professionals are great mentors as well, but, in general, industry professionals don't have experience teaching. And to be fair, teaching is not their job.[54]

Cooperative Education

The University of Cincinnati's Cooperative (co-op) Education Program integrates professional development throughout academic programming by integrating five co-op terms alternating with traditional classroom instruction. Initiated in 1906, the communication design program was adopted into the co-op in 1968 and is a mandatory component of the degree. Throughout the five-year course of study, students are placed into five co-op placements (usually repeating two terms with two employers and one term with one employer). A one-on-one meeting is scheduled after the completion of each placement to reflect on the work experience and design a new set of goals moving forward. These meetings offer a consistent point of contact and support for the student throughout the program at a university that enrolls over 40,000 students.

The program currently serves approximately 320 communication design students working about 400 co-op placements/semesters per year. Students receive not only the experience of working in the field of their study but are fairly compensated through required stipends paid by the employer. The program is a model of a college-industry partnership that is mutually beneficial to employers and students. Barlow and Juran write,

> Employers are providing real-world opportunities for students to test their theoretical knowledge and grow their professional skills. Students are bringing to the table, a fresh perspective, boundless energy and a desire to contribute. It is a give and take situation, but the mentorship and training our employers pay forward is priceless.[55]

Conclusion

The surge of enrollments in graphic design programs has been powered by an implicit promise that the degree equips students for careers in the field, and students increasingly view higher-education institutions as responsible for creating points of entry into the profession. The ambiguity surrounding the definition of a legal internship and the failure to regulate unethical employment practices paves the way for companies to continue unpaid internships, despite research documenting the detrimental effects on career outcomes for low-income students. As the past decade has shown, industry may pay lip service to a more diverse and inclusive graphic design community, but contribute to a culture of exclusion through the perpetuation of unpaid or low paid internships—a practice supported by many colleges and higher-education groups. Colleges that have benefited from increased enrollments in design programs may soon need to factor in the cost of providing experiential learning experiences that bridge academic studies with professional careers, carrying the challenge of establishing equitable access to paid design internships for populations historically marginalized. Failure to do so will only perpetuate the status quo, creating obstacles to the profession based on socioeconomic backgrounds rather than the potential to contribute meaningfully to the field.

Notes

1 Andrew Blauvelt and Ellen Lupton, *Graphic Design: Now in Production* (Minneapolis: Walker Art Center, 2012).

2 Ibid.

3 Douglas Belkin, "U.S. Colleges Are Separating Into Winners and Losers," *The Wall Street Journal*, February 21, 2018, www.wsj.com/articles/after-decades-of-growth-colleges-find-its-survival-of-the-fittest-1519209001

4   AIGA, "AIGA Designer 2025: Why Design Education Should Pay Attention to Trends," AIGA Design Educators Community, August 21, 2017, https://educators.aiga.org/wp-content/uploads/2017/08/DESIGNER-2025-SUMMARY.pdf

5   Hrridaysh Deshpande, *The Future of Design Education in India* (New Delhi: British Council and India Design Council, 2016), www.britishcouncil.org/education/ihe/knowledge-centre/national-policies/report-future-design-education-india

6   Paul O'Prey, "Patterns and Trends in UK Higher Education 2017," Universities UK, July 21, 2017, www.universitiesuk.ac.uk/facts-and-stats/data-and-analysis/Pages/patterns-and-trends-2017.aspx; HESA, "Higher Education Student Statistics: UK, 2016/17 – Summary," HESA, January 18, 2018, www.hesa.ac.uk/news/11-01-2018/sfr247-higher-education-student-statistics

7   Chen Huagang, "Chinese Contemporary Design Education: Situations and Expectations," interview by Clive Barstow, NITRO, last modified March 2, 2018, https://nitro.edu.au/articles/chinese-contemporary-design-education-situations-and-expectations

8   Bob Hildreth, "U.S. Colleges Are Facing a Demographic and Existential Crisis," *The Huffington Post*, July 5, 2017, www.huffingtonpost.com/entry/us-colleges-are-facing-a-demographic-and-existential_us_59511619e4b0326c0a8d09e9

9   Rachel Fishman, "College Decisions Survey: Deciding to Go to College," *New America*, May 18, 2015, www.newamerica.org/education-policy/edcentral/collegedecisions

10 Yojana Sharma, "What Do You Do with Millions of Extra Graduates?" *BBC News*, July 1, 2014, www.bbc.com/news/business-28062071

11 Philip Rose, "Internships: Tapping into China's Next Generation of Talent," *Asia-Pacific Journal of Cooperative Education* 14, no. 2 (2013); Devesh Kapur and Elizabeth J. Perry, *Higher Education Reform in China and India: The Role of the State* (Cambridge: Havard-Yenching Institute, 2015), http://nrs.harvard.edu/urn-3:HUL.InstRepos:14005052

12 Juliette Cezzar, Interviewed by author, April 4, 2018.

13 Mara Einstein, "Nothing for Money and Your Work for Free: Internships and the Marketing of Higher Education," *tripleC: Communication, Capitalism & Critique. Open Access Journal for a Global Sustainable Information Society* 13, no. 2 (2015): 25–32.

14 AIGA, "AIGA Designer 2025."

15 Nishan Kafle, "QC for Best Graphic Designing," *The QC Times*, 2018.

16 Yoko Akama and Carolyn Barnes, "Where Is Our Diversity? Questions of Visibility and Representation in Australian Graphic Design," *Research Journal of the Australian Graphic Design Association* 4, no. 1 (2009): 29–40.

17 Cheryl D. Miller, "Black Designers: Missing in Action," *Print Magazine*, June 27, 2016, accessed April 22, 2018, www.printmag.com/design-culture-2/history-2/blacks-in-design-1987/. Article was reprinted on Print Magazine's website on June 27, 2016.

18 Antionette Carroll, "Diversity & Inclusion in Design: Why Do They Matter?" AIGA, n.d., www.aiga.org/diversity-and-inclusion-in-design-why-do-they-matter

19 Ibid.

20 Design Council, *The Design Economy: The Value of Design to the UK* (London: Design Council, 2015).

21 Aboli Joshi, Interviewed by author, August 22, 2018.

22 Juliette Cezzar, Interviewed by author, April 4, 2018.

23 Chronicle of Higher Education, *The role of higher education in career development: employer perceptions* (Washington: Chronicle of Higher Education, 2012), http://chronicle.com/items/biz/pdf/Employers%20Survey.pdf

24 Delece Smith-Barrow, "Plan for Internships as a College Applicant," *U.S. News & World Report*, November 16, 2017, accessed April 24, 2018, https://www.usnews.com/education/best-colleges/art icles/2017-11-16/consider-internship-opportunities-during-a-college-search

25   Edwin Koc et al., *The Class of 2014 Student Survey Report: Results from NACE's Annual Survey of College Students* (Pennsylvania: National Association of Colleges and Employers, 2014).

26 Rebecca Montacute, *Internships: Unpaid, Unadvertised, Unfair* (The Sutton Trust, 2018), accessed September 16, 2018, suttontrust.com/research-paper/internships-unpaid-unadvertised-unfair/

27 Carys Roberts, *The Inbetweeners: The New Role of Internships in the Graduate Labour Market* (London: Institute for Public Policy Research, 2017), www.ippr.org/files/publications/pdf/inbetween ers-the-new-role-of-internships_Apr2017.pdf

28 C. M. Liu, Zu L. Wang, and Ji L. Chen, "Research on Characteristics and Models of China's Cooperative Education," *Applied Mechanics and Materials* 33 (2010): 598–601.

29 Aboli Joshi, Interviewed by author, August 22, 2018.

30 Xioameng Shi, Interviewed by author, August 18, 2018.

31 Phil Gardner, "The Debate over Unpaid College Internships," Intern Bridge, January 2010, www.ceri. msu.edu/wp-content/uploads/2010/01/Intern-Bridge-Unpaid-College-Internship-Report-FINAL.pdf

32 Maribeth Kradel-Weitzel, "The Cost of Free Labor," AIGA, March 29, 2011, www.aiga.org/the-cost-of-free-labor

33   **See** American Council on Education, "ACE Brief Stresses Importance of Internships to College Students," ACE, April 9, 2014, www.acenet.edu/news-room/Pages/ACE-Brief-Stresses-Importance-of-Internships-to-College-Students.aspx

34 Not-for-profit employers are not held to the same standards pertaining to unpaid internships as for-profit employers.

35 Rebecca Greenfield, "Unpaid Internships Are Back, with the Labor Department's Blessing," *Los Angeles Times*, January 13, 2018, www.latimes.com/business/la-fi-unpaid-internships-20180112-s tory.html

36 Alan Yuhas, "Condé Nast Pays Interns $5.8m to Settle Low-pay Lawsuit," *The Guardian*, November 14, 2014, www.theguardian.com/media/2014/nov/14/conde-nast-settles-lawsuit-interns

37 Julia E. Judish and Andrew J. Lauria, "Department of Labor Changes Rules on Unpaid Internships," *Pillsbury Law*, January 1, 2018, https://www.pillsburylaw.com/en/news-and-insights/department-of-labor-changes-rules-on-unpaid-internships.html

38 Greenfield, "Unpaid Internships Are Back."

39 BBC News, "Government Steps up Action on Unpaid Internships," *BBC News*, February 9, 2018, www.bbc.com/news/business-42997400

40 Internshala, "The Internship Sector in India: Unregulated and Largely Ignored," *Internshala Blog*, July 23, 2012, https://blog.internshala.com/2012/07/unfair-internships-laws

41 Grace Yang, "Student Interns in China," *China Law Blog*, December 20, 2015, www.chinalawblo g.com/2015/12/student-interns-in-china-the-china-employment-law-issues.html

42 Iam-chong Ip, "Negotiating Educated Subjectivity: Intern Labour and Higher Education in Hong Kong," *tripleC: Communication, Capitalism & Critique. Open Access Journal for a Global Sustainable Information Society* 13, no. 2 (2015): 501–8.

43 Ross Perlin, *Intern Nation: How to Earn Nothing and Learn Little in the Brave New Economy* (New York: Verso, 2014); Elaine Swan, "The Internship Class: Subjectivity and Inequalities—Gender, Race, and Class," in *Handbook of Gendered Careers in Management: Getting in, Getting on, Getting Out*, ed. Adelina Broadbridge and Sandra L. Fielden (Cheltenham: Edward Elgar, 2015); Roberts, *The Inbetweeners*.

44 Alexandre Frenette et al., *The Internship Divide: The Promise and Challenges of Internships in the Arts* (Bloomington: Indiana University Press, 2015).

45 Aggie Toppins, "Designers, Please Pay Your Interns," *Eye on Design*, last modified January 4, 2018, https://eyeondesign.aiga.org/designers-please-pay-your-interns

46 Kathryn Weinstein, "From College to Careers: Tracking the First Two Years for Graphic Design Graduates," *The International Journal of Visual Design* 12, no. 1 (2018): 1–22.

47 Ginia Bellafante, "Community College Students Face a Very Long Road to Graduation," *The New York Times*, October 3, 2014, www.nytimes.com/2014/10/05/nyregion/community-college-s tudents-face-a-very-long-road-to-graduation.html

48 New York City College of Technology (CUNY), Pratt Institute, Cooper Union, The School of Visual Arts and Fashion Institute (FIT), SUNY.

49 Genevieve M. Hitchings, "Career Opportunities: Connecting Design Students with Industry," *Procedia - Social and Behavioral Sciences* 228 (2016): 622–27.

50 Ibid.

51 Scott Carlson, *The Future of Work: How Colleges Can Prepare Students for the Jobs Ahead* (Washington DC: Chronicle of Higher Education, 2017), 4.

52 Shikha Anand, "Reservation in Higher Education: Category Wise Student Enrollment in Universities & Colleges," *Shiksha*, June 9, 2017, www.shiksha.com/humanities-social-sciences/articles/reservat ion-in-higher-education-category-wise-student-enrollment-in-universities-colleges-blogId-14557

53 Aboli Joshi, Interviewed by author, August 29, 2018.

54 C. J. Yeh, Interviewed by author, March 20, 2018.

55 Lisa Barlow, Interviewed by author, April 3, 2018.

21

Highlighting Race Issues Through Mentoring and Design

Sabrina Hall and Anjali Menon

Graphic design can play a positive role in sharing and promoting hope and humanity in troubled times. It can serve as a tool to highlight issues such as immigration, race, and religion and encourage a meaningful discussion among young adults. As seen in the Women's March on Washington in 2017, design played a significant role in representing the emotions of thousands of protestors' posters as highlighted in the *Huffington Post* article "The Poster at the Women's March on Washington Will Be Powerful."[1] These posters are an example of how design was harnessed to give the protest a powerful visual identity and send a strong message. It is this type of positive messaging that we would like to teach young adults. They are tomorrow's leaders and decision-makers, and with guidance, they can understand and develop their own opinions on the sociopolitical issues of generations past and present. Through the AIGA/NY Mentoring Program, we can encourage and empower students to become change-makers of tomorrow.

Online environments can provide support for many but have also become a place for hostility and harassment, with damaging consequences to students. Nationwide, about 21 percent of students aged between twelve and eighteen experience bullying.[2] Additionally, a 2017 study estimated that 14.9 percent of high school students experienced cyberbullying. Online hate crimes can be as bad as—if not worse than—ones committed in person because of the speed at which the abuse can spread. A single post attacking a person can be tagged and re-tagged, being widely disseminated in a matter of hours. Furthermore, online abuse can be more isolating and hurtful, with strangers also being perpetrators. It is essential, therefore, to engage in conversations with students to correct erroneous impressions, dispel biases, and learn how to recognize and help others. Designers and design educators can help students by providing a platform to share their experiences, which can lead to learning and healing.

The Mentoring Program

The AIGA/NY Mentoring Program was keen to incorporate an open dialogue in one of its annual workshops for students and mentors. The program aims to empower students with the essential tools needed to navigate their high school careers and beyond. These tools include (but are not limited to) a sound understanding of the world of design and all that it has to offer, as well as their available options for their future careers. It also aims to instill in them key values regarding relationships with their peers and mentors, as well as the importance of personal responsibility.

We felt that crafting a workshop to help them better understand current issues relating to race relations would fit nicely into our curriculum and allow the group to explore the role that graphic design can have in educating and sparking social change.

"Design Ignites Change" is an AIGA-led initiative that supports creative professionals, as well as students, who use design thinking, to improve the lives of individuals and communities. The workshops held were part of Make Art with Purpose (MAP)'s "Dialogues on Race," a nationwide public art and design initiative that founding director, Janiel Engelstad, designed to bring conversations about racial injustice into the public spaces such as billboards, murals, and other public art made by multi-racial teams (see Figure 21.1). "'Dialogues on Race'" aime[d] to advance racial injustice-related work through media, dialogue, and practice through producing collaborative initiatives in cities throughout the United States that informed, taught, and built relationships with the goal of strengthening the multi-racial and multi-ethnic fabric of our communities."[3] In our case, the teams—each made up of a mentor and student mentee—were required to create a poster addressing race and social injustice-related themes in compelling and thought-provoking ways.

The Healing Process

Healing can be fostered through openness in dialogue. Only when we start talking about issues facing society today can we bring like-minded people together. When one person fights for change, it's a cause; when people come together as a group, it's a movement. We need more movements because movements spread awareness, and increased awareness leads us closer to a solution. Racial issues are something that the United States has and continues to face as a nation. By creating a safe space through our mentoring program, we hope to help students express, process, and understand their feelings on these issues.

Education is a powerful tool that can be used to spread awareness and teach students the right way to participate in the societal conversations at hand. As Nelson Mandela said, "Education is the most powerful weapon which you can use to change the world."[4] Education from a young age is one way to ensure that we empower our youth with the knowledge necessary to deal with the experiences that come their way. These experiences might range from online abuse related to racism, homophobia, or sexism, to abuse at home or in the classroom. These conversations can begin at home, where parents and their children discuss instances of racial prejudice that they have witnessed or even experienced. Such conversations may continue in school and in after-school programs, where classmates can talk freely about their thoughts and feelings among their peers with teachers to guide the discussion. They can also take place through art and design projects, which may serve as a more approachable means for students to discuss and better understand an otherwise "heavy" topic.

FIGURE 21.1 *Make Art with Purpose (MAP) founding director Janiel Engelstad. Courtesy of Janiel Engelstad.*

With guidance from Janeil Engelstad of MAP and graphic design firm Worldstudio, we developed a workshop that focused on race relations and inequality called "Dialogues on Race." In the process, we created a safe space for students to have conversations about these difficult and often misunderstood social topics. One of our goals was to foster social and emotional growth for the students outside of the classroom setting by working and collaborating with their peers. This setting gave the students an opportunity to begin a dialogue without fear of making mistakes or of being judged. Instead, there would be sympathy and understanding.

Part of this process was setting up guidelines that taught students how to use "I" statements. An "I" message or "I" statement is a style of communication that focuses on the feelings or beliefs of the speaker rather than thoughts and characteristics that the speaker attributes to the listener.[5] This serves as a reminder to be respectful to one another, understanding and accepting discomfort, and fostering empathy.

Project Format

At the time of the project, there were many instances of social injustice being highlighted in the media, such as the statistics of shootings of unarmed black men in 2014 and 2015. "Despite making up only 2 percent of the total US population, African American males between the ages of 15 and 34 compromised more than 15 percent of all deaths logged."[6] Young black men were nine times more likely than other Americans to be killed by police officers in 2015 according to a study by *The Guardian*.[7] "Dialogues on Race" sought to help students understand and express their thoughts on these social and racial issues, and create a space for them to express some of their heightened emotions around these police/civilian encounters. We wanted to hear students' stories, learn from their experiences, and help them vocalize how they felt. The project also served as a means for expressing emotions through creativity, how we could elicit change, and to learn to support one another as well.

The discussion was divided into two parts. We began the conversation by asking the group the following questions:

1. Have you had any experiences that you felt were unjust or offensive?
2. What are some of the racial and social injustice issues you have seen or heard about in the media?
3. Are there any issues in the media you feel passionately about?
4. Are there any issues that have affected you, your family, or your friends?
5. How do these injustices make you feel?
6. What do you want to say about these issues?
7. Do you have an idea of how you may resolve such issues?

Students were encouraged to participate with the guidance of their mentors, who took the initiative to answer some of the questions posed. The students gradually opened up to participate by sharing their experiences. We then created a second part of the conversation by providing them with themes that corresponded with their responses. These included

1. Unity
2. Police Violence
3. Social Injustice
4. Tolerance
5. Racial stereotypes
6. Unconscious bias

During the process, students were provided with examples of social injustice posters from various campaigns.[8] These campaigns were chosen as examples because they highlighted issues through thoughtful creative direction, language that was clear and effective, and featured individuals with whom our mentors and students could relate. They were also diverse in expressing how these issues affect a wide range of audience.

Project Results

The act of creating these posters allowed students to process and express their fears, concerns, hopes, and other emotions in a methodical way. As coordinators, we supported the mentors by providing them with the tools they needed to guide their students in the best way possible during the creation process. We also helped them to talk about their own fears and uncertainties in facing these topics and any experiences they wished to share. Mentors supported students while also educating themselves on many of the obstacles faced by these students—mentors were equally involved in learning and providing guidance. The students were also able to speak with greater confidence about a topic of their choice and express their feelings clearly through the art they created with the support of their peers and mentors (see Figure 21.2).

When presenting their projects, one of the tools the students used was to speak with their "I" statements. This led to students speaking about their own experiences rather than generalizing. Students were empowered within a space of trust and community, knowing that the group would not pass judgment on their designs. Students learned how to explain the concept behind their pieces and how their ideas came about. Additionally, they were able to receive helpful feedback from their peers and learned how to share the stage with others.

As AIGA/NY Mentoring Program coordinators, we learned a lot about empathy and unconscious bias from the students' experiences. These young adults had strong opinions and emotions and were affected deeply by what was happening on a daily basis in the world around them. Their curiosity to learn about how best to express their feelings in a productive and mature manner was encouraging. The students, in turn, learned how to express their fears, concerns, and hopes to others without fear of judgment. They learned that their opinions were of value and should be taken seriously. When we had the chance to regroup with the students and their mentors, we found that many had learned about the power of their own voices through the workshop. The students expressed confidence in their ability to create a meaningful piece of design, which allowed them to process a negative social event.

[racism]

PROBLEM

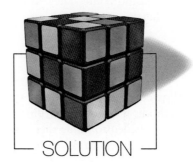

SOLUTION

FIGURE 21.2 *Poster by Leonora Gonzaque (Mentee) and Cathy Laskiewicz (Mentor). Courtesy of Leonora Gonzaque and Cathy Laskiewicz.*

This project showed us that tackling important racial and social issues is possible through design. Giving the students an "end goal" of creating a poster around the key topics allowed them to engage more during each session, knowing that they were working toward creating a work of art which they believed in, which had educational value, and which could possibly make a difference by changing biases. While some students had trepidations about expressing their emotions on social injustices, many were able to represent their feelings as an artistic concept better than in a formal "sit down" discussion.

The workshop was not without its challenges. The challenges we faced included finding ways to keep the conversation going outside of the workshop. Additionally, we realized that some students had never talked about social and/or racial injustices, and we wanted to ensure that they had a constructive space in which to do so. We hope to repeat this workshop in future years and highlight other important social and racial issues. Overall, we saw success as the students left with a deeper appreciation of the issues facing the community around them and an understanding of how to deal with them in a productive manner.

Notes

1 Katherine Brooks, "The Poster Art At The Women's March On Washington Will Be Powerful," *Huffington Post*, August 29, 2017, www.huffingtonpost.com/entry/womens-march-poster-art_us_5873c531e4b02b5f858a2b1d

2 United States Department of Justice, Office of Justice Programs, and Bureau of Justice Statistics, *National Crime Victimization Survey: School Crime Supplement, 2015* (Ann Arbor: Inter-university Consortium for Political and Social Research [distributor], 2016).

3 Make Art with Purpose, "Make Art with Purpose," MAP, n.d., http://makeartwithpurpose.net/projects.php?id=40

4 Nelson R. Mandela, "Lighting Your Way to a Better Future" (speech, Launch of Mindset Network, South Africa, July 16, 2003).

5 Good Therapy, "'I' Message, 'I' Statement," *Good Therapy*, February 14, 2018, www.goodtherapy.org/blog/psychpedia/i-message

6 Jon Swaine et al., "Young Black Men Killed by US Police at Highest Rate in Year of 1,134 Deaths," *The Guardian*, December 31, 2015, www.theguardian.com/us-news/2015/dec/31/the-counted-police-killings-2015-young-black-men

7 "The Counted: People Killed by Police in the US," *The Guardian*, June 1, 2015, www.theguardian.com/us-news/ng-interactive/2015/jun/01/the-counted-police-killings-us-database

8 Posters sourced from: thegraphicimperative.org, lookdifferent.org, and lovehasnolabels.com/

22

The Design Process is a Research Process: Students and the Ethics of Inquiry

David Gelb and Angela Norwood

Design education has long positioned itself as ethical because of its instilling in students the need to locate their practice in larger contexts to solve users' (individual and/or collective) problems. As the shift away from suggesting that well-designed, discrete artifacts provide solutions becomes reified in design programs, the role of a designer evolves to one of understanding and defining the conditions into which design can intervene and operate. Designers must understand how relevant contexts integrate and they must recognize the complexity of those relationships since "the designer's role has expanded from simply making what's requested to participating in discussions about what should be made."[1] Still, the persistence of debates about the definition and role of research among design educators manifests in students' attitudes, research tools, and orientation to making. If students misalign their project interests with inquiry-based practices, if they lose sight that the "frame of the design project is ethics, not technology,"[2] they lose the potential to give themselves an in-depth understanding through meaningful design exploration.

This study was inspired by concerns over how undergraduate students engage in primary research processes. Housed in a research university in Toronto, the students in this study are subject to ethics review board approval for projects that require human participants. As review forms adjudicators, the authors identified significant gaps between students' problem identification, appropriateness of research tools, and their agency as researchers to address their interests in ways that would result in meaningful projects. The authors sought to understand the range of student attitudes about design research. In recognition of the variety of methods and project structures available to students, they broadened their scope of inquiry beyond projects requiring ethics approval and asked the students to discuss design research in their own terms.

Research Study

The authors recruited upper-level students and their instructors for interviews through an online survey. The surveys were conducted early in the school year to capture initial attitudes and perceptions about how research would inform their projects. The follow-up interviews occurred in the second half of the year and gave students opportunities to reflect on their research activities. Of seventy-nine eligible students, thirty completed the survey questions and from this group, five participated in an interview.

A prominent theme that emerged from the data was the tendency to focus on research as a means for the express purpose of generating content to fulfill project goals. Twenty of the thirty respondents' answers to the question, "Who is design research for?" were variations on "designers, so they know what to make" or the "public, since the designed things that come out of it are for them." About one-quarter of those students acknowledged the role of research in defining the problem, so the designer can work to solve it. All these answers indicated the perception of research as informing content necessary to create solutions according to the desires and tastes of the end user.

The question, "What is the relationship between research and design work?" generated three categories of responses. Three respondents described research as being the element that separates art and design. Over one-half (seventeen) described research as the very first step in any design project. "The design process begins with research" and "it's important to gather as much research as possible at the beginning" represent the range of responses. When students believe research happens only at the project's beginning, they undermine the possibility of integrating research back into the design cycle at a later point. Ten respondents described the two—research and design practice—as being interrelated and supportive of each other. This vein of responses included several mentions of research as occurring at key points in a project, implying a process in which the design outcome responds to input throughout. These two latter categories also reflect limitations in the course structures of the program in this study. Often, there simply is not enough time to build in research in the forms of problem definition, generating design alternatives, prototypes, and user studies before the end of the course.

In the later interviews, students had more complex views of design research. Statements that referred to research as "a way to organize and formulate the design process" and "important to understand the users and people—how they interact in different situations and different objects" revealed expanded views of design research and alternative beliefs in student roles as designers and their relationship to research. However, the number of respondents who claimed never to have conducted primary research because they had not had time to do so negated the possibility that many students had been able to put their nuanced views into practice.

Concurrent to the student study, four out of six course instructors participated in both the survey and interview sessions. Reflective of a comprehensive design program, the views on research and how it is taught differ depending on the instructors' academic expertise and professional backgrounds. Instructional approaches range from directing students to use particular methods (e.g., expert interviews, audience surveys) to open-ended visual experimentation. Views around when to conduct research also varied among instructors. Responses like "research is a starting point where ideas form by looking at what has happened before" and it is "done to develop content and familiarize oneself with the topic" confirm the upfront approach of gathering material for concept development and creative direction.

Some participating instructors design their upper-level course projects to allow research to intersect at multiple intervals "based on students' interests and the way in which they want to conduct research." By actively "guiding them through the [ethics review] process" the instructor helps the students formalize their interests with disciplinary rigor. Both student and instructor then see the research plan as a tool with which to inform their work.

The study confirmed the need for primary research in design education, even though there was no consensus on its role in terms of timing, methods, or outcomes. The categories of responses from both students and instructors coalesced into two distinct conceptual models that help visualize both limitations and opportunities for expansion in design's ability to respond to current contexts.

The Ladder: A Graduated Model

With an emphasis on the project brief and ensuring that all students reach a similar product-oriented outcome, the expectation of variation in project results lies in visual differences. Students then use research as a content generator. In this model, like a ladder leading to the project outcome, all information gathered leads from one stage of the project to the next, building upon what is in place. It is a hierarchical process driven by the goals for the outcome. The higher up the ladder the student climbs in project development, the greater the risk posed by research findings or user input to dismantle the student's path to completion beyond aesthetic decisions. Research that reinforces design decisions limited to stylistic choices does not permit the intersection of design with other fields of study. The agency of the design student is diminished then, to ensuring the successful completion of an acceptable stylistic artifact. Instead, it becomes an onerous exercise to fulfill the institutions' demands, hived off from the creative aspects of the project.

In this model, primary research, particularly involving human participants requiring ethics review, may be perceived by both student and instructor as suppressing creativity. Design students know that they design artifacts for audiences. Students tend to believe that research is vital to understanding what audiences want. However, in the pursuit of an individual stylistic voice, the formal ethics review process is rarely recognized as an opportunity to inform design practice.

Network Models: Object and Relational

In a model that conceives of the problem space as an ecology into which design can exert influence, the components of a project are interconnected and adaptive to change. This arrangement of objects and their connections forms a network—a comprehensive entity comprised of individual units and their interactions. In the student's practice, the design process prioritizes either the *objects* themselves or the *relationships* between the objects (see Figure 22.1). These are two variations of the network model that both describe student agency in the design problem identification and their ability to respond to it.

The object network model pursues individual components as the highest priority in the development of a project. Emphasis is placed on the specific units (e.g., user interface, subject-matter content, visual treatment), with students recognizing that these elements are discrete but eventually must integrate and interact as a coherent whole as displayed (see Figure 22.2). As a network of objects, these items interoperate through visual devices and actions. However, their relationships to each other, or to users, are of less significance than their individual qualities. Modes of inquiry are aimed to further explore the problem space throughout the design process, and as new information is applied, these designed objects can be edited, refined, and returned into the network. Through this iterative process, the construction, revising, and rearranging of objects within the problem space can occur at various stages as the project evolves.

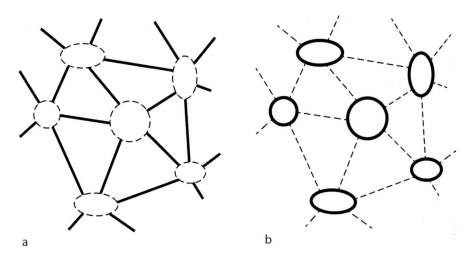

a   b

FIGURE 22.1 *Network models, c. 2018. Courtesy of David Gelb and Angela Norwood.*

The relational network model is also comprised of integrated objects, but the significant difference is rooted in the connections between objects as a means of addressing multifaceted and dynamic issues. The objects of design emerge by necessity at the intersections of these connections, made possible by foregrounding the interactions. By engaging in a design process that involves primary research that helps define the problem rather than provide content, the student can determine the design of these objects by considering the participants involved and their sociocultural contexts. Students who follow this model are often addressing problems that are many-sided and defy a concrete solution, as demonstrated in these design projects (see Figures 22.3 and 22.4). This relational network model supports the student's ability to design for variable conditions while fostering sensitivity to the limitations and opportunities for design to contribute and intervene in unexpected ways.

Both ways of interpreting these network models represent equally valid practices that are enriched by engaging in design research that propels the student beyond content seeking and creative direction. As the practice of design continues to expand beyond traditional boundaries, so has the requirement for students to explore new contexts of design. These models serve to enhance the research process through the discovery and integration of new information and begin to offer a framework for future designers facing more challenging and nuanced issues.

Conclusion

When they view primary research as content generation, students effectively limit the scope of their agency. In *The Philosophy of Design*, Glenn Parsons describes the "primacy of agency" as being a fundamental value in design.[3] He is referring to the user's agency to understand how they are being manipulated through embedded features that inherently impose certain value systems. However, the term resonates for this study for describing students developing into designers. Our notion of students' agency as designers is determined by their relationship to the design process, and whether they see it as something available to them to help shape the outcomes of their investigation. A critical aspect of design pedagogy is to instill in students an

FIGURE 22.2 *Voyager student project, c. 2018. Courtesy of Charlotte Lucas.*

awareness of both the existence of conventional value systems within the artifacts they design and simultaneously, their own agency as designers to transcend those values that are so often taken as norms.

   The authors learned that the conditions in which ethical design education can flourish are systemic and require complimentary, if not cohesive, views and attitudes from students and faculty about the potential for design research to expand the field. The authors do not claim that

FIGURE 22.3 *Chamos student project, c. 2018. Courtesy of Claudia Corrales Garrido.*

a graduated approach is unethical. They do argue that for a design program to call itself ethical—to prepare students to understand how to *act* through design rather than limit themselves to the *making* of designed artifacts[4]—it must prepare students to navigate "inherently unstable" ground.[5] An integrated approach that foregrounds primary research in the aid of problem definition in the design process expands the range of possibilities for students' roles as designers to devise unanticipated outcomes from an informed stance.

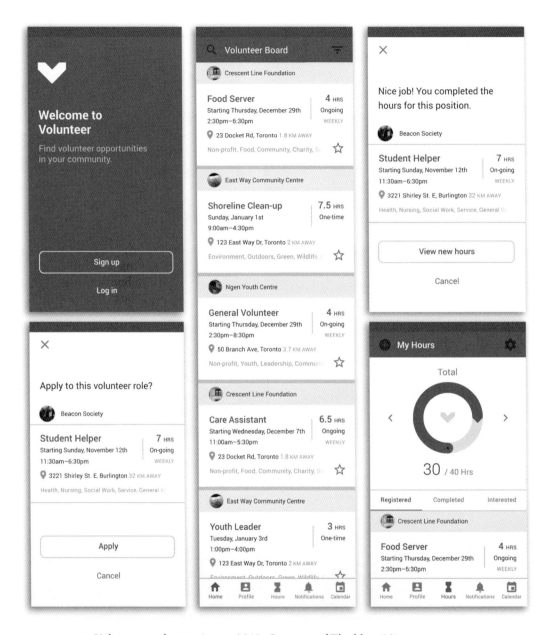

FIGURE 22.4 *Volunteer student project, c. 2018. Courtesy of Thaddeus Miya.*

Notes

1 Hugh Dubberly, "Connecting Things: Broadening Design to Include Systems, Platforms, and Product-Service Ecologies," in *Encountering Things: Design and Theories of Things*, ed. Leslie Atzmon and Prasad Boradkar (London: Bloomsbury, 2017), 153–66.

2 Alain Findeli, "Rethinking Design Education for the 21st Century: Theoretical, Methodological, and Ethical Discussion," *Design Issues* 17, no. 1 (2001): 5–17.

3 Glenn Parsons, *The Philosophy of Design* (Cambridge: Polity Press, 2016), 149.

4 Findeli, "Rethinking Design Education."

5 Meredith Davis, "Relevance in a Complex World — Icograda Design Education Manifesto," in *Icograda Design Education Manifesto*, ed. Russell Kennedy (Québec: International Council of Design, 2011): 73–75.

23

Home: The Ethics of Addressing In-equal Design

Peter Claver Fine

Sometimes, I have ruminated over whether social design projects are mere attempts to tug at the heartstrings of designers or perhaps attempts to save design itself, struggling to pull it ashore by those same thin heartstrings. I began writing this as an examination of a statewide project on homelessness done by a senior graphic design class I taught in 2015. Since then, the meaning of the project has evolved for me and with it, a desire to plumb the utility, the beauty, and the seeming futility of designing for good. Though I had worked on other social design projects, this was the first where I really engaged with what I call "in-equal design." I wrote the following in *Sustainable Graphic Design: Principles and Practice* to describe in-equal design projects:

> Projects like this raise the question of *value* where often no apparent goods possessing any exchange value exist and where people possess needs that no accounting can calculate. If design only defines things by their exchange value, it will find no value in people without the resources or the ability to produce goods for trade. Designers must, if they are to extend the work of graphic design beyond the theoretical and the purely profitable, see people as the principal resource and their creativity as the energy source for innovations that are profitable beyond a balance sheet.[1]

I want to be clear; projects that move beyond a classroom are hard, so any success or profits are hard won and often just as difficult to quantify. Through this project, I learned just how hard, partly because it raised an unforeseen ethical quandary for me personally. I want to take some time here in this chapter to talk more about the *in-equality* of design and the balancing act required if designers address it.

Baked into design, at least as I see it, is always the promise of doing some good or at least contributing something to some larger good even if only a little bit at a time. Despite whatever little success may be found or whatever failures may occur, some success is guaranteed by virtue of designing something for someone, or some group of persons. I should state that in my past writing, I made the case that failure is allowable in projects where non-prescriptive learning and experimentation are encouraged—in fact, it is quite relevant. In the case of this project, I, like my students, found myself outside of my comfort zone, somewhere between success and failure and really wondering how far to keep nudging students outside of theirs. Despite my best intentions, many of the social design projects I have initiated with students never came off as intended, succeeded in part, remained unfinished, or simply ended with the semester or the assignment. Optimistically, despite this, I have continued to seek them out and engage with others to see them through.

This particular social design project on homelessness was by standards of a graphic design course largely successful, but it did not acquire the legs to truly succeed beyond the classroom or beyond the limits of graphic design to then fully address in-equal design. This had to do with complications and limits beyond my control causing me to consider whether I should or could, ethically speaking, continue working on these types of projects despite my conviction that they were essential to holistic and human-centered design teaching and practice. If they were not being fully realized, perhaps the students and those we attempted to assist though design were not being well served. Victor Papanek thought that no matter whatever impossibilities might arise, design students should be exposed to thinking ethically about the inequality of design produced by capitalism.

> Even if the corporate greed of many design offices makes this kind of design impossible, students should at least be encouraged to work in this manner. For in showing students new areas of engagement, we may set up alternate patterns of thinking about design problems. We may help them to develop the kind of social and moral responsibility that is needed in design.[2]

I still very much want student projects to holistically address *in-equality* and confront the narrow confines of graphic design's assumed limitations, especially those imposed by the marketplace to find new ways of thinking about design. This project, serving the homeless, supplied these very expectations, which is why I chose to pursue it despite a consistent record of dissatisfaction on my part. It serves a population who are outside the marketplace, often entirely unable to labor, trade their labor for a wage, or maintain their relationship to earning and consuming in any consistent way. These students were learning design under affluent conditions and in almost every individual case, there was no sense of scarcity; they were now addressing the needs of those lacking even a roof over their heads. The homeless, on the other hand, do not possess any of the social or creative capital that my students do or that I do as an educator. In the case of the homeless, little or nothing is designed for them and literally speaking, they do not count in systems of design dependent on consumer capitalism. In many of the social design projects I have done with students, there was still some service or product to promote graphically, which would look like and perform as graphic design.

The overall low visibility of homelessness in Wyoming—a very large state with a population of just over half a million—made direct research a challenge, adding to the acute constraints that arose almost immediately in the research phase forcing changes to our approach. We were unable to conduct interviews with clients due to confidentiality, and there were few available local service providers to visit, including only one local shelter, a domestic violence shelter for women and children. The students, in general, did not initially appear to be interested in how graphic design could be used to address inequality, unlike my previous experience. In the past, student populations in the three other states where I had taught were enthusiastic about how sustainability and social design projects could change the way they thought about the nature of design. I was apprehensive as well because this population was also resistant to collaborative, semester-long projects even when it was made clear to them how a variety of different types of forms, media, and approaches would be used to produce distinct projects within the whole.

Two epiphanies happened in the course of the project, one which was positive and instructive, and another that made the whole enterprise seem problematic. In a discussion conducted by Paul Heimer, the director of the Wyoming Homelessness Collaborative, the "housing first" model, pioneered by Utah that the WHC was also proposing, came up. It was clear that some of the students were slightly incensed by the idea that the homeless would be housed regardless of present or future ability to pay for housing or contribute economically at all to the state. Paul led the group through one student's experiences with housing, asking her questions about how her parents were able to buy a home based on a subsidized federal loan system favoring the majority White population of the United States. Coming from an economically stable background in a suburban environment, she and the other students had never considered that they might have benefited from government help and perhaps had taken their middle-class status as somehow intrinsic to who they were, rather than a benefit of their economic and social class. This vital moment in the course connected the student's experience of a life with economic advantages, with the reality of how people living without those advantages are systematically excluded and that in a sense, this inequality occurs "by design."

The biggest hitch came at the semester's midpoint when we decided that the class should focus on developing a specific service-design solution for the local shelter for women and children suffering from homelessness due to domestic violence. We decided to focus on this facility because it was the only homeless shelter in the city of Laramie and where we had access to a former art student working for the shelter, able to provide insights through presentations and discussions. Within a short time, two students in the class revealed to me that they had recently suffered emotional abuse by romantic partners and would be unable to continue discussing the many nuances of domestic abuse in the immediate aftermath of their experiences. I briefly considered whether I should divide the small class of eight students in two and pursue a second project to reduce these students' exposure to such highly traumatic, personal experiences. I had to weigh the ethics of pursuing the subject at all beyond the research phase and basic graphic design deliverables. I normally would have seen this as a minor bump in the road and then made some reasonable adjustments to my expectations.

As it was, I too became a little undone by the subject matter, having been caught up in the same problem as a young child, an experience I had largely suppressed and rationalized as a surprise trip to a hotel in downtown Milwaukee where I got to watch reruns on the local UHF channel. I surprised myself for having suppressed my own experiences and embraced the project as if I had never been affected by domestic violence. I can, in fact, recall some of the events of that period of my life, beginning with a full day away from the house with my Mother and siblings, which I knew at the time was for the purpose of avoiding my father. I can recall in varying degrees of detail; returning for dinner on a warm day and my father coming home in the evening, quite drunk, slamming his hands on the table and shouting. Next, I can remember looking out the kitchen window from the second floor of the flat to see my mother running north on Oakland Avenue away from the back steps and her looking back over her shoulder at me. I assume I must have called down to her for her to turn her head back toward me. I then remember her coming in the front door the following morning and craning her head up the stairs at me looking down, where I must have heard her and was anticipating her return. What followed I can remember little of except staying at the hotel and the warm air and bright light common only to summer in such a cold climate. I know there were visits at various times by the police, called to interrupt the violence and a return to normal life. Somehow, in the intervening years, I had trivialized the events of that time, serious events affecting me directly and personally but which I was by late adulthood ignoring despite engaging directly with a project to provide services for people just like myself. The following year included a long separation from both my parents while living with an aunt in Kansas City while my parents divorced. I had experienced that liminal space between home and what lies outside of it and of being together with family and still separated from them.

In the end, the element I had not considered was myself and my emotional limitations; even those I had not considered might arise if I wanted to tackle tough subjects and address them through design. Excluding myself, I may have normally considered the ethics of the situation and divided the students into different groups to focus on other aspects of homelessness, but I found myself at sea emotionally. I remained stunned for several days and began to consider the ethics of exposing students and my own self to destabilizing subject matter that is complex and represents persistent, seemingly intractable social issues. The project stalled as I considered various solutions but, finally, I had to abandon the service-design component with hopes of returning to it at another time. I should say that in my writing, I have made the case for teaching to one's strengths when tackling thorny design problems even if this reveals one's own weaknesses. I think I was unprepared to deal with personal issues of such a traumatic nature. I was considering only the potential gaps in my own professional knowledge and experience over many years of design education, practice, and teaching—not the gaps that would reveal my own vulnerabilities. I am not sure I really understood the degree to which pedagogy is personal and not just a case of offering a critical point of view as a designer.

Despite the project not fully addressing the systemic issues that cause homelessness, it did make clear that ethics remain central to any design problem and this centers on the personal and intimate aspects of one's own life. The more profound moments in the class came not from designing alone but the process of designing and encountering for whom the how, why, when, and where from design matters. These variables, as it turned out, included ourselves, as well as some unplanned but not-entirely unexpected positive outcomes. The students proved articulate and empathetic when interviewed for the video shot and produced by my colleague Adam Herrera, showing the project had affected their exposure to complex socioeconomic issues generally limited by their relative isolation from urban centers. The posters and campaigns, focusing on the concept of home in conjunction with an annual statewide count of the homeless, were sensitive and elicited a compassionate and heartfelt response from viewers. Through this project, students were able to realize that design has an autonomous function that they can employ to assert their agency as designers to affect positive change without a prompt from a client but wherever they may see a need. It also created awareness for the first time among many in the state that graphic design as a discipline has value to local communities beyond providing typical graphic design outcomes. This is especially important in a state with one university and one graphic design program. The outcomes were by definition "good design" but not necessarily comprehensive enough to solve for in-equal design, a much broader definition that does not just address complex issues, but the designer's own relationship to complexity itself.

Notes

1   Peter Claver Fine, *Sustainable Graphic Design: Principles and Practices* (London: Bloomsbury, 2016), 90.

2   Victor Papanek, *Design for the Real World: Human Ecology and Social Change* (London: Thames & Hudson, 1972), 80–81.

24

Threading Ethics in a Design Curriculum

Paul J. Nini

Introduction

Design students' learning experiences in college-level curricula play a major role in shaping their careers. The approaches and underlying philosophies to which students are exposed can lead to specific opportunities in the field and help shape their mindsets as practitioners. While studies in traditional design disciplines concerned with products, spaces, and messages are still popular, there is also increasing student and institutional interest in educational programs that address issues of ethics in practice. This situation often presents educators with the challenge of incorporating such issues into existing design curricula.

The author and his faculty colleagues in the Department of Design at The Ohio State University have constructed an approach over several years where ethical concerns have been "threaded" into their programs.[1] Specifically, various issues are addressed over a program's sequence in a purposeful manner so that students are exposed to potential ethical choices in a variety of contexts. The focus of this chapter is geared toward sharing information concerning this approach primarily with the design education community, though the author hopes that any resulting insights will also be helpful to students and working designers who may wish to apply similar considerations.

What Do We Mean by "Ethical" Design?

The *Oxford Dictionaries* define "ethics" as "moral principles that govern a person's behavior or the conducting of an activity."[2] There are, of course, many interpretations of how this definition might be applied to design activities. Typically, design professional societies have framed ethics in the context of responsibilities to both clients and fellow professionals. For instance, the "Standards of professional practice" section of graphic design professional organization AIGA's online publication *Design Business + Ethics*[3] includes passages titled "The designer's responsibility to clients" and "The designer's responsibility to other designers." The first covers issues such as confidentiality of client information and potential conflicts of interest by consulting with competing businesses. The second concerns itself with issues related to fair competition among designers, honoring intellectual copyrights of other creators, etc. All of these are, of course, important ongoing issues and have traditionally been included in statements of professional ethics from societies representing multiple design disciplines throughout the world.

In 2004, the author published a piece on the AIGA website titled "In Search of Ethics in Graphic Design,"[4] which sought to prompt an expansion of the organization's *Design Business + Ethics* publication to address broader ethical issues. Following is a passage from that piece. Please note that the final three statements below were adapted from codes authored by ICSID, the International Council of Societies of Industrial Design, now known as the World Design Organization (WDO),[5] and the International Association of Business Communicators (IABC).[6] Of the many professional codes referenced at that time, these two groups were among the few to include any significant statements concerning responsibilities to the public.

The Designer's Responsibility to Audience Members and Users:

- Designers must recognize the need to include audience members and users whenever possible in the process of developing effective communications and to act as an advocate for their concerns to the client.

- The Designer's main concern must be to create communications that are helpful to audiences and users and that meet their needs with dignity and respect. Any communication created by a designer that intentionally misleads or confuses must be viewed as a negative reflection on the profession.

- Designers must not knowingly use information obtained from audience members or users in an unethical manner to produce communications that are unduly manipulative or harmful in their effect.

- Designers must advocate and thoughtfully consider the needs of all potential audiences and users, particularly those with limited abilities such as the elderly and physically challenged.

- Designers must recognize that their work contributes to the wellbeing of the public, particularly concerning health and safety and must not consciously act in a manner contradictory to this wellbeing.

- Designers uphold the credibility and dignity of their profession by practicing honest, candid and timely communication and by fostering the free flow of essential information in accord with the public interest.

Since the publication of that piece, significant discussion among the design professions has occurred, and the AIGA *Design Business + Ethics* publication has been updated to now include passages titled "The designer's responsibility to the public" and "The designer's responsibility to society and the environment." While both entries are somewhat general, they do address important issues and represent an example of a good-faith effort by one professional design society to promote potentially more informed and ethical behavior of its members.

A History of Advocacy for Ethics in Design

Notably, there have been several examples of individuals and groups throughout the history of the modern-day design professions that have promoted their visions of ethical practice. Many of these figures are fairly well documented, and the discussion of each here will be limited.

An important early effort is the *First Thing First Manifesto*,[7] published in 1964 by Ken Garland and signed by a group of British graphic designers, photographers, and students. They proposed that their efforts would be better spent on design that would "promote our trade, our education, our culture, and our greater awareness of the world." They were also critical of the advertising industry that had co-opted designers' talents to sell trivial things such as "cat food, stomach powders, detergent, hair-restorer, [and] striped toothpaste." The manifesto was then shared more widely, being published in *The Guardian* newspaper and other national publications. This effort was also taken up again in 2000 when an updated version appeared in the UK publication *Eye*[8] and was signed by a large international group of well-known graphic designers.

One of the more controversial individuals who advocated for a more ethical approach was the late industrial designer and educator Victor Papanek, who wrote the following in 1971, in his book *Design for the Real World*:

Advertising design, in persuading people to buy things they don't need, with money they don't have, in order to impress others who don't care, is probably the phoniest field in existence today. Industrial design, by concocting the tawdry idiocies hawked by advertisers, comes a close second.[9]

He also suggested a fairly radical model of practice, where designers would devote their efforts mainly to educational and health issues and play a significant role in advancing technologies helpful to those in the developing world. While there has been greater involvement by designers in these areas of practice since that time, much design activity still appears to contribute to consumer culture and over-consumption, as Papanek noted.

Well-known graphic designer Milton Glaser had the following to say about ethical issues, quoted from a 2016 interview with the UK web publication *It's Nice That*:

Your obligation is to the client, and not necessarily the public. In some cases, you're encouraging people to buy things that they don't need, or encouraging them to move in a direction that does not serve them. Frequently in advertising—and PR and journalism as well—we have to persuade people to do things that we don't really believe in and that they don't really believe in. Should you participate in something that encourages people to do something that is not good for them?[10]

Glaser appears to have had an ongoing concern with ethical considerations related to design. As one example, in a speech delivered at the AIGA 2002 Voice Conference,[11] he noted that "in the new AIGA's code of ethics, there is a significant amount of useful information about appropriate behavior towards clients and other designers, but not a word about a designer's relationship to the public." In fact, it was this statement that prompted the author to propose changes to the AIGA *Design Business + Ethics* publication as discussed earlier.

Another important figure in defining ethics in design is educator Jorge Frascara, whose 1988 article "Graphic Design: Fine Art or Social Science?" appeared in the journal *Design Issues*.[12] He urged graphic designers to move beyond issues of visual style and to consider their impact on the public. He proposed the following list of considerations:

Social responsibility in graphic design is a concern for the following:

- The impact of all visual communication on the community and the way its content influences people.

- The impact of all visual communication on the visual environment.
- The need to ensure that communications related to the safety of the community are properly implemented.

While Frascara addresses graphic design specifically in this article, the principles raised apply equally well to other design outcomes such as spaces, products, services, experiences, etc., and seem to suggest a general approach to ethics in design.

Human-centric Research and Ethical Design

If design efforts are to positively impact societies and communities, then efforts to understand people's needs and aspirations are required. Toward such ends, many of the design disciplines have embraced human-centric research approaches as significant parts of their practices. Today, it is common to see job titles such as "design researcher," and "user experience researcher," alongside traditional design position announcements. In fact, a recent web-search of the first term resulted in over 700 related job listings on the *LinkedIn* professional networking site[13]—a remarkable number for design roles that were uncommon years ago.

The design and innovation firm IDEO was an early adopter of a human-centered approach in design practice and has done much to popularize it through the various writings of the firm's principals. One such example is the *Human-Centered Design Toolkit,*[14] available as a free download via their website. IDEO's Jane Fulton Suri[15] is an early pioneer in this area along with the author's faculty colleague at the Department of Design at The Ohio State University, Elizabeth B.-N. Sanders, Ph.D., one of the first social scientists to work as a design researcher in the 1980s.

Fulton Suri, Sanders, and their various collaborators have also contributed to the development of many of the basic approaches used today in human-centric design research, including listening to what people say, observing what they do, and allowing them to make things to express aspirations for designed outcomes that serve their needs in a better way.[16] Sanders' book with coauthor Pieter Jan Stappers, *Convivial Toolbox: Generative Research for the Front End of Design,*[17] is a substantial guide for incorporating participatory design research activities in the design process.

While the human-centric research approach in design has been applied widely in commerce to develop innovative and effective products, spaces, messages, services, etc., it has also been used increasingly in "social innovation design," an emerging area of practice. One example of an education program devoted to this area is the MFA in Design for Social Innovation at The School of Visual Arts in New York City, chaired by Cheryl Heller, who states on the program's website:

Social Design is the creation of new social conditions—in cities, corporate cultures or communities—resulting in increased creativity, equity, social justice, greater resilience, and a healthy connection to nature. It is relevant to every business, government, city, neighborhood, and individual. It uses systems design, critical thinking, strategy, game mechanics, social movement design, collective leadership, imagination, and beauty to move people to think differently and become more resilient and resourceful themselves.[18]

This type of practice requires designers to collaborate closely with others from many disciplines— such as individuals typically found in government, nonprofits and NGOs, for-profit businesses, etc.—and the outcomes typically serve a broad spectrum of people. The scales of the problems addressed are often greater than those found in more traditional design projects and can involve a variety of coordinated efforts on many fronts that evolve over time. Some design consultancies also devote a portion of their efforts to this area, such as IDEO's *OpenIDEO*[19] web-platform that allows the firm to collaborate with a community of partners on a variety of projects. Social innovation design is a potentially more ambitious and complex undertaking that has drawn great interest from students and younger designers who wish to more positively impact the world through their developing design practices.

Preparing Students for "Ethical" Design Approaches

There are many possibilities for embedding content related to ethical issues in design curricula. At the Department of Design at The Ohio State University, we employ an approach where complementary content areas related to ethics are "threaded" through the various courses in our programs so that they can be strengthened and reinforced over time. Our current undergraduate programs in industrial design, interior design, and visual communication design are also highly interdisciplinary and include significant curricular overlap. There is a strong belief that students in our three programs should have a foundational knowledge of each discipline, and should be comfortable working with each other to create design solutions that successfully integrate products, spaces, messages, etc. There is also a substantial history of teaching human-centric design research courses and then employing those approaches in our studio courses—being, along with the Art Center College of Design in Pasadena, one of the few US design schools to have consistently integrated this subject in our curricula.[20]

Also, we attempt to enable a shift in mindset with our undergraduate students over their four-year experience in our programs—from thinking that design is mainly about creating an expressive visual form, to understanding that design foremost serves people, and can also be a proactive means to positively impact society. Our course sequences begin with students from the three programs mixed together in all first-year foundations courses. The general concept of "responsibility to others" is introduced to undergraduate students at that point—simply by stressing that there will always be people interpreting, experiencing, and using the things that they create. Projects throughout the curriculum include requirements that students identify those their designs will serve, interact with those people, and incorporate their feedback into the design development process.

Curricular Threads in Our Programs

Students in the three undergraduate programs are again mixed together after the first year and take two courses that are dedicated to human-centric design research, one in the second year, and another in the third year of studies. The first course deals with *evaluative* research[21] where student teams identify problems that occur in daily life. They often observe people experiencing such issues, and survey them to understand the specifics of what could be improved. Prototype designs are developed, and students then conduct an iterative process, having people evaluate a series of further-refined versions.

The second course focuses on *generative* research,[22] which typically allows stakeholders to contribute fully to design directions. Students often employ participatory, co-design research approaches, working closely with those involved to discover previously unmet needs. They then continue to work to develop design outcomes significantly shaped by the people who will ultimately experience them in use.

Each of the three undergraduate programs also provides discipline-specific course sequences that embed related content areas. For instance, the visual communication design program, in which the author mainly teaches, provides a thread over all four years of study that reinforces content related to the subject of User Experience (UX) Design.[23] Since this area of activity is particularly applicable to industrial design and visual communication design students, we introduce basic UX concepts during foundation studies, when all of the disciplines are mixed together in the courses. From there, the visual communication design program includes increasingly complex UX subject matter over the next three years—mainly through a sequence of media courses that involve designing for digital technologies, and include activities such as developing use scenarios and personas, conducting usability testing, etc.

The main sequence of visual communication design studio courses over years two, three, and four also address a variety of traditional practice activities—such as brand development, information design, packaging, environmental graphic design, etc. The third year also includes a collaborative studio experience where students from the three programs work in teams to develop more ambitious projects that integrate products, messages, spaces, services, etc. In all cases, human-centric research approaches are employed in both business and social innovation design contexts, with the goal of better serving those who will experience any designed outcomes. Likewise, a seminar course devoted to a variety of topics related to "designing for social good" exposes students to important readings, theories, and directions surrounding ethical issues. Undergraduate design students then create senior thesis projects in the fourth year, informed by both the seminar course and previous course experiences that have provided a grounding for ethical approaches to their work.

A similar seminar course for graduate students gives them the opportunity to explore potentially more ethical modes of practice than were experienced previously in the profession, and to incorporate those interests in longer-term, master-level research and writing efforts. As our graduate program is interdisciplinary in focus, students are encouraged to pursue academic research to advance issues applicable to all design disciplines—ethical issues being one of many broad topical areas.

Example of Student Projects

Following is an example of a visual communication design student's senior thesis project, which occurs over two-course experiences in the academic year. The first semester's course is devoted to identifying a problem area and conducting research with those involved to define a basic project direction. In the second term, the project is developed in detail, documented and exhibited. This student developed a responsive website named *Ballot* to address low voter turnout in young US adults. By working with this group, he determined that the system must include the ability to register to vote or update one's registration; nonpartisan information to make informed choices on issues and candidates; a complete checklist of intended voting to take into the ballot; and GPS information on voting location. While not implemented, the project provides a significant model for how voting could be made more convenient for this technology-savvy generation.

Two exploratory projects from graduate students in the previously mentioned seminar course are also shown. The first is a running shoe that combines an easily replaced, eco-friendly sole with a long-lasting, 3D-printed, woven "upper" piece that can be recycled after a considerably

FIGURE 24.1 *Ballot responsive website and its four main functions. Designer: Michael Booher.*

longer than normal use-life. The second project addresses young adults that often move from place to place, by proposing a group of "semi-nomadic" furniture pieces[24] (such as the table shown here) that can be easily assembled, disassembled, and flat-packed in their original packaging. As with the previous example, these projects have not been implemented, but do represent important future directions.

Conclusion

The programs, courses, subject matters, and ethical concerns that have been described are specific to the curriculum of one academic unit in a US public institution of higher learning.

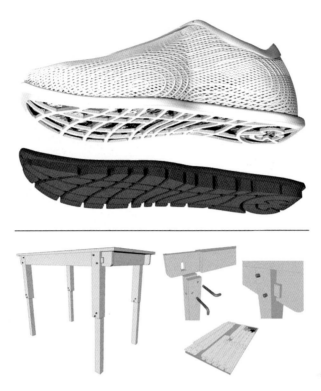

FIGURE 24.2 *Eco-friendly running shoe (top). Designer: Erika Braun. Semi-nomadic table (bottom). Designer: David McKenzie.*

Other types of educational programs exist in other contexts, and those faculty members would undoubtedly make different decisions on how to best integrate such issues into their unique situations and curricula. Regardless, the opportunity to embed ethical issues in design education programs exists and those educators who wish to provide this added dimension of learning to their students should embrace it.

In another piece published on the AIGA website titled "Graphic Design Family Values," the author noted:

> Being a professional designer means in part that we adopt values that are at the core of how we practice. Our profession is diverse, and there are varying beliefs that are reflected in our education programs. It's time for us as design educators to make the values of our programs obvious. Our students deserve to know a bit more about the kind of family they're joining when they embark on their design careers.[25]

Discussions concerning specific ethical issues to address, and what values to reflect in a curriculum should occur among faculty members so that a planned and cohesive approach can result. As educators, we can help shape our students' careers beyond the traditional subject matters of professional practices. At its best, design education leads the way to new areas for the profession to explore and develop. Ethics in design is one significant area deserving further consideration by all concerned.

Notes

1 T. J. Newcomb, B. R. Murphy, and J. M. Berkson, "Curricular Threads: Integrated Themes from Introductory to Capstone Courses," *Natural Resources and Environmental Issues* 9, no. 29 (2002): 32.

2 Oxford Dictionaries, "Definition of Ethics in English," *Oxford Dictionaries*, accessed March 15, 2018, https://en.oxforddictionaries.com/definition/ethics

3 AIGA, "Design Business and Ethics," *AIGA*, last modified 2009, www.aiga.org/design-business-and-ethics

4 Paul Nini, "In Search of Ethics in Graphic Design," *AIGA*, August 16, 2004, www.aiga.org/in-search-of-ethics-in-graphic-design

5 World Design Organization, "Code of Professional Ethics," *WDO*, n.d., http://uploads.wdo.org.s3.amazonaws.com/ProfessionalPractice/WDO_CodeofEthics.pdf

6 International Association of Business Communicators, "Code of Ethics for Professional Communicators," *IABC*, last modified 2004, iabc.com/about-us/governance/code-of-ethics

7 Victor J. Papanek, *Design for the Real World: Human Ecology and Social Change* (Chicago: Chicago Review Press, 2005).

8 Ken Garland, "First Things First Manifesto 2000," *Eye Magazine*, 1999, www.eyemagazine.com/feature/article/first-things-first-manifesto-2000

9 Ken Garland, "First Things First 1964 Manifesto," 1964, kengarland.co.uk/KG-published-writing/first-things-first

10 Nathalie Olah, "Milton Glaser: We Talk Drawing, Ethics, Shakespeare and Trump with the Graphic Design Legend," *It's Nice That*, May 17, 2016, www.itsnicethat.com/features/milton-glaser-ethics-design-170516

11 Milton Glaser, "This is what I have learned" (Paper presented at *Voice: AIGA National Design Conference*, New York, March 23, 2002).

12 Jorge Frascara, "Graphic Design: Fine Art or Social Science?" *Design Issues* 5, no. 1 (1988): 21–22.

13 "Design Researcher Jobs," *LinkedIn*, accessed March 15, 2018, linkedin.com/jobs/design-researcher-jobs

14 "Design Kit: The Human-Centered Design Toolkit," *IDEO*, August 31, 2018, ideo.com/post/design-kit

15 Jane Fulton Suri, "Interview with Jane Fulton Suri, Executive Design Director at IDEO," by DesignBoom, *DesignBoom*, April 25, 2016, designboom.com/design/jane-fulton-suri-interview-ideo-little-book-of-design-research-ethics-04-25-2016/

16 Elizabeth B. N. Sanders, "From User-centered to Participatory Design Approaches," in *Design and the Social Sciences: Making Connections*, ed. Jorge Frascara (London: Taylor & Francis, 2002).

17 Elizabeth B. N. Sanders and Pieter Jan Stappers, *Convivial Toolbox: Generative Research for the Front End of Design* (Amsterdam: BIS, 2014).

18 School of Visual Arts, "DSI/Social Design," date?, dsi.sva.edu

19 "Social Impact Powered by Design Thinking," *OpenIDEO*, accessed March 15, 2018, www.openideo.com

20 Katherine Bennett and Elizabeth Sanders, "Specialized Research Courses for Design Undergraduates," *IDSA Innovation* 33, no. 4 (2014): 40–41.

21 Liz Sanders, "ON MODELING: An Evolving Map of Design Practice and Design Research," *ACM Interactions* 15, no. 6 (2008): 13.

22 Ibid.

23 "What is User Experience (UX) Design?" *The Interaction Design Foundation*, accessed March 15, 2018, interaction-design.org/literature/topics/ux-design/

24 Rain Noe, "'Nomadic Furniture:' DIY Designs from the 1970s," *Core77*, November 9, 2015, www.core77.com/posts/42562/Nomadic-Furniture-DIY-Designs-from-the-1970s

25 Paul Nini, "Graphic Design Family Values," *AIGA*, last modified January 27, 2005, www.aiga.org/graphic-design-family-values

BIBLIOGRAPHY

Adar, Eytan, Desney S. Tan, and Jaime Teevan. "Benevolent Deception in Human Computer Interaction." In *Proceedings of the 2013 CHI Conference on Human Factors in Computing Systems*, edited by Orji Rita, Mandryk Regan, Vassileva Julita, and Gerling Kathrin, 1863. Paris: ACM, 2013.

Adno, Michael. "Robert Moses's Jones Beach." *Curbed NY,* June 21, 2017. https://ny.curbed.com/201 7/6/21/15838436/robert-moses-jones-beach-history-new-york-city.

Agamben, Giorgio. *Potentialities: Collected Essays in Philosophy*. Translated by Daniel Heller-Roazen. Stanford: Stanford University Press, 1999.

Agamben, Giorgio. *The Coming Community*. Translated by Michael Hardt. Minneapolis: University of Minnesota Press, 1993.

Aicher, Otl. *The World as Design*. Berlin: Ernst, Wilhelm & Sohn, 1994.

AIGA. "AIGA Designer 2025: Why Design Education Should Pay Attention to Trends." AIGA Design Educators Community, August 21, 2017. https://educators.aiga.org/wp-content/uploads/2017/08/D ESIGNER-2025-SUMMARY.pdf.

AIGA. "AIGA Standards of Professional Practice." AIGA. November 2010. www.aiga.org/standards-pr ofessional-practice.

Akama, Yoko, and Carolyn Barnes. "Where Is Our Diversity? Questions of Visibility and Representation in Australian Graphic Design." *Research Journal of the Australian Graphic Design Association* 4, no. 1 (2009), 29–40.

Amatullo, Mariana, Bryan Boyer, Liz Danzico, and Andrew Shea. *LEAP Dialogues: Career Pathways in Design for Social Innovation*. Pasadena: Designmatters at ArtCenter College of Design, 2016.

Amatullo, Mariana, Dan Gottlieb, Penny Herscovitch, and Susannah Ramshaw. "Educating the Next Generation of Social Innovators: Designmatters at ArtCenter." In *Public Interest Design Guidebook: Curricula, Strategies and SEED Academic Case Studies*, edited by Lisa M. Abendroth and Bryan Bell. London: Routledge, 2018.

Amatullo, Mariana, Penny Herscovitch, and Stella Hernadez. "Safe Niños, Designing Empathic Environments for Child Survivors." In Cumulus Working Papers 33/16: Cumulus Hong Kong 2016 – *Open Design for E-very-thing*, edited by Cecile Kung, Elita Lam, and Yanki Lee, 250–53. Hong Kong: Hong Kong Design Institute, 2016.

American Council on Education. "ACE Brief Stresses Importance of Internships to College Students." ACE. April 9, 2014. www.acenet.edu/news-room/Pages/ACE-Brief-Stresses-Importance-of-Internships -to-College-Students.aspx.

Anaissie, Tania. "Liberatory Design Thinking." Tania Anaissie. n.d. www.anaissie.com/liberatory-design.

Anand, Shikha. "Reservation in Higher Education: Category Wise Student Enrollment in Universities & Colleges." *Shiksha*. June 9, 2017. www.shiksha.com/humanities-social-sciences/articles/reservation-i n-higher-education-category-wise-student-enrollment-in-universities-colleges-blogId-14557.

Ancona, Laureen. "Sorry, I Should Be More Specific. This Is Peddling Anxiety, Not Information, and Disappointing to Say the Least." Twitter, November 8, 2016. https://twitter.com/laurenancona/status/ 796201871937511425.

Anderson, Stephen P. *Seductive Interaction Design: Creating Playful, Fun, and Effective User Experiences*. Berkeley: New Riders, 2011.

Angwin, Julia, Jeff Larson, Lauren Kirchner, and Surya Mattu. "Machine Bias? There's Software Used Across the Country to Predict Future Criminals. And It's Biased Against Blacks." *ProPublica*. May 23, 2016. www.propublica.org/article/machine-bias-risk-assessments-in-criminal-sentencing.

Arendt, Hannah. A Condição Humana. Lisbon: Relógio D'Água, 1958.

Arendt, Hannah. *Entre o passado e o futuro*. São Paulo: Perspectiva, 1972.

Arendt, Hannah, and Peter R. Baehr. *The Portable Hannah Arendt*. New York: Penguin Books, 2003.

Aristotle. *Metaphysics: Books VII-X, Zeta, Eta, Thetae, Iota*. Translated by Montgomery Furth. Indianapolis: Hackett, 1986.

Aristotle. *The Nicomachean Ethics of Aristotle*. Edited by Hugh Tredennick. Translated by J. A. K. Thomson. Lanham: Penguin Classics, 1976.

Arnaud, David, and Tim LeBon. "Key Concepts in Practical Philosophy: Practical and Theoretical Wisdom, And Moral Virtue, Practical Philosophy." *Practical Philosophy: Society for Philosophy in Practice* 3, no. 1 (March 2000), 6–9. http://society-for-philosophy-in-practice.org/journal/pdf/3-1%2006%20Arnaud%20-%20Practical%20and%20Theoretical.pdf.

Arnstein, Sherry R. "A Ladder of Citizen Participation." *Journal of the American Institute of Planners* 35, no. 4 (July 1969), 216–24.

Asad, Mariam, Christopher A. Le Dantec, Becky Nielsen, and Kate Diedrick. "Creating a Sociotechnical API: Designing City-Scale Community Engagement." In *Proceedings of the 2017 CHI Conference on Human Factors in Computing Systems*, edited by Gloria Mark, 295–306. New York: ACM, 2017.

Ashby, Michael F., Jordi Segalas Coral, and Didac Ferrer Balas. *Materials and Sustainable Development*. Amsterdam: Elsevier, Butterworth-Heinemann, 2016.

Asin, Iván. "The Sustainable Art Studio: Finding the Voice of Art in Education for Sustainable Development." *Green Teacher* 116 (Summer 2018), 12–15.

Aye, Sara Cantor. "The Gut Check." *Medium*, May 27, 2016. https://medium.com/greater-good-studio/the-gut-check-work-better-and-happier-by-formalizing-your-feelings-fe76a9854c2e.

Bach, Natasha. "Google Will Now Ask Users: 'Are You Depressed?'." *Fortune*, August 24, 2017. http://fortune.com/2017/08/24/google-depression-screening.

Baiocchi, Gianpaolo, Patrick Heller, and Marcelo Kunrath Silva. *Bootstrapping Democracy: Transforming Local Governance and Civil Society in Brazil*. Stanford, CA: Stanford University Press, 2011.

"Bait and Switch." Dark Patterns, n.d. https://darkpatterns.org/types-of-dark-pattern/bait-and-switch.

Balzarini, Rhonda N., Lorne Campbell, Taylor Kohut, Bjarne M. Holmes, Justin J. Lehmiller, Jennifer J. Harman, and Nicole Atkins. "Perceptions of Primary and Secondary Relationships in Polyamory." *PLoS One* 12, no. 5 (2017).

Baraniuk, Chris. "Google Responds on Skewed Holocaust Search Results." *BBC News*, December 20, 2016. www.bbc.com/news/technology-38379453.

Barker, Meg, and Darren Langdridge. *Understanding Non-Monogamies*. New York: Routledge, 2012.

Barocas, Solon, and Andrew D. Selbst. 'Big Data's Disparate Impact'. *California Law Review* 104 (2016), 671.

Bateman, Scott, Regan L. Mandryk, Carl Gutwin, Aaron Genest, David McDine, and Christopher Brooks. "Useful Junk? The Effects of Visual Embellishment on Comprehension and Memorability of Charts." In *Proceedings of the 28th International Conference on Human Factors in Computing Systems*, edited by Elizabeth Mynatt, 2573–82. New York: ACM, 2010.

Baudrillard, Jean. *Simulacra and Simulation*. Translated by Sheila Faria Glaser. Ann Arbor: The University of Michigan Press, 1994.

Baumer, Eric P. S., Vera Khovanskaya, Mark Matthews, Lindsay Reynolds, Victoria Schwanda Sosik, and Geri Gay. "Reviewing Reflection: On the Use of Reflection in Interactive System Design." In *Proceedings of the 2014 Conference on Designing Interactive Systems*, 93–102. New York: ACM, 2014.

Baumüller, Heike. "The Little We Know: An Exploratory Literature Review on the Utility of Mobile Phone-Enabled Services for Smallholder Farmers." *Journal of International Development* 30, no. 1 (2017), 134–54.

Bayard, Nicholas. "Valuing Nature in Environmental Education." *Green Teacher*, no. 79 (Summer 2006), 27.

BBC News. "Syria War: Russia Rejects Turkey's Calls for Idlib Truce." September 7, 2018. www.bbc.co m/news/world-middle-east-45444276.

BBC News. "Government Steps Up Action on Unpaid Internships." *BBC News*, February 9, 2018. www. bbc.com/news/business-42997400.

Beck, Julie. "People Are Changing the Way They Use Social Media." *The Atlantic*, June 7, 2018. theat lantic.com/technology/archive/2018/06/did-cambridge-analytica-actually-change-facebook-users-be havior/562154.

Belkin, Douglas. "U.S. Colleges Are Separating into Winners and Losers." *The Wall Street Journal*, February 21, 2018. www.wsj.com/articles/after-decades-of-growth-colleges-find-its-survival-of-the-f ittest-1519209001.

Bell, Ryan. "Temple Grandin, Killing Them Softly at Slaughterhouses for 30 Years." *National Geographic*, August 19, 2015. www.nationalgeographic.com/people-and-culture/food/the-plate/2015 /08/19/temple-grandin-killing-them-softly-at-slaughterhouses-for-30-years.

Bellafante, Ginia. "Community College Students Face a Very Long Road to Graduation." *The New York Times*, October 3, 2014, www.nytimes.com/2014/10/05/nyregion/community-college-students-face-a-very-long-road-to-graduation.html.

Belluck, Pam. "Hey Siri, Can I Rely on You in a Crisis? Not Always, a Study Finds." *Well*, March 14, 2016. https://well.blogs.nytimes.com/2016/03/14/hey-siri-can-i-rely-on-you-in-a-crisis-not-always-a-s tudy-finds.

Berdichevsky, Daniel, and Erik Neuenschwander. "Toward an Ethics of Persuasive Technology." *Communications of the ACM* 42, no. 5 (1999), 51–58.

Besbris, David. "AMP: Two Years of User-First Webpages." *Accelerated Mobile Pages Project* – AMP, May 15, 2018. ampproject.org/latest/blog/amp-two-years-of-user-first-webpages.

Biddle, Erika. "Info Nymphos." *Directory of Open Access Journals* 4, no. 1 (2013), 65–82.

Binder, Thomas, Giorgio De Michelis, Pelle Ehn, Giulio Jacucci, Per Linde, and Ina Wagner. *Design Things*. Cambridge: MIT Press, 2011.

Binder, Thomas, and Johan Redeström. "Programs, Experiments and Exemplary Design Research." In *Proceedings of Design Research Society Wonderground International Conference*, edited by K. Friedman, T. Love, and E. Corte-Real. Lisbon: Design Research Society, 2006.

Björgvinsson, Erling, Pelle Ehn, and Per-Anders Hillgren. "Participatory Design and Democratizing Innovation." In *Proceedings of the 11th Biennial Participatory Design Conference*, 41–50. ACM, 2010.

Black, Edwin. *IBM and the Holocaust*. New York: Crown, 2001.

Black, Richard, W. N. Adger, Nigel W. Arnell, Stefan Dercon, Andrew Geddes, and David Thomas. "The Effect of Environmental Change on Human Migration." *Global Environmental Change* 21, no. 1 (2011), S3–S11.

Blauvelt, Andrew, and Ellen Lupton. *Graphic Design: Now in Production*. Minneapolis: Walker Art Center, 2012.

Blom, Jonas N., and Kenneth R. Hansen. "Click Bait: Forward-Reference as Lure in Online News Headlines." *Journal of Pragmatics* 76 (2015), 87–100.

Boin, Arjen. "From Crisis to Disaster: Toward an Integrative Approach." In *What Is a Disaster?: New Answers to Old Questions*, edited by Ronald W. Perry and Enrico Louis Quarantelli, 153–72. Philadelphia, PA: Xlibris, 2005.

Boin, Arjen, and Paul 't Hart. "The Crisis Approach." In *Handbook of Disaster Research*, edited by Havidán Rodríguez, Enrico Louis Quarantelli, and Russell Rowe Dynes, 42–54. New York: Springer, 2007.

Bolter, Jay David, and Richard Grusin. *Remediation: Understanding New Media*. Cambridge: MIT Press, 2000.

Bonnefon, J. F., A. Shariff, and I. Rahwan. "The Social Dilemma of Autonomous Vehicles." *Science* 352, no. 6293 (2016), 1573–76.

Borenstein, Jason, Joseph R. Herkert, and Keith W. Miller. "Self-Driving Cars and Engineering Ethics: The Need for a System Level Analysis." *Science and Engineering Ethics* 25, no. 2 (2017), 383–98.

Borgmann, Albert. "The Moral Significance of Material Culture." In *Technology and the Politics of Knowledge*, edited by Andrew Feenberg and Alastair Hannay, 92. Bloomington: Indiana University Press, 1995.

Boyle, J. M. "Toward Understanding the Principle of Double Effect." In *The Doctrine of Double Effect: Philosophers Debate a Controversial Moral Principle*, edited by P. A. Woodward, 7–20. Notre Dame: University of Notre Dame Press, 2010.

Braiker, Harriet B. *Who's Pulling Your Strings?: How to Break the Cycle of Manipulation and Regain Control of Your Life*. New York: McGraw-Hill, 2004.

Brauneis, Robert, and Ellen P. Goodman. "Algorithmic Transparency for the Smart City." *Yale Journal of Law and Technology 103*, 20, no. 1 (2018), 103–76.

Brignull, Harry. "Dark Patterns: Deception vs. Honesty in UI Design." *A List Apart*, January 23, 2013. https://alistapart.com/article/dark-patterns-deception-vs.-honesty-in-ui-design.

Brignull, Harry. "Dark Patterns: Inside the Interfaces Designed to Trick You." *The Verge*, August 29, 2013. www.theverge.com/2013/8/29/4640308/dark-patterns-inside-the-interfaces-designed-to-trick-you.

Bromwich, Jonah. "Finding Love, the Old, Shallow Way." *The New York Times* (New York), October 25, 2013. https://www.nytimes.com/2013/10/27/nyregion/finding-love-the-old-shallow-way.html?

Brooks, Katherine. "The Poster Art at the Women's March on Washington Will Be Powerful." Huffington Post, August 29, 2017. www.huffingtonpost.com/entry/womens-march-poster-art_us_5873c531e4b02b5f858a2b1d.

Brown, Eliot. "Dockless Bike Share Floods into U.S. Cities, with Rides and Clutter." *The Wall Street Journal*, March 26, 2018. https://www.wsj.com/articles/dockless-bike-share-floods-into-u-s-cities-with-rides-and-clutter-1522076401.

Brownstone, Sydney. "Meet the Super Sexy, Super Conscious Humanitarians of Tinder." *Fast Company*, February 25, 2014. https://www.fastcompany.com/3026878/meet-the-super-sexy-super-conscious-humanitarians-of-tinder.

Buchanan, Richard. "Branzi's Dilemma: Design in Contemporary Culture." *Design Issues* 14, no. 1 (1998), 3.

Buchanan, Richard. "Design Ethics." In *Encyclopedia of Technology, Science and Ethics*, edited by Carl Mitcham. New York: Macmillan Reference, 2005.

Buchanan, Richard. "Wicked Problems in Design Thinking." *Design Issues* 8, no. 2 (1992), 5.

Bundy, Jonathan, Michael D. Pfarrer, Cole E. Short, and W. T. Coombs. "Crises and Crisis Management: Integration, Interpretation, and Research Development." *Journal of Management* 43, no. 6 (2016), 1661–92.

Buolamwini, Joy, and Timnit Gebru. "Gender Shades: Intersectional Accuracy Disparities in Commercial Gender Classification." *Proceedings of the 1st Conference on Fairness, Accountability and Transparency*, PMLR 81 (2018), 77–91.

Burghardt DuBois, William Edward. "The Development of a People." *Ethics* 14, no. 3 (1904), 292.

Burgoon, Judee K., and David B. Buller. "Interpersonal Deception Theory." *Communication Theory* 6, no. 3 (1996), 311–28.

Burn-Murdoch, John. "Why You Should Never Trust a Data Visualization." *The Guardian*, July 24, 2013. www.theguardian.com/news/datablog/2013/jul/24/why-you-should-never-trust-a-data-visualisation.

Butler, Samuel. *Erewhon*. London: Trübner, 1872.

Buwert, P. "Examining the Professional Codes of Design Organisations." In *Design Research Society International Conference* 2018, edited by Cristiano Storni, Keelin Leahy, Muireann McMahon, Peter Lloyd, and Erik Bohemia, 172–86. Limerick: Design Research Society, 2018.

Buwert, Peter M. "An/Aesth/Efthics: The Ethical Potential of Design." *Artifact* 3, no. 3 (2015), 4.

Buwert, Peter. "Potentiality: The Ethical Foundation of Design." *The Design Journal* 20, no. sup1 (2017), S4459–67.

Cammaerts, Bart. "Jamming the Political: Beyond Counter-Hegemonic Practices." *Continuum* 21, no. 1 (2007), 71–90.

Cammaerts, Bart, and Nico Carpenter. *Reclaiming the Media: Communication Rights and Democratic Media Roles.* Bristol: Intellect, 2007.

Caputo, John D. "The End of Ethics." In *The Blackwell Guide to Ethical Theory*, edited by Hugh LaFollette and Ingmar Persson, 1st ed., 111–28. Malden: Blackwell Publishers, 2000.

Cardullo, Paolo, and Rob Kitchin. "Being a 'Citizen' in the Smart City: Up and Down the Scaffold of Smart Citizen Participation in Dublin, Ireland." *GeoJournal* 84, no. 1 (2018), 1–13.

Carlson, Scott. *The Future of Work: How Colleges Can Prepare Students for the Jobs Ahead.* Washington, DC: Chronicle of Higher Education, 2017.

Carroll, Antionette. "Diversity & Inclusion in Design: Why Do They Matter?" AIGA., www.aiga.org/diversity-and-inclusion-in-design-why-do-they.matter.

Carson, Rachel. *Silent Spring.* Boston: Mariner Books (Houghton Mifflin), 1962.

Center for Humane Technology. "Home." Center for Humane Technology, http://humanetech.com.

Chalabi, Mona. "3 Ways to Spot a Bad Statistic." *TED: Ideas Worth Spreading*, February 2017. www.ted.com/talks/mona_chalabi_3_ways_to_spot_a_bad_statistic.

Chayka, Kyle. "Facebook and Google Make Lies as Pretty as Truth." *The Verge*, December 6, 2016. www.theverge.com/2016/12/6/13850230/fake-news-sites-google-search-facebook-instant-articles.

Chen, Yuyu. "Swipe Right to Buy: E-commerce Apps Take Design Cues from Tinder." *Digiday*, March 15, 2016. https://digiday.com/marketing/swipe-right-buy-e-commerce-apps-take-design-cues-tinder.

Chiang, Ted. *Stories of Your Life and Others.* London: Picador, 2015.

Chouldechova, Alexandra. "Fair Prediction with Disparate Impact: A Study of Bias in Recidivism Prediction Instruments." *Big Data* 5, no. 2 (2017), 153–63.

Chouldechova, Alexandra, Diana Benavides-Prado, Oleksandr Fialko, and Rhema Vaithianathan. "A Case Study of Algorithm-Assisted Decision Making in Child Maltreatment Hotline Screening Decisions." In *Conference on Fairness, Accountability and Transparency*, 81 (2018), 134–48.

Chronicle of Higher Education. "The Role of Higher Education in Career Development: Employer Perceptions." Washington: Chronicle of Higher Education, 2012. http://chronicle.com/items/biz/pdf/Employers%20Survey.pdf.

Churchman, C. West. *Prediction and Optimal Decision: Philosophical Issues of a Science of Values.* Englewood Cliff: Prentice-Hall, Inc., 1961.

Churchman, C. West. *The Systems Approach and Its Enemies.* New York: Basic Books, 1979.

Claire, Marie. "Tinder: The Online Dating App Everyone's Talking About." *Marie Claire*, November 28, 2017. www.marieclaire.co.uk/life/sex-and-relationships/tinder-the-online-dating-app-that-everyone-s-talking-about-112522.

Clarke, Alison J. "Actions Speak Louder." *Design and Culture* 5, no. 2 (2013), 151–68.

Clarke, Cody. "Humanitarians of Tinder." *H of T.*, n.d. http://humanitariansoftinder.com.

Clark, Garrette, Justin Kosoris, Long Hong, and Marcel Crul. "Design for Sustainability: Current Trends in Sustainable Product Design and Development." *Sustainability* 1, no. 3 (2009), 409–24.

Clark, Luke, Andrew J. Lawrence, Frances Astley-Jones, and Nicola Gray. "Gambling Near-Misses Enhance Motivation to Gamble and Recruit Win-Related Brain Circuitry." *Neuron* 61, no. 3 (2009), 481–90.

Coglianese, Cary, and David Lehr. "Regulating by Robot: Administrative Decision Making in the Machine-Learning Era." *The Georgetown Law Journal* 105, no. 5 (2017), 1147.

Common Practice. "23 Common Practices of Common Practice." Common Practice (blog), n.d. https://commonpractice.com/pages/23practices.

Conti, Gregory J. "Evil Interfaces: Violating the User." *HOPE*, July 2008.

Conti, Gregory J., and Edward Sobiesk. "Malicious Interface Design: Exploiting the User." In *Proceedings of the 24th International Conference on World Wide Web*, 271. New York: ACM Press, 2010.

Corinna, Heather. "Driver's Ed for the Sexual Superhighway: Navigating Consent." *Scarleteen*. www.s carleteen.com/article/abuse_assault/drivers_ed_for_the_sexual_superhighway_navigating_consent.

Correa, Sharon, and John Schlemmer. "Making Motion Meaningful." *Google Design* (blog), September 23, 2016. https://design.google/library/making-motion-meaningful.

Council of the European Union, and European Parliament. *Directiva 2011/83/UE del Parlamento Europeo y del Consejo, de 25 de octubre de 2011, sobre los derechos de los consumidores, por la que se modifican la Directiva 93/13/CEE del Consejo y la Directiva 1999/44/CE del Parlamento Europeo y del Consejo y se derogan la Directiva 85/577/CEE del Consejo y la Directiva 97/7/CE del Parlamento Europeo y del Consejo Texto pertinente a efectos del EEE*. The European Union, 2011. www.boe.es/doue/2011/304/L00064-00088.pdf.

Court of Justice of the European Union. "Judgment of the Court: Case C-131/12." *InfoCuria*, May 13, 2014. http://curia.europa.eu/juris/document/document.jsf?docid=152065&doclang=EN.

Cox, Amanda, and Josh Katz. "Presidential Forecast Post-Mortem." *The New York Times*, November 15, 2016. www.nytimes.com/2016/11/16/upshot/presidential-forecast-postmortem.html.

Cross, Nigel. *Developments in Design Methodology*. Ann Arbor: John Wiley & Sons, 1984.

Crouch, Christopher, and Jane Pearce. *Doing Research in Design*. Oxford: Bloomsbury Publishing, 2013.

Culier-Grice, Julia, Anna Davies, Robert Patrick, and Will Norman. *The Theoretical, Empirical and Policy Foundations for Building Social Innovation in Europe*. Brussels: European Commission, DG Research, 2012.

Côté, Denis, Anne Caron, Jonathan Aubert, Véronique Desrochers, and Robert Ladouceur. "Near Wins Prolong Gambling on a Video Lottery Terminal." *Journal of Gambling Studies* 19, no. 4 (November 2003), 433–38.

Dan-Cohen, Meir. "Responsibility and the Boundaries of the Self." *Harvard Law Review* 105, no. 5 (1992), 959.

Danner, Peter L. "Affluence and the Moral Ecology." *Ethics* 81, no. 4 (1971), 287–302.

Davies, William. "How Statistics Lost Their Power—And Why We Should Fear What Comes Next." *The Guardian*, January 19, 2017. www.theguardian.com/politics/2017/jan/19/crisis-of-statistics-big-data -democracy.

Davis, James A., Tom W. Smith, and Peter V. Marsden. *General Social Surveys, 1972–2004 [Cumulative File]*. Ann Arbor: Inter-university Consortium for Political and Social Research, 2005.

Davis, Meredith. "Relevance in a Complex World —Icograda Design Education Manifesto." In *Icograda Design Education Manifesto*, edited by Russell Kennedy, 72–75. Québec, International Council of Design, 2011.

"Defining Blight in Detroit." *The New York Times* - Breaking News, World News & Multimedia, May 27, 2014. www.nytimes.com/interactive/2014/05/27/us/Defining-Blight-in-Detroit.html.

"Definition of TRUST." Dictionary by Merriam-Webster. www.merriam-webster.com/dictionary/trust %20in.

Deleuze, Gilles, Félix Guattari, and Marie Maclean. *Kafka: Toward a Minor Literature: The Components of Expression*. Baltimore: Johns Hopkins University, 1985.

Dempsey, Samantha, and Ciara Taylor. "A Designer's Oath: Collaboratively Defining a Code of Ethics for Design." *Touchpoint: The Journal of Service Design* 7, no. 1 (2015), 29–31.

Den Hollander, Marcel. "Design for Managing Obsolescence: A Design Methodology for Preserving Product Integrity in a Circular Economy." Master's thesis, Delft University of Technology, 2018.

DePaul, Michael R., and Linda Zagzebski. *Intellectual Virtue: Perspectives from Ethics and Epistemology*. Oxford: Clarendon, 2003.

Deshpande, Hrridaysh. *The Future of Design Education in India*. New Delhi: British Council and India Design Council, 2016. www.britishcouncil.org/education/ihe/knowledge-centre/national-policies/rep ort-future-design-education-india.

Design Council. *The Design Economy: The Value of Design to the UK*. London: Design Council, 2015.

"Design Justice Network Principles." *Design Justice*, n.d. http://designjusticenetwork.org/network-princ iples.

Deterding, Sebastian, Dan Dixon, Rilla Khaled, and Lennart Nacke. "From Game Design Elements to Gamefulness: Defining 'Gamification.'" In *Proceedings of the 15th International Academic MindTrek Conference: Envisioning Future Media Environments*, 9–15. New York: ACM, 2011.

Dewey, John. *Ethics*. Read Books Limited, 2016.

Dilnot, Clive. "Ethics? Design?" In *The Archeworks Papers, vol. 1*, edited by Stanley Tigerman, 1–148. Chicago: Archeworks, 2005.

Dilnot, Clive. "Ethics in Design: 10 Questions." In *Design Studies: A Reader*, edited by Hazel Clark and David Eric Brody, 180–91. Oxford: Berg, 2009.

Dilnot, Clive. "Some Futures for Design History?" *Journal of Design History* 22, no. 4 (2009), 377–94.

Dilnot, Clive. "Sustainability and Unsustainability in a World Become Artificial: Sustainability as a Project of History." *Design Philosophy Papers* 9, no. 2 (2011), 103–55.

Dilnot, Clive. "The Critical in Design (Part One)." *Journal of Writing in Creative Practice* 1, no. 2 (2008), 177–89.

DiSalvo, Carl. *Adversarial Design*. Cambridge: MIT Press, 2012.

DiSalvo, Carl. "Design, Democracy and Agonistic Pluralism." In *Proceedings of the Design Research Society Conference*, 366–71. Montreal: Design Research Society, 2010.

"Disguised Ads." Dark Patterns, n.d. https://darkpatterns.org/types-of-dark-pattern/disguised-ads.

Dobransky, Kerry, and Eszter Hargittai. "Unrealized Potential: Exploring the Digital Disability Divide." *Poetics* 58 (2016), 18–28.

Domonoske, Camila. "Bike-Share Firm Hits the Brakes in France After 'Mass Destruction' of Dockless Bikes." *National Public Radio*, February 26, 2018. www.npr.org/sections/thetwo-way/2018/02/26/58 8901870/bike-share-firm-hits-the-brakes-in-france-after-mass-destruction-of-dockless-bik.

Doorn, Neelke. "The Blind Spot in Risk Ethics: Managing Natural Hazards." *Risk Analysis* 35, no. 3 (2014), 354–60.

Dormer, Peter. *Design Since 1945*. London: Thames & Hudson, 2003.

Dove, Michael, and Daniel Kammen. "The Epistemology of Sustainable Resource Use: Managing Forest Products, Swiddens, and High- Yielding Variety Crops." *Human Organization* 56, no. 1 (1997), 91–101.

Drennen, D. A. *Barron's Simplified Approach to the Methodical Philosophy of René Descartes*. Woodbury, Barron's Educational Series, 1969.

Drucker, Johanna. *Graphesis: Visual Forms of Knowledge Production*. Cambridge: Harvard University Press, 2014.

Drucker, Johanna. *SpecLab: Digital Aesthetics and Projects in Speculative Computing*. Chicago: University of Chicago Press, 2009.

Dubberly, Hugh. "Connecting Things: Broadening Design to Include Systems, Platforms, and Product-Service Ecologies." In *Encountering Things: Design and Theories of Things*, edited by Leslie Atzmon and Prasad Boradkar. London: Bloomsbury, 2017.

Dunne, Anthony, and Fiona Raby. *Speculative Everything: Design, Fiction, and Social Dreaming*. Cambridge: MIT Press, 2013.

Dunn, Halbert L. "High-Level Wellness for Man and Society." *American Journal of Public Health and the Nation's Health* 49, no. 6 (1959), 786–92.

Dyson, Freeman. "Technology and Social Justice." Lecture, The Fourth Louis Nizer Lecture on Public Policy, Carnegie Council on Ethics and International Affairs, November 5, 1997.

Eco, Umberto. *Travels in Hyper-Reality Essays*. London: Pan Books, 1987.

Eco, Umberto. *Toward a Semiolical Guerrilla Warfare*. 1976. www.kareneliot.de/downloads/Umberto Eco_Towards%20a%20Semiological%20Guerrilla%20Warfare.pdf.

The Editorial Board. "Hillary Clinton for President." *The New York Times*, September 24, 2016. www.n ytimes.com/2016/09/25/opinion/sunday/hillary-clinton-for-president.html.

The Editorial Board. "Why Donald Trump Should Not Be President." *The New York Times*, September 25, 2016. www.nytimes.com/2016/09/26/opinion/why-donald-trump-should-not-be-president.html.

Ehn, Pelle. *Work-Oriented Design of Computer Artifacts*. Stockholm: Arbetslivcentrum, 1989.

Einstein, Mara. "Nothing for Money and You're Work for Free: Internships and the Marketing of Higher Education." *Communication, Capitalism & Critique. Open Access Journal for a Global Sustainable Information Society* 13, no. 2 (2015), 471–85.

Eisenhardt, Kathleen M., and Melissa E. Graebner. "Theory Building from Cases: Opportunities and Challenges." *Academy of Management Journal* 50, no. 1 (2007), 25–32.

Ekstrand, Susie Stærk, and Kristine Lilholt Nilsson. "Greenwashing?" *European Food and Feed Law Review* 6, no. 3 (2011), 167–73.

Ellis, Susie. "Wellness, Well-Being . . . And What about Spa?" Huffington Post (blog), April 9, 2017. www.huffpost.com/entry/wellness-wellbeingand-wha_b_9641722.

Ellul, Jacques. *The Technological Bluff*. Grand Rapids: W.B. Eerdmans, 1990.

Enfield, Nick. "We're in a Post-truth World with Eroding Trust and Accountability. It Can't End Well." *The Guardian*, November 16, 2017. www.theguardian.com/commentisfree/2017/nov/17/were-in-a-post-truth-world-with-eroding-trust-and-accountability-it-cant-end-well.

Escobar, Arturo. *Designs for the Pluriverse: Radical Interdependence, Autonomy and the Making of Worlds*. Durham: Duke University Press, 2018.

ESilverStrike Consulting Inc. "Tinder Information, Statistics, Facts and History - Dating Sites Reviews." Dating Sites Reviews, n.d. datingsitesreviews.com/staticpages/index.php?page=Tinder-Statistics-Facts-History.

Eubanks, Virginia, and Teri Schnaubelt. *Automating Inequality How High-Tech Tools Profile, Police, and Punish the Poor*. Old Saybrook: Tantor Media, 2018.

Facebook. "Company Info." Facebook Newsroom. n.d. newsroom.fb.com/company-info.

Featherstone, Mark. "The Eye of war: Images of Destruction in Virilio and Bataille." *Journal for Cultural Research* 7, no. 4 (2003), 433–47.

Feltham, Jamie. "VRChat Dev Vows to Address 'Harmful' User Behavior in Open Letter." UploadVR (blog). January 12, 2018. uploadvr.com/vrchat-dev-vows-address-harmful-users-open-letter.

Felton, Emma, Oksana Zelenko, and Suzi Vaughan. *Design and Ethics: Reflections on Practice*. London: Routledge, 2012.

Fernandez, Kenneth, Susie Wise, and David Clifford. *Empathy Techniques for Educational Equity*. Stanford: Hasso Plattner Institute of Design at Stanford University, 2017. dschool.stanford.edu/resources/empathy-techniques-for-educational-equity.

Findeli, Alain. "Rethinking Design Education for the 21st Century: Theoretical, Methodological, and Ethical Discussion." *Design Issues* 17, no. 1 (2001), 5–17.

Fine, Peter Claver. *Sustainable Graphic Design: Principles and Practices*. London: Bloomsbury, 2016.

Firth, Richard, Einar Stoltenberg, and Trent Jennings. "Using an Outdoor Learning Space to Teach Sustainability and Material Processes in HE Product Design." *International Journal of Art & Design Education* 35, no. 3 (2016), 327–36.

Fishman, Elliot. "Bikeshare: A Review of Recent Literature." *Transport Reviews* 36, no. 1 (2015), 92–113.

Fishman, Rachel. "College Decisions Survey: Deciding to Go to College." New America (blog), May 18, 2015. www.newamerica.org/education-policy/edcentral/collegedecisions.

Flores, Anthony W., Kristin Bechtel, and Christopher T. Lowenkamp. "False Positives, False Negatives, and False Analyses: A Rejoinder to 'Machine Bias: There's Software Used Across the Country to Predict Future Criminals. And It's Biased Against Blacks.'" *Federal Probation Journal* 80, no. 2 (September 2016), 38.

Flusser, Vilém. "The Ethics of Industrial Design?" In *The Shape of Things: A Philosophy of Design*, 66–69. London: Reaktion Books, 1999.

Flusser, Vilém. *Writings*. Edited by Andreas Ströhl and Erik Eisel. Minneapolis: University of Minnesota Press, 2002.

Fogg, B. J. *Persuasive Technology: Using Computers to Change What We Think and Do*. San Francisco: Morgan Kaufmann Publishers, 2003.

Folmer, Eelke. *The Glossary of Human Computer Interaction*. Edited by Bill Papantoniou, Mads Soegaard, Julia Reinhard Lupton, Mehmet Goktürk, David Trepess, Dirk Knemeyer, Eric Svoboda, Thomas Memmel, Eelke Folmer, Hatice Gunes, Martin Harrod, Frank Spillers, and Eva Hornecker. The Interaction Design Foundation, 2015. www.interaction-design.org/literature/book/the-glossary -of-human-computer-interaction/interaction-design-patterns.

Fong, Katrina, and Raymond A. Mar. "What Does My Avatar Say about Me? Inferring Personality from Avatars." *Personality and Social Psychology Bulletin* 41, no. 2 (2015), 237–49.

Frazer, Elizabeth. "Max Weber on Ethics and Politics." *Politics and Ethics Review* 2, no. 1 (2006), 19–37.

Frenette, Alexandre, Amber D. Dumford, Angie L. Miller, and Steven J. Tepper. *The Internship Divide: The Promise and Challenges of Internships in the Arts*. Bloomington: Indiana University Press, 2015.

Friedman, Jaclyn, and Jessica Valenti. *Yes Means Yes!: Visions of Female Sexual Power et a World Without Rape*. Berkeley: Seal Press, 2008.

Friend, Cecilia, and Jane B. Singer. *Online Journalism Ethics: Traditions and Transitions*, 2nd ed. Hove, East Sussex: Routledge, 2015.

Fuad-Luke, Alastair. *Design Activism: Beautiful Strangeness for a Sustainable World*. Sterling: Earthscan, 2009.

Fulton, Janet M., and Marjorie D. Kibby. "Millennials and the Normalization of Surveillance on Facebook." *Continuum* 31, no. 2 (2016), 189–99.

Gale, Elan. *Tinder Nightmares*. New York: Harry N. Abrams, 2015.

Gardner, Phil. "The Debate over Unpaid College Internships." Intern Bridge. 2011. www.ceri.msu.edu/ wp-content/uploads/2010/01/Intern-Bridge-Unpaid-College-Internship-Report-FINAL.pdf.

Georgia Institute of Technology's Public Design Workshop, and Center for Urban Innovation. *Fictions of a Smart Atlanta: An Anthology of Smart City Use Cases*. 2018. Atlanta: Georgia Institute of Technology.

Giraud, Stéphanie, Pierre Thérouanne, and Dirk D. Steiner. "Conceptualization of a Technical Solution for Web Navigation of Visually Impaired People." In *27ème conférence francophone sur l'Interaction Homme-Machine*, w3. Toulouse: ACM, 2015.

Giroux, Henry, and Brad Evans. "Disposable Futures." Truthout (blog), June 1, 2014. truthout.org/article s/disposable-futures.

Glabau, Danya. "Fancy Feast: The Aspirational Fantasies in Photogenic Food." *Real Life*, September 21, 2017. reallifemag.com/fancy-feast/.

Glaser, Milton. "Ambiguity & Truth." Milton Glaser. n.d. www.miltonglaser.com/milton/c:essays/#.

Glaser, Milton, Mirko Iliⵥ, Tony Kushner, and Steven Heller. *The Design of Dissent: Socially and Politically Driven Graphics*. Beverly: Rockport Publishers, 2017.

Good Therapy. "'I' Message, 'I' Statement." Good Therapy, February 14, 2018. www.goodtherapy.org/ blog/psychpedia/i-message.

Goodman, Bryce W. "A Step towards Accountable Algorithms? Algorithmic Discrimination and the European Union General Data Protection." In *29th Conference on Neural Information Processing Systems (NIPS 2016)*. Barcelona: NIPS Foundation, 2016.

Google. "Google Transparency Report." Google Transparency Report, n.d. https://transparencyrepor t.google.com/eu-privacy/overview.

Gordon, David, John Michael Kittross, John Calhoun Merrill, and Carol Reuss. *Controversies in Media Ethics*, 3rd ed. Thousand Oaks: Routledge, 2011.

Gottlieb, Dan, Penny Herscovitch, and Stella Hernandez. "Why Safe Niño? Empathy, Connection and a Safe Space to Heal." In Safe Niños: *Design for Holistic Healing*, 26–48. Designmatters, ArtCenter College of Design, n.d. https://4eyos01khlgv2ccw28adjy2x-wpengine.netdna-ssl.com/wp-content/up loads/2016/11/SafeNinos_Complete_Web.pdf.

Government Digital Services. "Government Digital Service Design Principles." GOV.UK, April 2, 2012. www.gov.uk/design-principles.

Graham, Stephen, and Simon Marvin. *Splintering Urbanism: Networked Infrastructures, Technological Mobilities and the Urban Condition*. London: Routledge, 2001.

Greenfield, Rebecca. "Unpaid Internships Are Back, with the Labor Department's Blessing." *Los Angeles Times*, January 13, 2018. www.latimes.com/business/la-fi-unpaid-internships-20180112-story.html.

Grieb, Suzanne M., Molly Reddy, Brittany Griffin, Arik V. Marcell, Sophie Meade, Becky Slogeris, Kathleen R. Page, and Jacky M. Jennings. "Identifying Solutions to Improve the Sexually Transmitted Infections Testing Experience for Youth Through Participatory Ideation." *AIDS Patient Care and STDs* 32, no. 8 (2018), 330–35.

Grigoriadis, Vanessa. "Inside Tinder's Hookup Factory." *Rolling Stone Magazine* (blog), October 27, 2014. rollingstone.com/culture/culture-news/inside-tinders-hookup-factory-180635.

Griswold, Alison. "Are You 30? Tinder Has Officially Decided You're Old." *Slate Magazine*, March 2, 2015. https://slate.com/business/2015/03/tinder-plus-pay-for-passport-rewind-and-unlimited-right-swipes.html.

GroundUp. "GroundUp: Another Abahlali baseMjondolo Member Assassinated." *Daily Maverick*, October 2, 2014. www.dailymaverick.co.za/article/2014-10-02-groundup-another-abahlali-basemjondolo-member-assassinated.

The Guardian. "The Counted: People Killed by Police in the US." June 1, 2015. www.theguardian.com/us-news/ng-interactive/2015/jun/01/the-counted-police-killings-us-database.

Hall, Edward T. *The Hidden Dimension: An Anthropologist Examines Man's Use of Space in Public and Private*. New York: Anchor Books, 1982.

Hall, Edward T. "A System for the Notation of Proxemic Behavior." *American Anthropologist* 65, no. 5 (1963), 1003–26.

Hall, Peter. "Bubbles, Lines, and String: How Information Visualization Shapes Society." In *Graphic Design: Now in Production*, edited by Andrew Blauvelt and Ellen Lupton, 170–85. Minneapolis: Walker Art Center, 2012.

Hampton, Keith, Lee Raine, Weixu Lu, Inyoung Shin, and Kristen Purcell. *Psychological Stress and Social Media Use*. Pew Research Center, January 15, 2015. pewinternet.org/2015/01/15/psychological-stress-and-social-media-use-2.

Han, Hahrie. *How Organizations Develop Activists: Civic Associations and Leadership in the 21st Century*. Oxford: Oxford University Press, 2014.

Hanouch, Michel. "What Is USSD & Why Does It Matter for Mobile Financial Services?" CGAP, March 8, 2017. www.cgap.org/blog/what-ussd-why-does-it-matter-mobile-financial-services.

Hardin, R. "Institutional Morality." In *The Theory of Institutional Design*, edited by Robert E. Goodin, 126–53. Cambridge: University Press, 1996.

Hardin, Russell. *Indeterminacy and Society*. Princeton: Princeton University Press, 2013.

Hardin, Russell. *Trust*. Cambridge: Polity, 2008.

Harris, Tristan. "What Is Time Well Spent (Part 1): Design Distinction?" Tristan Harris, September 30, 2015. tristanharris.com/tag/time-well-spent/.

Harvey, David. *Spaces of Hope*. Berkeley: University of California Press, 2008.

Hassenzahl, Marc. "The Thing and I: Understanding the Relationship between User and Product." In *Funology 2: From Usability to Enjoyment*, edited by Mark A. Blythe and Andrew Monk, 301–13. Springer International Publishing, 2018.

Hassenzahl, Marc. "User Experience (UX): Towards an Experiential Perspective on Product Quality." In *Proceedings of the 20th International Conference of the Association Francophone D'Interaction Homme-Machine*, edited by Éric Brangier, 11–15. New York: ACM, 2008.

HESA. "Higher Education Student Statistics: UK, 2016/17-Summary." HESA, 2018. www.hesa.ac.uk/news/11-01-2018/sfr247-higher-education-student-statistics.

Heskett, John. *Toothpicks and Logos: Design in Everyday Life*. Oxford: Oxford University Press, 2003.

Hewitt, Kenneth, editor. *Interpretations of Calamity from the Viewpoint of Human Ecology*. Boston: Allen & Unwin, 1983.

"Hidden Costs." Dark Patterns, n.d. https://darkpatterns.org/types-of-dark-pattern/hidden-costs.

Hiesinger, Kathryn B., and George H. Marcus. *Landmarks of Twentieth Century Design: An Illustrated Handbook*. Abbeville Press, 1993.

Hildreth, Bob. "U.S. Colleges Are Facing a Demographic and Existential Crisis." The Huffington Post, July 5, 2017. https://www.huffingtonpost.com/entry/us-colleges-are-facing-a-demographic-and-existen tial_us_59511619e4b0326c0a8d09e9.

Hitchings, Genevieve M. "Career Opportunities: Connecting Design Students with Industry." *Procedia - Social and Behavioral Sciences* 228 (2016), 622–27.

Holmes, Nigel, and Steven Heller. *Nigel Holmes: On Information Design*. New York: Jorge Pinto Books, 2006.

Hooks, Bell. *Feminism Is for Everybody: Passionate Politics*, 2nd ed. New York: Routledge, 2015.

Hooks, Bell. *Teaching Community: A Pedagogy of Hope*. Hoboken: Taylor and Francis, 2013.

Hopkins, Michael S. "How Sustainability Fuels Design Innovation." *MIT Sloan Management Review* 52, no. 1 (Fall 2010), 75–81.

Huagang, Chen. "Chinese Contemporary Design Education: Situations and Expectations." By Clive Barstow. NITRO, March 2, 2018. https://nitro.edu.au/articles/chinese-contemporary-design-educati on-situations-and-expectations.

Huff, Darrell. *How to Lie with Statistics*. New York: W. W. Norton & Company, 1954.

Idris, Nurul Hawani, Mike Jackson, and Robert J. Abrahart. "Map Mash-Ups: What Looks Good Must Be Good?" In *GISRUK Conference* 2011, 1–8.GISRUK, Portsmouth, 2011.

Ijeoma, Ekene. "Ekene Ijeoma Combines Data and Design to Tackle Pressing Global Issues." *Design Indaba*, December 2017. www.designindaba.com/videos/conference-talks/ekene-ijeoma-combines-dat a-and-design-tackle-pressing-global-issues.

Interaction Design Association. "Interaction 16." Interaction 16. Last modified 2016. interaction16.ixda. org/.

International Council of Design. *Model Code of Professional Conduct for Designers*. Brussels: ICSID, 1976.

International Data Corporation. "Worldwide Semiannual Smart Cities Spending Guide." IDC. n.d. www. idc.com/tracker/showproductinfo.jsp?prod_id=1843.

Internshala. "The Internship Sector in India: Unregulated and Largely Ignored." Internshala Blog, July 23, 2012. https://blog.internshala.com/2012/07/unfair-internships-laws.

Invision. "Design Disruptors: The Future Is Designed." *DESIGN DISRUPTORS*. July 7, 2016. www. designdisruptors.com.

Ip, Iam-chong. "Negotiating Educated Subjectivity: Intern Labour and Higher Education in Hong Kong." *tripleC: Communication, Capitalism & Critique. Open Access Journal for a Global Sustainable Information Society* 13, no. 2 (2015), 501–8.

Jackson, David, and Gary Marx. "Data Mining Program Designed to Predict Child Abuse Proves Unreliable, DCFS Says." *Chicago Tribune*, December 6, 2017. www.chicagotribune.com/news/wa tchdog/ct-dcfs-eckerd-met-20171206-story.html.

Jackson, Mark. "Ethics of Design." *Scope (Art & Design)* 4 (2009), 179–87.

James, William. *The Will to Believe, and Other Essays in Popular Philosophy*. New York: Longmans, Green, and Co, 1907.

Jarwala, Alisha. "Minority Report: Why We Should Question Predictive Policing." *Harvard Civil Rights- Civil Liberties Law Review* (blog), December 4, 2017. harvardcrcl.org/minority-report-why-we-s hould-question-predictive-policing/.

Jefferson, Thomas. *Notes on the State of Virginia*. Virginia: Prichard and Hall, 1781.

Jewell, Matthew. "Contesting the Decision: Living in (and Living with) the Smart City." *International Review of Law, Computers & Technology* 32, no. 2–3 (2018), 210–29.

Jordan, Tim, and Gül Çağalı Güven. *Activism! Direct Action, Hacktivism and the Future of Society*. İstanbul: Kitap, 2002.

Joseph, Gail E., Phil Strain, Tweety Yates, and Mary Louise Hemmeter. *Social Emotional Teaching Strategies*. Nashville, Center on the Social and Emotional Foundations for Early Learning, 2012. http: //csefel.vanderbilt.edu/modules/module2/script.pdf.

Judish, Julia E., and Andrew J. Lauria. "Department of Labor Changes Rules on Unpaid Internships." *Pillsbury Law*, January 1, 2018. www.pillsburylaw.com/en/news-and-insights/department-of-labor-changes-rules-on-unpaid-internships.html.

Julier, Guy. "From Design Culture to Design Activism." *Design and Culture* 5, no. 2 (2013), 215–36.

Jégou, François, and Ezio Manzini. *Collaborative Services: Social Innovation and Design for Sustainability*. Milano: Edizioni Polidesign, 2008.

Kafle, Nishan. "QC for Best Graphic Designing." *The QC Times*, 2018.

Kahn, Mattie. "Jewish Rituals Are the Hot New Thing in Wellness." BuzzFeed News (blog), December 18, 2017. www.buzzfeednews.com/article/mattiekahn/goop-shabbos.

Kallus, Nathan, and Angela Zhou. "Residual Unfairness in Fair Machine Learning from Prejudiced Data." In *Proceedings of the 35th International Conference on Machine Learning*, PMLR 80 (2018), 2439–48..

Kaptelinin, Victor. "Affordances." In *Encyclopedia of Human Computer Interaction*, edited by Mads Soegaard and Rikke Friis Dam. Hershey: Idea Group Reference, 2013.

Kapur, Devesh, and Elizabeth J. Perry. *Higher Education Reform in China and India: The Role of the State*. Cambridge: Havard-Yenching Institute Working Papers, 2015. http://nrs.harvard.edu/urn-3:HUL.InstRepos:14005052.

Kastrenakes, Jacob. "Adoptly, the Tinder for Adoption, Was Actually an Art Project." *The Verge*, January 31, 2017. www.theverge.com/2017/1/31/14455622/adoptly-app-tinder-child-adoption-art-project-reveal.

Keshavarz, Mahmoud. "Design-Politics Nexus: Material Articulations and Modes of Acting." In *Design Ecologies: Conference Program and Abstracts*. Stockholm: Konstfack, 2015.

Kim, Jong-Jin, and Brenda Rigdon. *Sustainable Architecture Module: Introduction to Sustainable Design*. Ann Arbor: National Pollution Prevention Center for Higher Education, 1998.

Kim, Minsoo. *Exploring the Design Culture of the 21st Century*. Seoul: Greenbi, 2002.

King, Gary, Jennifer Pan, and Margaret E. Roberts. "How Censorship in China Allows Government Criticism but Silences Collective Expression." *American Political Science Review* 107, no. 2 (2013), 326–43.

Kitchin, Rob. "The Ethics of Smart Cities And Urban Science." *Philosophical Transactions of the Royal Society* 374, no. 2083 (2016).

Kleinherenbrink, Arjen. "Fields of Sense and Formal Things: The Ontologies of Tristan Garcia and Markus Gabriel." *Open Philosophy* 1, no. 1 (2018), 129–42.

Koc, Edwin, Andrea Koncz, Kenneth Tsang, and Anna Longenberger. *The Class of 2014 Student Survey Report: Results from NACE's Annual Survey of College Students*. Pennsylvania: National Association of Colleges and Employers, 2014.

Koerner, Brendan I. "Why ISIS Is Winning the Social Media War'And How to Fight Back." *WIRED*, April 2016. wired.com/2016/03/isis-winning-social-media-war-heres-beat/.

Korenhof, Paulan, Jef Ausloos, Ivan Szekely, Meg Ambrose, Giovanni Sartor, and Ronald Leenes. "Timing the Right to Be Forgotten: A Study into 'Time' as a Factor in Deciding About Retention or Erasure of Data." *Law, Governance and Technology Series*, 2014, 171–201.

Korten, David C. *The Great Turning: From Empire to Earth Community*. San Francisco, CA: Berrett-Koehler, 2006.

Kradel-Weitzel, Maribeth. "The Cost of Free Labor." AIGA, March 29, 2011. www.aiga.org/the-cost-of-free-labor.

Krug, Steve. *Don't Make Me Think!: A Common Sense Approach to Web Usability*. Berkeley: New Riders, 2006.

Kuder, Nick. "Deep Ruts: The Impact of Stigmergic Mechanisms on Cigarette Design (Among Other Things)." *LIVD* 15, no. 2 (2017), 7–11. http://pdxscholar.library.pdx.edu/livd.

Kuo, Andrew. "Charlie Rose Tomorrow—Andrew Kuo." By Charlie Rose. http://www.charlierose.com/view/interview/89567. February 23, 2008.

Kuo, Andrew. "Charting Odd Future." ArtsBeat (blog), April 3, 2012. artsbeat.blogs.nytimes.com/201
2/04/03/charting-odd-future/.

Kuo, Andrew. "Artist Talk: Andrew Kuo." By RxArt, November 8, 2011. rxart.net/blog/artist-talk-
andrew-kuo.

Kurzweil, Ray, and Alan Sklar. *The Age of Spiritual Machines: When Computers Exceed Human
Intelligence*. New York: Penguin Audiobooks, 1999.

Labos, Christopher. "There's an App for That Medical Issue. Should You Use It?" *Macleans*, April 11,
2016. www.macleans.ca/society/health/the-problem-with-wildly-inaccurate-health-apps.

Lacy, P., J. Keeble, R. McNamara, J. Rutqvist, T. Haglund, M. Cui, P. Buddemeier, et al. *Circular
Advantage: Innovative Business Models and Technologies to Create Value in a World without Limits
to Growth*. Chicago: Accenture, 2014.

Lang, Peter, and William Menking. *Superstudio: Life without Objects*. Milano: Skira, 2003.

Latour, Bruno. "A Cautious Prometheus? A Few Steps toward a Philosophy of Design (With Special
Attention to Peter Sloterdijk)." In *Proceedings of the 2008 Annual International Conference of the
Design History Society (UK) University College Falmouth, 3–6 September. HAL CCSD*, edited by
Fiona Hackne, Jonathn Glynne, and Viv Minto, 2–10. Falmouth: Universal Publishers, 2008.

Lawson, Shaun, Ben Kirman, Conor Linehan, Tom Feltwell, and Lisa Hopkins. "Problematising
Upstream Technology through Speculative Design: The Case of Quantified Cats and Dogs." In
Proceedings of Conference on Human Factors in Computing Systems (CHI), 2663–2672. New York:
ACM, 2015.

Lenskjold, Tau U., Sissel Olander, and Joachim Halse. "Minor Design Activism: Prompting Change from
Within." *Design Issues* 31, no. 4 (2015), 67–78.

Lepore, Jill. "Politics and the New Machine." *New Yorker*, November 16, 2015. www.newyorker.com/ma
gazine/2015/11/16/politics-and-the-new-machine.

Lessig, Lawrence. *Code: Version 2.0*. New York: Basic Books, 2006.

"Let us introduce a new Pans-CJK (汎韓中日) font of Google." Google Developers Korea Blog, July 16,
2014. https://developers-kr.googleblog.com/2014/07/cjkfont.html.

Libert, Timothy. "Privacy Implications of Health Information Seeking on the Web." *Communications of
the ACM* 58, no. 3 (2015), 68–77.

Linebaugh, Peter. *The Magna Carta Manifesto: Liberties and Commons for All*. Berkeley: University of
California Press, 2009.

Lin, Patrick. "Why Ethics Matters for Autonomous Cars." In *Autonomous Driving: Technical, Legal and
Social Aspects*, edited by Markus Maurer, J. Christian Gerdes, Barbara Lenz, and Hermann Winner,
69–85. Berlin: Springer, 2015.

Liu, C. M., Zu L. Wang, and Ji L. Chen. "Research on Characteristics and Models of China's
Cooperative Education." *Applied Mechanics and Materials* 33 (2010), 571–74.

Loo, Stephen. "Design-Ing Ethics: The Good, the Bad and the Performative." In *Design and Ethics:
Reflections on Practice*, edited by Emma Felton, Oksana Zelenko, and Suzi Vaughan, 10–20. London:
Routledge, 2012.

Lorenz, Taylor. "Here's What Happened When I Was Surrounded by Men in Virtual Reality." Mic (blog),
May 26, 2016. https://mic.com/articles/144470/sexual-harassment-in-virtual-reality#.zqMVIy4Hh.

Lum, Kristian, and William Isaac. "To Predict and Serve?" *Significance* 13, no. 5 (2016), 14–19.

Lévinas, Emmanuel. *Totality and Infinity: An Essay on Exteriority*. Pittsburgh: Duquesne University
Press, 1969.

Macdonald, Nico. "Can Designers Save the World? (And Should They Try?)." In *Looking Closer 4:
Critical Writings on Graphic Design*, edited by Michael Bierut, William Drenttel, and Steven Heller.
Princeton, Recording for the Blind & Dyslexic, 2002.

MacLachlan, Alice. "An Ethic of Plurality: Reconciling Politics and Morality in Hannah Arendt." In
In History and Judgement: IWM Junior Visiting Fellows' Conferences, Vol. 21, edited by Vienna A.
MacLachlan and I. Torsen. Vienna: Institut für die Wissenschaften vom Menschen, 2006.

Madary, Michael, and Thomas K. Metzinger. "Real Virtuality: A Code of Ethical Conduct: Recommendations for Good Scientific Practice and the Consumers of VR-Technology." *Frontiers in Robotics and AI* 3 (2016).

Madsen, Peter. "Responsible Design and the Management of Ethics." *Design Management Review* 16, no. 3 (2010), 37–41.

Maeda, John. *Fresh Dialogue Nine: New Voices in Graphic Design: In/Visible: Graphic Data Revealed - New Voices in Graphic Design*. New York: Princeton Architectural Press, 2009.

Make Art with Purpose. "Make Art with Purpose." MAP. n.d. http://makeartwithpurpose.net/projects. php?id=40.

Maldonado, Tomás. *Design, Nature, and Revolution: Toward a Critical Ecology*. New York: Harper & Row Publishers, 1972.

Maltbie, Benjamin. "Powerful Illusions: Addressing the Code of Ethics for VR." *UploadVR*, April 16, 2017. https://uploadvr.com/ethics-vr-research-concerns.

Mandela, Nelson R. "Lighting Your Way to a Better Future." Speech, Launch of Mindset Network, South Africa, July 16, 2003.

Manzini, Ezio. *Design: When Everybody Designs. An Introduction to Design for Social Innovation*. Translated by Rachel Coad. Cambridge: MIT Press, 2015.

Manzini, Ezio, and Eduardo Staszowski, eds. *Public and Collaborative: Exploring the Intersection of Design, Social Innovation and Public Policy*. DESIS Network, 2013.

Manzini, Ezio, and Francesca Rizzo. "Small Projects/Large Changes: Participatory Design as an Open Participated Process." *CoDesign* 7, no. 3–4 (2011), 199–215.

Manzini, Ezio, and Victor Margolin. "Open Letter to the Design Community: Stand Up For Democracy." Democracy and Design Platform, March 5, 2017. www.democracy-design.org/open-letter-stand-up -democracy.

Marcum, James W. "Design for Sustainability." *The Bottom Line* 22, no. 1 (2009), 9–12.

Margalit, Liraz. "Tinder And Evolutionary Psychology." TechCrunch (blog), September 27, 2014. https:// techcrunch.com/2014/09/27/tinder-and-evolutionary-psychology/?ncid=rss.

Margolin, Victor. *Design e risco de mudança*. Vila do Conde: Verso da História, 2014.

Margolin, Victor, Douglas Garofalo, Eva Maddox, and Stanley Tigerman. *Healing the World: A Challenge for Designers*. Chicago: Archeworks, 2004.

Marketplace, and Edison Research. "Economic Anxiety Index." October 2016. https://cms.marketplace.o rg/sites/default/files/anxiety-index-data.pdf.

Markussen, Thomas. "The Disruptive Aesthetics of Design Activism: Enacting Design between Art and Politics." *Design Issues* 29, no. 1 (2013), 38–50.

Martucci, Leonardo A., Simone Fischer-Hübner, Mark Hartswood, and Marina Jirotka. "Privacy and Social Values in Smart Cities." In *Designing, Developing, and Facilitating Smart Cities: Urban Design to IoT Solutions*, edited by Vangelis Angelakis, Elias Tragos, Henrich C. Pöhls, Adam Kapovits, and Alessandro Bassi, 89–107. Thousand Oaks: Springer, 2017.

"MATCH GROUP, INC. (MTCH) IPO." NASDAQ.com. Accessed September 20, 2018. https://www.nas daq.com/markets/ipos/company/match-group-inc-905768-79612.

Maureira, Marcello Gómez, Jeroen van Oorschot, Matei Szabo, and Cors Brinkman. "Tender - It's How People Meat." Vimeo, 2014. https://vimeo.com/111997940.

Mays, Erin. "Design Activism." *Print Magazine* (blog), January 3, 2014. printmag.com/featured/design-activism.

McDonough, William, and Michael Braungart. *Cradle to Cradle: Remaking the Way We Make Things*. London: Vintage, 2009.

McDonough, William, and Michael Braungart. *The Hannover Principles: Design for Sustainability*. New York: W. McDonough Architects, 1992.

McLaughlin, Dorothy. "Special Reports - Silent Spring Revisited." Public Broadcasting Service, August 24, 2010. www.pbs.org/wgbh/pages/frontline/shows/nature/disrupt/sspring.html.

Meng, Amanda, and Carl DiSalvo. "Grassroots Resource Mobilization through Counter-Data Action." *Big Data & Society* 5, no. 2 (2018).

Mersini-Houghton, L., and R. Holman. "'Tilting' the Universe with the Landscape Multiverse: The 'Dark' Flow." *Journal of Cosmology and Astroparticle Physics* 2009, no. 02 (2009), 006, https://iopscience.iop.org/article/10.1088/1475-7516/2009/02/006

Metzinger, Thomas. *Being No One: The Self-Model Theory of Subjectivity*. Cambridge: MIT Press, 2006.

Meyer, Christian. "Concrete Materials and Sustainable Development in the USA." *Structural Engineering International* 14, no. 3 (2004), 203–7.

Milgram, Stanley. "Behavioral Study of Obedience." *The Journal of Abnormal and Social Psychology* 67, no. 4 (1963), 371–78.

Millar, Jason. "Ethics Settings for Autonomous Vehicles." In *Robot Ethics 2.0: From Autonomous Cars to Artificial Intelligence*, edited by Patrick Lin, Keith Abney, and Ryan Jenkins, 20–34. New York: Oxford University Press, 2017.

Miller, Alex P. "Want Less-Biased Decisions? Use Algorithms." *Harvard Business Review*, July 26, 2018. https://hbr.org/2018/07/want-less-biased-decisions-use-algorithms.

Miller, Cheryl D. "Black Designers: Missing in Action." *Print Magazine*, June 27, 2016. www.printm ag.com/design-culture-2/history-2/blacks-in-design-1987.

Miller, James William. "Wellness: The History and Development of a Concept." *Spektrum Freizei* 27, no. 1 (2005), 84–102.

Miner, Adam S., Arnold Milstein, Stephen Schueller, Roshini Hegde, Christina Mangurian, and Eleni Linos. "Smartphone-Based Conversational Agents and Responses to Questions About Mental Health, Interpersonal Violence, and Physical Health." *JAMA Internal Medicine* 176, no. 5 (2016), 619.

Miquel-Ribé, Marc. "Throwing Light on Dark UX with Design Awareness." *UX Magazine*, no. 1268 (July 2014). https://uxmag.com/articles/throwing-light-on-dark-ux-with-design-awareness.

Miquel-Ribé, Marc. "Using Open Experience Design and Social...Ing to Stamp Out Dark UX." *UX Magazine*, no. 1508 (July 2015). https://uxmag.com/articles/using-open-experience-design-and-social-networking-to-stamp-out-dark-ux.

"Misdirection." Dark Patterns. n.d. https://darkpatterns.org/types-of-dark-pattern/misdirection.

Mitcham, Carl. "Ethics into Design." In *Discovering Design Explorations in Design Studies*, edited by Richard V. Buchanan and Victor Margolin, 173–89. Chicago: The University of Chicago Press, 1995.

Mitcham, Carl. "Os Desafios Colocados pela Tecnologia à Responsabilidade Ética." *Análise Social* 41, no. 181 (2006), 1127–41.

Mitrašinoviⵡ, Miodrag, and Gabriela Rendón, eds. *Cooperative Cities: Journal of Design Strategies, Volume 9*. New York: School of Design Strategies, The New School, 2017.

Montacute, Rebecca. "Internships: Unpaid, Unadvertised, Unfair." The Sutton Trust, January 30, 2018. https://www.suttontrust.com/research-paper/internships-unpaid-unadvertised-unfair.

Morrison, Julia Frances. "Pedagogies of Consent: What Consent teaches us about Contemporary American Sexual Politics." Master's thesis, Wesleyan University, 2017. https://wesscholar.wesleyan.ed u/etd_hon_theses/1736.

Moulaert, Frank, Flavia Martinelli, Erik Swyngedouw, and Sara Gonzalez. "Towards Alternative Model(s) of Local Innovation." *Urban Studies* 42, no. 11 (2005), 1969–90.

Moxie0. "Saying Goodbye to Encrypted SMS/MMS." Signal Messenger (blog),. March 6, 2015. https://signal.org/blog/goodbye-encrypted-sms.

Mudhar, Raju. "Tinder's Swipe Interface Gets Swiped by Other Apps." *The Star*, August 6, 2014. https://www.thestar.com/life/technology/2014/08/06/tinders_swipe_interface_gets_swiped_by_other _apps.html.

Mugge, Ruth. "Product Design and Consumer Behaviour in a Circular Economy." *Sustainability*10, no. 10 (2018), 3704.

Murray, Martin J. "Waterfall City (Johannesburg): Privatized Urbanism in Extremis." *Environment and Planning A* 47, no. 3 (2015), 503–20.

Murray, Robin, Julie Caulier-Grice, and Geoff Mulgan. *The Open Book of Social Innovation*. London: National Endowment for Science, Technology and the Art, 2010.

National Institutes of Health, and the National Institute on Deafness and Other Communication Disorders. "Guidelines on Communicating Informed Consent for Individuals Who Are Deaf or Hard-of-Hearing and Scientists." National Institutes of Health (NIH) (blog), February 16, 2016. www.nih.gov/health-information/nih-clinical-research-trials-you/guidelines-communicating-informed-consent-individuals-who-are-deaf-or-hard-hearing-scientists.

Natividad, Angela. "The World's Most Eligible Bachelor on Tinder Is Literally the Last of His Kind." *Adweek*, May 25, 2017. www.adweek.com/creativity/the-worlds-most-eligible-bachelor-on-tinder-is-literally-the-last-of-his-kind.

Navarro, M. V., and J. R. Martínez. "Diseño sostenible: herramienta estratégica de innovación." *Revista legislativa de estudios sociales y de opinión pública* 4, no. 8 (2011), 47–88.

Neihardt, John Gneisenau, Philip Joseph Deloria, and Raymond J. DeMallie. *Black Elk Speaks*. Albany: Excelsior, 2008.

Nielsen, Jakob. "The Power of Defaults." Nielsen Norman Group (blog), September 26, 2005. nngroup.com/articles/the-power-of-defaults/.

Nightingale, Sophie J., Kimberley A. Wade, and Derrick G. Watson. "Can People Identify Original and Manipulated Photos of Real-World Scenes?" *Cognitive Research: Principles and Implications* 2, no. 1 (2017).

Nikolewski, Rob. "How Can Dockless Bike and Scooter companies Make Money?" *The San Diego Union-Tribune*, April 15, 2018. www.sandiegouniontribune.com/business/energy-green/sd-fi-dockless-profitable-20180415-story.html.

Nini, Paul. "In Search of Ethics in Graphic Design." AIGA, August 16, 2004. www.aiga.org/in-search-of-ethics-in-graphic-design.

Noble, Safiya Umoja. *Algorithms of Oppression: How Search Engines Reinforce Racism*. New York: New York University Press, 2018.

Nodder, Chris. *Evil by Design: Interaction Design to Lead Us into Temptation*. Indianapolis: Wiley, 2013.

Noothigattu, Ritesh, Snehalkumar Neil. Gaikwad, Edmond Awad, Sohan Dsouza, Iyad Rahwan, Pradeep Ravikumar, and Ariel D. Procaccia. "A Voting-Based System for Ethical Decision Making." *arXiv preprint arXiv:1709.06692*, 2017.

Norman, Donald A., and Roberto Verganti. "Incremental and Radical Innovation: Design Research vs. Technology and Meaning Change." *Design Issues* 30, no. 1 (2014), 78–96.

Norton, Aaron M., and Joyce Baptist. "Couple Boundaries for Social Networking in Middle Adulthood: Associations of Trust and Satisfaction." *Cyberpsychology: Journal of Psychosocial Research on Cyberspace* 8, no. 4 (2014).

Nyholm, Sven, and Jilles Smids. "The Ethics of Accident-Algorithms for Self-Driving Cars: An Applied Trolley Problem?" *Ethical Theory and Moral Practice* 19, no. 5 (2016), 1275–89.

Obama, Barack. "Remarks by President Obama and Chancellor Merkel of Germany in a Joint Press Conference." Whitehouse.gov., November 17, 2016. https://obamawhitehouse.archives.gov/the-press-office/2016/11/17/remarks-president-obama-and-chancellor-merkel-germany-joint-press.

Oberhaus, Daniel. "We're Already Violating Virtual Reality's First Code of Ethics." Motherboard (blog), March 6, 2016. https://motherboard.vice.com/en_us/article/yp3va5/vr-code-of-ethics.

O'Connor, Richard. *Undoing Perpetual Stress: The Missing Connection between Depression, Anxiety, and 21st Century Illness*. New York: Berkley Books, 2005.

Orr, David W. *The Nature of Design: Ecology, Culture, and Human Intention*. Oxford, Oxford University Press, 2002.

Ortutay, Barbara. "Tech Companies Banishing Extremists after Charlottesville." Associated Press (New York), August 17, 2017. www.apnews.com/09e4a4b1fb664b5a947ec23fc988ef07.

Ostrom, Elinor. *Governing the Commons: The Evolution of Institutions for Collective Action*. Cambridge: Cambridge University Press, 2008.

Outlaw, Jessica. "Virtual Harassment: The Social Experience of 600+ Regular Virtual Reality (VR) Users." The Extended Mind (blog),. April 4, 2018. https://extendedmind.io/blog/2018/4/4/virtual-harassment-the-social-experience-of-600-regular-virtual-reality-vrusers.

O'Prey, Paul. "Patterns and Trends in UK Higher Education 2017." Universities UK. July 21, 2017. www.universitiesuk.ac.uk/facts-and-stats/data-and-analysis/Pages/patterns-and-trends-2017.aspx.

Page, Tom. "Skeuomorphism or Flat Design: Future Directions in Mobile Device User Interface (UI) Design Education." *International Journal of Mobile Learning and Organisation* 8, no. 2 (2014), 130.

Papanek, Victor J. *The Green Imperative: Natural Design for the Real World*. New York: Thames and Hudson, 1995.

Papanek, Victor. *Design for the Real World: Human Ecology and Social Change*. Chicago: Academy Chicago Publishers, 1971.

Pappas, Gregory Fernando. "To Be or to Do. John Dewey and the Great Divide in Ethics." *History of Philosophy Quarterly* 14, no. 4 (1997), 447–72.

Parkinson, Hannah Jane. "Tinder Nightmares founder: 'I Hate Dating so Much.'" *The Guardian*, December 7, 2015. www.theguardian.com/technology/2015/dec/07/elan-gale-tinder-nightmares-interview.

Parsons, Glenn. *The Philosophy of Design*. Cambridge, Polity Press, 2016.

Pasquale, Frank. *Black Box Society: The Secret Algorithms That Control Money and Information*. Cambridge: Harvard University Press, 2015.

Paunovic, Goran. "The Bottom Line: Why Good UX Design Means Better Business." *Forbes*, March 23, 2017. www.forbes.com/sites/forbesagencycouncil/2017/03/23/the-bottom-line-why-good-ux-design-means-better-business/#943104f23960.

Pedersen, Jens. "War and Peace in Codesign." *CoDesign* 12, no. 3 (2015), 171–84.

Peixoto, Tiago, and Jonathan Fox. "When Does ICT-Enabled Citizen Voice Lead to Government Responsiveness?" *IDS Bulletin* 41, no. 1 (2016), 23–39.

Peretó, Juli, Jeffrey L. Bada, and Antonio Lazcano. "Charles Darwin and the Origin of Life." *Origins of Life and Evolution of the Biosphere* 39, no. 5 (October 2009), 395–406.

Perlin, Ross. *Intern Nation: How to Earn Nothing and Learn Little in the Brave New Economy*. New York: Verso, 2014.

Pickert, Kate. "The Mindful Revolution." *Time*, February 3, 2014. http://content.time.com/time/subscriber/article/0,33009,2163560,00.html.

Playfair, William. *The Commercial and Political Atlas: Representing, by Means of Stained Copper-Plate Charts, the Exports, Imports, and General Trade of England, at a Single View*. London: J. Debrett, 1786.

Pogue, David. "Apple's 5 Worst Attempts at Digital Realism." *Scientific American* (blog), February 1, 2013. www.scientificamerican.com/article/pogue-apples-5-worst-attempts-at-digital-realism.

Popper, Karl. *The Poverty of Historicism*. London: Routledge, 2002.

"Privacy Zuckering." Dark Patterns, n.d. https://darkpatterns.org/types-of-dark-pattern/privacy-zuckering.

Protzen, Jean-Pierre, and David J. Harris. *The Universe of Design: Horst Rittel's Theories of Design and Planning*. Hoboken: Taylor & Francis, 2010.

Putnam, Robert D. *Bowling Alone: The Collapse and Revival of American Community*. New York: Touchstone, 2001.

Rahwan, Iyad. "Society-in-the-Loop: Programming the Algorithmic Social Contract." *Ethics and Information Technology* 20, no. 1 (2017), 5–14.

Rakowski, Eric. "Introduction." In *The Trolley Problem Mysteries*, edited by Frances M. Kamm, 1–7. New York: Oxford University Press, 2016.

Rams, Dieter. "The Power of Good Design." Vitsœ. n.d. www.vitsoe.com/us/about/good-design.

Rancière, Jacques, and Steve Corcoran. *Dissensus: On politics and Aesthetics*. London: Continuum, 2010.

Rand, Paul. *Paul Rand: A Designer's Word*. New York: School of Visual Arts, 1998

Rath, Tom, and James K. Harter. *Wellbeing: The Five Essential Elements*. New York: Gallup Press, 2010.

Rendón, Gabriela Pere. *Cities for or Against Citizens? Socio-Spatial Restructuring in Low-Income Neighborhoods and the Paradox of Citizen Participation*. Delft: AB+B Series, 2018.

Revolvy LLC. "R V Sussex Justices, Ex P McCarthy." Revolvy, October 17, 2018. www.revolvy.com/page/R-v-Sussex-Justices%2C-ex-p-McCarthy.

Rezai, Maziar, and Mitra Khazaei. "The Challenge of being Activist-Designer. An Attempt to Understand the New Role of Designer in the Social Change Based on Current Experiences." *The Design Journal* 20, no. sup1 (2017), S3516–35.

Rittel, Horst W. J., and Melvin M. Webber. *Dilemmas in a General Theory of Planning*. Berkeley: University of Urban and Regional Development, 1973.

"Roach Motel." Dark Patterns, n.d. https://darkpatterns.org/types-of-dark-pattern/roach-motel.

Roberts, Carys. *The Inbetweeners: The New Role of Internships in the Graduate Labour Market*. London: Institute for Public Policy Research, April 2017. www.ippr.org/files/publications/pdf/inbetweeners-the-new-role-of-internships_Apr2017.pdf.

Roberts, Jeff. "A Top Google Result for the Holocaust Is Now a White Supremacist Site." *Fortune*, December 12, 2016. fortune.com/2016/12/12/google-holocaust.

Robertson, Toni, and Ina Wagner. "Ethics: Engagement, Representation and Politics-In-Action." In *Routledge International Handbook of Participatory Design*, edited by Jesper Simonsen and Toni Robertson, 64–85. New York: Routledge, 2013.

Robertson, Toni, and Jesper Simonsen. "Participatory Design: An Introduction." In *Routledge International Handbook of Participatory Design*, edited by Jesper Simonsen and Toni Robertson. Thousand Oaks: Routledge, 2012.

Rock, Michael. "Since When Did USA Today Become the National Design Ideal?" *I.D. Magazine*, March/April 1992. 2x4.org/ideas/12/since-when-did-usa-today-become-our-national-design-ideal.

Rosen, Marc A., and Hossam A. Kishawy. "Sustainable Manufacturing and Design: Concepts, Practices and Needs." *Sustainability* 4, no. 2 (2012), 154–74.

Rose, Philip. "Internships: Tapping into China's Next Generation of Talent." *Asia-Pacific Journal of Cooperative Education* 14, no. 2 (2013), 89–98.

Roth, Dik, and Jeroen Warner. "Rural Solutions for Threats to Urban Areas: The Contest over Calamity Polders." *Built Environment* 35, no. 4 (2009), 545–62.

Rowe, Christopher J., and Sarah Broadie, editors. *Nicomachean Ethics*. London: Oxford University Press, 2002.

Rushe, Dominic. "Why Can't We Have Nice Things: Dockless Bikes and the Tragedy of the Commons." *The Guardian* (Washington), November 5, 2017. www.theguardian.com/politics/2017/nov/05/why-we-cant-have-nice-things-dockless-bikes-and-the-tragedy-of-the-commons.

Sadowski, Jathan, and Frank Pasquale. "The Spectrum of Control: A Social Theory of the Smart City." *First Monday* 20, no. 7 (2015).

Sanders, Elizabeth B., and Pieter J. Stappers. "Probes, Toolkits and Prototypes: Three Approaches to Making in Codesigning." *CoDesign* 10, no. 1 (2014), 5–14.

Sanders, Elizabeth B., and Pieter J. Stappers. *Convivial Toolbox: Generative Research for the Front End of Design*. Amsterdam: BIS, 2013.

Sanghani, Radhika. "These Countries Tried Women-Only Transport. Here's What Happened." *The Telegraph*, August 16, 2015. www.telegraph.co.uk/women/womens-life/11824962/Women-only-trains-and-transport-How-they-work-around-the-world.html.

Saunders, Jessica, Priscillia Hunt, and John S. Hollywood. "Predictions Put into Practice: A Quasi-Experimental Evaluation Of Chicago's Predictive Policing Pilot." *Journal of Experimental Criminology* 12, no. 3 (2016), 347–71.

Sauro, Jeff, and James R. Lewis. *Quantifying the User Experience: Practical Statistics for User Research*. San Diego: Elsevier Science, 2016.

Sayer, Andrew. "Moral Economy and Political Economy." *Studies in Political Economy* 61, no. 1 (2000), 79–103.

Sayer, Andrew. "Moral Economy as Critique." *New Political Economy* 12, no. 2 (2007), 261–70.

Scalin, Noah, and Michelle Taute. *The Design Activist's Handbook: How to Change the World (or at Least a Part of It) with Socially Conscious Design.* Cincinnati: How Books, 2012.

Scarry, Elaine. *The Body in Pain: The Making and Unmaking of the World.* Oxford: Oxford University Press, 1985.

Schön, Donald A. *The Reflective Practitioner: How Professionals Think in Action.* New York: Basic Books, 1984.

Schroeder, Ralph. "Social Interaction in Virtual Environments: Key Issues, Common Themes, and a Framework for Research." *The Social Life of Avatars*, 2002, 1–18.

Schul, J. J. "Sostenibilidad en el diseño y ejecución de proyectos: Implicaciones prácticas." *Información Comercial Española*, 2002, 123–38.

Schulte, Paul A., Rebecca J. Guerin, Anita L. Schill, Anasua Bhattacharya, Thomas R. Cunningham, Sudha P. Pandalai, Donald Eggerth, and Carol M. Stephenson. "Considerations for Incorporating 'Well-Being' in Public Policy for Workers and Workplaces." *American Journal of Public Health* 105, no. 8 (2015), e31–e44.

Schwab, Katharine. "VR Has A Harassment Problem." Fast Company. April 4, 2018. www.fastcodesign.com/90166592/vr-has-a-harassment-problem.

Schweber, S. S. *In the Shadow of the Bomb: Oppenheimer, Bethe, and the Moral Responsibility of the Scientist.* Princeton: Princeton University Press, 2007.

Sclater, Madeleine. "Sustainability and Learning: Aesthetic and Creative Responses in a Digital Culture." *Research in Comparative and International Education* 13, no. 1 (2018), 135–51.

Scott, Susie. "Re-clothing the Emperor: The Swimming Pool as a Negotiated Order." *Symbolic Interaction* 32, no. 2 (2009), 123–45.

Scruton, R. *On Human Nature.* Princeton: Princeton University Press, 2017.

Sebastian Boring, Jo Vermeulen, and Jakub Dosta. "Dark Patterns in Proxemic Interactions - a Critical Perspective." In *Proceedings of the 12th ACM Conference on Designing Interactive Systems*, edited by Saul Greenberg, 523–32. New York: ACM, 2014.

Seeger, Matthew W., Timothy L. Sellnow, and Robert R. Ulmer. "Communication, Organization, and Crisis." *Annals of the International Communication Association* 21, no. 1 (1998), 231–76.

Segal, Leslie A. "Introduction." In *Graphis Diagrams: The Graphic Visualization of Abstract Data*, edited by Walter Herdeg. Zürich: Graphis Press, 1983.

Shahani, Aarti. From Hate Speech to Fake News: The Content Crisis Facing Mark Zuckerberg." National Public Radio, November 17, 2016. https://one.npr.org/?sharedMediaId=495827410:502402451.

Sharma, Yojana. "What Do You Do with Millions of Extra Graduates?" *BBC News*, July 1, 2014. www.bbc.com/news/business-28062071.

Shaw, Joe, and Mark Graham. "An Informational Right to the City? Code, Content, Control, and the Urbanization of Information." *Antipode* 49, no. 4 (2017), 907–27.

Shearer, Elisa, and Jeffrey Gottfried. "News Use Across Social Media Platforms 2017." Pew Research Center Journalism Project, September 7, 2017. www.journalism.org/2017/09/07/news-use-across-social-media-platforms-2017.

Shontell, Alyson. "Ousted Tinder Cofounder Sues For Sexual Harassment, And She's Using These Nasty Texts As Evidence." *Business Insider*, July 1, 2014. businessinsider.com/tinder-lawsuit-and-sexual-harassment-text-messages-2014-7.

Shroff, Ravi. "Predictive Analytics for City Agencies: Lessons from Children's Services." *Big Data* 5, no. 3 (2017), 189–96.

Simon, George K. *In Sheep's Clothing Understanding and Dealing with Manipulative People.* Little Rock: A.J. Christopher, 1996.

Simon, Herbert Alexander. *The Sciences of the Artificial.* Cambridge: MIT Press, 1969.

Simonsen, Jesper, and Toni Robertson, editors. *Routledge International Handbook of Participatory Design.* Thousand Oaks: Routledge, 2012.

Sim, Stuart. *Derrida and the End of History*. Duxford: Icon Books, 2000.

Slater, M. "Place Illusion and Plausibility Can Lead to Realistic Behaviour in Immersive Virtual Environments." *Philosophical Transactions of the Royal Society B: Biological Sciences*364, no. 1535 (2009), 3549–57.

Slovák, Petr, Christopher Frauenberger, and Geraldine Fitzpatrick. "Reflective Practicum: A Framework of Sensitizing Concepts to Design for Transformative Reflection." In *Proceedings of the 2017 CHI Conference on Human Factors in Computing Systems*, edited by Gloria Mark, 2696–707. New York: ACM, 2017.

Smart Cities Connect Conference and Expo. Smart Cities Connect Conference and Expo, 2018. https://spring.smartcitiesconnect.org.

Smith-Barrow, Delece. "Plan for Internships as a College Applicant." *U.S. News & World Report*, November 16, 2017. www.usnews.com/education/best-colleges/articles/2017-11-16/consider-internship-opportunities-during-a-college-search.

Smith, Tania H. "Sustainable design and the design curriculum." *Journal of Design Research* 7, no. 3 (2008), 259.

Speer, Albert. *Inside the Third Reich*. New York: Avon, 1971.

"SPJ Code of Ethics." Society of Professional Journalists, September 6, 2014. www.spj.org/ethicscode.asp.

Steele, Julie, and Noah Iliinsky. *Designing Data Visualizations: Representing Informational Relationships*. Sebastopol: O'Reilly Media, 2011.

Sterling, Bruce. "Dark Patterns: User Interfaces Designed to Trick People." *WIRED* (blog), February 10, 2014. wired.com/2014/02/dark-patterns-user-interfaces-designed-trick-people.

Stinson, Elizabeth. "Koko Is a New Social Network Designed to Help You Deal with Stress." *WIRED*, December 16, 2015. wired.com/2015/12/a-new-social-media-network-to-help-you-deal-with-stress.

Stoyanovich, Julia. *Testimony of Julia Stoyanovich before the New York City Council Committee on Technology Regarding Automated Processing of Data (Int. 1696–2017)*, 2017. https://dataresponsibly.github.io/documents/Stoyanovich_VaccaBill.pdf.

Strohecker, James. *A Brief History of Wellness*. HealthWorld Online, 2006. www.mywellnesstest.com/certResFile/BriefHistoryofWellness.pdf.

Subrahmanyam, Kaveri, David Smahel, and Patricia Greenfield. "Connecting Developmental Constructions to the Internet: Identity Presentation and Sexual Exploration in Online Teen Chat Rooms." *Developmental Psychology* 42, no. 3 (2006), 395–406.

Swaine, Jon, Oliver Laughland, Jamiles Lartey, and Ciara McCarthy. "Young Black Men Killed by US Police at Highest Rate in Year of 1,134 Deaths." *The Guardian*, December 31, 2015. www.theguardian.com/us-news/2015/dec/31/the-counted-police-killings-2015-young-black-men.

Swan, Elaine. "The Internship Class: Subjectivity and Inequalities—Gender, Race, and Class." In *Handbook of Gendered Careers in Management: Getting in, Getting on, Getting Out*, edited by Adelina Broadbridge and Sandra L. Fielden, 30–43. Cheltenham: Edward Elgar, 2015.

Swann, Cal. *Language and Typography*. Translated by Sungjae Song. Seoul: Communication Books, 2003.

Sweeney, Latanya. "Discrimination in Online Ad Delivery." *Communications of the ACM* 56, no. 5 (2013), 44.

Sweeting, Ben. "Wicked Problems in Design and Ethics." In *Systemic Design: Theory, Methods, and Practice*, edited by Peter Jones and Kyoichi Kijima. Japan: Springer, 2018.

Swilling, Mark. *The United Democratic Front and Township Revolt in South Africa*. Johannesburg: Association for Sociology in Southern Africa, 1987.

Thackara, John. *Design after Modernism: Beyond the Object*. New York: Thames and Hudson, 1988.

Thackara, John. *How to Thrive in the Next Economy: Designing Tomorrow's World Today*. London: Thames & Hudson, 2015.

Thackara, John. *In the Bubble: Designing in a Complex World*. Cambridge: MIT Press, 2006.

Thaler, Richard H., Cass R. Sunstein, and Sean Pratt. *Nudge: Improving Decisions about Health, Wealth, and Happiness*. New Haven: Yale University Press, 2008.

Thomas, Angharad. "Design and Sustainable Development What Is the Contribution That Design Can Make? A Case Study of the Welsh Woollen Industry." In Design *Research Society Conference*, 16–19 July 2008. Sheffield: The University of Salford, 2008.

Thorpe, Ann. "Defining Design as Activism." *Journal of Architectural Education*, 2010.

Thorpe, Ann. "Design as Activism: A Conceptual Tool." In *Changing the Change: Design, Visions, Proposals and Tools*, edited by Carla Cipolla and Pier Paolo Peruccio, 127. Turin: Icsid, 2008.

Tidwell, Jenifer. *Designing Interfaces: Patterns for Effective Interaction Design*. Sebastopol: O'Reilly Media, 2005.

Tinder Inc. "Tinder on the App Store." App Store, August 3, 2012. https://itunes.apple.com/ke/app/tinder/id547702041?mt=8.

"Tinder | Swipe. Match. Chat." Tinder (blog), n.d. https://tinder.com/?lang=en.

Toker, Alp. "Looking for Trends in @nytimes's Presidential Forecast Needle? Don't Look Too Hard - The Bounce Is Random Jitter from Your PC, Not Live Data pic.twitter.com/pwcV6epee7." Twitter, November 8, 2016. https://twitter.com/atoker/status/796176641600974851/photo/1.

Tonkinwise, Cameron. "Ethics by Design, or the Ethos of Things." *Design Philosophy Papers* 2, no. 2 (2004), 129–44.

Toppins, Aggie. "Designers, Please Pay Your Interns." Eye on Design, January 4, 2018. https://eyeondesign.aiga.org/designers-please-pay-your-interns.

Travis, John W., and Regina Sara Ryan. *Wellness Workbook: How to Achieve Enduring Health and Vitality*, 3rd ed. Berkeley: Celestial Arts, 2004.

"Trick Questions." Dark Patterns, n.d. https://darkpatterns.org/types-of-dark-pattern/trick-questions.

Trybe. "Trybe." n.d. www.trybe.us.

Tufekci, Zeynep. "Facebook Said Its Algorithms Do Help Form Echo Chambers, and the Tech Press Missed It." *New Perspectives Quarterly* 32, no. 3 (2015), 9–12.

Tufekci, Zeynep. *Twitter and Tear Gas: The Power and Fragility of Networked Protest*. New Haven: Yale University Press, 2017.

Tufekci, Zeynep. "The Latest Data Privacy Debacle." *The New York Times*, January 30, 2018. www.nytimes.com/2018/01/30/opinion/strava-privacy.html.

Tufte, Edward R. *The Visual Display of Quantitative Information*, 2nd ed. Cheshire: Graphics Press, 2001.

Tufte, Edward R. *Envisioning Information*. Cheshire: Graphics Press, 1990.

Tullo, Carol, ed. *Mental Capacity Act*. London: The Stationery Office, 2005.

"Two Dots: Free Puzzle Game for IOS and Android." Dots, n.d. https://www.dots.co/twodots.

UNESCO. *Education for Sustainable Development: Sourcebook*. Paris: UNESCO, 2012.

United Nations General Assembly, editor. *Report of the World Commission on Environment and Development: Our Common Future*. Oslo, Norway: United Nations General Assembly, 1987.

United States Department of Justice, Office of Justice Programs, and Bureau of Justice Statistics. *National Crime Victimization Survey: School Crime Supplement, 2015*. Ann Arbor: Inter-University Consortium for Political and Social Research, 2016.

Universidad de Palermo. *Introducción a la investigación: Diseño gráfico sustentable*. Buenos Aires, 2015.

"Urban Dictionary: Tindering." Urban Dictionary. n.d. www.urbandictionary.com/define.php?term=Tindering.

Vaithianathan, Rhema, Emily Putnam-Hornstein, Nan Jiang, Parma Nand, and Tim Maloney. *Developing Predictive Models to Support Child Maltreatment Hotline Screening Decisions: Allegheny County Methodology and Implementation*. New Zealand: Centre for Social Data Analytics, 2017. www.alleghenycountyanalytics.us/wp-content/uploads/2017/04/Developing-Predictive-Risk-Models-package-with-cover-1-to-post-1.pdf.

Valtonen, Anna. "Back and Forth with Ethics in Product Development: A History of Ethical Responsibility as a Design Driver." In *Opening the Black Box: Moral Foundation of Management Knowledge*, 13–14. Paris: EIASM, 2006.

Van den Hoven, Jeroen. "Introduction." In *Designing in Ethics*, edited by Jeroen Van den Hoven, Seumas Miller, and Thomas Pogge, 1–10. Cambridge: Cambridge University Press, 2017.

Van Heerden, Ferdi. "Foreword." In *Data Flow: Visualizing Information in Graphic Design*, edited by Robert Klanten, Nicolas Bourquin, Thibaud Tissot, and Sven Ehmann. Berlin: Gestalten, 2006.

Van Kessel, Ineke. *Beyond Our Wildest Dreams The United Democratic Front and the Transformation of South Africa*. Charlottesville: University Press of Virginia, 2000.

Veale, Michael, Max Van Kleek, and Reuben Binns. "Fairness and Accountability Design Needs for Algorithmic Support in High-Stakes Public Sector Decision-Making." In CHI 2018 *Proceedings of the 2018 CHI Conference on Human Factors in Computing Systems*, 440. Montreal: ACM, 2018.

Vignelli, Massimo. "Massimo Vignelli's A Few Basic Typefaces." Fonts in Use. August 13, 2016. https://fontsinuse.com/uses/14164/massimo-vignelli-s-a-few-basic-typefaces.

Von Holdt, K., and Adèle Kirsten. *The Smoke That Calls: Insurgent Citizenship, Collective Violence and the Struggle for a Place in the New South Africa: Eight Case Studies of Community Protest and Xenophobic Violence*. Johannesburg, South Africa: Centre for the Study of Violence and Reconciliation, 2011.

Vosoughi, Soroush, Deb Roy, and Sinan Aral. "The Spread of True and False News Online." *Science* 359, no. 6380 (2018), 1146–51.

Wallach, Wendell, and Colin Allen. *Moral Machines: Teaching Robots Right from Wrong*. New York: Oxford University Press, 2010.

Wansink, Brian, and Katie Love. "Slim by Design: Menu Strategies for Promoting High-Margin, Healthy Foods." *International Journal of Hospitality Management* 42 (2014), 137–43.

Warby, Mark. *Judgment by the High Court of Justice, Citation #: [2018] EWHC 799 (QB)*. London: Royal Courts of Justice, 2018.

Wartik, Nancy. "NYT Needle Returns to the Spotlight. The Internet Notices." *The New York Times*, December 14, 2017. www.nytimes.com/2017/12/14/reader-center/nyt-needle-election.html.

Webster, Dennis. "Unfreedom Day Rally: Freedom a Figment of Elite Imagination, Say 50,000 Shack Dwellers." *Daily Marveric*, April 24, 2018. www.dailymaverick.co.za/article/2018-04-24-freedom-a-figment-of-elite-imagination-say-50000-shack-dwellers

Weinschenk, Susan. *100 Things Every Designer Needs to Know About People*. Berkeley, CA: New Riders, 2011.

Weinstein, Kathryn. "From College to Careers: Tracking the First Two Years for Graphic Design Graduates." *The International Journal of Visual Design* 12, no. 1 (2018), 1–22.

Wender, Miriam, Uta Brandes, and Sonja Stich. *Design by Use: The Everyday Metamorphosis of Things*. Basel: De Gruyter, 2009.

"What Are Dark Patterns?" Dark Patterns, n.d. https://darkpatterns.org/.

Whitbeck, Caroline. *Ethics in Engineering Practice and Research*. Cambridge: Cambridge University Press, 2011.

Whiteley, Nigel. *Design for Society*. London: Reaktion Books, 1993.

Wilkie, Alex, Martin Savransky, and Marsha Rosengarten. "The Lure of Possible Futures: On Speculative Research." In *Speculative Research: The Lure of Possible Futures*, 1–17. London: Routledge, Taylor & Francis Group, 2017.

Willett, Cynthia, Ellie Anderson, and Diana Meyers. "Feminist Perspectives on the Self." In *Stanford Encyclopedia of Philosophy*, edited by Edward N. Zalta, 3rd ed. Stanford: Stanford University. The Metaphysics Research Lab, 2016.

Williams, Bernard Arthur Owen. *Ethics and the Limits of Philosophy*. Abingdon: Routledge, 2006.

Williams, Felicia. "Tinder Wins Best New Startup of 2013 | Crunchies Awards 2013." TechCrunch, February 11, 2014. techcrunch.com/video/tinder-wins-best-new-startup-of-2013-crunchies-awards-2013.

Wineburg, Sam, and Sarah McGrew. "Lateral Reading: Reading Less and Learning More When Evaluating Digital Information." Stanford History Education Group Working Paper No. 2017-A1, October 2017.

Wineburg, Sam, Sarah McGrew, Joel Breakstone, and Teresa Ortega. *Evaluating Information: The Cornerstone of Civic Online Reasoning*. Stanford: Stanford Digital Repository, 2016. http://purl.stanford.edu/fv751yt5934.

Winner, Langdon. "Do Artifacts Have Politics?" *Daedalus* 109, no. 1 (Winter 1980), 121–36.

Winston, Ali. "Palantir Has Secretly Been Using New Orleans to Test Its Predictive Policing Technology." *The Verge*, February 27, 2018. www.theverge.com/2018/2/27/17054740/palantir-predictive-policing-tool-new-orleans-nopd.

Workman, Dean. "R2K: South African Govt is Spying on Mobile Users." IT News Africa, August 24, 2017. www.itnewsafrica.com/2017/08/r2k-south-african-govt-is-spying-on-mobile-users.

Wright, Diana, and Donella H. Meadows. *Thinking in Systems: A Primer*. Hoboken: Taylor & Francis, 2012.

Yang, Grace. "Student Interns in China." *China Law Blog*, December 20, 2015, www.chinalawblog.com/2015/12/student-interns-in-china-the-china-employment-law-issues.html.

Yang, Qian, Alex Scuito, John Zimmerman, Jodi Forlizzi, and Aaron Steinfeld. "Investigating How Experienced UX Designers Effectively Work with Machine Learning." *Proceedings of the 2018 on Designing Interactive Systems Conference* 2018 - DIS '18, 2018.

Yates, Joshua J. "Saving the Soul of the Smart City." *The Hedgehog Review* 19, no. 2 (2017), 18–35.

Yelavich, Susan, Barbara Adams, and Cameron Tonkinwise. "Design Away." In *Design As Future-Making*, 198–213. London: Bloomsbury Academic, 2014.

Yin, Robert K. *Case Study Research: Design and Methods*. Thousand Oaks, CA: Sage Publications, 2014.

Yuhas, Alan. "Condé Nast Pays Interns $5.8m to Settle Low-pay Lawsuit." *The Guardian* (New York), November 14, 2014. www.theguardian.com/media/2014/nov/14/conde-nast-settles-lawsuit-interns.

Yury, Carrie. "Turning Desire into an App: 5 Questions for Sean Rad, CEO of Tinder." The Huffington Post, June 7, 2014. https://www.huffingtonpost.com/carrie-yury/sean-rad-ceo-of-tinder-on_b_5087420.html.

Zagal, José Pablo, Staffan Björk, and Chris Lewis. "Dark Patterns in the Design of Games." In *Proceedings of the 8th Conference on Foundations of Digital Games 2013*. Gothenburg, Sweden: Department of Applied Information Technology, University of Gothenburg, 2013.

ZDNet Korea, "A Record on Struggle for Developing 3 Nations, Korean-Chinese-Japanese Fonts." September 23, 2014. zdnet.com/topic/korea.

Zerzan, John. *Twilight of the Machines*. Port Townsend: Perseus Book LLC, 2009.

Zhao, Jieyu, Tianlu Wang, Mark Yatskar, Vicente Ordonez, and Kai-Wei Chang. "Men Also Like Shopping: Reducing Gender Bias Amplification Using Corpus-Level Constraints." In *Proceedings of the 2017 Conference on Empirical Methods in Natural Language Processing*, 2979–89, 2017, Copenhagen, Denmark.

Ziva Meditation. "Ziva Meditation." n.d. https://zivameditation.com.

AUTHOR BIOGRAPHIES

Mariana Amatullo, PhD, is an associate professor of strategic design and management at Parsons School of Design, The New School. Amatullo is the cofounder of Designmatters, the social innovation department of ArtCenter College of Design. Amatullo lectures internationally about the role of design in social innovation and serves on the Executive Board of Cumulus as president (2019–22 term); she holds a PhD in management from the Weatherhead School of Management at Case Western Reserve University, an MA in art history and museum studies from the University of Southern California, and a licence en lettres degree from the Sorbonne University, Paris.

Iván Asin is an NYC-based art educator from Santiago, Chile. His work focuses on establishing connections between art education and Education for Sustainable Development (ESD). He studied Visual Arts and Marketing at Montclair State University, earned a master's degree in art and design education from Pratt Institute and is currently a doctoral candidate in the Art and Art Education Program at Teachers College, Columbia University. He was awarded the title of "Master Environmental Educator" by the Colorado Alliance for Environmental Education in 2017 and is currently in the Fulbright specialist roster 2019–22. Since 2010, Iván has taught visual arts in the New York City public school system and community-based art programs in Amsterdam and New York. As the founder and leading art educator of the Center for Art Education and Sustainability (CAES), Iván has taught workshops in Argentina, Peru, Colombia, Mexico, and the United States and has carried out professional development for art educators at conferences and higher-education institutions.

Rachel Berger is a designer in Oakland, California, and associate professor and chair of graphic design at California College of the Arts. Her work focuses on identity design, information systems, visual and technological experimentation, and writing. She holds an MFA in graphic design and a BA in American studies, both from Yale University.

Peter Buwert is a design educator and researcher based at Edinburgh Napier University, Scotland. He achieved his PhD in 2016 (Gray's School of Art, Robert Gordon University) for his work exploring and unpacking the implications of the idea that design is always inherently ethical. His work continues to focus on the ethical dimensions and implications of visual communication design, with broad interests in the connections between design, aesthetics, ethics, and politics in society.

Jeffrey Chan is assistant professor in the Humanities, Arts and Social Sciences cluster (HASS) at the Singapore University of Technology and Design (SUTD). He researches on design ethics in the context of urban built environments. He is also author of the monograph "Urban Ethics in the Anthropocene," published by Palgrave in 2019.

Michelle Cortese is a Canadian virtual reality designer, artist, and futurist currently residing in Brooklyn, New York. She splits her professional time between leading VR design for Oculus social products at Facebook and teaching 3D design and creative technology at Queens College CUNY and NYU Steinhardt. Most of her work, both art and design, investigates the transmutation of human communication across new technologies and formats. Michelle was previously a design technologist at Refinery29; an experiential art director at the *New York Times*' Fake Love; and has exhibited work at CES, Tribeca Film Festival, SXSW, and at the Sundance Film Festival.

Samantha Dempsey is a human-centered designer and researcher co-creating experiences, services, and products that promote equitable and healthy communities. Her experience includes designing at Hennepin Healthcare System's Upstream Health Innovations, the Mayo Clinic Center for Innovation, and Mad*Pow. Samantha has also served as the co-curator of the "Designer's Oath" and sits on the board of the nonprofit Creature Conserve advocating for collaboration between artists and scientists. She holds a BFA from the Rhode Island School of Design. When she is not designing, Samantha enjoys embroidering patterns of bacteria onto household objects.

Andrew DeRosa is an assistant professor of design at Queens College, City University of New York. His work balances studio practice, design education, and research related to design thinking, design ethics, pedagogy, and creative process. He holds a master of fine arts degree in 2D Design from Cranbrook Academy of Art.

Johanna Drucker is the Breslauer Professor of Bibliographical Studies in the Department of Information Studies at UCLA. She is internationally known for her work in artists' books, the history of graphic design, typography, experimental poetry, fine art, and digital humanities. Her work is represented in special collections in museums and libraries in the North American and Europe. Her recent titles include *Downdrift: An EcoFiction* and *The General Theory of Social Relavity*, both published in 2018. She is currently the Inaugural Beinecke Fellow in Material Cultures at Yale.

Sara Velez Estêvão is head of the Multimedia Design master's program and assistant professor in design at the University of Beira Interior. She is also a researcher with the LABCOM.IFP research unit at the same university. She holds a PhD in communication design from the Faculty of Fine Arts, University of Lisboa, with a thesis about Vilém Flusser and his contributions to a communication design theory. She has discussed this subject in different conferences and has published works on it. Her research on design theory focuses around a critical view of the mediation of design objects and the political issues related to it.

Peter Claver Fine is the author of *Sustainable Graphic Design: Principles and Practice*, published by Bloomsbury Academic in 2016. He also writes, curates, teaches, and produces creative work on the subject of race and representation, culminating in his book *The Design of Race: How Visual Culture Shapes America* to be published in 2020. He is an associate professor of graphic design at the University of Wyoming where he teaches studio courses in design, design history, and visual culture, emphasizing the role of the designer past, present, and future.

David Gelb is a designer and educator who explores the potential of technology and pedagogical experimentation with a focus on ethical interfaces, artifact collaboration, and building design knowledge. He resides in Toronto, Ontario, Canada, where he is an associate professor in the Department of Design at York University, teaching digital product design, user-centered research, and interaction design theory.

Sabrina Hall is an interdisciplinary art director and creative leader living in NYC. With a career spanning over fourteen years, she has done work for companies of all sizes. Sabrina graduated from The School of Visual Arts with a BFA in graphic design, and is a continual learner with classes on UX/UI, accessibility, and product design. For the past five years Sabrina has served as co-chair of AIGA NY's Mentoring Program. She is passionate about creating opportunities for young designers from underrepresented groups within the field of design. Sabrina frequently visits college classrooms to speak about design and can be found on Twitter discussing her ideas.

Meredith James is a researcher with a focus on design theory and on how to develop a culture of design that is more reflective, equitable, humanist, and self-aware. She has presented and published her work across the United States and Europe, speaking in cities such as New York, Los Angeles, Brighton, and Paris. Additionally, James is an award-winning practicing designer who has worked on projects for some of the world's more well-known companies. She also currently serves as an associate professor in the graphic design program at Portland State University. James received her MFA degree from Cranbrook Academy of Art.

Suna Jeong 정선아 majored in visual communication design as an undergraduate. She received her MFA degree in design history and culture (Seoul National University, Republic of Korea). Now she is a doctoral candidate and is preparing a dissertation about a history of Korean modern typography, specifically in relation with Russian constructivism. She has researched on the history of Korean school emblem design, the spectacle of "Science Day" in colonial Korea, the adaptation of Russian constructivism in Korean typographic culture in the colonial era, and the meaning of the integrated font.

Luke Jordan is the founder and CEO of Grassroot, a nonprofit technology start-up in South Africa. Grassroot's vision is a nation self-organizing from the ground-up. It deploys simple, purpose-built tools that enable ordinary people to initiate, lead, and participate in community organizations and social movements, with little to no bandwidth or resources. Since late 2015 it has reached over 500,000 people and been used for over 35,000 activities, from meetings to volunteer calls. Prior to starting Grassroot, Luke worked at the World Bank in India and Afghanistan from 2011–14, and at McKinsey & Company in China and South Africa from 2005–10.

Tau U. Lenskjold is associate professor at the University of Southern Denmark. His work investigates design collaborations with disadvantaged groups and collective engagements around ecological issues. Drawing on participatory and experimental practices from co-design, speculative prototyping, and activism, his research explores design as an inquiring approach toward social and environmental sustainability.

Michael A. Madaio is a PhD candidate in human-computer interaction at Carnegie Mellon University. His research focuses on human-centered machine-learning systems used in education and the public sector. He is a fellow in the IES Program for interdisciplinary education research, where he researches educational technologies for developing contexts, and he is a PI for the Metro21 Smart Cities Institute, where he researches the impact of machine learning on civic decision-making. He holds a master's in digital media from Georgia Institute of Technology and a master's in education from the University of Maryland, College Park. He is a former public school teacher.

Sarah Edmands Martin is a designer, storyteller, and assistant professor of graphic design at Indiana University in Bloomington. Sarah's work employs diverse processes in printmaking, animation, and early photographic methods. She has two other degrees in English literature and painting from the University of Maryland, has taught design at the University of Notre Dame and Missouri University of Science and Technology, and continues to balance an active studio practice with both research and pedagogy. Her international portfolio of clients include Citibank, AMC's the Walking Dead, the University of Notre Dame, Cook Medical, and Whirlpool—to name a few.

Anjali Menon was born and raised between India and Singapore, and is currently Creative Director at COTY where she develops packaging and 360° campaigns for fragrance brands. She holds a BFA in Communication Design from the School of Visual Arts in New York and a Diploma in Communication Design from the LaSalle College of the Arts in Singapore. Ms. Menon has been an active member of the AIGA NY since 2005, first as a mentor and currently as co-chair in the Mentoring Program. In this role, she develops programming and activities which positively impacts the next generation of designers by providing them with unique opportunities that empower them and develop their careers.

Marc Miquel-Ribé is a PhD researcher and lecturer on user experience in both video games and websites. Previously, he has worked in the gaming industry as a user researcher and has collaborated with the website darkpatterns.org in an effort to stamp out user interfaces designed to trick people and to improve the web. His research focuses on the study of user engagement and Wikipedia. In his free time, he also created the project Catalan Games to disseminate Catalonia's culture in a funny way.

Paul J. Nini is professor and past chairperson in the Department of Design at The Ohio State University, United States. His writings have appeared in a variety of publications, and he has presented at numerous national and international design and education conferences. He has served on AIGA's Design Educators Community Steering Committee; as an editorial board member of the ico-D journal *Communication Design*; and as an advisory board member for the AIGA journal *Dialectic*.

Angela Norwood is a designer and educator whose interests lie in the consideration of design practice as evidence of externalized knowledge. Currently exploring the intersection of design epistemologies with traditional knowledge systems, she believes that such an approach allows for more equitable learning experiences and nuanced outcomes. She is an associate professor in the Department of Design at York University, Toronto, Canada, where she teaches across the curriculum with an emphasis on visual literacy and data visualization.

Sissel Olander is associate professor at the Royal Danish Academy of Fine Arts, School of Design. She holds a PhD in co-design and design anthropology. Her research explores participatory processes as experimental forms of knowing and making that tie together the empirical with the speculative. For many years, Olander has worked in practice-based research projects dealing with issues of community building and democratic representation in collaboration with public libraries and cultural institution. In her research, she highlights how co-design approaches, design experimentation, and design encounters hold the potential to stage critical and post-critical strategies that can challenge the aesthetics of bureaucracy.

Andréa Poshar holds a PhD in communication design—title granted by the Politecnico di Milano, Italy. She is a member of CARISM—Interdisciplinary Center for Research and Analysis of Media at Université Paris 2, Pantheon-Assas, Sorbonne Universities, and she also collaborates with the Research Lab on Typography and Graphic Language, Design Program at Senac University Center, São Paulo, Brazil. Poshar is also one of the current editorial members of *DESIGNABILITIES—Design Research Journal for Social, Cultural and Political Discourse, Transformation & Activism*. She develops her research on creative resistance, design activism, media activism, and social and cultural changes. She teaches aesthetics of visual communication, art and media history, and creative processes on advertising and design schools.

Maziar Rezai is a design-activist, design researcher, design strategist, and film critic. Holding a master's degree in industrial design from the Islamic Azad University in Tehran and having studied as a PhD joint student at Köln International School of Design (KISD), he currently is a PhD candidate at The Braunschweig University of Art (HBK) and also a guest lecturer at the Art University of Tehran. He has given lectures and published numerous papers and articles in both English and Persian on a range of topics including issues of sustainable design and design activism. Besides his more academic work, he also works as an art director and design counselor and has led several consulting projects in Iran.

Laura Scherling is an interactive designer, researcher, and educator. Scherling is an adjunct associate faculty at Columbia University in the City of New York and an instructor at Columbia University Teachers College. She holds a BFA in communication design from the School of Visual Arts and a MA in media studies from The New School, and is completing a doctorate Columbia University Teachers College. Scherling researches emerging technologies, design, education, sustainability, applied ethics, and analytics. Scherling is the co-founder of GreenspaceNYC, a sustainability and design collective. Her work has been published in *Design and Culture, Design Observer, Spark Journal, Interiors: Design/Architecture/Culture* and the *Futures Worth Preserving Cultural Constructions of Nostalgia and Sustainability*. Her work can be viewed at laurascherling.info.

David Stairs is the founder of Designers Without Borders, founding editor of the Design-Altruism-Project blog, and writer/director of the social design documentary *Digging the Suez Canal With a Teaspoon*. For over twenty years Stairs has worked at the confluence of design and social enterprise, contributing numerous articles to *Design Issues*, *Design Observer*, and various other periodicals and websites. While teaching graphic design and design history at Central Michigan University, Stairs has received several research fellowships to Africa and India. He makes his home in Mount Pleasant, Michigan.

Ciara Taylor is CXO at Cream of the Crop Gardens and part-time designed objects faculty at the School of the Art Institute of Chicago. She is a passionate and creative design leader with expertise in designing engaging digital and physical experiences in the realm of healthcare, wellness, financial services, education, and technology. She leverages a unique and thoughtful approach to experience design, integrating game design and play while acting as creative catalyst to challenge traditional methods and encourage innovation. She loves collaborating with her team, teaching students, and spending time at the zoo learning about animal behavior, conservation, and welfare.

Kathryn Weinstein is associate professor of graphic design at Queens College, CUNY. Her work spans media, including web interface design, print design, and photography. Much of her work has focused on not-for-profit institutions, including arts foundations, local health and housing services, legal defense, and youth services. She has received funding from CUNY Workforce Development Initiative, PSC CUNY, and CUNY Service Corps to implement internship programs and track career pathways of former interns. She is co-founder of Design Incubation and serves on the advisory board of *Designer Magazine*.

Andrea Zeller writes and designs for social AR/VR experiences with Facebook. She earned a BFA from NYU in Film and Television and an MA from the University of Washington in digital media. After spending a decade working on documentary films, she led several content teams at Expedia. Invited to teach at the University of Washington, her class evolved into the first online certificate program for storytelling and content strategy. As a filmmaker she began to think about perception and participation in experiences, which led to early thinking about writing beyond the screen. This passion has now extended to designing safe and respectful experiences in AR/VR. She lives on the west coast with her husband and two kids.

INDEX